Lecture Notes of the Institute
for Computer Sciences, Social Informatics
and Telecommunications Engineering 9

Anton Nijholt   Dennis Reidsma
Hendri Hondorp (Eds.)

Intelligent Technologies
for Interactive Entertainment

Third International Conference, INTETAIN 2009
Amsterdam, The Netherlands, June 22-24, 2009
Proceedings

 Springer

Volume Editors

Anton Nijholt
Dennis Reidsma
Hendri Hondorp
PO Box 217
7500 AE, Enschede, The Netherlands
E-mail: {a.nijholt; d.reidsma; g.h.w.hondorp}@ewi.utwente.nl

Library of Congress Control Number: Applied for

CR Subject Classification (1998): K.8, I.2.1, H.5, H.1.2, J.5

ISSN   1867-8211
ISBN-10   3-642-02314-2 Springer Berlin Heidelberg New York
ISBN-13   978-3-642-02314-9 Springer Berlin Heidelberg New York

springer.com

© Springer-Verlag Berlin Heidelberg 2009
Printed in Germany

Typesetting: Camera-ready by author, data conversion by Scientific Publishing Services, Chennai, India
Printed on acid-free paper   SPIN: 12697731   06/3180   5 4 3 2 1 0

Preface

These are the proceedings of the 3rd International Conference on Intelligent Technologies for Interactive Entertainment (INTETAIN 09). The first edition of this conference, organised in Madonna di Campiglio, saw the gathering of a diverse audience with broad and varied interests. With presentations on topics ranging from underlying technology to intelligent interaction and entertainment applications, several inspiring invited lectures, a demonstration session and a hands-on design garage, that first edition of INTETAIN generated a lot of interaction between participants in a lively atmosphere. We hope that we have managed to continue this direction with the third edition, which will take place in Amsterdam, following the second edition held in Cancún. The submissions for short and long papers this year show a certain focus on topics such as emergent games, exertion interfaces and embodied interaction, but also cover important topics of the previous editions, such as, affective user interfaces, story telling, sensors, tele-presence in entertainment, animation, edutainment, and (interactive) art. The presentation of the accepted papers, together with the many interactive demonstrations of entertainment and art installations, and other participative activities to be held during the conference, should go some way towards recreating the open and interactive atmosphere that has been the goal of INTETAIN since its beginning.

In addition to the aforementioned papers and demonstrations, we are happy to present contributions from three excellent invited speakers for INTETAIN 09. Matthias Rauterberg of Eindhoven University, in his contribution titled "Entertainment Computing, Social Transformation and the Quantum Field", takes a broad view as he discusses positive aspects of entertainment computing regarding its capacity for social transformation. Michael Mateas, of the University of California, Santa Cruz, talks about his work in interactive art and storytelling. Antonio Camurri, of InfoMus Lab, Genova, discusses an approach to Human Music Interaction that assigns a more active role to users listening to and interacting with music, in his contribution titled "Non-verbal full body emotional and social interaction: a case study on multimedia systems for active music listening".

This conference would not have been possible without the help of many people. In the first place, there are the members of the Program Committee, who did a very good job of providing authors with constructive feedback. Their dedication results in the kind of review process that improves the quality of a conference. We also extend our thanks to the additional reviewers who contributed their specific expertise on certain papers. In alphabetical order, these were: Betsy van Dijk, Wim Fikkert, Matthias Kranz, Frank Nack, Mannes Poel, Ronald Poppe, Sara Streng, Ivo Swartjes, Dhaval Vyas, and Herwin van Welbergen. We would also like to acknowledge the generous support of our sponsors and technical sponsors. ICST and CREATE-NET supported the organisational process, BNVKI-AIABN provided us with financial support, and GATE, NWO, and IIP-CreaTe made it possible to organise special activities during the conference. Finally, this conference would not have been organised but for the unflagging technical and organisational support of Charlotte Bijron, Lynn Packwood and Alice Vissers-Schotmeijer.

June 2009   Anton Nijholt
                                                                             Dennis Reidsma
                                                                             Hendri Hondorp

Organization

INTETAIN 2009 is organized by Human Media Interaction (HMI) which is part of the Department of Electrical Engineering, Mathematics and Computer Science, (EEMCS) at the University of Twente in cooperation with the Institute for Computer Sciences, Social-Informatics and Telecommunications Engineering (ICST).

Executive Committee

Conference Chair:	Anton Nijholt (Human Media Interaction, University of Twente, The Netherlands)
Local Chair:	Dennis Reidsma (Human Media Interaction, University of Twente, The Netherlands)
Local Chair, Web Master and Publication Chair:	Hendri Hondorp (Human Media Interaction, University of Twente, The Netherlands)
ICST Conference Coordinator:	Maria Morozova (Institute for Computer Sciences, Social-Informatics and Telecommunications Engineering, Hungary)
Steering Committee Chair:	Imrich Chlamtac (CREATE-NET Research Consortium, Trento, Italy)

Program Committee

Stefan Agamanolis	Distance Lab, Forres, UK
Elisabeth André	Augsburg University, Germany
Tilde Bekker	University of Eindhoven, The Netherlands
Regina Bernhaupt	University of Salzburg, Austria
Kim Binsted	University of Hawai, USA
Tony Brooks	Aalborg University Esbjerg, Denmark
Andreas Butz	University of Munich, Germany
Yang Cai	Visual Intelligence Studio, CYLAB, Carnegie Mellon, USA
Antonio Camurri	University of Genoa, Italy
Marc Cavazza	University of Teesside, UK
Tat-Jen Cham	Nanyang Technological University, Singapore
Keith Cheverst	University of Lancaster, UK
Berry Eggen	University of Eindhoven, The Netherlands
Arjan Egges	University of Utrecht, The Netherlands

Sponsoring Institutions

GATE: GAme research for Training and Entertainment

The Netherlands Organization for Scientific Research (NWO)

The Netherlands ICT Research and Innovation Authority (ICT Regie: IIP-Create)

ICST: Institute for Computer Sciences, Social-Informatics and Telecommunications Engineering

BNVKI-AIABN: Benelux Association for Artificial Intelligence

Technical sponsor: CREATE-NET Center for REsearch And Telecommunication Experimentation for NETworked communities

Table of Contents

Short Papers

Entertainment Computing, Social Transformation and the Quantum Field

Matthias Rauterberg

Industrial Design, Eindhoven University of Technology, The Netherlands

Abstract. The abstract should summaritinment computing is on its way getting an established academic discipline. The scope of entertainment computing is quite broad (see the scope of the international journal Entertainment Computing). One unifying idea in this diverse community of entertainment researchers and developers might be a normative position to enhance human living through social transformation. One possible option in this direction is a shared 'conscious' field. Several ideas about a new kind of field based on quantum effects are presented and discussed. Assuming that social transformation is based on a shared collective unconscious I propose designing entertainment technology for a new kind of user experience that can transform in a positive manner the individual unconscious and therefore the collective unconscious as well. Our ALICE project can be seen as a first attempt in this direction.

Keywords: culture, social responsibility, entertainment, computing, quantum field.

1   Introduction

The scope of the research and development arena 'entertainment computing' is quite broad[1]: computer, video, console and internet games; digital new media for entertainment; entertainment robots; entertainment technology, applications, application program interfaces, and entertainment system architectures; human factors of entertainment technology; impact of entertainment technology on users and society; integration of interaction and multimedia capabilities in entertainment systems; interactive television and broadcasting; methodologies, paradigms, tools, and software/hardware architectures for supporting entertainment applications; new genres of entertainment technology; simulation/gaming methodologies used in education, training, and research. A remaining question is how to bring this community together based on shared and hopefully unifying ideas? In Nakatsu, Rauterberg and Vorderer [20], Nakatsu, Rauterberg and Salem [19] and Rauterberg [27] we started to sketch the scene. I discussed in Rauterberg [25,26] the pros and cons of games and social behaviour worldwide: while in Western countries the discussion is focussing on violent game and media content, the discussion in Asia is on intensive game usage and the impact on the

---

[1] See at www.elsevier.com/locate/inca/717010.

A. Nijholt, D. Reidsma, and H. Hondorp (Eds.): INTETAIN 2009, LNICST 9, pp. 1–8, 2009.

intellectual development of children. A lot is already discussed on the harmful and negative effects of entertainment technology on human behaviour; therefore we decided to focus primarily on the positive effects. In Rauterberg [25,26] a first overview over positive effects of entertainment technology on human behaviour is presented and discussed. The drawn recommendations can support developers and designers in entertainment industry. This paper tries to go a step further by including the idea of social transformation (Drucker [6]). Engeström [8] argues for the mediating effect of activities with and around artefacts. In the scope of his paper we can look at entertainment technology as an important mediating factor to influence social transformations.

2   How Can Social Transformation Be Achieved?

Van Loon [31] relates an analysis of risk arising from electronic media to that of a transformation in the societal organization of aesthetic experience. His central assumption is "that particular risks cannot be understood independently from the media by which they have been generated" (p. 166). The sets of connections electronic communications have made possible have amplified not only our capacity to transcend many of the physical limitations of spatio-temporal relations, but also fundamentally transformed the sense of being human. Van Loon argues that in the age of cybernetic reproduction it is no longer helpful or adequate to discuss risks in term of reality versus representation. The notion of 'virtual risks' could be used to discuss the relationships between science, politics, economics, law, the media and popular culture as part of one and the same complexity of connections. Van Loon argues that by following mechanical reproduction and extending it into the organic realm itself, informational reproduction implies a fundamentally new moment. The unity beneath the old dualism between humanism and technocracy needs to be exposed as unethical! We currently face the most critical virtual risks: the death of the human. He concludes: let us "cultivating a responsive sensibility to effect a disclosure of the transgressive implications of the mediation of technology (...) on subjective and biographic experiences" (p. 180).

Maton [16] proposes a multidisciplinary and multilevel framework for social transformation, encompassing the following foundational goals: (1) capacity-building, (2) group empowerment, (3) relational community-building, and (4) culture-challenge. He presents and discusses examples to illustrate the synergistic relationship among the four foundational goals, which is the core of the social transformation process. He concludes with three challenges to guide our efforts to build the new century: "(1) to move social transformation to the center of our consciousness as a field; (2) to articulate jointly with allied disciplines, organizations, and citizen groups an encompassing, multidisciplinary, and multilevel framework for social transformation; and (3) to do the above with heart, soul, and humility" (Maton [16] p.25).

In passing from history to nature, myth acts economically: it abolishes the complexity of human acts, it gives them the simplicity of essences, it does away with all dialectics, with any going back on what is immediately visible, it organizes a world which is without contradiction because it is without depth, a world which is open and wallowing in the evident, it establishes a blissful clarity: things appear to mean something by themselves. If we think that the heterogeneous, polyvalent world is a separate structure in its own right, law is disruptable; i.e., the carnival can be held on the church steps. But if this is not the case, if the carnival and the church do not exist independently of each other, then the only way we can challenge the church is from within an alternative symbolic universe. We cannot choose the imaginary, the semiotic, the carnival as an alternative to the law. It is set up by the law precisely in its own ludic space, its area of imaginary alternative, but not as a symbolic alternative. So that, politically speaking, it is only the symbolic, a new symbolism, a new law that can challenge the existing dominant law.

According to Mulvey [18] are three different change processes: (1) order and disorder, (2) liminality, (3) festivals of the oppressed (e.g. carnival). I will focus on (2): Rituals guide an individual through the transitional moments of life, marking the disruption and difficulty of change and reintegration back into the ordered life of a community. There are rites of separation that initiate the process and put the person concerned into a state of privilege or crisis outside the norms of everyday existence. These are followed by transitional rites, during which the person is in a liminal relation to the world, in a no-man's-land, that may well be marked literally by a particular relationship to place ('transitional periods that require a certain autonomy'). These rites are followed by those of re- incorporation.

Liminal and trance are altered states of consciousness which individuals can enter through a variety of techniques, including hypnotism, drugs, sound (particularly music, percussive drumming etc.), sensory deprivation, physical hardships (eg. flagellation, starvation, exhaustion) and vigorous exercise (particularly dance). People can also use trance, particularly in the context of 'ritual' events, to learn new strategies of thinking or of relating to one another. There are different types of learning: for example 'conscious learning' is a transaction between consciousness, the environment and memory; and 'unconscious learning', which takes place with the addition of 'outer' and 'inner' ways of learning. These arise through the interaction of consciousness with transpersonal mass/collective consciousness (c.g. Jung's [13] "collective unconscious"). The feedback link between consciousness and unconsciousness gives rise to inner experiential learning or tuning-in to the dynamics of meta-systems transcending man and his immediate environment. It may be enhanced by various techniques, mostly developed in connection with Eastern philosophies (e.g. Jantsch and Waddington, Varela, Thompson and Rosch [12,32]). As the arguments concerning the attainment of liminal and trance states indicate, it is often an advantage to utilize the whole body in order to achieve them; consciousness is a function of the body as a whole neuronal and bio-chemical energy system. Consciousness involves both sensory feedback mechanisms and imaginative practices based in fields of signification which are culturally determined. Significant mental effects can be obtained when the entire physical organism is utilised.

There are several phenomena like psycho kinesis, telepathy, out-of-body experiences, unidentified flying objects, near death experience, time travel, etc. that are waiting for some explanations (Talbot [29]). Despite its apparent materiality, the universe looks like a kind of 4-D projection and is ultimately no more real than a hologram, a 4-D image projected in space and time. Using this holographic model Talbot [29] has developed a new description of reality. It encompasses not only reality as we know it, including hitherto unexplained phenomena of physics, but is capable of explaining such occurrences as telepathy, paranormal and out-of-the-body experiences, 'lucid' dreaming and even mystical and religious traditions such as cosmic unity and miraculous healings.

Mitchell [17] believes that all psychic phenomena involve nonlocal resonance between the brain and the quantum vacuum, and consequent access to holographic, nonlocal information. In his view, this hypothesis could explain not only psycho kinesis and extra sensorial perception, but also out-of-body and near-death experiences, visions and apparitions, and evidence usually cited in favor of a reincarnating soul. One has to admit that these theories are often seen as speculative and not yet part of main stream science.

3   A 'Conscious' Field and Quantum Physics

Turing used the concept 'machine' for describing mechanical processes and did not emphasize any distinction between a human 'worker-to-rule' and a physical system. If Turing was thinking about mental operations, it is unclear what he thought the brain was doing when it saw the truth in a manner that could not be modeled computably. Turing explained the principle that his universal machine could simulate any machine, if the behavior of these machines is in principle predictable by calculation, in contrast to the indeterminacy principle in quantum mechanics where such kind of predictions is even theoretically impossible. At the end of his life he came up with his 'Turing Paradox': that the standard principles of quantum mechanics imply that in the limit of continuous observation a quantum system cannot evolve. Turing's 'paradox (also know as the 'watched pot problem') in quantum measurement theory, is now called the *quantum Zeno effect* (Itano, Heinzen, Bollinger & Wineland [11]). This effect is relevant to the new technology of quantum 'interaction free measurement' (Hodges [9]). The quantum Zeno effect states that if we find a system in a particular quantum state, and repeatedly check whether it is still in that state, it will remain in that state. The watched quantum pot never boils (Vaidman [30]). This looks as if human actions -although indirectly- can have an influence on quantum states (Nelson et al [24]). Recent experimental evidence in physics suggests quantum non-locality occurring in [sub]conscious and unconscious brain function, and functional quantum processes in molecular biology are becoming more and more apparent. Moreover macroscopic quantum processes are being proposed as intrinsic features in cosmology, evolution and social interactions (Nelson [21,22,23]).

Quantum and vacuum physics shows that there is an *interconnecting layer* in nature, beyond the connectivity we are familiar with. Einstein claimed that no connection between particles can be achieved beyond light speed (the 'local' hypothesis); on the other side it seems to be possible to synchronize quantum states immediately (the 'non-local' hypothesis; see Aspect et al [2,3], Aspect [1]). Bohm [4] laid most of the theoretical foundations for the Einstein, Podolsky and Rosen [7] experiments performed by Aspect et al [2,3]. These experiments demonstrated that if two quantum systems interact and then move apart, their behavior is correlated in a way that cannot be explained in terms of signals traveling between them at or slower than the light speed. This phenomenon is known as *non-locality*, and is open to two main interpretations: (1) it involves unmediated, instantaneous action at a distance, or (2) it involves faster-than-light signaling. For if nonlocal connections are propagated not at infinite speeds but at speeds greater than that of light through a 'quantum ether' (a sub-quantum domain where current quantum theory and relativity theory break down) then the correlations predicted by quantum theory would disappear if measurements were made in periods shorter than those required for the transmission of quantum connections between particles. The alternative position is that information always takes time to travel from its source to another location, that information is stored at some para-physical level, and that we can access this information, or exchange information with other minds, if the necessary conditions of 'sympathetic resonance' exist (see also the 'morphic resonance' concept of Sheldrake [28]).

As for *precognition* one possible explanation is that it involves direct, 'non-local' access to the actual future. Alternatively, it may involve a new kind of perception (beyond the range of ordinary perception) of a probable future scenario that is beginning to take shape on the basis of current tendencies and intentions, in accordance with the traditional idea that coming events cast their shadows before them; such foreshadowing takes place deep in the implicate order which some mystical traditions would call the astral or Akashic realms (Laszlo [14]). We can assume that there eventually exists an interconnecting cosmic field at the foundation of reality that conserves and conveys information. This cosmic field looks like a possible candidate for our required 'supranatural' memory. Recent discoveries in the field of vacuum physics show that this Akashic field is real and has its equivalent in the zero-point field that underlies space itself. This field consists of a subtle 'sea of fluctuating energies' from which all things arise: atoms and galaxies, stars and planets, living beings, and even [un]consciousness. This zero-point Akashic-field is not only the original source of all things that arise in time and space; it is also the constant and enduring memory of the universe. It holds the record of all that ever happened in life, on Earth, and in the cosmos and relates it to all that is yet to happen.

4   Discussion and Conclusions

We started the cultural computing project ALICE as an interactive, entertaining experience (see Nakatsu, Rauterberg & Vorderer [20]) inspired from 'Alice in Wonderland' (Carroll [5]). In the scope of this project interactive adventures are experiences provided by an augmented reality environment based on selected parts from Lewis Carroll's book 'Alice's Adventures in Wonderland'. The user assumes the role of Alice and explores this interactive narrative. ALICE is an exploration of interactive story-telling in augmented reality (Hu et al [10]). By exploiting the unique characteristics of augmented reality compared to established media such as film and interactive media, the project uses augmented reality as a new medium for edutainment and entertainment as a particular carrier for cultural transformations. Innovations include the refashioning of conventions used in film and interactive tools for the development of an augmented reality narrative, and the use of simple artificial virtual and real characters (avatar and robot respectively) to create an immersive interactive experience.

In ALICE real and virtual agents (i.e. rabbit and caterpillar robot, Cheshire cat) act as characters who lead the user through virtual and real locations, moral choices and emotional states. The narrative is a surreal quest, sometimes funny, sometimes disturbing. The character White Rabbit (representing the concept of time) introduces him and joins with the user in a series of absurdist challenges. ALICE is an educational journey towards the user's heart's desire, designed to provoke self-reflection on a number of other issues: bullying and trusting others; selfish- and selflessness; enjoying the moment or sublimating pleasure. The user is given the opportunity to occupy and experience any of these mental and emotional positions. ALICE can be used to give interesting examples of many of the basic concepts of adolescent psychology. Alice's experiences can be seen as symbolic depictions of important aspects of adolescent development, such as initiation, identity formation, and physical, cognitive, moral, and social development (Lough [15]). Alice's adventures are de- and reconstructive in nature and as such are directly challenging the strongly held belief of a linear, single track and sequential reality.

Acknowledgements

I am very grateful to my colleagues who made it possible: Sjriek Alers, Dimar Aliakseyeu, Chet Bangaru, Christoph Bartneck, Razvan Cristescu, Jun Hu, Elco Jacobs, Joran Jessurun, Tijn Kooijmans, Hao Liu, Jeroen Peerbolte, Ben Salem, Christoph Seyferth, Vanessa Sawirjo, Joran van Aart, Dirk van de Mortel, Geert van den Boomen, Ton van der Graft, Arrens van Herwijnen, Tijn van Lierop, CheeFai Tan. I have also to thank Microsoft Research in Cambridge and my department of Industrial Design for the financial support.

References

1. Aspect, A.: Quantum mechanics: to be or not to be local. Nature 446, 866–867 (2007)
2. Aspect, A., Dalibard, J., Roger, G.: Experimental test of Bell's inequalities using time-varying analyzers. Physical Review Letters 49(25), 1804–1807 (1982)

3. Aspect, A., Grangier, P., Roger, G.: Experimental realization of Einstein-Podolsky-Rosen-Bohm Gedankenexperiment: a new violation of Bell's inequalities. Physical Review Letters 49(2), 91–94 (1982)

4. Bohm, D.J.: Quantum theory. Prentice-Hall, Englewood Cliffs (1951)

5. Carroll, L.: Alice's adventures in wonderland. Macmillan, Basingstoke (1865)

6. Drucker, P.: The age of social transformation. The Atlantic Monthly 11 (1994) (online)

7. Einstein, A., Podolsky, B., Rosen, N.: Can quantum-mechanical description of physical reality be considered complete? Physical Review 47(10), 777–780 (1935)

8. Engeström, Y.: Activity theory and individual and social transformation. In: Engeström, Y., Miettinen, R., Punamaki, R.-L. (eds.) Perspectives on Activity Theory, pp. 19–38. Cambridge University Press, Cambridge (1999)

9. Hodges, A.: Alan Turing, logical and physical. In: Cooper, S.B., Löwe, B., Sorbi, A. (eds.) New computational paradigms, pp. 3–15. Springer, Heidelberg (2008)

10. Hu, J., Bartneck, C., Salem, B., Rauterberg, M.: ALICE's adventures in cultural computing. International Journal of Arts and Technology 1(1), 102–118 (2008)

11. Itano, W.M., Heinzen, D.J., Bollinger, J.J., Wineland, D.J.: Quantum Zeno effect. Physical Review A 41(5), 2295–2300 (1990)

12. Jantsch, E., Waddington, C.H. (eds.): Evolution and consciousness: Human systems in transition. Addison-Wesley, Reading (1976)

13. Jung, C.G.: Die Archetypen und das kollektive Unbewußte. Gesammelte Werke, vol. 9/I, Walter (1934)

14. Laszlo, E.: Science and the Akashic field: an integral theory of everything. Inner Traditions (2004)

15. Lough, G.C.: Alice in Wonderland and cognitive development: teaching with examples. Journal of Adolescence 6(4), 305–315 (1983)

16. Maton, K.I.: Making a difference: The social ecology of social transformation. American Journal of Community Psychology 28(1), 25–57 (2000)

17. Mitchell, E.: The way of the explorer: An Apollo astronaut's journey through the material and mystical Worlds, Putnam (1996)

18. Mulvey, L.: Thoughts on Myth, Narrative and Historical Experience. History Workshop (23), 3–19 (1987)

19. Nakatsu, R., Rauterberg, M., Salem, B.: Forms and theories of communication From multimedia to Kansei mediation. Multimedia Systems 11(3), 304–312 (2006)

20. Nakatsu, R., Rauterberg, M., Vorderer, P.: A new framework for entertainment computing: from passive to active experience. In: Kishino, F., Kitamura, Y., Kato, H., Nagata, N. (eds.) ICEC 2005. LNCS, vol. 3711, pp. 1–12. Springer, Heidelberg (2005)

21. Nelson, R.: EGGs in a global basket. The Golden Thread (5), 8–12 (2002)

22. Nelson, R.: The global consciousness project-part 2. The Golden Thread (8), 6–10 (2002)

23. Nelson, R.: The global consciousness project-part 3. The Golden Thread (11), 30–31 (2002)

24. Nelson, R.D., Radin, D.I., Shoup, R., Bancel, P.A.: Correlations of continuous random data with major world events. Foundations of Physics Letters 15(6), 537–550 (2002)

25. Rauterberg, M.: Positive effects of entertainment technology on human behaviour. In: Jacquart, R. (ed.) Building the Information Society, pp. 51–58, IFIP. Kluwer Academic Press, Dordrecht (2004)

26. Rauterberg, M.: Positive Effects of VR Technology on Human Behavior. In: Proceedings of The 14th International Conference on Artificial Reality and Telexistence, ICAT 2004, pp. 85–88, KAIST & VRSJ (2004)
27. Rauterberg, M.: Hypercomputation, unconsciousness and entertainment technology. In: Markopoulos, P., De Ruyter, B., IJsselsteijn, W., Duncan, R. (eds.) Fun and Games 2008. LNCS, vol. 5294, pp. 11–20. Springer, Heidelberg (2008)
28. Sheldrake, R.: New science of life: the hypothesis of morphic resonance. Blond & Briggs (1981)
29. Talbot, M.: The holographic universe. HarperCollins (1991)
30. Vaidman, L.: Quantum mechanics: evolution stopped in its tracks. Nature 451, 137–138 (2008)
31. Van Loon, J.: Virtual risks in an age of cybernetic reproduction. In: Adam, B., Beck, U., van Loon, J. (eds.) The risk society and beyond: Critical issues for social theory, pp. 165–182. Sage, Thousand Oaks (2000)
32. Varela, F., Thompson, E., Rosch, E.: The embodied mind. MIT Press, Cambridge (1991)

Non-verbal Full Body Emotional and Social Interaction: A Case Study on Multimedia Systems for Active Music Listening

Antonio Camurri

InfoMus Lab – Casa Paganini Intl Research Centre
DIST- University of Genova
Piazza Santa Maria in Passione 34, 16123 Genova, Italy
antonio.camurri@unige.it

Abstract. Research on HCI and multimedia systems for art and entertainment based on non-verbal, full-body, emotional and social interaction is the main topic of this paper. A short review of previous research projects in this area at our centre are presented, to introduce the main issues discussed in the paper. In particular, a case study based on novel paradigms of social active music listening is presented. Active music listening experience enables users to dynamically mould expressive performance of music and of audiovisual content. This research is partially supported by the 7FP EU-ICT Project SAME (Sound and Music for Everyone, Everyday, Everywhere, Every Way, www.sameproject.eu).

Keywords: non-verbal full-body multimodal interfaces, emotion, social signals, sound and music computing, active listening.

1   Introduction

Entertainment applications characterized by full-body engagement of users has emerged in the recent years. The Nintendo Wii and the diffusion and familiarity by users with interactive art multimedia installations (e.g. in museums and science centers, in public spaces) are examples that bear witness of the diffusion of such "embodied" applications. Art and entertainment is contributing to move toward more effective, user-centric, embodied paradigms of interaction with multimedia content. In a broader scenario, we can envisage future internet networked media enabling users within the next 5-10 years to be fully immersed with 3D audiovisual content, using natural interfaces sensitive to the context and to full-body multimodal expressive intentions, and with the highest degrees of physical as well as social engagement. See for example the User Centric Media EU FP7 ICT projects for a state of the art on these visions.

Already in the sixties, the choreographer Merce Cunningham and the composer John Cage developed an artistic project where a dancer could move in a sensitive space, where his body could modify electronically generated music: this was a sort of a large scale Theremin musical instrument, and we can consider it as a pioneer work

A. Nijholt, D. Reidsma, and H. Hondorp (Eds.): INTETAIN 2009, LNICST 9, pp. 9–18, 2009.
© ICST Institute for Computer Sciences, Social Informatics and Telecommunications Engineering 2009

anticipating current trends of interactive entertainment, interactive dance and music systems, and interactive installations. Many attempts have been done by researchers, artists, and practitioners until nowadays in this direction. International conferences such as ISEA (International Symposium on Electronic Arts), NIME (New Interfaces for Musical Expression, www.nime.org), and ICMC (International Computer Music Conference) bear witness of these developments along more than three decades. A number of challenging and significant examples of cross-fertilization between artistic and scientific/technological research emerged: one example among the several available, can be found in "digital luthery", where the longstanding experience of traditional lathery, developed in many centuries of evolution of musical instruments, is exploited for enhancing and developing not only novel digital musical instruments, but also novel human-computer interfaces and interaction paradigms.

We focus here on innovative multimedia and multimodal human-computer interfaces and systems for performing arts, museums, audience and spectators interfaces, systems for therapy and rehabilitation (we may call it "entertherapy"): these systems are characterized by non-verbal, full-body, emotional, and social interaction. We aim at understanding, modeling, and exploiting the non-verbal expressive gestures (e.g. [1]) and social signals (e.g. [2]), to develop innovative intelligent interfaces and multimedia systems. Our approach is based on the cross-fertilization of scientific and artistic research. Artistic productions [3, 4], museum and science-centre applications [5], therapy and rehabilitation ("entertherapy") [6], and music and multimedia industry entertainment [7, 8] are the main targets where our research results are applied and validated. At the same time, artistic and humanistic theories are often sources of inspiration for scientific research. For example, the Theory of Effort by the choreographer Rudolf Laban has been utilised to design computational models of expressive gesture. In another occasion, important inspiration to scientific research came from the Morphology theory by the French composer Pierre Schaeffer (e.g. [1, 4]).

Given these premises, we briefly sketch in Section 2 a few examples from our research, started in the eighties, toward interactive systems for performing arts and entertainment, based on non-verbal, multimodal, expressive and emotional interaction. Then, the paper considers a main case study on social active music listening, one of our current research project at Casa Paganini – InfoMus Lab. Novel paradigms for social active music experience, based on the dynamic moulding of audiovisual content and expressive music performance are described. This research finds its origins from previous projects (the EU Esprit Project MIAMI – Multimodal Interaction for Advanced Multimedia Interfaces, 1995-1997; the EU CRAFT Project U-CREATE: the EU IST Project MEGA – Multisensory Expressive Gesture Applications, www.megaproject.org), and it is the core topic of the recently started 7FP EU-ICT Project SAME (Sound and Music for Everyone, Everyday, Everywhere, Every Way, www.sameproject.eu). Further, the case study has been designed and developed using the EyesWeb XMI open software platform (www.eyesweb.org).

2   Previous Research and Systems

Since the late eighties, research at InfoMus Lab (www.infomus.org) was directed to the study of sound and music computing, focusing on the understanding of sonic and music communication. This was since the beginning grounded on the hypothesis that knowledge about sound and music must include models on both the motion alluded, evoked by music and the real motor behavior needed to produce the music: music originates by movement, music evokes movement (e.g. in dance), the gestural component is fundamental to understand sonic and music content, up to the expressive subtleties typical of music interpretation in a performance [13].

The HARP approach and system [7] originated a number of entertainment and artistic applications in which music content is related to motor activity. Figure 1 shows the conceptual model of the HARP system. In [7] a series of interactive applications emerging from the research on HARP were proposed (see figure 2): the SoundCage system was based on a sort of sensorized cage equipped with about 80 IR sensors and floor tiles (see figure 2, on the left), capable to reconstruct approximated features of the movement of a human moving inside the "cage"; the HARP/Vscope was based on the V-Scope sensor system, characterized by IR / US wearable wireless markers able to track human behavior; the HARP/DanceWeb was based on a cluster of US sensors directed vertically from the ceiling to the floor, integrated with sensorized pressure tiles. Description of the latter two systems are available in [5] and in [3]. Main ideas were to influence and modify the music listened by dancing, and to develop novel concepts of games, we called them "audiogames", where sonic and music material were the main content, addressed and manipulated by the non-verbal full-body behavior, keeping into account memory and context. HARP was a hybrid system to support the development of interactive gesture- and sound-driven interactive stories. We proposed several proptotypes and museum applications based on HARP, for example an application able to re-mix and re-structure in real-time MIDI-based music

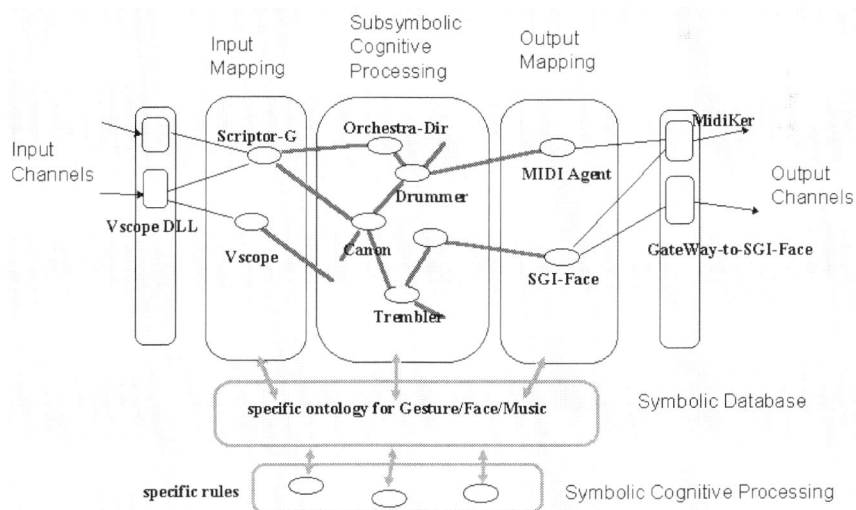

Fig. 1. The HARP model for an application where human gesture controls both the synthesis of the emotion of an artificially synthesized 3D human face and the interpretation of a computer-generated music [7]. This was designed in the MIAMI EU Esprit project (1994-1997).

Fig. 2. Three interactive dance-music systems: the HARP/DanceWeb (in the picture, it is the "start"-like structure hanging on the right from the ceiling), the HARP/Vscope (in the centre, on the floor the receivers of the signals from wireless markers are shown), and the SoundCage interactive dance-music machine (the sensorized "cage" on the left and behind the column), at the EC EITC'95 Exhibition as entertainment tools in the CyberCafé' area (Brussels Congress Centre, 27-29 Nov.1995.

pieces, thus obtaining a sort of "dance karaoke", where orchestration, tuning, quality of the sound depends on the quality of dance. The diverse scenarios of entertainment applications can be found in [3, 7].

The idea of active experience of audiovisual content was also the basic idea for the museum project described in [5]: the "Music Atelier" of the "Città dei Bambini" science center in Genoa included a series of interactive installations: one was based on the HARP/DanceWeb for interactive audio-based storytelling, to explore and experience physically sound and music content. Further, a simple mobile robot, based on Stanford Research Institute "Pioneer 1" platform, was acting in the "Music Atelier" as a mobile installation, a companion of children, talking and interacting with them and the other installation of the atelier. The Music Atelier was active for five years from 1997, and was one of the first projects of our Centre for science-centres and museums.

From 1997 to 2004 InfoMus Lab was hosted at the Genoa Opera House - Teatro Carlo Felice: this collaboration included a lab site at the theatre and joint activities, including projects involving scientific experiments within artistic productions of the Opera House. This was very productive for maturing experience on scientific and technological research development cycle, grounded on the cross-fertilisation of artistic and scientific research. For example, we had the opportunity to participate to

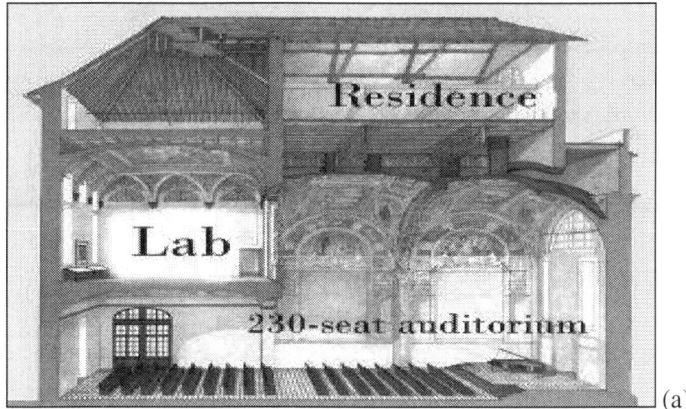

(a)

Fig. 3. (a) the layout of two of the rooms of *Casa Paganini – InfoMus Intl Centre of Excellence*: one of the main Lab rooms (Matroneo) is in a space not visible from the auditorium but allowing a full control of what happens on stage: this allows researchers to perform ecological experiments on emotion and empathy (among musicians, dancers, or between performers and the audience) without any perturbation. (b) the experiment in 2006, in occasion of the *Intl Violin Competition "Premio Paganini"* and the *EU Summer School of the Network of Excellence HUMAINE*: selected violinists were measured in different conditions (eye Vs no-eye contact; induced Vs simulated emotion; etc.), in order to create a dataset to study emotions and in particular emotional entrainment between musicians [12], and with the audience during a concert. The view of the stage is as it is seen from the Lab/Matroneo.

the artistic project of the "lighting keyboard" for the Scriabin's "Promethee" symphonic poem, performed with the orchestra of the Opera House. Here the interaction was between the colors evoked by the "light keyboard", one of the instruments of the orchestra (for more details, see www.infomus.org), and its relations with the music and the concert hall of the opera house, providing interesting insights on interactive systems for multiple users (the audience of the concert) integrating sound and color.

Since 2005, InfoMus Lab has its new premises in the recently restored monumental building of S.Maria delle Grazie La Nuova - Casa Paganini. This new site is determinant to contribute to the growth of the process of cross-fertilisation between artistic and scientific research (see figure 3).

3 Case Study: Social Active Music Listening

We recently started a project on active music listening (www.sameproject.org; [8]). Music making and listening are a clear example of interactive and social activity. However, nowadays mediated music making and listening is usually still a passive, non–interactive, and non-context sensitive experience. The current electronic technologies, with all their potential for interactivity and communication, have not yet been able to support and promote this essential aspect of music making and listening. This can be considered a degradation of traditional listening experience, in which the public can interact in many ways with performers to modify the expressive features of a piece.

The need of recovering such active attitude with respect to music is strongly emerging, and novel paradigms of active experience are going to be developed. With *active experience* and *active listening* we mean that listeners are enabled to interactively operate on music content, by modifying and molding it in real-time while listening. Active listening is the basic concept for a novel generation of interactive music systems [9], which are particularly addressed to a public of beginners, naïve and inexperienced users, rather than to professional musicians and composers.

Active listening is also a major focus for the EU-ICT Project SAME (Sound and Music for Everyone, Everyday, Everywhere, Every Way, www.sameproject.eu). SAME aims at: (i) defining and developing an innovative networked end-to-end research platform for novel mobile music applications, allowing new forms of participative, experience-centric, context-aware, social, shared, active listening of music; (ii) investigating and implementing novel paradigms for natural, expressive/emotional multimodal interfaces, empowering the user to influence, interact, mould, and shape the music content, by intervening actively and physically into the experience; and (iii) developing new mobile context-aware music applications, starting from the active listening paradigm, which will bring back the social and interactive aspects of music to our information technology age.

The Orchestra Explorer [8] allows users to physically navigate inside a virtual orchestra, to actively explore the music piece the orchestra is playing, to modify and mold in real-time the music performance through expressive full-body movement and gesture. Concretely, the virtual orchestra is spread over a physical surface (see figure 4). By walking and moving on the surface, the user discovers each single instrument or section and can operate through her expressive gestures on the music piece the instrument is playing.

The Orchestra Explorer is not a simple reproduction or remixing of multiple audio tracks, nor a full automatic conducting system. It is something in between these two extremes. On the one hand, it provides the active listener with means for operating on the sound and music content that are not available in simple (passive) reproduction or remixing of multiple audio tracks. On the other hand, it does not provide the full control of the performance as in traditional conducting systems (e.g., see Lee et al., 2006). This approach is motivated by our aim of developing a new paradigm which, while actively engaging listeners, is at the same time different from traditional metaphors such as conducting, and enabled by recent research on expressive multimodal interfaces. The user really becomes an explorer of sound and music, i.e., she discovers the content step by step; she gradually understands how music performance works; she learns how to operate on the content. Figure 4 shows a sketch of the Orchestra Explorer paradigm.

We developed another active music listening paradigm, starting from the *Orchestra Explorer*, characterized by social interaction among users. We applied this paradigm for the design of a multimedia installation and a performance for dancers and singers: *Mappe per Affetti Erranti* [11]. It extends and enhances the *Orchestra Explorer* in two major directions. On the one hand it reworks and extends the concept

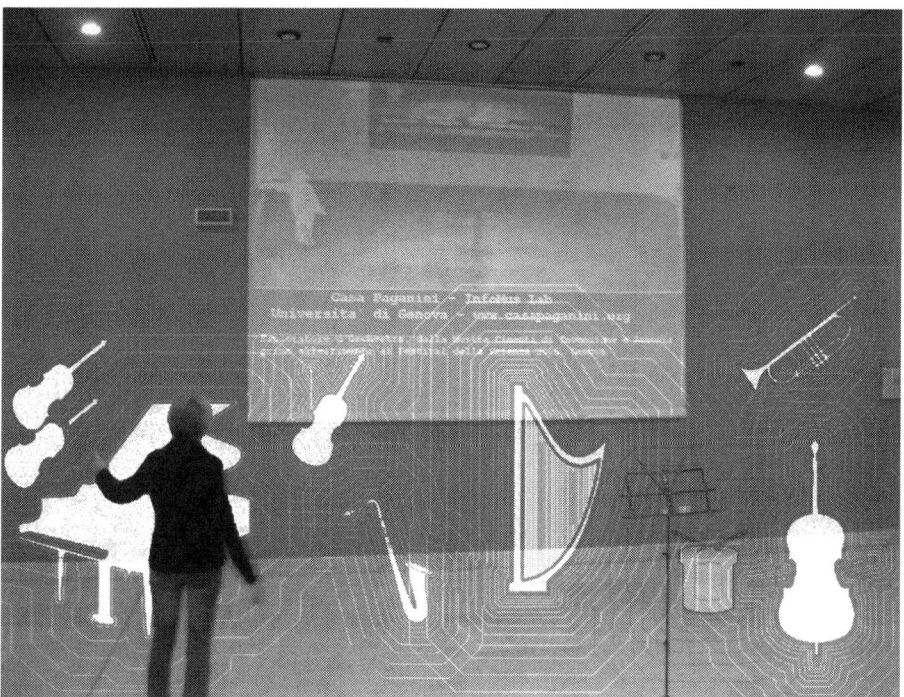

Fig. 4. An example of implementation of the paradigm of the active music listening paradigm: the "orchestra explorer" at Accademia di Santa Cecilia in Rome (2007). (Photo by Corrado Canepa)

Fig. 5. The paradigm of active music listening with social interaction: each user "embodies" a music section of the piece, and her behavior influences the expressive interpretation of her associated music section. We adopted vocal music pieces in our experiments: so each of the four users "embodies" one of the specific voices of the music piece (baritone, tenore, contralto, and soprano). The music is pre-recorded. The users can intervene to modify the voices with various degrees of freedom. For example, if a user moves shy and hesitant, her associated voice changes, e.g. toward a more intimate and whispering interpretation. If she moves aggressive, her voice performance becomes loud, extrovert, and angry. Emotion models from experimental psychology are here utilized. To obtain a coherent performance, all the users must converge to behave with similar, coherent behavior. Otherwise, the different voices remain unsynchronized and with separate, contrasting interpretations.

of navigation of a virtual orchestra by introducing multiple levels: from the navigation in a physical space populated by virtual objects or subjects (as it is for the musical instruments in the *Orchestra Explorer*) up to the navigation in virtual affective, emotional spaces populated by different expressive performances of the same music piece. Users can navigate such affective spaces by their expressive movement and gesture. On the other hand, *Mappe per Affetti Erranti* explicitly addresses the fruition by multiple users and encourages collaborative behavior: only collaboration among users brings toward aesthetically pleasant reconstructions of the music piece. In other words, while users explore the physical space, the (expressive) way in which they move and the degree of collaboration between them allow them to explore at the same time an affective, emotional space. On the one hand, the new system exploits a refined set of features for expressive gesture classification, including a new model for measurement of impulsiveness and features for analysis of the behavior of a group of users as a whole. On the other hand, it supports adaptation to context, i.e., it can change inputs, outputs, analysis and mapping strategies according to what is needed in the different situations For example, during a performance the interaction rules may change according to the evolution of the music piece. In a situation of shared/social active listening, the situation can adapt to the type and behavior of users.

The case studies described in this section (as well as all the research prototypes and applications we developed in the last ten years) have been developed with the EyesWeb open software platform. The latest version, EyesWeb XMI, is available for download from www.eyesweb.org.

4 Discussion

The social active listening paradigm described in the previous section opens new perspectives for both research and applications. We studied and developed a number of techniques for measuring social signals, resulting in a new library for our EyesWeb XMI open software platform (www.eyesweb.org). A novel approach and novel algorithms for the analysis of social behavior, and in particular of human emotional synchronization has been developed [12]. In a recent experiment, gestures from a duo of violin players were collected (see figure 3b) and analysed to detect occurrences of emotional-based Phase Synchronisation. The analysis of gesture is conducted using Recurrence Plot and Recurrence Quantification Analysis methods, and a statistical validation of results is done exploiting a surrogate data approach. For example, in this experiment, some of the results show that emotional entrainment occur preferably when players can communicate only by sound, and that positive emotions such as Serenity and Joy seem to promote this coordination better than negative emotions like, for example, Anger and Sadness.

Current research work is directed toward the refinement and extension of social descriptors for empathy, emotional entrainment, leadership, and attention. Two papers in preparation describe the results available so far.

We deem that the inclusion of social signals in the design of multimodal interfaces and systems such as the examples presented in this paper is important to move toward a novel generation of user-centric, embodied artistic and entertainment applications characterized by non-verbal, full-body interaction.

Acknowledgements

I am deeply grateful to my colleagues and friends Corrado Canepa, Paolo Coletta, Gualtiero Volpe, for their invaluable contribute to the development of the active music listening project. I wish to thank also the other colleagues and friends at InfoMus Lab, and in particular Nicola Ferrari, Donald Glowinski, Alberto Massari, Barbara Mazzarino, Maurizio Mancini, Giovanna Varni.

This research is partially supported by the 7FP EU-ICT Project SAME (Sound and Music for Everyone, Everyday, Everywhere, Every Way, www.sameproject.eu). SAME is coordinated by Casa Paganini – InfoMus, and the partners are Nokia Research Centre, Ircam, KTH – Stockholm, TKK – Helsinki Institute of Technology.

References

1. Camurri, A., Mazzarino, B., Volpe, G.: Expressive Interfaces. In: Marti, P. (ed.) Cognition Technology & Work, special issue on "Presence: design and technology challenges for cooperative activities in virtual or remote environments", vol. 6, pp. 15–22. Springer, Heidelberg (2004)
2. Pentland, A.: Socially aware, Computation and Communication. Computer. IEEE CS Press, Los Alamitos (2005)
3. Camurri, A., Ferrentino, P.: Interactive Environments for Music and Multimedia. ACM Multimedia Systems, Special issue on Audio and Multimedia 7(1), 32–47 (1999)
4. Camurri, A., De Poli, G., Leman, M., Volpe, G.: Toward Communicating Expressiveness and Affect in Multimodal Interactive Systems for Performing Art and Cultural Applications. IEEE Multimedia 12(1), 43–53 (2005)
5. Camurri, A., Coglio, A.: An Architecture for Emotional Agents. IEEE Multimedia 5(4), 24–33 (1998)
6. Camurri, A., Mazzarino, B., Volpe, G., Morasso, P., Priano, F., Re, C.: Application of multimedia techniques in the physical rehabilitation of Parkinson's patients. Journal of Visualization and Computer Animation 14(5), 269–278 (2003)
7. Camurri, A.: Interactive Dance/Music Systems. In: Proc. Intl. Computer Music Conference ICMC 1995, The Banff Centre for the arts, Canada, ICMA-Intl. Comp. Mus. Association, September 3-7, pp. 245–252 (1995)
8. Camurri, A., Canepa, C., Volpe, G.: Active listening to a virtual orchestra through an expressive gestural interface: The Orchestra Explorer. In: Proc. Intl Conf. NIME 2007 New Interfaces for Music Expression, New York University (2007)
9. Rowe, R.: Interactive music systems: Machine listening and composition. MIT Press, Cambridge (1993)
10. Lee, E., Karrer, T., Borchers, J.: Toward a Framework for Interactive Systems to Conduct Digital Audio and Video Streams. Computer Music Journal 30(1), 21–36 (2006)
11. Camurri, A., Canepa, C., Coletta, P., Mazzarino, B., Volpe, G.: Mappe per Affetti Erranti: a Multimodal System for Social Active Listening and Expressive Performance. In: Proc. Intl Conf. NIME 2008 – New Interfaces for Musical Expression, Casa Paganini, University of Genoa (2008), http://www.nime.org
12. Varni, G., Camurri, A., Coletta, P., Volpe, G.: Emotional Entrainment in Music Performance. In: Proc. 8th IEEE Intl Conf. on Automatic Face and Gesture Recognition, Amsterdam, September 17-19 (2008)
13. Camurri, A., Morasso, P., Tagliasco, V., Zaccaria, R.: Dance and Movement Notation. In: Morasso, P., Tagliasco, V. (eds.) Human Movement Understanding, pp. 85–124. North Holland, Amsterdam (1986)

Home Exercise in a Social Context:
Real-Time Experience Sharing Using Avatars

Yasmin Aghajan[1,*], Joyca Lacroix[1], Jingyu Cui[2], Aart van Halteren[1],
and Hamid Aghajan[2]

[1] Philips Research, Eindhoven, The Netherlands
[2] Stanford University, USA

Abstract. This paper reports on the design of a vision-based exercise monitoring system. The system aims to promote well-being by making exercise sessions enjoyable experiences, either through real-time interaction and instructions proposed to the user, or via experience sharing or group gaming with peers in a virtual community. The use of avatars is explored as means of representation of the user's exercise movements or appearance, and the system employs user-centric approaches in visual processing, behavior modeling via history data accumulation, and user feedback to learn the preferences. A preliminary survey study has been conducted to explore the avatar preferences in two user groups.

Keywords: Exercise monitor, avatars, pose analysis, experience sharing, social networks, user acceptance.

1 Introduction

A plethora of published research in the past years has underscored the relationship between regular physical activity and physical as well as mental well-being [15]. As a consequence of these findings, public awareness and efforts to promote exercise behavior at home and in fitness centers has considerably increased. The focus on a healthier lifestyle and on increased physical fitness has prompted people to introduce exercise programs into their daily lives. Nevertheless, while the benefits of exercise are widely known, preoccupation with career demands and other daily obligations and activities have caused difficulty for many in finding time to incorporate regular exercise at the gym or outside the home into their schedules. Exercising at home is a viable alternative, but it has two main disadvantages compared to exercising in the gym. The first disadvantage concerns the absence of human coaches that guide a person in following an effective exercise program and provide motivational and educational feedback. The second disadvantage concerns the lack of social factors that may be helpful to enhance motivation and realize commitment to previously formulated exercise intentions such as the company of other exercisers or an exercise friend.

Modern technology opens an enormous space of possibilities for enabling such coaching, motivational and social support in situations where human face-to-face contact is unavailable. Many technological solutions aimed at enriching the

---

* Yasmin Aghajan did an assignment at Philips Research.

A. Nijholt, D. Reidsma, and H. Hondorp (Eds.): INTETAIN 2009, LNICST 9, pp. 19–31, 2009.

exercise experience have been developed to monitor the user's exercise behavior and physiological variables relevant for exercising (e.g., heart rate). These developments are supported with studies from the field of traditional sports and exercise psychology that showed the importance of feedback for motivation and performance [5]. In several studies, it was shown that measuring physical activity (e.g. with pedometer, activity monitor, or self-report) and providing feedback about measured activity enhances physical activity participation (e.g., [11]). Based on the literature we believe that enhancing the concept of exercising at home with interactive elements (e.g., monitoring movements and feedback) and with elements of social connectedness (e.g., connecting with a coach or other exercisers) may be a powerful way to provide the coaching and social support that motivate people to stay with their exercise routine. An important element in the overall user experience is the entertainment factor. In [14], the authors present a comprehensive survey of the area of computational entertainment with several examples spanning the concept of entertainment in ambient intelligence environments, both within and beyond the smart home.

One way to monitor and provide feedback about the exercise movements of an exerciser, while also introducing the notion of entertainment and gaming, is through the use of a real-time image processing system. A camera and a display unit can be used to build an avatar model of the user and project the model and its body movements onto a screen. This system may be used not only to give feedback about exercise motions to the exerciser, but also to share the exerciser's model with relevant others, such as a trainer/coach, an exercise buddy or a group of other exercisers in a virtual community. Depending on user preferences, the graphical model can be displayed at various levels of abstraction through an avatar, ranging from a de-personalized avatar, to a semi-personalized body model avatar, or a personalized view similar to a mirror image.

In such a system, avatars have two roles: i) offering the exerciser immediate visual feedback, and (ii) serving as a communication token that finds relevance in a social context, or where others (e.g., a coach or other exercisers) can see the avatar. In a study experimenting with the former role, it was found that people who watched an avatar that looked similar to themselves and ran on a treadmill for approximately five minutes exercised more the next day than people whose avatars weren't similar in appearance to themselves with regards to body weight, height, and age. Also, those who viewed their avatars lounging around exercised less than those whose avatars were active [3]. Displaying exercise movements through a personal avatar and sharing it with a coach or with other exercisers is expected to enhance the user's awareness of his/her appearance, body shape and movements. Therefore, the level of satisfaction with one's own appearance and body shape and the level of self-confidence about one's own exercise capabilities may impact user preferences with respect to the degree of personalization of the avatar, i.e., the degree to which the avatar reflects the bodily characteristics (i.e., appearance) of the user. Moreover, levels of preferred personalization may vary across different social contexts (defined as the groups with whom the avatar is shared). In short, we expect that user characteristics and the type of social

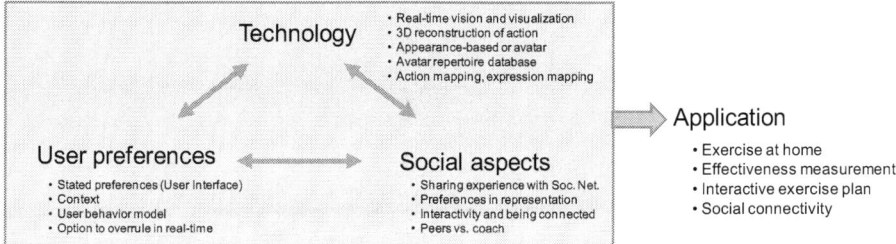

Fig. 1. Interactive design of technology based on user preferences and social aspects

context affect the preferences with respect to the level of personalization of the avatar. Therefore, it is important to gain insight into the relationship between avatar preferences and relevant user characteristics in various social contexts.

In this paper, we propose a design for a home exercise monitoring system that incorporates the notions of interaction with the user and communication with others into a real-time avatar-based representation of the user's exercise. Fig. 1 illustrates our approach to system design for this application, regarding user preferences and social aspects as important factors. In addition, this paper presents a preliminary exploration study into user preferences with respect to avatar types employed in an exercise sharing context. The system offers instructions to the user, measures the movements, and allows sharing the avatar with others, hence providing an enjoyable exercise experience.

In section 2 an overview of the user interface and vision processing modules is presented. The use of avatars as a means of visual connectedness is explained and the visualization options are described. Section 3 introduces user characteristics believed to influence the acceptance of the technology and affect the choice of visual communication through avatars. In particular, we discuss self-image/body-image and gender. We also present our study methodology aimed at gaining insight into avatar preferences by users, and discuss the results of user study surveys conducted with different age groups on the avatar-based exercise experience. Section 4 offers some concluding remarks.

2 Exercise Monitoring System

In order to realize a home exercise system that allows for visual feedback of the user's movements and the possibility of sharing these movements in a social network setting, we need to consider: 1) technology for monitoring the body and the body movements of the exerciser, and 2) possibilities to display the monitored data in a user-friendly way. The system is composed of an interactive module that detects the user's gesture and measures the exercise actions in real-time, and a communicative module that transmits a visual representation of the user to others according to the selection of avatar graphics made by the user. Fig. 2 illustrates the relationship between the different components of the system.

The use of camera and computer vision technology presents a wide scope of possibilities for monitoring the user during exercising. Video taken of the user

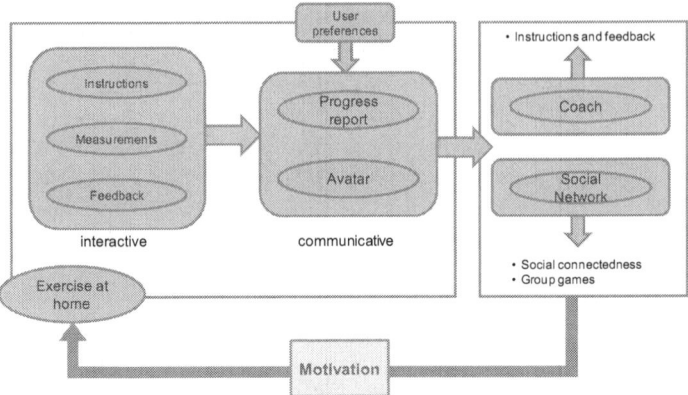

Fig. 2. The overall system block diagram showing the interactive gesture analysis module and the communicative module connecting the user to the outside world. Social connectedness provides further motivation for exercising.

by a camera as he performs exercises can be displayed to him in real-time as a simple means of visual feedback. Such video can be processed locally to extract measurements of the user's body movements such as the number of repetitions and the relative position of joints. In addition, the actions of the exerciser can be mapped onto an 3d model displayed through an avatar in real-time, allowing the user to receive visual feedback which may be augmented with annotations related to the performance or deviations from the ideal routine. The processing involves methods of human pose and gesture analysis. Such methods which are based on extracting positions of the body joints as the user movements are registered between video frames have been reported extensively in the literature [4,16,17,19,20]. Multi-camera implementations in real-time using embedded

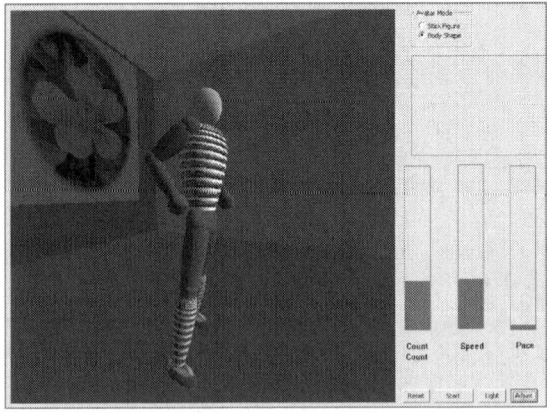

Fig. 3. The interactive module of the system offers measurements such as count, speed, and pace of specific exercise routines

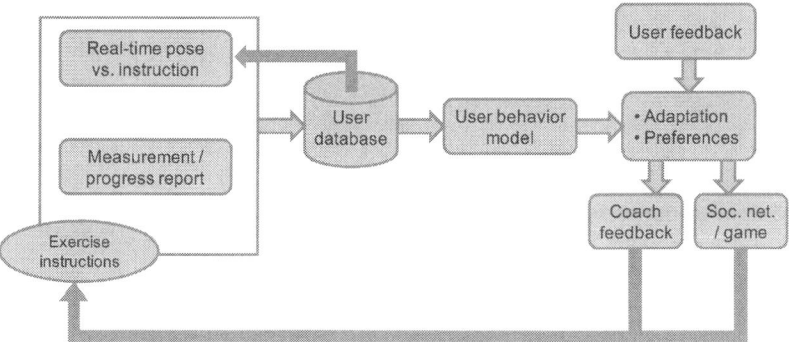

Fig. 4. Schematic overview of the employed mechanisms: pose analysis, behavior modeling, user preference assessment, and creation of exercise instructions

processing have also been reported, for example in multi-player games with networked cameras [25].

The pose estimation output is used to map the user's actions onto an avatar, while analytic measurements are also obtained from the observations. Fig. 3 displays a screen shot of an exercise plan in which the measurements of the count, speed, and pace of the exercise are recorded in the interactive module.

2.1   System Design

The design employs several mechanisms based on the observations and specific behavior models and explicit input from the user. These methods are illustrated in Fig. 4 and briefly described in this section.

Pose estimation: The system suggests an exercise routine to the user, which is displayed on an avatar for the user to follow. The user's pose is detected via a silhouette matching operation using banks of saved silhouettes (see Fig. 5). The knowledge of the specific exercise action being suggested to the user is employed

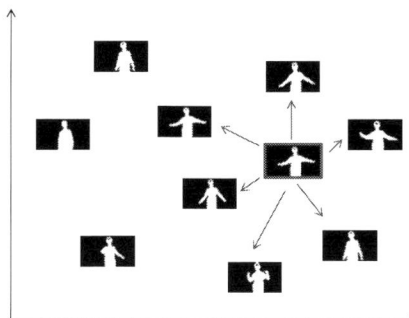

Fig. 5. User's pose is detected using a database of silhouettes accumulated from the user

as prior knowledge to limit the search for matching silhouettes. This yields a processing efficiency gain, enabling a real-time markerless vision-based operation. The silhouettes are created and collected for each exercise routine based on a two-layered method. A generic set of silhouettes is created and embedded in the system for each exercise routine. Then, at the initialization stage of the system the user is asked to follow a simple exercise action through which the system captures the observed silhouettes from the user and builds up a user-specific silhouette set. This silhouette set is used to perform matching in the subsequent instances of the same exercise routine, and the system updates and refines the user silhouette bank for the exercise over time.

Behavior model: The system measures and stores the analytics of the exercise in a database. These include the frequency, duration, pace, and other numeric measurements obtained by visual processing of the exercise and the progress made for each specific routine. The behavior model is used to keep a progress report and to suggest further exercise routines aligned with user's progress. The behavior model also maintains the history of the exercise plan which can be accessed by the user or by a trainer if the user opts for that. Further application of the accumulated data from the user is the subject of our on-going development.

User feedback: The system inquires from the user about the preferences both in the exercise content and in the mode of communication with the outside world. The user's choice of the exercise level and the pace of advancing to higher exercise levels can be adjusted by a simple menu, and the mode of communication offers a choice between sharing the mirror image, a semi-personalized body shape avatar, and a de-personalized, skeletal avatar.

2.2   Representation by Avatars

The experience of the user is determined partly by the graphical representation that is communicated to the user and to the user's social network. Privacy issues as well as cognitions and confidence regarding body image and comfort of exposing one's self to other people may impact a user's willingness to use personal avatars as a visual representation both when exercising alone or in a social context.

The use of avatars has been studied extensively within the domain of virtual communities. Avatars can range from imaginary to realistic, depending on the application, system design and user preferences. The most popular use of avatars has been on instant messaging services in cyberspace. People can use avatars to build their own different identity [7,8]. More recently, the use of avatars has been considered for virtual reality applications such as Second Life (www.secondlife.com) [1] and Qwaq Forum (www.qwaq.com) [24]. Fitness applications for avatars have also been explored to motivate healthy practices by creating and keeping track of a body model avatar online.Interactive avatar applications for exercising have appeared based on devices held by or attached to the body of the user. Gaming platforms such as the Nintendo $WiiFit^{TM}$ have been used for interactive exercise sessions involving the display of an avatar [18].

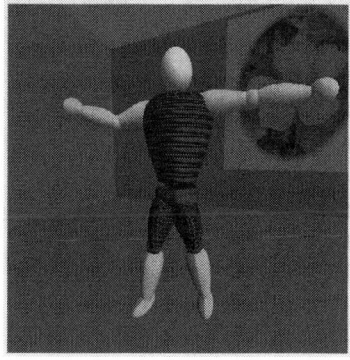 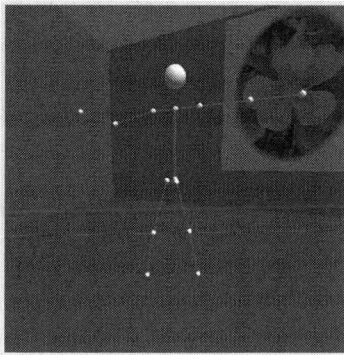

Fig. 6. The user can select a semi-personalized (muscle model) avatar or a de-personalized (skeletal model) avatar for sharing with the social network

The communication function of avatars is most relevant in a social context where others can see the avatar. Considering the identity-expressive properties of an avatar, we expect that avatar preferences vary with certain user characteristics as discussed in section 3. In the context of exercise monitoring applications, it is expected that the use of an avatar and the preferences for the type of avatar become specifically relevant when others (coach, exercising friends) are watching.

In our development, 3 types of representations are available to the user:

- Mirror image (raw video with optional superimposed annotations)
- Semi-personalized avatar (called body shape or muscle avatar)
- De-personalized avatar (called skeletal or stick figure avatar)

Fig. 6 displays examples of the muscle model and skeletal model avatars. The avatars are displayed in a three-dimensional room and the system offers the following flexibilities and selections for the avatar appearance as well as the appearance of the room:

- The viewing angle to the avatar can be set by the user or changed during the session (Fig. 7).
- The user can choose various clothing colors and preset textures for the muscle model avatar (Fig. 7).
- Based on the user input the system can represent the muscle model avatar with body size and proportions reflecting those of the user. The body part proportions can be individually set or a whole body configuration can be selected from a set of sizes from skinny to muscular (Fig. 8).
- The virtual room can be decorated with wall posters and different lighting backgrounds by the user (Fig. 7).

2.3   Current State and Work in Progress

The system operates in real-time on a laptop computer equipped with a regular webcam at the VGA resolution. Operation runs at around 15 frames per second.

Fig. 7. The user can select various clothing configuration for the avatar. The viewpoint, lighting condition, and wall posters can also be set by the user.

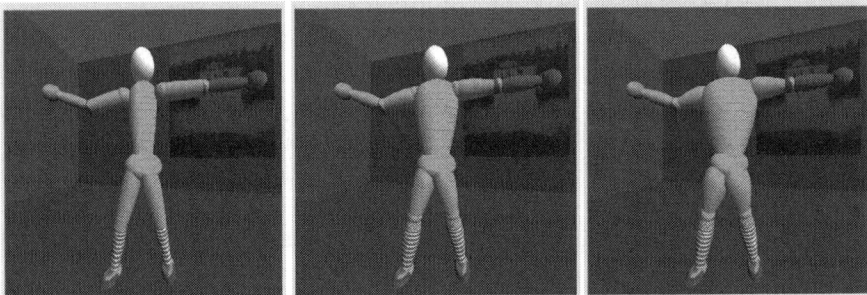

Fig. 8. The body size and proportions of the avatar can be selected by the user or be set to reflect the user's build or fitness indexes such as BMI and WHR

The existing exercise set involves upper body movements, while on-going work consists of embedding several exercise routines in the silhouette database bank, extending the analysis to full body, and the mapping of user's body proportion and fitness information such as body mass index (BMI) and waist-to-hip ratio (WHR) values. The current vision processing for gesture extraction is based on a single camera, restricting the type of the exercises to those occurring in a plane parallel to the image plane. Although an extension to a multi-camera setup may allow more complex exercise routines, the complexities associated with installation, calibration and processing load may introduce disadvantages in home-based applications. A stereo camera system may offer a compromise, and is the subject of further development.

3   Preliminary User Preferences Study

The study entails an initial exploration into user preferences for the degree of personalization of the graphical image (avatar) across different social contexts. It is expected that user characteristics impact these preferences as well as the acceptance of the technology and willingness to use it in the home. The user characteristics that may play a role in shaping these preferences include self-image/body-image (including social physique anxiety (SPA)), personality traits (extraversion, openness), age, self-confidence, self-efficacy, and gender. For our current explorations we focus specifically on self-image/body-image (in particular level of SPA) and gender, to observe preference trends for avatars in different social contexts. We briefly describe the role of these characteristics in influencing user preferences.

Self-image is the way in which a person perceives himself, either physically or as a concept. Self-image has important implications in a person's self-esteem and confidence.Body-image is the feeling a person has specifically about his physical appearance.Related to body-image is the concept of social physique anxiety (SPA). SPA indicates how anxious an individual may be about his body when around others. Although related to self-image and self-esteem, SPA is different in that it is the comfort level of an individual when there are others present. In an experiment regarding social physique anxiety and exercise behavior, it was found that individuals with high SPA were less likely to participate in exercise in situations where their bodies could be criticized [12]. Lantz's results may imply that an individual with high SPA will feel uncomfortable exercising in a social environment where others can see his physique. Such an individual may for example not feel comfortable sharing his mirror-image avatar with a coach or exercise friends.

Several studies have shown that men and women can differ in motivation and reasons to exercise, body perceptions and cognitions, and willingness to engage in competition and comparison with others [2,10,13,21,22]. While these factors may be indicative of gender differences in preferences for the avatar type, no study we know of has directly assessed gender differences in avatar preferences in the field of exercise. However, several studies have examined the correlation between gender and avatar preferences in the context of communication in virtual communities. For example, in a study about the use of avatars in computer-mediated communication, females were more likely to use avatars that were less similar to themselves, whereas males didnt mind using avatars that were somewhat representative of reality [8].

3.1 User Survey

While many types of user characteristics may affect a user's avatar preferences in various social contexts, the survey in this work focuses on the relationship of avatar preferences with gender and body-image (in particular level of SPA). We would like to explore to what extent preferences for avatar type and avatar privacy in the exercise monitoring application vary with gender and level of SPA.

For our survey, we included questions inquiring about user preferences for three types of avatars: skeletal "stick-figure", body-shaped "muscle", and mirror-image. The questions related to the degree of acceptance for sharing each avatar type with a coach, peers in the user's network, and other unknown people. Factors such as enjoyment, comfort, and helpfulness of using an avatar when exercising were also included in the questionnaire.

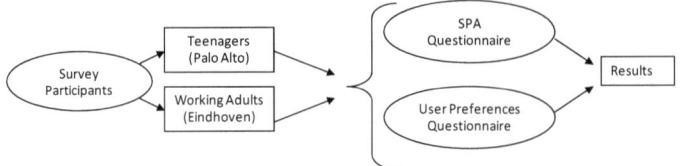

Fig. 9. Components of the user preference survey

We administered an anonymous survey to males and females of two different age groups, namely high school students in California and working adults in the Netherlands. The survey introduced the exercise monitoring project and provided the participants with images of the three types of avatars. Survey takers then proceeded to answer questions rating their view of each type of avatar to see, to share with a coach, exercising friends, or others. Then, we measured their SPA using the 12-point SPA questionnaire [6]. Fig. 9 illustrates the components of the survey.

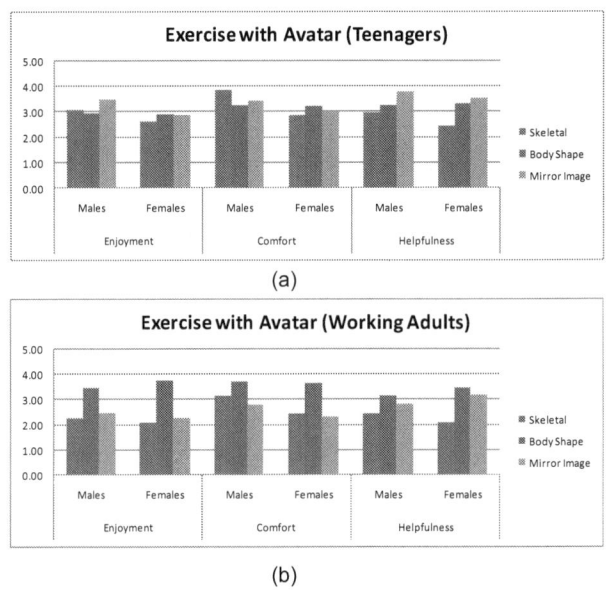

Fig. 10. Opinions on exercise with avatars in different survey groups

3.2   Survey Results

A summary of the survey results is presented in the graphs of Figs. 10 and 11. The most significant observation from these results is the noticeable preferences in the Working Adults group for the body shape (muscle model) avatar, while the interest in the Teenagers group is on the mirror image followed by the body shape avatar. Skeletal avatar receives favorable views only when sharing the exercise experience with unknown others. Other observations from the graphs include:

- Males have a more favorable view of the skeletal avatar than females (Fig. 10).
- Males more easily share mirror image avatar with coach and friends than females (Fig. 11(a)).
- Males and females have somewhat similar view of body shape avatar (Fig. 10).
- Body shape avatar is preferred over skeletal avatar when sharing avatar with coach and friends (Fig. 11(a),(b)).
- Mirror image is not favored when sharing avatar with unknown others (Fig. 11 (a),(b)).
- Skeletal avatar is least preferred except for when sharing with unknown others (Fig. 11(a),(b)).
- Among high SPAs, body shape avatar is more preferred in Working Adults sample than in Teenagers sample (Fig. 11(b)).
- Among high SPAs, skeletal avatar is more preferred in Teenagers sample than in Working Adults sample (Fig. 11(b)).

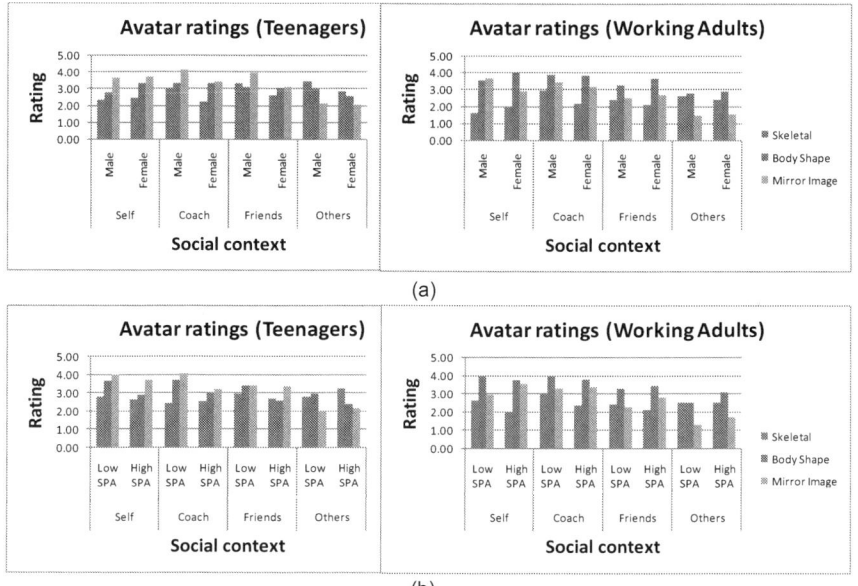

Fig. 11. Avatar type preferences in different survey groups

4   Conclusions

Experience sharing has been a driving force for many of today's social networks applications. As interesting a real-time connectedness concept involving visualization of participants might sound, venturing to develop such a technology calls for a careful system and interface design that closely registers and follows the user preferences for representation and privacy. The work reported in this paper aims to address such a design. An important design element concerns the user's preferences with respect to an avatar through which exercise behavior can be communicated to the user and to peers. Also the avatar can be shared with a coach to receive feedback. This is supported by other system elements, which employ vision to extract the user's pose in real-time, and offer instructions based on history, as well as group gaming options to the user.

References

1. Bell, L.: Who's on third in second life? Online Magazine (July/ August 2007), http://basie.exp.sis.pitt.edu/1904/1/Who's_On_Third.pdf (Retrieved December 31, 2008)
2. Bowden, R., Lanning, B., Irons, L., Briggs, J.: Gender comparisons of social physique anxiety and perceived fitness in a college population. Research Quarterly For Exercise and Sport 73(1), 87 (2002)
3. Dell, K.: How second life affects real life. Time Magazine (2008), http://www.time.com/time/health/article/0,8599,1739601,00.html (Retrieved January 1, 2009)
4. Dimitrijevic, M., Lepetit, V., Fua, P.: Human body pose detection using Bayesian spatio-temporal templates. CVIU (104), pp. 127–139 (2006)
5. Hagger, M.S., Chatzisarantis, N.L.D.: Intrinsic Motivation and Self-determination in Exercise and Sport. Human Kinetics, Champaign, IL (2007)
6. Hart, E.H., Leary, M.R., Rejeski, W.J.: The measurement of social physique anxiety. Journal of Sport and Exercise Psychology 11, 94–104 (1989)
7. Jordan, T.: Cyber Power: The Culture and Politics of Cyberspace and The Internet. Routledge, New York (1999)
8. Kang, H., Yang, H.: The visual characteristics of avatars in computer-mediated communication: Comparison of Internet Relay Chat and Instant Messenger as of 2003. International Journal of Human-Computer Studies 64, 1173–1183 (2006)
9. Kilpatrick, M., Bartholomew, J., Riemer, H.: The measurement of goal orientations in exercise. Journal of Sport Behavior 26, 121–130 (2003)
10. Koivula, N.: Sport participation: Differences in motivation and actual participation due to gender typing. Journal of Sport Behavior 22, 360–381 (1999)
11. Lacroix, J., Saini, P., Homles, R.: The Relationship between Goal Difficulty and Performance in the Context of a Physical Activity Intervention Program. In: Proc. of the 10th Int. Conf. on Human-Computer Interaction with Mobile Devices and Services (MobileHCI) (2008)
12. Lantz, C.D., Hardy, C.J.: Social physique anxiety and perceived exercise behavior. Journal of Sport Behavior 20, 83–93 (1997)
13. Martin Ginis, K.A., Prapavessis, H., Haase, A.M.: The effects of physique-salient and physique non-salient exercise videos on women's body image, self-presentational concerns, and exercise motivation. Body Image 5, 164–172 (2007)
14. Nijholt, A., Reidsma, D., Poppe, R.: Games and Entertainment in Ambient Intelligence Environments. In: Aghajan, H., Delgado, R.L.-C., Augusto, J.C. (eds.) Human-centric Interfaces for Ambient Intelligence. Academic Press, London (2009)
15. Penedo, J.R., Dahn, F.J.: Exercise and well-being: A review of mental and physical health benefits associated with physical activity. Current Opinion in Psychiatry 18, 189–193 (2005)

16. Rittscher, J., Blake, A., Roberts, S.: Towards the automatic analysis of complex human body motions. Image and Vision Computing (12), 905–916 (2002)
17. Robertson, C., Trucco, E.: Human body posture via hierarchical evolutionary optimization. In: British Machine Vision Conference, vol. III: 999 (2006)
18. Schiesel, S.: O.K., avatar, work with me. New York Times (2008), http://www.nytimes.com/2008/05/15/fashion/15fitness.html (Retrieved December 31, 2008)
19. Sigal, L., Black, M.J.: Predicting 3d people from 2d pictures. In: Conference on Articulated Motion and Deformable Objects, Mallorca, Spain (2006)
20. Sminchisescu, C., Triggs, B.: Kinematic jump processes for monocular 3d human tracking. In: Computer Vision and Pattern Recognition, Madison, USA (2003)
21. Smith, A.: Measurement of social physique anxiety in early adolescence. Med. Sci. Sports Exerc. 36, 475–483 (2004)
22. Sorgen, C.: His and hers fitness (2004), http://www.webmd.com/fitness-exercise/guide/his-hers-fitness (Retrieved July 11, 2008)
23. Taylor, A.: Gender differences in exercise motivation. Tarleton Journal of Student Research 1, 18–23 (2006)
24. Vesperini, E. (ed.): Virtual laboratories and virtual worlds. International Astronomical Union, Princeton (2008)
25. Wu, C., Kleihorst, R., Aghajan, H.: Real-time human posture reconstruction in wireless smart camera networks. In: Information Processing in Sensor Networks St. Louis, USA (2008)

Generating Instructions in a 3D Game Environment: Efficiency or Entertainment?

Roan Boer Rookhuiszen and Mariët Theune

Human Media Interaction
University of Twente
P.O. Box 217
7500 AE Enschede
The Netherlands
a.r.boerrookhuiszen@student.utwente.nl, m.theune@ewi.utwente.nl

Abstract. The GIVE Challenge was designed for the evaluation of natural language generation (NLG) systems. It involved the automatic generation of instructions for users in a 3D environment. In this paper we introduce two NLG systems that we developed for this challenge. One system focused on generating optimally helpful instructions while the other focused on entertainment. We used the data gathered in the Challenge to compare the efficiency and entertainment value of both systems. We found a clear difference in efficiency, but were unable to prove that one system was more entertaining than the other. This could be explained by the fact that the set-up and evaluation methods of the GIVE Challenge were not aimed at entertainment.

Keywords: instructions, 3D environment, Natural Language Generation, game, evaluation, efficiency vs. entertainment.

1 Introduction

Natural Language Generation (NLG) is the automatic conversion of some non-linguistic representation of information to written text in natural language (e.g., English). Most NLG systems focus on efficiency and effectiveness, generating texts that are aimed at getting the information across in an optimal way. Common applications of NLG are the generation of weather forecasts and various other kinds of reports. NLG is also used for the generation of system utterances in dialogue systems such as interactive travel guides or virtual tutors. So far, NLG has rarely been used in entertainment-oriented applications such as games.

In this paper, we present the NLG systems we developed for the Challenge on Giving Instructions in Virtual Environments (GIVE), an NLG evaluation challenge to generate instructions for users in a game-like 3D environment. We participated in the GIVE Challenge with two NLG systems: one system that was focused on generating maximally helpful instructions (the Twente system) and one that was intended to be more game-like and thus entertaining (the Warm/Cold system). Although the GIVE Challenge was presented as a game

A. Nijholt, D. Reidsma, and H. Hondorp (Eds.): INTETAIN 2009, LNICST 9, pp. 32–43, 2009.

to its users, who were invited to 'play a game', the evaluation criteria used in the Challenge still focused on effectiveness and efficiency of the generated instructions. In other words, the NLG systems were evaluated as if used in a serious application rather than a game. Nevertheless, in this paper we will try to use the data collected in the evaluation period of the GIVE Challenge to compare our own systems in terms of not only efficiency, but also entertainment.

Overview of Paper. We introduce the GIVE Challenge in more detail in Section 2. In Section 3 we describe the NLG systems we have developed. Our hypotheses on the differences between the systems, and the methods to measure those differences are discussed in Section 4. The evaluation results of our systems are provided in Section 5 and we conclude with a discussion in Section 6.

2   The GIVE Challenge

The GIVE Challenge was designed for the evaluation of automatically generated instructions that help users carry out a task in a game-like 3D environment. We participated in the first installment of the Challenge: GIVE-1 [1].

The GIVE Challenge tries to tackle a difficult problem in the field of natural language generation: evaluation. Since multiple outputs of an NLG system may be equally good (the same information can be expressed in natural language in a variety of ways), it is difficult to automatically evaluate generated texts against a 'gold standard' of texts written by humans. Therefore, the evaluation in GIVE is done based on performance data and subjective ratings gathered with a user questionnaire. Because the GIVE game could be played in an ordinary web browser, it was expected that a large amount of data and human judgements could be collected relatively easily [2]. A website was set up with some short instructions and the game. Players were recruited via (mainly NLG related) email distribution lists and postings on other Internet websites. In total 1143 games were played by people from all over the world, with the largest number of users coming from the USA, Germany and China.

2.1   The Task

Users of the GIVE system were asked to perform a task in a game-like 3D virtual environment. To 'win' the game, they had to follow the instructions that the NLG system produced.

The 3D environment presented to the player of the GIVE-game consists of one or more rooms, connected with doors. There are some objects (e.g. a chair, a lamp) in the world that can be used as 'landmarks' for navigation. On several walls there are buttons of various colors. The objective of the GIVE-game for the player is to find a trophy without triggering an alarm. The trophy is hidden in a safe behind a picture on one of the walls. The safe can only be opened by pressing multiple buttons in the right order. The user has a first person view of the world and can walk through it and turn to left or right (but he cannot walk through walls and closed doors). The user can also press buttons. The function

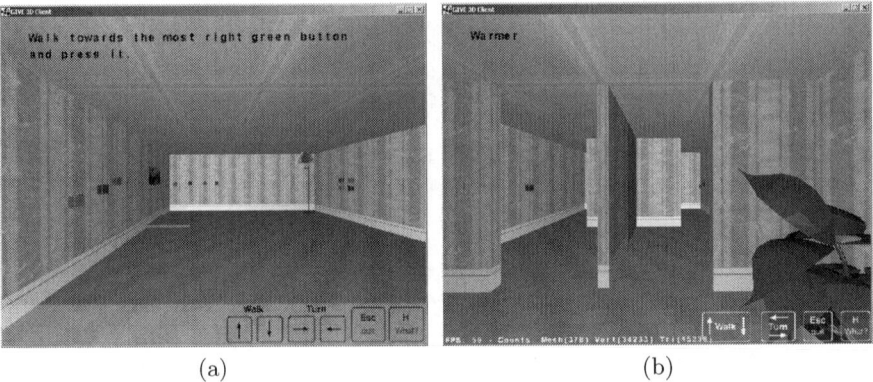

(a)   (b)

Fig. 1. Screenshots of the GIVE game, showing instructions from the Twente system (a) and the Warm/Cold system (b)

of each button however is unknown to the user: a button can open a door, move a picture, but also trigger an alarm. If the user is in the wrong location and passes a detector the alarm is also triggered. It is sometimes necessary to press multiple buttons in a specific order to perform one of the actions described above.

The interface for the user is shown in Figure 1. At the top of the screen instruction sentences are presented to the user. These instructions tell the user which actions he should perform and help him to achieve the goal. The NLG system that generates those instructions has complete knowledge of the world and the actions to be performed in order to win the game; see section 2.2. There are three different game worlds available; for each game one is randomly selected. The worlds have a different layout and provide different levels of difficulty for the instruction-giving system.

2.2   Architecture

The goal of the GIVE Challenge was to develop an NLG system and not to implement a whole client-server architecture. Each participant of the challenge only had to implement the language generation part of the game. All other software needed to run the game was provided by the GIVE organizers. Below we list the main components of the GIVE game environment.

The Client. The client is the actual program the users used to play the game. It could be started from the GIVE website. The client displayed the 3D environment in which a user could walk around and perform several actions. It also displayed the text generated by the NLG system. Before and after the game, the client presented the users with a questionnaire (see section 2.3).

The Matchmaker. During the evaluation period of the GIVE Challenge (7 November 2008 - 5 February 2009), the GIVE organizers ran a matchmaker server. This server held a list of all NLG systems made by the participants of the challenge. As soon as a user started a client, the matchmaker randomly assigned a NLG system to this client. After the game was finished (with or without success), a complete log of all actions performed by both the NLG system and the user was saved in a database for later evaluation.

The NLG System. The language generation part of the game was implemented by each team participating in the Challenge. The input for language generation consisted of a plan containing the sequence of actions the user should perform to successfully achieve the task (i.e., win the game). This plan was updated after each user action. Furthermore the system had complete knowledge of the virtual environment; it knew the position and properties of all objects in the environment, and which objects were currently visible to the user. Based on this information it generated sentences informing the user about what he had to do. The only feedback on the system's instructions were the actions a user performed after having received the instruction, and a notification whenever the user pressed a 'Help' button.

7-point scale items
overall: What is your overall evaluation of the quality of the direction-giving system? (1 = very bad, 7 = very good)

5-point scale items
task difficulty: How easy or difficult was the task for you to solve? (1 = very difficult, 5 = very easy)

goal clarity: How easy was it to understand what you were supposed to do? (1 = very difficult, 5 = very easy)

play again: Would you want to play this game again? (1 = no way!, 5 = yes please!)

instruction clarity: How clear were the directions? (1 = totally unclear, 5 = very clear)

instruction helpfulness: How effective were the directions at helping you complete the task? (1 = not effective, 5 = very effective)

choice of words: How easy to understand was the system's choice of wording in its directions to you? (1 = very unclear, 5 = very clear)

referring expressions: How easy was it to pick out which object in the world the system was referring to? (1 = very hard, 5 = very easy)

navigation instructions: How easy was it to navigate to a particular spot, based on the system's directions? (1 = very hard, 5 = very easy)

friendliness: How would you rate the friendliness of the system? (1 = very unfriendly, 5 = very friendly)

Nominal items
informativity: Did you feel the amount of information you were given was: too little / just right / too much

timing: Did the directions come: too early / just at the right time / too late

Fig. 2. The post-game evaluation questions

In total 4 teams participated in the Challenge, with 5 different NLG systems [3]. As our contribution we created two NLG systems, discussed in this paper.

2.3   Questionnaire

Before and after the game, the user was confronted with an optional questionnaire. This questionnaire was designed by the organizers of the GIVE Challenge; it was the same for each NLG system. Before the game, the user was asked for the following personal information: age, profession, level of computer expertise, level of proficiency in English, and experience playing video games. Then the user played a game, with a randomly assigned combination of game world and NLG system. After the game was finished, the user was asked to rate various aspects of the game experience such as the clarity and helpfulness of the instructions, and the friendliness of the system. The user was also asked to rate the quality of the direction-giving system with an overall score. Most questions had to be answered with a rating on a 5-point scale. The full list of questions asked in the post-questionnaire can be found in Figure 2.

3   Our NLG Systems

For the Challenge, we designed two NLG systems, each with a different goal:

1. The Twente system, focusing on efficiency
2. The Warm/Cold system, focusing on entertainment

The first system, the Twente system, is purely task-oriented and tries to guide the user through the game as efficiently as possible. The Warm/Cold system on the other hand tries to make the game more entertaining for the user even if a consequence is a decrease of the efficiency. Below we describe both systems. A more detailed description of the systems' designs is given in [4].

3.1   The Twente System

The organization of the GIVE Challenge provided all participating teams with an example implementation of an NLG system. This system was very basic and gave only one instruction at a time. This was easy to understand, especially for new users; however it was very annoying for more experienced users. In our first attempt at implementing our own NLG system, all instructions to get to a button were combined into one sentence. More experienced users did perform better with this system than with the example system (they used less time, and found the instructions clearer), but inexperienced users could not handle the increased complexity of the instructions. Because of this difference between new and more experienced users we decided to design a framework with three different levels. The first level generates very basic instructions, explicitly mentioning every step of the plan. The higher levels generate more abstract, global instructions that are expressed using more complex sentences. Some example sentences generated by the different levels:

- Level 1: Only one instruction at a time: "Walk forward 3 steps", "Press the blue button", "Turn right."
- Level 2: A combination of a walk instruction and another action instruction: "Walk forward 3 steps then press the button."
- Level 3: Also a combination, but only referring to objects when the user can see them: "Turn right and walk forward", followed by "Press the blue button." See Figure 1(a) for an example.

In the third level we thus do not give the exact route to the next button to be pushed, but try to encourage users to walk to it on their own. Only whenever the user goes into the wrong direction the system will give an extra instruction.

Our framework is adaptive; the NLG system will try to fit the level to the user's needs. It is expected that novice users learn while they are playing the game. The system is *able to detect* the level of experience of the user and automatically change the level during the game. When the game starts the level used is 2. Every second, the system checks the number of actions the user performed in the last 5 seconds. Whenever this number exceeds a certain threshold the user will probably perform better on a higher level, so the level is switched upward. On the other hand the level is switched down as soon as the number of actions is low or the user presses the 'Help' button.

All levels are generated using the same general framework. The sentences generated by the different levels are very similar. Certain actions are the same for all levels: interpreting events, the generation of referring expressions ("The blue button") and the check whether users are performing the right actions. Only the timing and specific realization of a sentence is different between levels. In our framework a new level can simply be added by making a new class containing the functions that realize the text of all types of sentences. It is very easy to switch between two levels: only the realization of the sentence is different.

We asked a few users to play each level of the game separately (no automatic switching of levels). These test users suggested several small adaptations. For example, in our first version of level 2 a sentence consisted of an action followed by a move instruction. For example:"Turn right then walk 3 steps". People found it more natural and easier to understand when the order was changed to having a move followed by an action: "Walk 3 steps then turn right."

3.2   The Warm/Cold System

To make the task more interesting for the users, we created a more game-like situation with a system that tries to simulate a warm/cold game. Instead of telling the user exactly what to do, the only instructions given are "warmer" and "colder" to tell the user if he comes closer to the next button to be pushed, "turn" to indicate that the user only has to turn to see that button and of course the instruction to push it. Before the user gets his first 'hint', he has to walk around in any direction. To find the next button it is not always enough to follow the instruction "warmer". Sometimes the user has to make a small detour to get around a wall or another obstacle. To encourage the user, some exaggerated statements are used when the user is very close to the target ("Feel the heat!"). The instructions do not prevent the user from triggering an alarm while walking around. As soon as he triggers an alarm he has lost the game.

In short, the system does not exactly tell the user where to go but leaves the navigation choices open. This is illustrated in Figure 1(b): the user is warned that he is getting closer ("warmer") to the button to be pushed, but he still has to decide for himself whether to go left or right. It is expected that this makes it more interesting to play the game, although it will probably decrease the efficiency and increase the playing time. As game studies have shown, player enjoyment increases if a game is more challenging, and if the players have more control and freedom to play the game in the way they want [5].

It was not expected that the Warm/Cold system would perform well in the GIVE Challenge, because the GIVE evaluation focused on efficiency and clarity of instructions. The overview of the results of all participating systems confirms this expectation [3].

4   Evaluation

To test if our systems have achieved their respective goals (being efficient versus being entertaining), we evaluate them using the data collected for our systems in the GIVE Challenge, including the action logs of the system and the answers to the questionnaires. We will compare the results of the Twente system and the Warm/Cold system in light of the two goals. Our main hypotheses are:

Hypothesis 1 - The Twente system is more efficient than the Warm/Cold system.

Hypothesis 2 - The Warm/Cold system is more entertaining than the Twente system.

To test these hypotheses, the only information we have available are the data collected in the GIVE Challenge. A disadvantage is that the evaluation questions used in the Challenge were about clarity and task performance rather than the users' experiences. This means they are most suitable to test Hypothesis 1, whereas for Hypothesis 2 we will have to rely on more indirect clues. Below, we describe how we intend to measure the efficiency and entertainment value of our NLG systems in terms of the data available from GIVE.

4.1   Measuring Efficiency

The efficiency of a system can be measured objectively by using the logged performance results. One system is more efficient than another if using this system, the users successfully performed the task in *less time* and with less detours (i.e., using *fewer steps*) than when using the other system. We also take *task success rate* as an objective indicator of efficiency.

Most questions in the post-questionnaire (Figure 2) deal with the subjective perception of efficiency. We assume that one system is perceived as more efficient than another if it scores better on *task difficulty, goal clarity, instruction clarity, instruction helpfulness, choice of words, referring expressions, navigation instructions, informativity* and *timing*. Also the overall rating of the quality of the direction-giving system *(overall)* is expected to be better, based on the assumption that the users mostly based this rating on the clarity and helpfulness of the instructions, rather than on the entertainment value of the game.

4.2 Measuring Entertainment

It is expected that users find a game more interesting if they have to try harder to finally achieve the goal of the game, as is the case in the Warm/Cold system when compared to the Twente system. The GIVE action logs provide some information that may indicate how entertaining the users found each game. First, *cancellation frequency*: if the user is more interested in the game he is less likely to cancel it. Second, *playing time until cancellation*: if the user does cancel, this is expected to be after a longer period.

As said, the GIVE questionnaire was primarily aimed at measuring clarity and effectiveness of the system's instructions. However, one of the questions can be directly related to the system's entertainment value: if the game is entertaining, the user is more likely to want to play it again. So, in the user questionnaire we expect to find that the score given for *play again* is higher for Warm/Cold than for Twente, even after the user has lost the game.

Finally, we think that if users find a game entertaining, they are at least as interested in the process of playing as in the outcome of the game. Therefore we expect that the more entertaining the users find a system, the less they care about losing. Overall, our prediction is that when the 'game-play' merely consists of carrying out instructions (as with the Twente system), failing to achieve the task ('losing' the game) will negatively influence the users' subjective judgement of the system, whereas in a more entertaining situation (as with the Warm/Cold system) the users' judgement will be much less influenced by the game's outcome.

5 Results

The results presented here are based on the data gathered in the GIVE Challenge. The subjective user ratings for the Twente and Warm/Cold systems, given in Table 1, and a few other results reported here, were taken from the overview paper [3] discussing the outcomes of the Challenge. We computed the other results presented in this section from the raw evaluation data for our two systems, which were made available to us by the GIVE organizers.

Roughly one third of the games was played from an IP address in the USA, another third from Germany and the rest from other countries. Around 80% of the games were played by male users, 10% by female users and for 10% the gender was not specified. Unfortunately we were unable to determine whether all

Table 1. Results of the GIVE user questionnaire taken from [3]. Results that are **significantly different** (with $p < 0.05$) are given in bold face. For *informativity* and *timing* we give the percentages of "just right" answers; these were computed for successful games only.

Question	Twente	Warm/Cold
overall	**4.3**	**3.6**
task difficulty	**4.0**	**3.5**
goal clarity	**3.9**	**3.3**
play again	2.4	2.5
instruction clarity	**3.8**	**3.0**
instruction helpfulness	**3.6**	**2.9**
choice of words	**4.1**	**3.5**
referring expressions	3.7	3.5
navigation instructions	**4.0**	**3.2**
friendliness	3.1	3.1
informativity	51%	51%
timing	60%	49%

games also represent different users, as the GIVE Challenge only distinguished between game plays, not between users. It is possible that users played a game with another NLG system before they used one of our systems.

In Table 1, the results from the questionnaire are reported as the mean ratings given by the users of each system. Each mean value was calculated from roughly 50 answers. Significance was tested by using Tukey tests. The means that are significantly different (with $p < 0.05$) are shown in bold face.

Hypothesis 1. The Twente system is more efficient than the Warm/Cold system if we look at the objective measurements: the task is performed in less time (207.0 vs. 312.2 seconds), using fewer steps (160.9 vs. 307.4). Also the task success rate is significantly higher (35% vs. 18%) [3].

As we have seen in Section 4.1, most of the questions in the questionnaire consider the subjective perception of efficiency. The results shown in Table 1 clearly show that for all questions related to efficiency, except *referring expressions*, there is a significant difference between the means of the two systems.

Hypothesis 1 is confirmed: the Twente system is more efficient than the Warm/Cold system.

Hypothesis 2. In relation to this hypothesis, we predicted that when a game is more entertaining, the player is less likely to cancel it. However, the game logs show almost no difference: 25.8% of the games with the Twente system were cancelled, against 24.6% of the games with the Warm/Cold system. We also expected that entertaining games would be cancelled after a longer period. However, the mean playing time before cancellation was 234 seconds for the Twente system and 233 seconds for the Warm/Cold system. These results contradict our expectation; there is no significant difference between the two systems. The scores for *play again* are not significantly different either (see Table 1).

We also suggested that when a game is entertaining, the outcome is less important than when it is not. To investigate the extent to which the outcome influenced the subjective ratings of each system, we compared our systems' ratings for the games in which the user won and the games in which the user lost. For each system, we tested the significance of the differences between the means of the successful and lost games by using Tukey tests. In Table 2 the means with a significant or near-significant difference are indicated by ** (with $p < 0.05$) or * (with $p < 0.10$). For the Twente system, *task difficulty*, *play again*, *instruction clarity* and *referring expressions* show a significant difference between the user ratings, when distinguishing between won and lost games. This shows that losing a game did cause users to judge the Twente system more negatively on these aspects, whereas for the Warm/Cold system no such negative influence of losing was found. This is in line with our hypothesis. However for one question, *goal clarity*, a significant difference between won or lost games was found for the Warm/Cold system, but not for the Twente system. We will try to give an explanation for this in the discussion.

Based on these results, we can neither confirm nor reject Hypothesis 2.

Table 2. Results of the GIVE user questionnaire. Significant differences are indicated by ** (with $p < 0.05$) and * (with $p < 0.10$)

Question	Twente		Warm/Cold	
	Won	Lost	Won	Lost
overall	4.34	4.26	3.93	3.60
task difficulty	**2.15**	**3.83** **	3.55	3.57
goal clarity	4.10	3.64 *	**3.62**	**2.94** **
play again	**2.14**	**3.06** **	2.56	2.54
instruction clarity	**4.06**	**3.46** **	3.22	2.93
instruction helpfulness	3.64	3.64	3.02	2.91
choice of words	4.22	3.74 *	3.89	3.62
referring expressions	**3.96**	**3.33** **	3.76	3.36
navigation instructions	3.96	3.76	3.38	3.29
friendliness	3.27	2.94	3.29	3.07
informativity	2.26	2.08	1.67	1.69

6   Discussion

Some of the results presented in the previous section differ from what we expected. For example, Table 2 shows a significant difference in *goal clarity* between lost and successful games for the Warm/Cold system, but not for the Twente system. Our hypothesis however was that this should be the other way around. We can explain this because in the GIVE Challenge, the users were led to expect a system aimed at efficiency. The Warm/Cold system has another goal, but this was not (clearly) communicated to the user. It seems that the users were confused about the goal of the Warm/Cold game, and 'blamed' the explanation after losing a game.

In general, the evaluation results for both systems were probably strongly influenced by the users' expectations. In the introduction of the GIVE game, the NLG system was presented to the user as a 'partner' or 'assistant' who would "tell you what to do to find the trophy. Follow its instructions, and you will solve the puzzle much faster." In short, all information provided to the users suggested that the instructions would be as helpful as possible. The players thus expected a co-operative assistant that would obey the Cooperative Principle proposed by the philosopher Grice: "Make your conversational contribution such as is required, at the stage at which it occurs, by the accepted purpose of the talk exchange in which you are engaged." ([6], p. 45). In accordance with the Cooperative Principle, Grice proposed four conversational maxims:

- Maxim of Quantity: Make your contribution as informative as needed, but not more informative than required
- Maxim of Quality: Do not say what you believe to be false or for which you lack adequate evidence
- Maxim of Relation: Be relevant
- Maxim of Manner: Be perspicuous, and avoid ambiguity.

These maxims can be seen as rules a co-operative speaker uses in a conversation. They underlie most work in NLG, and we have obeyed them for the instructions generated by the Twente system. In contrast, we intentionally failed to fulfill some of the maxims to make the Warm/Cold system more challenging. We flouted the Maxim of Manner: our instructions were obscure, and we introduced ambiguity in our direction giving. This is also in violation of the Maxim of Quantity: we gave less information than we could. This made it much harder for the users to understand the direction giving instructions of the system. Instead of just blindly following the instructions, in the Warm/Cold version the user should think of a strategy to be able to win the game, which we expected would make the game more entertaining.

Note that the conversational behaviour of the Warm/Cold system could still be seen as cooperative, in the sense that its instructions were "such as is required (...) by the accepted purpose of the talk exchange" if this purpose was defined as achieving entertainment. However, as mentioned above, this purpose was not clearly presented to the users of the GIVE game. Rather, the accepted purpose was to guide the users as efficiently as possible to the trophy. This probably explains the lower ratings on all questions for the Warm/Cold system compared to the Twente system.

In short, the GIVE Challenge was set up to measure efficiency-related quality aspects of generated instructions. In this paper, we have tried to extract the level of entertainment provided by our systems' instructions from data that were not fully suitable to measure this. In future editions of the GIVE Challenge, it would be good if the participating teams could adapt the user questionnaire to their own research questions. In our case, this would allow us to use better methods for measuring entertainment value, such as the FUN questionnaire developed by Newman [7]. This questionnaire was designed to evaluate player enjoyment in roleplaying games, measuring the degree in which (1) the user lost track of time while playing, (2) felt immersed in the game, (3) enjoyed the game, (4) felt engaged with the narrative aspects of the game, and (5) would like to play the game again. The FUN questionnaire looks like a good starting point for our evaluation purposes, and could easily be adapted to our own game context, as was also done by Tychsen et al. [8].

Acknowledgements. We thank Michel Obbink for his contribution to the development and testing of the Twente system. We are also grateful to the organizers of the GIVE Challenge for the development of the framework and for collecting the evaluation data. In particular we thank Alexander Koller for his quick responses to all our questions. This research has been supported by the GATE project, funded by the Netherlands Organization for Scientific Research (NWO) and the Netherlands ICT Research and Innovation Authority (ICT Regie).

References

1. Koller, A.: First NLG Challenge on Generating Instructions in Virtual Environments (GIVE-1),
   http://www.give-challenge.org/research/page.php?id=give-1-index
   (last visited March 20, 2009)
2. Koller, A., Moore, J., di Eugenio, B., Lester, J., Stoia, L., Byron, D., Oberlander, J., Striegnitz, K.: Instruction Giving in Virtual Worlds. In: Dale, R., White, M. (eds.) Report of the Workshop on Shared Tasks and Comparative Evaluation in NLG, pp. 48–55 (2007)
3. Byron, D., Koller, A., Striegnitz, K., Cassell, J., Dale, R., Moore, J., Oberlander, J.: Report on the First NLG Challenge on Generating Instructions in Virtual Environments (GIVE). In: Proceedings of the 12th European Workshop on NLG, special session on Generation Challenges (2009)
4. Rookhuiszen, R.B., Obbink, M., Theune, M.: Two Approaches to GIVE: Dynamic Level Adaptation versus Playfulness. GIVE-1 Report (2009),
   http://www.give-challenge.org/research/files/
   GIVE-09-Twente-WarmCold.pdf
5. Sweetser, P., Wyeth, P.: GameFlow: A Model for Evaluating Player Enjoyment in Games. ACM Computers in Entertainment 3(3) (2005)
6. Grice, H.P.: Logic and Conversation. In: Cole, P., Morgan, J.L. (eds.) Syntax and Semantics 3: Speech Acts, pp. 41–58. Academic Press, New York (1975)
7. Newman, K.: Albert In Africa: Online Role-Playing and Lessons From Improvisational Theatre. ACM Computers In Entertainment 3(3) (2005)
8. Tychsen, A., Newman, K., Brolund, T., Hitchens, M.: Cross-Format Analysis of the Gaming Experience in Multi-Player Role-Playing Games. In: Situated Play, Proceedings of DiGRA 2007 Conference, pp. 49–57 (2007)

Interactive Documentary: A Production Model for Nonfiction Multimedia Narratives

Insook Choi

Emerging Media Technologies, Department of Entertainment Technology
New York City College of Technology of the City University of New York
300 Jay Street V411, Brooklyn, NY 11201, USA
ichoi@CityTech.CUNY.edu

Abstract. This paper presents an interactive production model for nonfiction multimedia, referred to as interactive documentary. We discuss the design of ontologies for authoring interactive documentary. A working prototype supports the use of reasoning for retrieving, composing, and displaying media resources in real-time. A GUI is designed to facilitate concept-based navigation which enables queries across media resources of diverse types. A dual-root-node data design links ontological reasoning with metadata, which provides a method for defining hybrid semantic-quantitative relationships. Our application focuses on archiving and retrieving non-text based media resources. The system architecture supports sensory-rich display feedback with real time interactivity for navigating documents' space. We argue an experience of narratives evolves through the performitivity in the interactive narrative structure when the constituents are mediated by common ontology. The consequential experience identifies a renewed practice of oral tradition where the accumulative sensorial propositions inform narratives, such as in performance practice.

Keywords: Documentary, ontology, authoring, media production, cognitive architecture, oral tradition, GUI, interaction design.

1 Introduction

Documentary in film practice is an established genre. Yet its definition often undergoes a discursive path. Two factors play consistently in various definitions: 1) reality is captured in some forms of documents and 2) the documents are subjected to assemblage to serve a larger context. This paper proposes a production model of documentary with respect to the emerging practices with interactive technologies. As a starting position the paper adopts the simplest task definition of traditional documentary, that of Vertov: "to capture fragments of reality and combine them meaningfully" [1]. We attribute Grierson's "the creative treatment of actuality" [1] to be at the heart of documentary practice for both spectators and authors. In this spirit we facilitate interactivity to reduce the gap between the two poles in documentary culture, between users and producers, between production and reproduction, and between authoring and an act of inquiry.

A. Nijholt, D. Reidsma, and H. Hondorp (Eds.): INTETAIN 2009, LNICST 9, pp. 44–55, 2009.
© ICST Institute for Computer Sciences, Social Informatics and Telecommunications Engineering 2009

The construction of the documentary utilizes both physical and literary narrative devices, found in many forms of storytelling. The devices are engaged by information sources such as first-person accounts to anchor them in factual circumstances. The result is a narrative about factual objects and events which include original and reconstructed documents and representations of them. The work of narrative relies significantly upon human memories for reconstructing observations and experiences. In terms of narrative structure, these basic cognitive functions create a unique role of the narrator as a direct or indirect subject in the narrative.

An act of authoring involves grounding perspectives and rationales as in storytelling. Storytelling in turn is an act of authoring of performance instances. In interactive documentary the performance is an act of authoring parallel to illustrated storytelling or annotating a flow of media resources. In our architecture, the use of ontologies is brought to organize the references and media resources. Currently the working prototype includes 2D images and videos, 3D graphic models and scenes, simulations, and data-driven and procedural auditory and visual processing of resources.

The remaining part of Section 1 covers related works through a comparative analysis with respect to the proposed system. Section 2 describes the production model in our system and we work through the definition of an interactive documentary. Section 3 describes the working prototype focusing on 1) the role of path-making for generating narrative recall, 2) the use of interactive reasoning to retrieve media resources, and 3) a graphical user interface design for queries across media resources of diverse types. Section 4 describes the design of ontological data, specifically a dual-root-node data design linking ontological reasoning with metadata, which also serves as a method for defining hybrid relationships of semantic and quantitative data.

1.1 Related Work

Interactive Documentary combines elements of generative storytelling systems with an interaction framework related to live media, virtual reality performances, and installations. The present application of semantic networks came about while developing generative models for interactive media performance [2]. Bocconi's "Vox Populi" [3] has similarities to the interactive documentary concept in terms of functional goals for preparing semantics. One common goal is to provide production-level access to documentary material for community exploration and reconfiguration beyond the constraints of pre-determined linear presentations. Another similarity is the role of an initial design phase to specify a semantic context that will result in a graph structure of semantic units. This phase is parallel to "pre-authoring," discussed in Section 2. Bocconi describes semantic annotation of individual media resources; we use a process of grouping resources to concepts, rather than annotation of each resource. Vox Populi uses a thesaurus of rhetorical constructs to determine the point of view expressed in spoken text. In distinction our structured vocabulary of concepts describes contents of media resources ("traffic downtown") and real-world objects depicted in media resources ("my car"; "6th avenue and 42nd street"). Both projects generate data-driven media sequences by navigating a graph structure; our prototype operates in real-time with navigation controlled by an observer. Vox Populi is highly specific for rhetorical relationships in video sequences, whereas we utilize a *display grammar* that generates "display prosody" in real-time for multiple types of media, dynamically determining durations and inter-media composition and tempos. Prosody is determined through ontology of qualitative aspects of media resources such as tone, duration, and other sensorial properties, accounted in the display grammar.

"Evolving Documentary" [4] and "Multi-Threaded Stories" [5] propose models for documentaries that can be modified in successive presentations as situations evolve and new media resources are available. This is similar to our model of an observer with an authored work creating alternate semantic "paths" to customize and extend the work. "Very Distributed Storytelling" [6] sketches an idea of widely embedded interactive media governed by a central narrative production system. Installation-based narratives are similar to our previous work applying motion-sensing and pattern-recognition to observers' movements in a gallery to generate paths through a semantic network [7].

Interactive Documentary most notably differs from previous work in its focus on the integration of media resources of multiple types with semantic composition and real-time interaction. This follows from a body of applications and research in live performance for virtual reality and interactive media installation [8]. Mutual interests shared by these research histories indicate a likelihood of productive exchanges in the areas of semantic computing, media resource analysis and signal processing across multiple display devices and modalities.

1.2 Production in a Heterogeneous Media Ecosystem

Today media content is often created as a convergence of diverse media types deployed on diverse devices. Display systems such as personal communications devices can differ considerably from the production systems where media resources originate. And their roles can be reversed: personal devices can generate media in consumer formats that are repackaged and distributed by media syndication. It is an open, multi-platform ecosystem. Media can be authored to combine resources that are pre-selected with resources that are automatically searched and pulled from diverse providers. Authoring combined with semi-automation can re-use media resources to create new content. Social networks represent heterogeneous communities of media end-users as producers where oral histories are widely exchanged in multiple media formats. These practices may be formalized through a model for interactive documentary production. The model presented here is designed to support a heterogeneous media capacity by systematizing semantic authoring functionality:

1. Common representations for reasoning over media of unlike types;
2. Semantic representations of authored media shared by multiple observers;
3. Ability to author multiple versions from shared semantic structure;
4. Ability to modify the semantic structure without changing the media resources;
5. Ability to modify the media resources without changing the semantic structure.

2 Interactive Documentary Production Model

As a working definition, Interactive Documentary is a production model for telling and retelling nonfiction narratives by means of interactive recall for retrieving media resources in an open data space. Nonfiction refers to representations of real-world artifacts. Narrative is synthesized through composite interactions of components and constituent media resources. Authoring in the context of interactive media refers to the design of instruction sets integrating contents of multiple types, media devices in an anticipation of observers' actions to realize terminal presentations. The instruction sets are embedded with media content or otherwise transmitted to display systems and devices. An authoring process configures initial conditions, combinations of media resources and conditional procedures for generating program contents. Authoring anticipates actions of observers who are sensed by the system.

Our prototype system combines a capacity for (1) *authoring interactive media* with (2) an *interactive authoring process*. The first refers to production of procedures for processing media resources while responding to observers' actions. The second refers to an authoring environment supported by real-time media processing to display results of procedures. The objective is to support both capacities in close proximity with proper system architecture and performance.

When a system enables interactive authoring with real-time feedback, the authoring process is similar in many ways to a presentation process, placing the author in a role akin to a presenter or a performer who is rehearsing and modifying their material. This quality of performativity emphasizes similarities to oral tradition. For system configuration some aspects of planning, source material acquisition and concept design are not feasible for real-time semantic interaction. These are prepared in advance in a process we refer to as *pre-authoring*. Figure 1 illustrates an interactive documentary production model comprised of a pre-authoring phase and an interactive authoring phase.

Pre-authoring tasks consist of

- Review and ingest media resources to an ontological repository
- Define concept vocabulary
- Assert membership of resources to concepts (i.e. identify concepts that describe the media resources)
- Design *display grammar* for the automated display of resources.

The interactive authoring tasks consist of

- Access the concept graph structure through an interface
- Explore structured vocabulary of concepts
- Generate queries to display media resources associated with a concept
- Explore paths of queries previously authored
- Modify existing paths or create new paths by arranging concept nodes
- Define new concepts by applying logical expressions to existing concepts.

3   Interactive Documentary Prototype

In Figure 1 three layers of function modules in the architecture relate to control flow and data flow with temporal differentiation. Active Observation modules support fine-grained scheduling for immediate action-feedback response in the GUI and media displays. Working memory modules weigh relationships among concepts and media contents and provide heuristics for displaying these relationships. Long-term memory

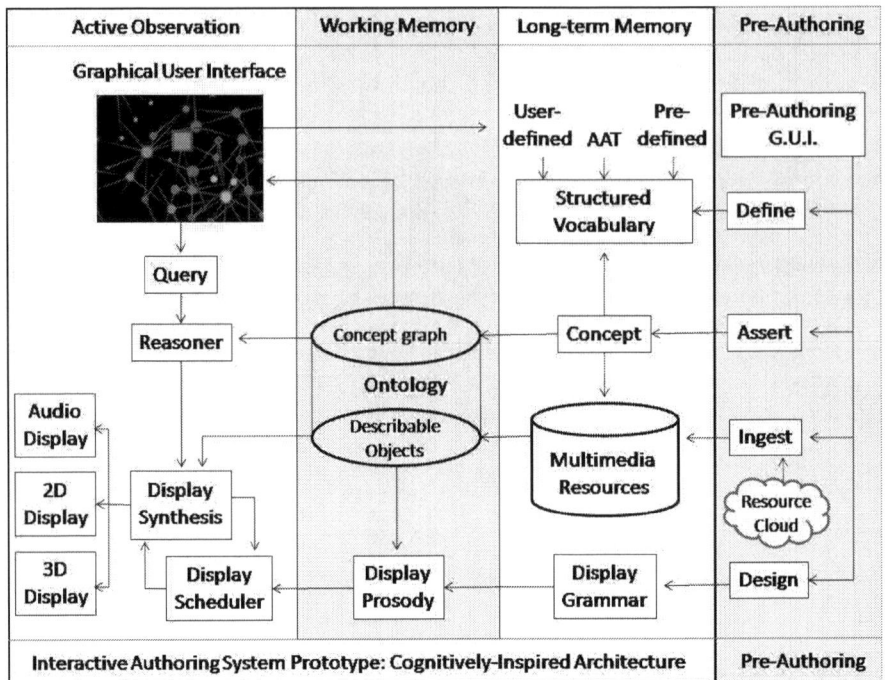

Fig. 1. Interactive Documentary Production Model

modules represent deep structure and media assets supplying production capacity. Semantic and media assets are brought into relationships in the computational workflow.

We describe the architecture as cognitively-inspired in reference to our system design criteria to facilitate concept formation, computational inference, and the observer's cycle of discovery, prediction, and path refinement. Von Foerster draws a distinction between the "invariance of quality" in storage and retrieval, and the synthesis of information in recognition and recall [9]. He regards perception, memory, and inference (prediction) as the requisite components of cognitive processes. The pre-authoring phase supporting the composition of a concept graph indicates a strong role for prediction in the process of interactive exploration and path-making. To design a concept graph is to predict as well as to perceive. To explore a concept graph is to predict as well as to discover. To traverse a path is to recall a sequence of predictions in the form of queries. While computational inference supports storage and retrieval, an author's concept designs and path-making constitute recognition and recall. Paths are coupled to the production architecture for observers' dispositions for learning through ontological inference.

For semantic organization and reasoning we have adopted an ontological data design. The authoring process is formalized as path planning through a semantic data structure—an ontology describing media resources of diverse types. Ontological structure is defined as a set of logical expressions that may be interpreted as a directed graph of concept nodes, where edges represent relatedness of concepts. Structure is encoded in OWL file format using an open source editing tool [10] [11].

3.1   Graphical User Interface: Path-Making for Interactive Authoring

The path-making process is supported by a graphical user interface. A media scheduling engine displays the results of each query as a real-time mixture of media resources. The ontological graph is visualized in the GUI as a 2D network of nodes and edges. Figure 2 shows the GUI as a collection of dynamic nodes; visible nodes represent a limited region of a much larger ontology. Several levels of interaction are defined. Mouse-over a node displays its concept name. Double-click on a node selects that node to generate a resource query and modifies the display to reveal all nodes that are nearest neighbors. Nodes remain hidden until a nearest neighbor is selected. Nodes are displayed with animated ball-and-spring dynamics, aiding visual identification of relationships. The "current location of the user" is defined as the most recently selected node. The square node is anchored; it is a member of an authored path.

The idea of making paths through a digital document space can be traced to multiple sources, including the Memex technology proposed by Bush in the late 1940's [12]. These proposals focus on "trails of documents" using text processing for cross referencing and indexing to achieve more efficient storage and retrieval. Our prototype differs from "trails of documents" proposals by implementing *paths of queries;* paths through concept space generating queries as acts of creative inquiry, recalling in real-time sequences of composite displays of resources, functioning both as dynamic media content and as semantic navigation feedback to an observer.

Figure 2 represents the current prototype interface for query paths. A vertical array on the left of the GUI is a sequence of concept nodes arranged as a path. The path can be traversed in order or explored out of order. In the main GUI a selected path member displays a square anchor node and a concept neighborhood. Any node in the concept neighborhood can be expanded for exploration. Clicking on anchor nodes

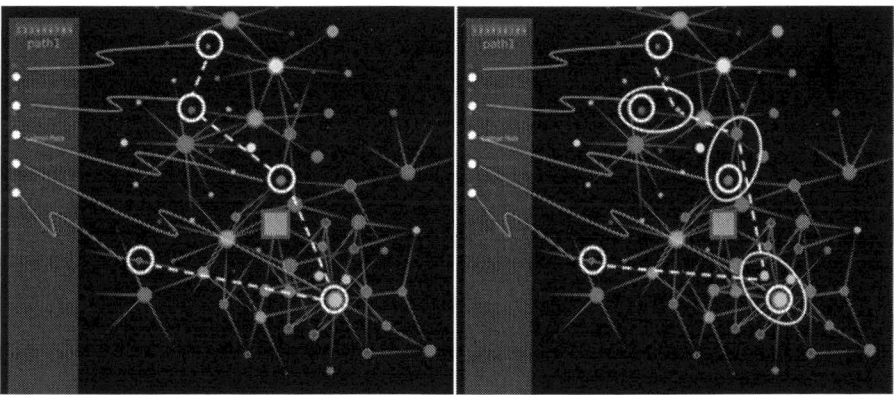

Fig. 2. Graphical User Interface representing concepts as interactive nodes. Size of node indicates number of links to a node. Color indicates subclass-superclass relationship. A Path of nodes is presented in separate vertical array on the left. **2A (left)**: White circles show graph positions of each path node; dotted lines indicate non-adjacent links across semantic regions. **2B (right):** A second narrative instance of the path utilizing alternate nodes in semantic regions of the original path nodes.

generates the queries selected by the path author. Clicking on a non-anchor node returns a related set of media resources and expands the graph visualization to reveal the concept neighborhood of the selected node. Exploration of neighboring nodes produces further queries returning related resources.

We advance the principle of paths of queries not only for initial creative acts but as the regular and normative use model for experience of Interactive Documentary. This is to say that an Interactive Documentary is generated and re-generated through path recall, and the distinction between authors and observers is fluid. An observer may follow a path verbatim or introduce variations, which can be fleeting or result in multiple path versions we refer to as *narrative instances*.

3.2 Interactive Media Use Case

To develop examples of nonfiction narratives, a set of media resources was gathered in reference to present-day and historical Brooklyn [13]. A tiled large-screen format is used to display 2D images and 3D scenes. The GUI is accessed at a small kiosk. To render a path, the system responds to queries by scheduling the concurrent display of sounds, 2D images, and 3D virtual camera movements.

In an example query path the first node is the concept "FultonStreet2000toPresent"; it returns photographs of storefronts, sounds of bus traffic, pedestrians and street vendors captured 2006-08 on Fulton Street, and a 3D camera movement slowly "flying" (tracking) along virtual Fulton street. Selecting a second path node while these resources are displayed, "BoroHall2000toPresent" introduces new photos and sounds, with smooth visual and audio cross-fades effecting the transition. The 3D camera movement interpolates from Fulton Street to a new position hovering above the model of Borough Hall. A subset of images and sounds may be common to both queries; these are brought forward in the display to effect smooth transition. The third path node "FultonStreet1880to1920," sends the 3D camera to resume a flyover of Fulton Street; the 3D scene now includes a model of the Brooklyn elevated train from the early 20th century, and postwar buildings are removed. Photographs of hip-hop shops and cell phone vendors are replaced by historical drawings, lithographs, and photos including images of the elevated train that were used as references for modeling its 3D graphics counterpart. Sounds captured on Fulton Street are replaced by sounds from a SFX library: horses, carriages, a steam engine, and pedestrians on a boardwalk.

Durations and transitions in each media display are qualitative and critical to narrative interpretation. Transitions are computed dynamically in reference to qualitative data of media resources, using metadata stored as properties of individuals. We introduce the term *Display Grammar* for heuristics of display signal processing and resource scheduling. We refer to *Display Prosody* as the application of heuristics with respect to qualitative properties of resources. These subsystems are well-developed for signal processing in computational performance media though not semantically well-formed for reasoning. We advance them as architecturally essential for interactive documentary.

3.3 Narrative Instances

A media archive is like memory without recall; media resources cannot encode their meaning as metadata. Archaeology (cognition) is required to determine or assert what resources may mean. An author performs an archaeology reflecting upon what is recognized and drawing associations to account for what is missed; these constitute the author's perspective in associative aspects. Interactive recall is a retelling accompanied by retrieval of media resources. To traverse a path of queries is to recall the narrative that binds them and entails a performative quality shared by path authors and observers retracing paths.

Our system architecture and graphical interface are designed to facilitate performance aspects for observers to extend and vary the experience. Paths make leaps of narrative association to nonadjacent graph regions. A path member centers a semantic region; within a region there may be multiple nodes that support associative coherence. Multiple narrative instances are generated from a pool of neighboring concepts creating variations in a query path. Figure 2A shows the nonadjacent graph members' narrative associations in a query path. Figure 2B represents a narrative instance of the query path in Figure 2A.

4 Ontological Data Design for Narrative Association among Media of Multiple Types

Authoring applied to media of multiple types requires structured access to diverse media resources; it is desirable to develop uniform and extensible authoring procedures rather than tailoring a process for each media type. Ontological data design provides a means for designing uniform criteria for organizing media resources of multiple types.

Ontologies are relationships of concepts that describe media resources. "Describe" is a principle of set membership: concepts describe sets; resources are unordered members of one or more sets. "Relatedness" may be hierarchical in the form of set membership or non-hierarchical in the form of semantic associations. Navigation of an ontological data structure involves traversing subclass-superclass relationships and non-hierarchical associations. This flexibility is desirable for authoring both level-of-detail and narrative.

Concepts represent queries that retrieve media resources by assertion and by inference. Assertion is a direct assignment of set membership when a resource is entered into the data set. Inference is a computational evaluation that mines relationships to be discovered by an observer. Ontological reasoning combines both types of discovery.

4.1 Dual Root Data Design Relating Concepts to Individual Media Resources

Figure 3 summarizes the main components in the ontology: a dual-root node structure of Concepts and Describable Objects. *Concepts* describe media resources of multiple types. *Describable Objects* are classed as individual media *Resources*, or as *Content Objects*—entities depicted by resources. *Properties* designate metadata of individual resources or relationships between individuals, rather than between individuals and concepts. Media metadata is stored as Properties of individual resources, and Properties may store other types of keywords, labels and numerical data.

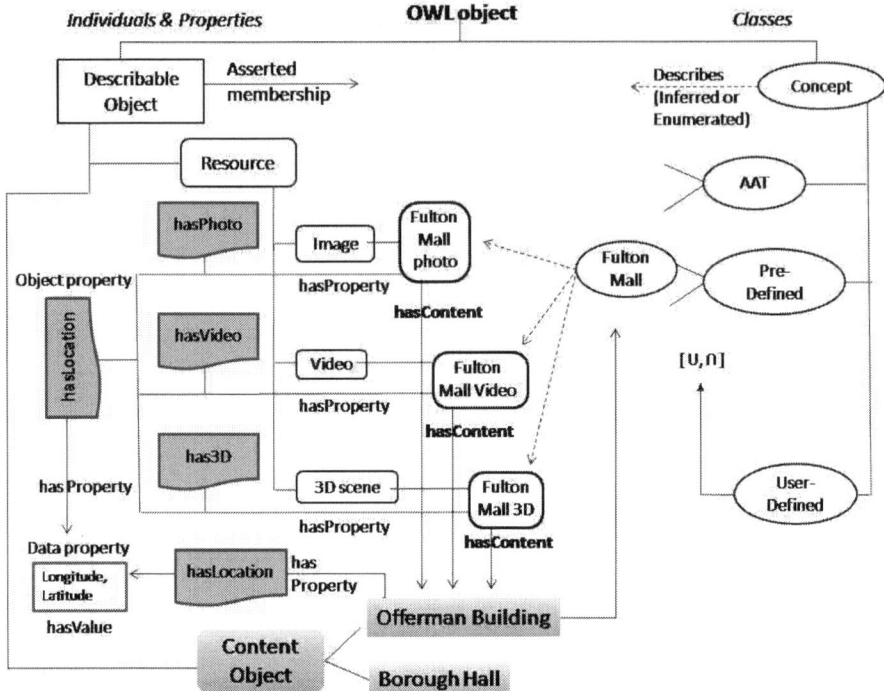

Fig. 3. A photograph, a video and a 3D scene are Resources inferred as members of "Fulton Street." The inference evaluates the GPS metadata encoded in the "hasLocation" Data property, and matches it with the location data of the "Offerman Building" Content Object that is independently asserted as a member of "Fulton Street." The Offerman Building is depicted in the three Resources.

Object Properties are extensible and inferable: they may refer to other properties; or to metadata common to multiple types of media resources. *Data Properties* are terminal, not extensible, and may be asserted only, not inferred. Figure 3 illustrates this relationship: several resources of different types have an object property "hasLocation," which links to the Data property "hasValue" where an asserted set of GPS metadata are stored. This data matches the location data of the Content Object "Offerman Building," an entity depicted in each of the resources. "Offerman Building" is asserted as a member of the Fulton Mall concept, and this enables the inference that the other resources are also members of "Fulton Street" even though their membership was not previously asserted.

Concepts may have relationships asserted to specific media resources. However many concepts have relationships only to other concepts. The dual-root design enables modifiable concept relationships without affecting the representations of individual media resources. By minimizing direct dependencies between concepts and resources, the concept graph can be changed without modifying resources. Reciprocally, resources can be changed without modifying the concept graph.

4.2 Structured Concept Vocabulary

A controlled vocabulary provides semantic constraints for resources depicting downtown Brooklyn. The Getty Art and Architectural Thesaurus (AAT) [14] provides both hierarchical and associative relationships among 35,000 concepts. We presently use about 3000 concepts in the ontology. The AAT serves as a semantic anchor for describing the built environment. However the AAT does not provide all concepts needed for structuring queries to support media authoring. For example dates independent of cultural and historical periods are not part of the AAT. So we complement the AAT with Predefined concepts.

Predefined_concepts are an application-specific vocabulary specified by the system designers to meet the narrative needs of projects. Predefined_concepts group media resources under complex logical relationships that are not easily represented as a graph nor easily manipulated using a GUI.

User-defined concepts are created on-the-fly by selecting available concepts and applying operations such as unions and intersections, or filters on metadata values. Combinations of predefined concepts and AAT concepts may be grouped in real-time while using the GUI to explore media resources. Examples of metadata filters in user-defined concepts include dates, GPS locations, polygon counts, and focal length settings.

5 Concluding Remarks and Future Direction

Documentary practice is growing beyond its roots in cinematic apparatus. The impulse may be recognized in blog journalism and social networks linked to web media archives. Distributed communities' discourses are decentralized, bringing oral traditions into a leading role. Models of media authoring can facilitate continuity in a distributed participatory documentary production. Continuity is a sense of experience through the assemblage of fragments and redundant structure when entered into an observer's sensory faculty. A garden variety of sensors, processing engines, and media displays may be brought into an interactive structure to support multiple modalities of an observer's senses and actions. In return an observer may actively seek to synthesize media processing layers. To produce coherent works, an authoring model can anticipate distributed collections of devices and processes for generating alternatives.

The described Interactive Documentary system facilitates observation as an act of narrative synthesis. Building upon the multimodal interaction paradigms illuminated in previous performance system research, the present creative pursuit often orients itself towards the narrative objective of intensification, the techniques to intensify the perception of events. The following design requirements facilitate such an objective:

1. Respect tempo: Temporality of media artifacts is surrogated in the tempo of the perception of the events while the events are assimilated by an observer's traces.
2. Empower memory: Respect for practice of oral tradition provides mechanisms for appropriating an observer's memory for generating new media experiences. It is necessary to place the function of memory as an active agent for generating new materials and experiences for both a human agent and system agents.

3. Automate subsystems: Access and analysis mechanisms for acquiring media resources and for streaming from archives into a display subsystem can be managed computationally. Automated subsystems can be optimized for cognitive priority and for system performance to deliver the responsiveness to observers' actions.

Future development depends upon assessment of interface design and computational performance. Feasibility of interactive recall as a vehicle of community narrative requires field study. Open contribution of media resources is desirable and can be facilitated by minimizing the complexity of data entry. The capacity to combine multiple structured vocabularies to define domains of ontology, suggests the value of investigating self-organizing methods. Finally, we look toward an extended repertoire of distributed interactive display devices that can host the documentary process, to enable interactive documentary work cycles across a wider community.

Acknowledgments. Thanks to Arthur Peters for API and software development, Robin Bargar for software design and project supervision, and Brian Macmillan and Marius Schebella for module implementations. Tatiana Malyuta contributed insights toward the potential of ontological reasoning. Robert Zagaroli and students provided archival documents of Brooklyn; Robin Michals and students provided photography; Mark Skwarek and students provided 3D models.

References

1. Barnouw, E.: Documentary: a History of the Non-fiction Film. Oxford University Press, Oxford (1993)
2. Choi, I.: Gestural Primitives and the context for computational processing in an interactive performance system. In: Battier, Wanderly (eds.) Trends in Gestural Control of Music. IRCAM, Paris (2000)
3. Bocconi, S.: Vox Populi: generating video documentaries from semantically annotated media repositories. PhD Thesis, Technical University of Eindhoven (2006)
4. Davenport, G., Murtaugh, M.: ConText towards the evolving documentary. In: Proceedings of the Third ACM International Conference on Multimedia, San Francisco, pp. 381–389 (1995)
5. Halliday, M.: Digital Cinema: an Environment for Multi-Threaded Stories. MSMAS Thesis, Massachusetts Institute of Technology (1993)
6. Davenport, G., Agamanolis, S., Barry, B., Bradley, B., Brooks, K.: Synergistic storyscapes and constructionist cinematic sharing. IBM Systems Journal 39(3&4), 456–469 (2000)
7. Choi, I., Zheng, G., Chen, K.: Embedding a sensory data retrieval system in a movement-sensitive space and a surround sound system. In: Proceedings of the 2000 International Computer Music Conference, pp. 141–144. International Computer Music Assoc., Berlin, Germany (2000)
8. Choi, I., Bargar, R.: Human-Machine Performance Configuration for Multidimensional and Multi-modal Interaction in Virtual Environments. In: Proceedings of the 4th Annual Symposium on Human Interaction with Complex Systems. IEEE Computer Society, Dayton (1998)

9. von Foerster, H.: What is Memory that It May Have Hindsight and Foresight as well? In: Understanding Understanding, pp. 101–131. Springer, New York (2002)

10. W3C: OWL Web Ontology Language Overview (2004),
    `http://www.w3.org/TR/owl-features/`

11. Protégé Ontology Editor and Knowledge Acquisition System,
    `http://protege.stanford.edu/`

12. Bush, V.: As We May Think. Atlantic Monthly (July 1945)

13. Choi, I.: idBrooklyn, an Interactive Virtual Media Presentation. In: Music and the Moving Image Conference. New York University (2008)

14. Paul, J.: Getty Trust: Art and Architecture Thesaurus (2005)

A Design Approach to Decentralized Interactive Environments

Harm van Essen, Pepijn Rijnbout, and Mark de Graaf

Department of Industrial Design, Eindhoven University of Technology
P.O. Box 513, 5600 MB Eindhoven, The Netherlands
{h.a.v.essen,p.rijnbout,m.j.d.graaf}@tue.nl

Abstract. We are exploring a design approach to the implementation of decentralized intelligent environments. We adopt the research through design process by creating an infrastructure of physical, interactive objects and explore the potential of a decentralized philosophy in four design iterations. Open-ended play serves as a fruitful context for design cases. Iterations of prototyping and user testing facilitate the exploration of emergence. One of the design outcomes is a simple decentralized system for soccer training which proved to be very successful on challenge and motivation, and inspired players to invent a range of games, both competitive and cooperative.

Keywords: open-ended play, decentralized systems, research-through-design, ubiquitous computing.

1 Introduction

In open-ended play, the goal of a game is not specified in detail. Tools and materials for open-ended play leave room for imagination, meaning giving, exploration and experimentation. A traditional example is construction material like Lego. SPORE [15] is a recent computer game that facilitates open-ended gaming. Open-endedness is an issue in designing intelligent play objects [1, 17]. If in a given physical context people start interacting with a number of such objects, the whole of objects and users forms an intelligent system, and the domain of open-ended play becomes connected to the domain of ubiquitous computing. This is the type of intelligent environments this paper is about.

The field of ubiquitous computing or ubicomp aims at a technology saturated future, in which the numerous computers that have invaded the environment we live in, are woven into the fabric of everyday life. They have become invisible to the users, they become connected in a ubiquitous network and will profoundly change the way we live [18]. In this paper, we are exploring the design of *decentralized* interactive environments. The potential of decentralized solutions has been explored successfully for a wide variety of contexts, such as sensor networks [10], P2P web crawlers [14], and robot swarms [13]. In these applications, the role of the user interacting with the objects is very limited. In the work presented here, the users are considered to be active, influential agents in the system.

A. Nijholt, D. Reidsma, and H. Hondorp (Eds.): INTETAIN 2009, LNICST 9, pp. 56–67, 2009.

In our view, entertainment and play is an excellent test ground for ubicomp research. It is often considered to be a good metaphor for "real" life: there are people with motivations and intentions, interactions, rules, and there is a physical environment. Compared to real life, all these aspects are strongly simplified. This is a favorable condition for the exploration of fundamental aspects of ubiquitous computing. Ubiquitous computing also offers excellent perspectives for open-ended play. In the dialogue with the environment, players can give new meaning to interactions taking place in the game, and new forms of play can be invented.

As a working method, we adopt the research through design process. In our interpretation, this encompasses an iterative approach based on extensive experiments with hardware objects interacting with real users. By designing objects and analyzing the interaction with users we investigate fundamental aspects of decentralized systems. Observing users' behavior and experience in different settings aids to an understanding how decentralized systems could be designed for applications in intelligent environments. Our final goal is to derive design heuristics.

Novel in this work is the combination of the important role of the users in the system, the decentralized implementation, and the design perspective. This paper aims to explore the potential of this focus on several levels. First, does the design approach work for decentralized interactive environments? Second, does it open new directions for interactive open-ended play? And finally, can the lessons learned be generalized to design heuristics for similar decentralized environments for open-ended play?

In the following section, we will go deeper into the roots and potential of the decentralized design method. Next, we will discuss the research through design approach method in more detail. Finally we will report and discuss three completed iterations of this process and formulate further steps.

2   Decentralized Systems

Decentralized systems consists of a number of (identical or different) components (objects, devices, or agents) that can have mutual interactions (i.e. communicate, coordinate, negotiate) with each other and with their common environment, according to basic (local) interaction rules. Grouped together these components form a system; this overall system demonstrates a global functionality (or reaches a goal) that single components are never able to accomplish. This behavior emerges from interaction dynamics and is called emergent behavior. Emergent behavior of a system is not explicitly described by the behavior/design of the individual components, and these components do not have knowledge about desired system behavior. The global behavior is not predictable as the sum or a function of the local behavior.

Well known and inspirational examples of Emergent Behavior are found in nature (ants [4], bee hive [12], flocks of birds and schools of fish [11], but also heart beat and brain rhythm [2]) but also in large cultural systems (traffic [7], economy [9], etc). In recent years, the principles of these multi agent systems are better understood. Many researchers like Steven Strogatz [16] and John Holland [8] have proved underlying mechanisms like self organization, clustering and coordination. For emergent behavior to occur, a relatively large number of more or less identical agents, gradient fields (like accumulation, pheromone traces etc.), multiple and intensive interactions, feedback loops, and finally, some amount of randomness are required.

A large number of interactions can be achieved by many agents having a few interactions, or few agents having many interactions, or anything in between. Ubicomp typically focuses on environments like a home or an office. The number of agents will be limited and the diversity will be high. In terms of a decentralized system this is characterized as small and heterogeneous, as opposed to the large and homogeneous systems known from nature. The low number of agents and the heterogeneity hampers the intensity of interactions. If such a system had to be self sustaining, there would be little chance of successful emergence. However, the active presence of (human) users makes the essential difference here: our decentralized system is sustained by user interactions.

The user input is a necessary condition to achieve emergence. The user introduces "order" into the system by his decisions and strategies. In a sense the decentralized systems that we strive for are no longer "closed", autonomous systems, and different conditions for the emergence of interesting behavior might be applicable. Moreover, the perception and experience of the users are more important than autonomy, stability, or extinction of interesting behavior; it is the user who drives the system. This opens perspectives for a designers approach.

Methodologies for decentralized systems' design have been developed [5, 6]. The designer of a system is interested in designing the global behavior of a system, in order to reach an overall design goal. For a decentralized system, the real challenge is how to define the (local) interaction/communication behavior ("the rules") between separate objects such that, when taken as a whole, they self-organize and demonstrate the desired global behavior.

When human users are involved, also the interaction between the users and the system, and the interaction between users needs to be designed. An interesting question is what the elementary requirements on the interactions rules of the agents are. A first, undisputable, requirement is that for determining the values of the output of a particular agent only information is used that is available within that agent at that time. This information can be based on (previous received) inputs or on autonomous change of internal variables. The update can be static, or dynamic, i.e. based on a history of previous input and conditions. Another requirement could be that that agents are not allowed to give direct instructions related to the output of other agents (in a hierarchical order). These basic requirements rule out that individual agents have a "global" overview of the status of other agents or the overall system (like a central database), and they also avoid properness errors, i.e. using information that is not available yet.

The expected advantages of a decentralized system are in:

- transparency (both from a user as well as from a designers' point of view, simple objects with limited functionality, simple local interaction rules instead of complex overall programs),
- scalability (add or remove objects without the need for reconfiguration),
- adaptivity (self organizing systems adapt easily to changing environments and different modes of use, also if they have not been foreseen by the designers),
- robustness (malfunction of one agent will not have large effects on the system behavior).

3   Research-through-Design Approach

Decentralized systems can and are explored from many different perspectives. These range from strictly mathematical, i.e. studying the dynamic behavior of coupled differential equations [16], via computational, e.g. verifying design goals by extensive simulations (e.g. traffic management [3]), to a merely observational approach, i.e. analyzing and mimicrying (biological) mechanisms and phenomena [4, 12]. Borrowing from all those disciplines, we choose to approach this problem from a design point of view.

Design refers to the process of creating and developing new objects or services. Designing requires considering aesthetic, usability, functional, and contextual aspects of a system or service. Working in a realistic context, relevant design goals and a specific user group needs to be formulated and evaluated. User needs and user capabilities are central in our view on design. Design research typically produces heuristics rather than mathematical relationships.

In our opinion, the research-through-design method is appropriate for the challenge at hand here. Research through design implies an explorative and iterative approach. Short cycles of design and reflection on design are used to generate research output. Reflection is driving the iterations. To investigate the (effect) of interaction, real objects are needed in a realistic use context. Concretely, in this project sets of physical agents are built and used in several consecutive design cases.

4   Design of the Objects

Before starting the actual design iterations we need an infrastructure of physical, communicating and interactive objects to work with. A set of requirements has been formulated, based on our vision on designing for interactive decentralized systems presented above.

The objects should be autonomous, it should be possible to spatially distribute the objects over a space, and the objects should be able to exhibit real interaction with each other and with human users. This means that agents have to be able to receive input from other agents and to communicate output with other agents, and that agents have to be able to receive input from users and to communicate output which is perceptible for users. The agents should be able to autonomously compute their current output based on (past) inputs and interaction rules.

Because we intend to explore the system in different contexts, the agents need to be easy to handle and have a neutral design. It should be possible to change the behavior of the individual agents by changing the interaction rules. Agents should have a flexible, easily adaptable functionality, while the interaction modalities should be abstract (for instance colored LED lighting instead of signals that are meaningful in a single context). Heterogeneity can be implemented by the flexible functionality: Objects could be "sensing" input in a subset of modalities, while being "active" in another subset of modalities.

Twenty agents have been built. This number of agents is a compromise between effort of building, interaction opportunities, assumed probability of emergent behavior, and perception of users. The number fits well in the range of small number decentralized systems. The intensity of mutual interaction is of course influenced by software. In the perception of users, a set of 10 to 15 agents (when placed close enough together), is already experienced as 'a group' of agents. Interacting with a group, it is more likely that users perceive group output instead of output from individual objects. This perception obviously fits better the principles of emergent behavior.

As casing, standard, low cost containers (12x8x8 cm) are used in which a Plexiglas frame is fitted on which all components are mounted. All parts are shielded and protected by the box, including the battery pack. A robust on/off switch is positioned on the bottom of the agent. All agents are identical and the design is neutral. Power supply of the agents is arranged with batteries, which allows flexible positioning of the agents. As low battery voltage causes unpredictable behavior, a battery voltage monitor indicates if the voltage drops below a critical value.

 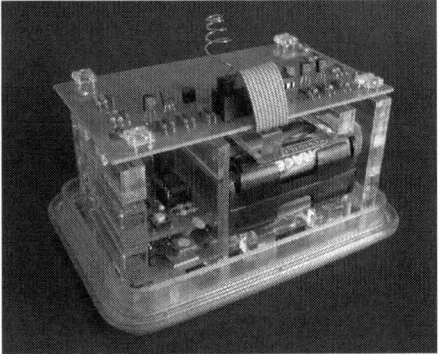

Fig. 1. Pictures of an agent, (left) closed with indicated LED lights and opened

In every agent the following modules are implemented on separate printed circuit boards: microcontroller module, input/output module, XBee module, battery voltage monitor, and a battery pack. The agents are equipped with a standard PIC microcontroller board. In most cases the interaction rules are simple and the required amounts of computing power and memory needed are limited. The opportunities for interaction with the user are implemented on a separate I/O PCB (which can be adapted to different contexts). The agents are able to give output which is perceptible for users. This is implemented with two sets of RGB LEDs. As different colors or patterns can have different meaning, this symbolic output provides sufficient output possibilities. Although the agents are physically identical, different input/output modes can simulate heterogeneity. The agents are able to receive input from users. A straightforward solution of one touch sensor (one bit output) on top of the object has been selected.

Interaction between agents is implemented with XBee wireless RF communication modules. The ZigBee protocol supports a peer-to-peer network configuration. When the module is configured correctly, communication is arranged by the module without interference of the microcontroller. In experiments with intensive data communication, occasional data loss was encountered. Although data loss can be part of a decentralized system, it can be avoided by including a handshake procedure. Also more advanced communication protocols can be implemented.

As a matter of fact, the input of an agent is the output of another agent. In our case, agents should have light and color sensitive sensors. Instead of real sensors, the RF communication emulates input of agents, agents are connected by communication. As an example, when a red LED of a particular agent shines, this agent communicates that it is emitting red light to all other agents. Whether an agent is able to receive this signal is determined in software. An advantage of an emulated sensor is that the communication can be programmed freely; there is no measurement noise or problems with line of sight. It provides extra flexibility, because no sensors or different types of sensor are needed.

The microcontroller and communication software are written in C. In a discrete time frame, the output of the agent for the next sample time is computed according to the local interaction (or input/output) rules. Different methods are available for programming the local interaction rules of the agents: It is possible to program dedicated algorithms for learning or pattern recognition in the agents; it is also possible to select a generic structure for the software which can (easily) be adapted to different cases.

5 Research-through-Design: Case Studies

The above described abstract interactive objects were the starting point for a still ongoing iterative research-through-design process. The design cases represent simplified implementations of decentralized systems in a specific context. The first case, the coming home ritual, was chosen as a typical example of a repetitive, rather stable pattern in a relevant ubicomp context, home. Consecutive design cases were formulated based on the evaluation of the proceeding ones. This is the nature of the research-through-design process. The first three iterations have been finished and are concisely presented. The next planned iteration is described. As we found out with interactive simulations earlier, interactive decentralized systems are hard to imagine for people. Fast iterations of prototyping and testing allow people to experience such systems.

5.1 Coming Home Ritual

This design case is based on a simple scenario: a user arrives at home, opens the front door, puts his coat at the hall stands, switches on the lights in the living room, gets a soda from the fridge, and goes to the living room to watch TV. The scenario is simplified to a set of 6 simple agents, having binary output states. One agent represents the front door (open or closed), another the light switch (on or off position), and so on.

The agents are identical to the ones described above, and programmed with an associative memory: they can perceive short series of events, and in the case of repeating patterns in which they take part, memorize them. The concrete implementa-tion is as follows. Users can toggle the state of the agents by touching the touch sensor of the agents. The toggle signal is broadcasted, so other agents can perceive it. Whenever an agent's state is toggled, it reinforces the pattern from its short-term memory into its long term memory. This way, it gradually learns to recognize repeating patterns, in which it takes part. At a certain level of reinforcement, the agent will toggle itself when the recognized pattern comes along.

Agents can only learn short fragments of patterns: the long term memory can allocate memory chains of three transitions preceding their own transition. Longer patterns can develop in this system as a whole, but cannot be known to any of the agents. Users can train a pattern by just touching the objects repeatedly in a specific order and frequency and the system demonstrates to be capable to reproduce the pattern autonomously. As can be expected, when different patterns are trained simultaneously, or if the end of a certain pattern is coupled to the start of another, the system can exhibit unexpected interfering repeating patterns.

5.2 Smartgoals

The coming home case taught us that having embodied prototypes turned out to make all the difference to our test users. Suddenly the concept of a decentralized approach came to live. It also taught us that the context was abstracted too much to be experienced as realistic by test persons.

Therefore, for the second iteration, a realistic, but simple, context has been selected: sport, soccer training to be specific. Soccer training has all the aspects we have to deal with in a complex human environment like a home or an office: people with intentions and motivations, physical space, rules, interactions. The associative memory is modified: only the strongest ten patterns will be remembered. Patterns slowly fade unless reinforced. With these starting points, the Smartgoals have been developed.

Fig. 2. Smartgoals field test

The Smartgoals game is played with 6 interactive goals randomly positioned on a space of 50 to 100 square meters. At every moment, a fixed number of goals (usually one or two) are "active". The lights on that goal are on, and if a ball passes an active goal it is counted as a score. Whenever a score occurs, the goal at which the score happened is deactivated and another goal is activated. A possible goal of the game is to score as much as possible in a set time. The game can be played alone, in couples or with teams. It can be cooperative or competitive, depending on the interpretation

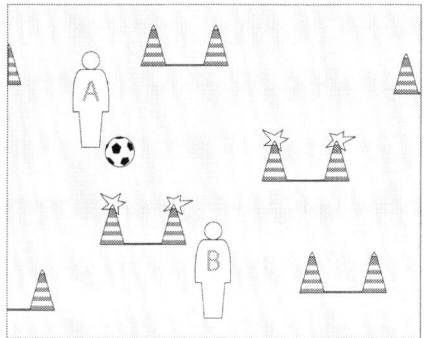 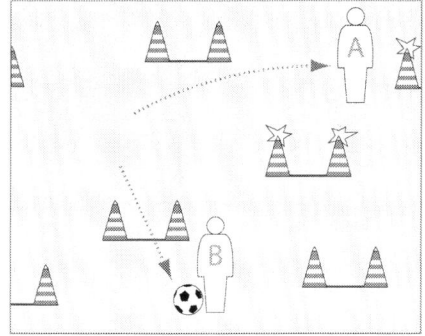

Fig. 3. A game variant with two players cooperating, and two active goals. In the left figure, the players choose the left active gate. Immediately after passing the ball, player A chooses position at the other active goal. When the ball passes the gate, it is deactivated and another goal becomes active.

trainers and players give to it. User can try to anticipate to the expected system behavior, the actual behavior strongly depends on the users actions.

A single Smartgoal has no knowledge of the intentions of the users, it does not know how many other Smartgoals are in the system, and it does not know its users. Yet, it turned out that even a system of only 6 goals can form a highly challenging, interactive training setup. With changes in the spatial configuration, the initial states of the individual agents, the number of players, or small changes in rules for agent behavior, a wide range of exercise forms could be generated. Currently, this concept is developed further for a startup company.

5.3 Synchronizing Fireflies

Reflecting on the Smartgoals, we conclude that this game clearly demonstrates the potential of the simplicity of a decentralized system, once it is brought alive by interaction with users. Moreover, the context of sports and games seems very appropriate for involving users in the research process. The decentralized implementation adds challenge, surprise, and user anticipation to a "traditional" game. A shortcoming of this iteration is that our approach to programming the behavior of the agents has been rather ad hoc. As our goal is to obtain understanding and derive heuristics for the design of decentralized systems also in other applications and contexts, we need knowledge that can be generalized. Therefore more transparent descriptions of the relations between the agent's input and output are required, which can be mapped with observed (emergent) system behavior.

We decided to start exploring more formal descriptions of the agents' interaction rules. In particular we apply generic state descriptions. Apart from its flexibility, the use of state descriptions in the agents is also useful because it corresponds to approaches in different fields of research. As a design case, we have implemented the synchronizing behavior of fireflies in order to demonstrate emergent behavior in small sets of physical agents. The relatively simple system dynamics of synchronizing fireflies and the clearly recognizable emergent behavior makes it a suitable case. In this particular exploration interactions with users are not yet implemented.

A firefly is a bug that can emit periodic light flashes using a chemical process called bioluminescence. Large groups of fireflies have the property that they can synchronize their flashes. Strogatz [16] analyzed that an individual fly can be seen as an agent. The input of this agent is the detection of light emission by other fireflies. Output is the light emission of the fly itself. The system is formed by the population of fireflies reacting on each other. The (simplified) individual firefly can be modeled as a pulse generating oscillator.

The state description is one of the most general and transparent ways of describing interaction rules. States allow dynamical updates, which imply that agents can have memory. Memory is locally stored in state variables. In a difference equation, the new values of the states are computed based on the current values of the states and new values of the inputs (which are related to outputs of other agents and direct input from users). The new outputs are a function of the updated states.

Many phenomena in decentralized systems are based nonlinear mechanisms, such as threshold values, discontinuities, local extremes etc. Therefore it is necessary to introduce nonlinear equations. To allow a generic and flexible state description, in the implementation a strict separation between non-linear functions X and linear state functions Q has been made:

$$X_q(T) = f\left(input_p(T), Q_n(T)\right)$$
$$Q_n(T + \Delta t) = A + B \cdot Q_n(T) + C \cdot input_p(T) + D \cdot X_q(T)$$
$$output_m(T + \Delta t) = E \cdot Q_n(T + \Delta t)$$

In which: q is the number of non-linear functions, n is the number of state variables, p is the number of inputs, m is the number of outputs, and the matrices A [1xn], B [nxn], C [pxn], D [qxn], and E [mxn] define the constant parameters in the linear state functions. Note that due to the time discretization, the value of Δt is encapsulated in the parameter values in the matrices.

Three states are used to describe the behavior of the firefly-agent in the generic state description. The first state variable Q_1, represents the firefly's building up of charge. A constant increase combined with a dissipation factor results in a basic exponential increase of charge. When the energy level reaches a certain threshold value, the fly will flash, and the charge level drops down. When an agent 'detects' the light flash of another agent, it can make a little extra step (effort) in charging. This results in a tiny extra increase in charge. The interaction with other agents in the form of an extra charge pulse eventually results in a synchronization of the light pulses of a group of agents.

The discharge threshold level is represented by the second state variable Q_2. In case the initial value (or the natural frequency) of this threshold varies over the separate objects, a dynamic adaptation mechanism of the value of Q_2 allows for synchronization. The threshold is a non-linear component creating a periodical discharge. The nonlinear threshold function X_1 indicates the timeslot in which the fly fires (the int operator truncates the sub decimal values variable to the nearest integer value below).

$$X_1(T) = Q_1(T) \cdot \text{int}\left[\frac{Q_1(T)}{Q_2(T)}\right]$$

The third state variable Q_3, is the flash indicator. In fact Q_3 equals the nonlinear state function and is only required to link the flash indicator to the linear output equation.

In order to test the implementation and demonstrate the opportunities of the agents for emergent behavior, three different firefly models are implemented in the agents. The models differ in synchronization mechanism (adaption speed, adaptation of capacitor charge and adaption of pulse frequency) resulting in different nonlinear functions and parameter sets in the matrices. Every model has a slightly different approach on achieving synchronization. The experimental results are compared with computer simulation results, based on virtual agents with a similar state description.

Experiments proved that it is possible to construct this self-synchronizing system with a set of general state descriptions in the hardware set of agents. The use of state description proved to be generic and flexible. The transparent description allows for a better insight in the mapping between model parameters and the resulting dynamic behavior of the complete decentralized system. Preliminary comparisons between computer simulations and the hardware agent experiments proved similar results.

5.4   Next Iteration: Interactive Objects for Open-Ended Play

The Smartgoals design case proved that the context of games and play provides great opportunities to explore decentralized interactive concepts with users. The system is open-ended to a certain extent: players or trainer might define the rules and the goals to be achieved in the game in many different ways. However, once defined, rules and the goals were not likely to evolve during play.

In a broader interpretation of open-ended play, exploration and discovery are more important than reaching a specific goal. The next design case aims at this broader interpretation by designing interactive play objects which, in interaction with playing users, demonstrates these opportunities of open-ended play. The decentralized systems approach seems especially appropriate to develop open-endedness. The assumption is that the dynamically changing behavior enabled by the interaction with the objects creates inspiring and unpredictable open-ended play opportunities. We will use the framework for successful design of an intelligent, interactive playground from Sturm [17]. An important aspect will be the balance between predictability and surprise. To deal with the expected increase in complexity, we build upon the work on formal descriptions of interaction rules. This will enable better mapping between parameter settings, system behavior, and experience of the user.

The expectation is that interactive objects, designed to facilitate emergent behavior, will be more exciting and fun to play with. We also expect that open-ended play stimulates children to develop their social skills, because they need to communicate and negotiate about the goals and rules of the game to play. Although we have just started this design case by creating scenarios and context studies, the interesting combination between new implementation methods and social, interactive opportunities of game design to conquer societal problems like loneliness, isolation and obesity offers great opportunities.

6 Conclusions

The research-through-design approach works. The first iteration helped to understand and communicate the concept of a decentralized approach to intelligent interactive environments. The approach allowed developing new directions and it enabled other researchers to imagine what is possible with decentralized systems, and thus opened opportunities for inspiring cooperation. The second iteration, the Smartgoals, demonstrates the surprisingly high potential to motivate and engage users, it also demonstrates the opportunities of realizing emergent behavior brought alive by interactions with users. It demonstrates that the user is an unpredictable, but essential element in our approach which cannot be captured with standard frameworks for multi agent systems. The third iteration proved to be a step in demonstrating emergence related to more formal and theoretical frameworks. In general, the context, the prototyping, and solving practical problems in all iterations contribute not only to our insight, but also allow users and colleagues to experience such systems.

Does the decentralized approach open new directions for open-ended play? The answer to this question is positive. The Smartgoals were a convincing demonstrator of the potential of even a simple system consisting of a handful of identical agents, one or a few users and a simplified use context. Still, a big challenge remains, when a broader interpretation (exploration and discovery) of open-endedness is chosen. The next design case aims to address this issue.

The research goal is to derive design heuristics for the design of decentralized systems. Although the presented design cases are just a first step, it is possible to make some interesting observations. The exploration of memory in the agents indicates that memory of agents may be a key to stabilizing a decentralized system. A more structured use of memory forces the system to converge to a limited set of repeating patterns, as we explored in the first and second design case. This implies that factors like surprise and predictability can be tuned by balancing randomness and the strength of the associative memory. Challenge, an important factor in games, appears to be related to surprise.

Another issue explored is choice and (perceived) user control. In the soccer game, if only one goal at a time is active, players have no choice and the game basically is about skills in passing and stopping. If two goals at a time are active, players start communicating about possible strategies. The nature of the interactions between players changes with this simple parameter. Especially the notion of user control in relation to system behavior will be explored in the next iterations on open-ended play.

After three research-through-design iterations we feel we are on a challenging, engaging, and definitely open-ended road, which is worth to be explored for new intelligent play solutions. Eventually, insights developed in sports and play concepts also contribute to intelligent interactive environments in other contexts.

Acknowledgments. We thank Maarten de Jager, Chris Heger, Sjef Fransen and Vic Hensberg for their substantial contributions to the design iterations. Tilde Bekker and Janienke Sturm have inspired us with their ideas on open-ended play.

References

1. Bekker, M.M., Sturm, J., Wesselink, R., Groenendaal, B., Eggen, J.H.: Play Objects and the effects of open-ended play on social interaction and fun. In: Proceedings of ACE, International Conference on Advances in Computer Entertainment Technologies (2008)
2. Camazine, S., et al.: Self-Organisation in Biological Systems. Princeton University Press, Princeton (2003)
3. Dresner, K., Stone, P.: Multiagent Traffic Management: An Improved Intersection Control Mechanism. In: AAMAS 2005, Utrecht, Netherlands (2005)
4. Franks, N.R.: Army Ants: A Collective Intelligence. American Scientist 77(2)
5. Fromm, J.: The Emergence of Complexity. Kassel University Press (2004)
6. Fromm, J.: On Engineering and Emergence (2006),
   http://arxiv.org/ftp/nlin/papers/0601/0601002.pdf
7. Herman, R., Gardels, K.: Vehicular Traffic Flow. Scientific American 209, 6 (1963)
8. Holland, J.H.: Emergence, From chaos to order. Perseus Books (1998)
9. Krugman, P.: The Self-organizing Economy. Blackwell, Malden (1996)
10. Mainland, G., Parkes, D.C., Welsh, M.: Decentralized, Adaptive Resource Allocation for Sensor Networks. In: Proceedings of the 2nd conference on Symposium on Networked Systems Design & Implementation, vol. 2 (2005)
11. Reynolds, C.W.: Flocks, Herds, and Schools: A Distributed Behavioral Model. Computer Graphics 21(4) (1987) (SIGGRAPH 1987 Conference Proceedings)
12. Seeley, T.D.: The Honey Bee Colony as a Super Organism. American Scientist 77 (1989)
13. Settembre, G., Scerri, P., Farinelli, A., Sycara, K., Nardi, D.: A Decentralized Approach to Cooperative Situation Assessment in Multi-Robot Systems. In: Proceedings of International Conference on Autonomous Agents and Multiagent Systems, Portugal (2008)
14. Singh, A., Srivatsa, M., Liu, L., Miller, T.: Apoidea: A Decentralized Peer-to-Peer Architecture for Crawling the World Wide Web. In: Callan, J., Crestani, F., Sanderson, M. (eds.) SIGIR 2003 Ws Distributed IR 2003. LNCS, vol. 2924, pp. 126–142. Springer, Heidelberg (2004)
15. SPORE, Electronic Arts Inc (2007), http://www.spore.com
16. Strogatz, S.: Sync, the emerging science of spontaneous order. Penguin books (2003)
17. Sturm, J., Bekker, M.M., Wesselink, R., Groenendaal, B., Eggen, J.H.: Key issues for the successful design of an intelligent, interactive playground. In: Proceedings of the Interaction Design and Children Conference (IDC 2008), Chicago, IL, USA, June 10-13 (2008)
18. Weiser, M.: The Computer for the 21st Century. Mobile Computing and Communications Review 3(3) (1991)

Accessible Gaming through Mainstreaming Kinetic Controller

Yolanda Garrido, Álvaro Marco, Joaquín Segura, Teresa Blanco, and Roberto Casas

Tecnodiscap Group, University of Zaragoza
María de Luna 1, Ed. Ada Byron, 50018 Zaragoza, Spain
{ygarrido,amarco,jsegura,teresa.blanco,rcasas}@unizar.es

Abstract. Leisure is a very important aspect in our everyday life; and gaming is one of the main ways to it. Depending on the particular situation of each person, the way of playing could be very different. Motivation, preferences, skills, knowledge are some of the factors that influences this experience. When the person has a disability, additional agents come to scene such as cognitive level and mobility. Besides the design of the game, these factors clearly affect how the person interacts with the game; its user interface. In this paper we present a tool that allows people with disabilities to play games with a normalized user interface. This tool a) manages several wireless kinetic remote controllers, e.g. the Wiimotes; b) can be configured to capture any voluntary movements users could do and c) convert them into the specific inputs required by existing adapted games. As a result, users with disabilities can experience and enjoy games that were previously inaccessible to them.

Keywords: user interface, people with disabilities, accessibility, games, kinetic controllers, design for all.

1 Introduction

Nowadays the "design for all" concept is arriving to many fields including ICT, industrial design, etc. Nevertheless, this is not being applied in leisure and gaming because these businesses have to be very innovative. As a result, universal design is relegated to a second place hindering access of people with disabilities people to games [1].

Leisure is an important part of everyday life allowing us to mix with other people, relax, have fun, etc. And these factors are of special importance in the case of elderly and disabled people. In the case of children and teenagers is also relevant the interrelationship that comes with the games. Games lead them to share experiences, practice together; in other words, socializing. As a result from not doing games accessible, children with disabilities are not able to play and consequently not included [2].

Games, are not only for having fun, they have many others important applications. As a powerful motivation tool that helps children to learn and also motivates people with disabilities and elderly [3]; for example, Groenewegen et al. use games to teach

A. Nijholt, D. Reidsma, and H. Hondorp (Eds.): INTETAIN 2009, LNICST 9, pp. 68–77, 2009.

activities of the daily life such as shopping or preparing the meal [4]. Finally, gaming may also have a strong cognitive and physical therapeutic contribution [5, 6].

Currently there are some systems developed to provide alternative access to the games and include people with physical disabilities in the use of computers [2].

Waber et al. use a webcam to have an accurate head tilt detection as a mouse system [7]. Other head tracking driven camera mouse system, called HMouse calculates the user's head roll, tilt, yaw, scaling, horizontal, and vertical motion for further mouse control [8]. Others camera mouse systems based on visual face tracking [9, 10] and eye tracking [5].

Capturing biological signals is also used when the user can hardly make a controlled movement [11]. As a quite common alternative, brain-computer interfaces provide good results when user is not able to move at all [12].

Different interfaces for people with visual disabilities have been described by Alonso [13] and Miller [14] who use auditory and haptic displays. Raisamo uses a low cost vibro-tactile device [15].

In the following sections we present the requirements from which we started our project and the approach we decided. In section 3, the architecture of the solution is showed. Section 4 outlines the evaluation procedure we underwent and finally, the conclusions are stated in section 5.

2 Requirements from the End Users and Approach

The final objective we had from the beginning of the project was to enable people with a wide range of disabilities to enjoy themselves with games. It is evident that to play an electronic game, the user has to command a machine (computer, video console, etc.). This commanding has to be done through specific actions done by the user; pressing a button, moving him/herself, etc. This interaction has to be ruled by user's cognitive procedures stimulated by the game. Thus, to enjoy games, people need to understand and know how to interact with the game and be able to command it according to their thoughts.

We collaborated closely with a special education school where very diverse physical and cognitive disabilities exist. It is clear that games have to be adapted to the user's cognitive capacities to allow proper interaction. This is solved adapting the game to the user's motivation and intellectual level. We considered developing adapted games to be used with video consoles, but we discarded it because it is complicated and expensive to get game-developer licenses and it would force us to use a specific platform. Thus we decided to use the games already used in the school that the children knew very well. Most of these games are designed for PC platform (Windows and Linux).

Choosing the right game has the same importance as selecting the appropriate user interface to the user's kinetic capacities. These capacities can be very diverse depending on the user disability. Nevertheless, regardless of this diversity, we found common features transversal to the disabilities that helped us in the decision about the final design. For example, some users with physical disabilities can do movements but not controlling their strength or direction; in the end, these users just can do intentionally few movements. Others can only perform very small movements but very precise, for example slightly move a finger. Others don't have any control on their upper limbs or cannot move them at all; but they can intentionally move the head, foot or knee.

In the disability world, capture of these movements is done by means of different adapted switches connected to a computer. The professionals working with the end users wanted **one common interface** for the majority of the children. It had to be **able to interact with existing software, cheap, wireless and easily configurable** to be robust to hits, sensible to slight movements and immune to tremors. Moreover, it was desired that **several interfaces could be connected simultaneously** to play collaborative games.

In our research team we have big experience working with sensors, wireless communication, digital electronics, etc. Thus we started the design of an interface fulfilling the requirements...till we realized that we were reinventing the wheel. What users were demanding was a cheap, wireless device able to capture a wide range of movements (push of buttons, movement of head, hands, foot, etc) and able to be personalized to interact with existing games in a PC. Thus we decided to use the kinetic controllers used in some commercial video consoles (Miwi, Technigame or the better known Wii from Nintendo) to control the already existing games in a PC. In particular, due to its availability, global development community and accessories we selected the Wiimote and Nunchuk.

Wii remote controls also offer some extra advantages, thanks to its innovative physical interface, rather distant from traditional consoles. The Wiimote is fairly light and compact, which allows an easier attachment to any member of the human body. It can be handled with only one hand. Its use is intuitive and usually requires no previous experience. On the other hand, it may seem that its nine buttons are too much for some users; when most games used by people with disabilities just would need one or two of them. Also, its configuration is enough versatile to allow the user to understand its layout horizontally or vertically. In addition, the remote control has two non-visual communication elements—sound and vibration—both essential for adaptations for people with visual disabilities.

There are many projects that connect the Wiimote to a computer, but none of them fulfill the functionalities required. Most of them are not suited for people with disabilities; being not versatile enough or too complicated for non computer experts (some are just source code) [16]. Others, specially developed to enhance computer accessibility of people with disabilities, are too specific and have limited functionalities; e.g. adapted text-entry interface [17], mouse pointer emulator [18].

3 System Architecture

As we have said in last section, all the target games run in a PC being controlled by means of keyboard and mouse. Thus, the objective is to connect the controller to the PC and translate its outputs to keyboards and mouse events that would be sent to the game (see fig. 1). Specifically the actions would be the following:

- Buttons in the controller would be mapped to any keyboard or mouse event: move cursor to any direction and quantity of pixels, any keystroke, any mouse button or wheel event, execution of an application or command or any combination of them; e.g. key bindings.

- Acceleration ranges would be mapped to any of the preceding events and it also should be possible to emulate the mouse movement. Customizing acceleration thresholds, it is possible to tune the application to the user needs. It can be sensible to slight movements using low thresholds, or immune to large tremors using higher ones.
- Infrared pointer should be able to emulate the mouse movement.

Each user has different ways of interaction with the Wiimote. Besides the software configuration we just described, a physical adaptation of the device can be required; some examples following. A user totally paralyzed that can just do slight finger movements will control the knob in the Nunchuk that has to be placed under his/her hand. A user that can only control the head movement can wear a cap with the Wiimote attached and translate acceleration movements. Other user that can just move a leg can have the Wiimote tied and also capture the accelerations.

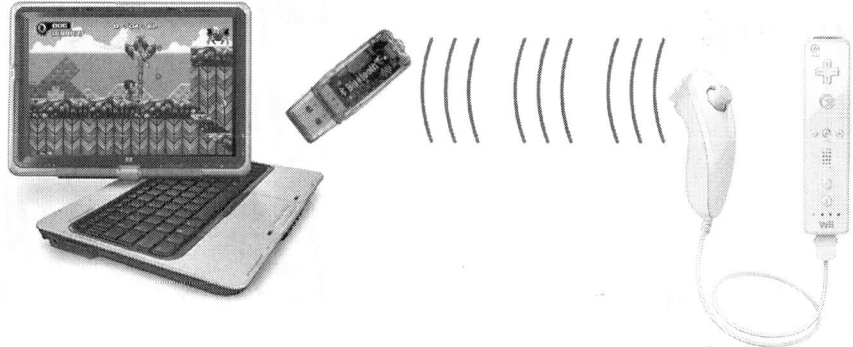

Fig. 1. System architecture. The Wiimote and the Nunchuk are connected to the computer through Bluetooth.

Wiimotes use Bluetooth as wireless communication protocol to connect to the video console. Thus, besides the physical controller for each user, the host PC where the game runs has to be Bluetooth enabled (see fig. 1).

3.1 Software Architecture

We identify two different scenarios where the system will run. One is when the educator first shows the game to the child; where it will be necessary to configure the tool to recognize the user specific actions and map them to the desired keyboard and mouse events. Resulting from this configuration stage, there will be different configuration files pairing users and games. This is motivated because each user will have different ways to interact the computer, and each game will have different controls.

Once these configuration files are created, the second scenario would be when the user plays the game. In this stage, the game is running, the tool captures the outputs from the interface and—according to the configuration file—translates them into the

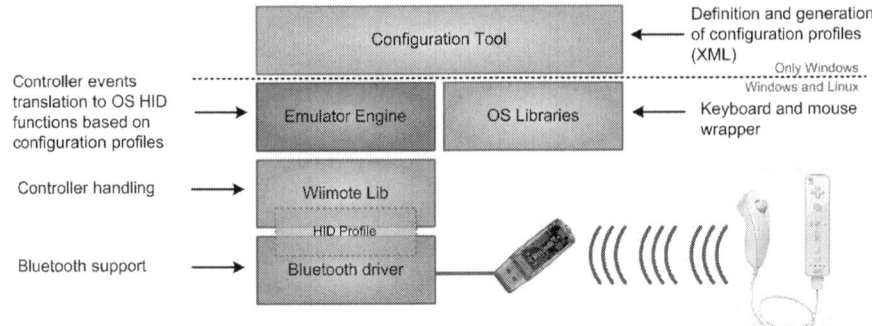

Fig. 2. Software architecture. Most of the components that compound the system are multiplatform and works on Windows and Linux, whereas Configuration Tool is only available on Windows.

adequate keyboard and mouse events. In figure 2 we can see the software architecture that supports these two scenarios.

As already said, the connection between the PC and the Wiimote uses Bluetooth thus, in the lower layer it is needed a Bluetooth driver that grants this communication. As each manufacturer can incorporate different stacks (Toshiba, Widcomm...) on their drivers, it is needed that the connection is configured through the operating system.

Above the driver there is a Wiimote library that handles communication with the controller, which care of which buttons were pressed or what accelerations are registered by the Wiimote or the Nunchuk. This library access the controller as a Human Input Device (HID) through the Bluetooth HID profile, which is intended to provide access to devices such as keyboards, joysticks, etc.

The core part of the system is the Emulator Engine, which is responsible of translate the actions performed with the controller to HID actions in the Operative System. The Emulator Engine determines which actions must be performed on each controller event, regarding the user profile configuration loaded from the XML file.

Although configuration will be mainly defined to work with a specific game, it will not be controlled by the emulator, but the actions are sent directly to the OS which will drive the game. This task is accomplished by the OS Libraries component that provides such functions to inject HID events into the OS. Actually, if the Emulator Engine translates a button push to any keystroke, the following event is indistinguishable from the real keystroke.

These components are the ones required by the second scenario, and are available for both Windows and Linux OS, but for the first scenario, it is needed a Configuration Tool that allows to define the user profile configuration files. That tool currently is only implemented on Windows, but generated configuration files are also suitable for Linux.

3.2 Configuration Tool

The purpose of the system presented is to enable people with disabilities using mainstreaming PC games, looking for accessibility. But it is also important that the

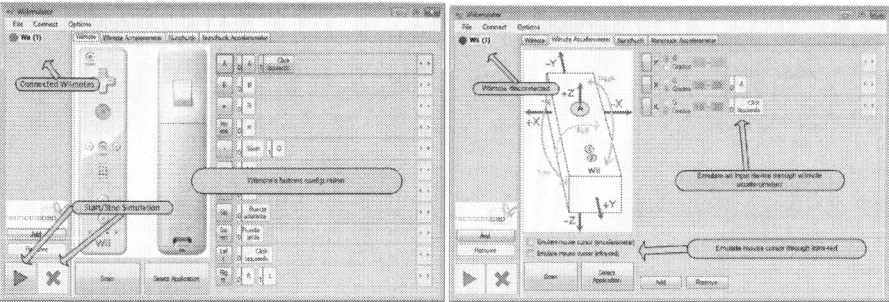

Fig. 3. Configuration tool. It allows assigning keystroke sequences and other OS events to controller actions such as push of buttons or controller movements.

```
<wiiconfig>
  <Peripheral Type="controller">
    <Device Type="button|accelerometer|IR ">
      <emulation>keystroke|mouse event|app. path</emulation>
            ...
    </Device>
        ...
  <Peripheral Type="Nunchuk">
    <Device Type="button|accelerometer|joystick">
      <emulation>keystroke|mouse event|app. path</emulation>
            ...
    </Device>
        ...
  </Peripheral>
</wiiconfig>
```

Fig. 4. Configuration file. Controller actions are mapped to OS events such as keystrokes, mouse events or application launching.

system itself is accessible too. For that reason, an effort was done in the configuration tool to ensure that definition of configuration files can be easily done, especially for people that are not supposed to have high informatics skills.

The tool shows a list where connected Wiimotes are listed (it is possible to have more than one controller connected with the same PC), and allows assigning OS events to every button in both Wiimote and Nunchuk as well as to some movement patterns (see fig. 3). The operation is quite simple: the user has to indicate the button it wants to assign a SO event—by clicking on the button list or directly in the controller image—, and press the "Scan" button, after which the tool will wait for a PC event from the keyboard or the mouse. When that event occurs, the tool grabs it and assigns it to the previously selected button. It is possible to assign a sequence of events to a controller action, for instance a sequence of keystrokes for writing a word or performing an actions-combo in the active game. It is possible also to assign the launching of an application to an action, so the game can be started directly with the controller.

Acceleration measurements from the controller can be used to trigger events when some thresholds are exceeded, or to drive mouse pointer as a virtual joystick and infrared sensor can be used as mouse pointer too, which will require a led bar like the one supplied with the Nintendo Wii to work.

The tool allows checking that the configuration generated works properly with the game desired, and in that case, generate the respective XML configuration file (see fig. 4), that can be used with the emulation tool in both Windows and Linux Platforms.

4 System Evaluation

Our work and experience in Tecnodiscap has taught us that any technological development is useless if user has not been taken into account. Therefore, the assessment of services and devices that we implement is made through a final user evaluation. There, we consider all the potential users involved in all steps of use of the product (carers and other professionals that give support to the beneficiary user, the beneficiary user himself, the family...).

To conclude and check the service as a whole, we have applied the principles of "Design for All" as a work guide, and we followed the criteria of ISO 9126 as a quality foundation to be met.

Thus, the evaluation of this project was conducted with the professional advice of the experts who originally participated in the project requirements, and the involvement of two children from the center, each one of them with some different features and needs. One of these children (male, aged 11) had mild cognitive disability and no physical disabilities. The second one (male, aged 13) besides a mild cognitive disability, also had an important physical disability (very reduced mobility, with high spasticity in upper limbs). Two games were tried; one to learn drawing and the other emulating a football penalty round. In both cases the software was firstly explained to the children. First one, they had to copy different forms choosing colors from a palette. Both children used the mote as a mouse; first with the pointer and second with the accelerometer. They also used one button to change color. Second game just required the children to press the space bar to kick the ball; we associated this key press through an accelerometer threshold and with one button.

Always looking toward both types of user (carers and end users), the assessment was tackled from several perspectives, which allowed us to check the interface possibilities from the following points of view:

-    **Interface usability (Carer):** The overall impression was in every case very favorable. All users highlighted the simplicity of programming and learning the management of the interface, and its intuitive use. They found the program very efficient, with a high degree of consistency between the appearance and the operations requested, and all of them maintained that they had felt comfortable with the application. It was checked that the graphic design was clear and practical for all users, and they all considered it attractive and clean.

-    **Improvement in quality of life (End user):** Through this assessment, we could also show a clear improvement in quality of life of the end user, in this case children with diverse disabilities. This interface allowed both children participate in gaming and learning activities that were previously inaccessible to them, and could be optimally adapted to the particular needs of each one. This was especially relevant for the child with severe physical disability.

In this sense, the experts reported that this tool could also help them to develop more easily their "curricula tracking for the end users" and also they pointed out that it could have more applications in their daily work, especially in physiotherapy and physical education.

Currently we are facing a more extensive and long term evaluation. In the school many other children are using the tool during this academic year; also a research group from the Royal Institute of Technology (KTH) in Sweden is testing the it with elderly people with very good results; and our research group is delivering it to any user interested.

5   Conclusions

In this paper we have described an innovative tool that allows people with disabilities to play games. There is no restriction in the games that could be played, they have to run in a PC (Windows or Linux) and be controlled with keys or mouse. Although technically possible, we found that users with disabilities are not usually able to play fast games or those needing large combinations of buttons; but this is mainly because of their physical or cognitive disabilities. This tool also improves the computer accessibility disabled people as it can be also used to control any application such as word processor, navigator, e-mail client, etc. So far, we have successfully tried flash games, specific adapted-for-disability games, mainstreaming games (pinball, arkanoid, sims, etc.) and other applications such as text editor and browser. Although not already evaluated with elderly users in Spain, we can say that this tool is also very useful for then due to the good results from the experiments being done in Sweden.

Several users with diverse disabilities can play simultaneously using different wireless kinetic controls, and also they can share the game and compete against other persons without disabilities, inside or outside the family. This is a very important step in the integration and socialization of people with disabilities. We have developed the system to be used with the Wii's remote controller, although it could be used with any other. The person specific disabilities highly condition how he/she can interact with the controller: slight and precise movements of just a finger, head inclination, brusque arm movements, etc. Our tool personalizes this interaction and translates it to any input required by the game.

We have successfully tried the tool with users with disabilities and games that were previously inaccessible to them. Thus, following the "design for all" principles, we have extended the target users of an already existing product.

Inherent to the gaming experience, this tool also allows therapeutic leisure, because this way of interaction stimulates the physical movement and empowers socialization.

We also realized that this tool can be also used in other fields of interest such as turning more enjoyable and funnier the initiation to computers for elderly and disabled. It is obviously more intuitive to point where you want to go than move the mouse. It also enhances the accessibility of computers for disabled people offering an alternative way of interaction.

Summarizing, we can say that this tool can improve the quality of life of elderly and disabled people allowing them, among other activities, new gaming experiences. Moreover this is done in a cost effective way; just using mainstreaming and cheap devices and free software that can be downloaded from our research group site (http://tecnodiscap.unizar.es/)

Acknowledgments. We would like to thank to the special education school of Alborada in Zaragoza for their unconditional collaboration in this work. This work was partially supported by the EU under MonAMI (IST-5-035147) and EasyLine+ (IST-045515) projects and by the Spanish Ministry of Science and Technology under the AmbienNET Project (TIN2006-15617-C03-02).

References

1. Tollefsen, M., Flyen, A.: Internet and accessible entertainment. In: Miesenberger, K., Klaus, J., Zagler, W.L., Karshmer, A.I. (eds.) ICCHP 2006. LNCS, vol. 4061, pp. 396–402. Springer, Heidelberg (2006)
2. Iacopetti, F., Fanucci, L., Roncella, R., Giusti, D., Scebba, A.: Game Console Controller Interface for People with Disability. In: Proceedings of the 2008 international Conference on Complex, intelligent and Software intensive Systems. CISIS, pp. 757–762. IEEE Computer Society, Washington (2008)
3. Pearson, E., Bailey, C.: Evaluating the potential of the Nintendo Wii to support disabled students in education. In: ICT: Providing choices for learners and learning. Proceedings Ascilite, Singapore (2007)
4. Groenewegen, S., Heinz, S., Fröhlich, B., Huckauf, A.: Virtual world interfaces for special needs education based on props on a board. Comput. Graph. 32(5), 589–596 (2008)
5. Lin, C., Huan, C., Chan, C., Yeh, M., Chiu, C.: Design of a computer game using an eye-tracking device for eye's activity rehabilitation. Optics and Lasers in Engineering 42(1), 91–108 (2004)
6. Foulds, R., Saxe, D., Joyce, A., Adamovich, S.: Sensory-motor enhancement in a virtual therapeutic environment. Virtual Reality 12(2), 87–97 (2008)
7. Waber, B., Magee, J., Betke, M.: Fast Head Tilt Detection for Human-Computer Interaction. In: Proceedings of the ICCV Workshop on Human Computer Interaction, Beijng, China. Springer, Heidelberg (2005)
8. Fu, Y.; Huang, T. S.: hMouse: Head Tracking Driven Virtual Computer Mouse. In: Proceedings of the Eighth IEEE Workshop on Applications of Computer Vision WACV. IEEE Computer Society, Washington, DC, 30 (2007)
9. Tu, J., Tao, H., Huang, T.: Face as mouse through visual face tracking. Comput. Vis. Image Underst. 108(1-2), 35–40 (2007)
10. Shin, Y., Ju, J.S., Kim, E.Y.: Welfare interface implementation using multiple facial features tracking for the disabled people. Pattern Recogn. Lett. 29, 1784–1796
11. Shima, K., Bu, N., Okamoto, M., Tsuji, T.: A universal interface for video game machines using biological signals. In: Kishino, F., Kitamura, Y., Kato, H., Nagata, N. (eds.) ICEC 2005. LNCS, vol. 3711, pp. 88–98. Springer, Heidelberg (2005)

12. Nijholt, A., Tan, D., Allison, B., del, R., Milan, J., Graimann, B.: Brain-computer interfaces for HCI and games. In: CHI 2008 Extended Abstracts on Human Factors in Computing Systems CHI 2008, Florence, Italy, pp. 3925–3928 (2008)
13. Alonso, F., Fuertes, J.L., Martínez, L., Szabo, H.: Design Guidelines for Audio–Haptic Immersive Applications for People with Visual Disabilities. In: Miesenberger, K., Klaus, J., Zagler, W.L., Karshmer, A.I. (eds.) ICCHP 2006. LNCS, vol. 4061, pp. 1071–1078. Springer, Heidelberg (2006)
14. Miller, D., Parecki, A., Douglas, S.A.: Finger dance: a sound game for blind people. In: Proceedings of the 9th international ACM SIGACCESS Conference on Computers and Accessibility Assets 2007, Tempe, AZ, pp. 253–254 (2007)
15. Raisamo, R., Patomäki, S., Hasu, M., Pasto, V.: Design nd evaluation of a tactile memory game for visually impaired children. Interact. Comput. 19(2), 196–205 (2007)
16. http://www.wiili.org/index.php/Main_Page (2009)
17. http://www.inference.phy.cam.ac.uk/dasher/DasherSummary.html (2009)
18. González, M.L., Muñoz, A., Valero, M.A.: A low-cost multimodal device for web accessibility. In: 6th Collaborative Electronic Communications and ecommerce Technology and Research Conference (2008)

Interactive Play Objects: The Influence of Multimodal Output on Open-Ended Play

Eva Hopma, Tilde Bekker, and Janienke Sturm

Industrial Design, Eindhoven University of Technology
Den Dolech 2, 5612 AZ Eindhoven, The Netherlands
E.E.Hopma@student.tue.nl, {M.M.Bekker,J.Sturm}@tue.nl

Abstract. In this paper we investigate how providing multiple output modalities affects open-ended play with interactive toys. We designed a play object which reacts to children's physical behavior by providing multimodal output and we compared it with a unimodal variant, focusing on the experience and creativity of the children. In open-ended play children create their own games inspired by the interaction with a play object. We show how the modalities affect the number of games played, the type and diversity of games that the children created, and the way children used the different feedback modalities as inspiration for their games. Furthermore, we discuss the consequences of our design choices on open-ended play.

Keywords: open-ended play, creativity, social interaction, interactive toys, children, multimodality, design.

1 Introduction

Children like to play: it is a vital aspect in their development and an important element in their daily lives. Open-ended play is a form of play where game rules and goals are not predetermined. Instead, the players can create their own (emerging) game goals [1], inspired by the interaction with one or multiple play objects. The goal of open-ended play is to allow children to explore and learn by creating their own game rules, by providing a simple design with many play opportunities [2]. Previous research has shown that open-ended play provides opportunities for diverse play patterns like physically active play, fantasy play, and games with rules [3]. When an object allows for creativity, children may consider it more fun and fun for a longer period of time [4]. It keeps the children focused and involved in the game. Open-ended play also offers opportunities for children to practice social behaviors – like negotiating and solving problems – while discussing about the different game rules.

We design and do research with *interactive* play objects that can be used for open-ended play. We assume that interactive toys are interesting and fun for children in exploring the possibilities of the toy (especially on the long run), because they offer many interaction possibilities to which the children can assign meaning. In [5] the authors describe how technology (sensors and actuators) in toys can stimulate children to practice both physical and social skills. In interactive open-ended play the

A. Nijholt, D. Reidsma, and H. Hondorp (Eds.): INTETAIN 2009, LNICST 9, pp. 78–89, 2009.

players create their own games and rules based on the feedback from the interactive toys on their behavior; this stimulates the children's creativity in inventing new games. In previous studies (as described in [3]) we have shown that children are able to create different games inspired by their interaction with relatively simple interactive play objects, without predefined game rules.

The design cases discussed in previous publications [1, 2, 3] all use interactive play objects with light feedback as the only output modality. However, the question remains how the use of diverse output modalities influences the games that children come up with. We expect that multimodal feedback will have a positive impact on players' experience and inspiration, because it offers more diverse forms of output to which the players can assign meaning. Every single modality has its own specific characteristics [6]. For instance, visual feedback is always present and requires being in the field of vision; auditory feedback however is transient and the play objects do not need to be visible; haptic feedback is personal (bodily) and invisible. We expect that the qualities of the type of output will trigger particular behavior of the players and eventually affect the type of games they create. For example, objects that provide haptic feedback may trigger more secretive games than objects that emit light, because of the invisible and mysterious character of the feedback. The type of games that children play both depends on the specific characteristics of the signal (*invisibility*) and the meaning that the players assign to that signal (*mystery*). Another example: for a game based on the auditory signal the children do not necessarily need to see each other, thus facilitating a game in which the children are blindfolded, which would be impossible when light is offered as only output modality. In summary, richer output may eventually lead to more fun and more diverse games than less rich feedback, because there are more states that the players can assign meaning to.

This paper describes the design of an open-ended interactive toy which provides multimodal output. We present the set-up and results of a study in which we compared a unimodal version of the interactive play object with the multimodal variant – focusing on the experience and creativity of the children. We explored how the feedback modalities of the interactive toys affect the number of games played, the type and diversity of games that the children create, and the way children use the different forms of output in these games. On the basis of a description of children's play behavior we discuss the design considerations of such interactive toys. With this paper we take the opportunity to share the consequences of our design choices on open-ended play as inspiration for the future development of open-ended play objects.

2 Related Work

In a previous project on open-ended play a handheld interactive play object (the ColorFlare [7]) was created as a research vehicle for open-ended play and the Intelligent Playground [1]. The ColorFlare is designed to support open-ended play, and thus also social interaction and physical play. Direct manipulation of the prototype is possible by rolling it (*changing color*) and shaking it (*flashing color*). Multiple ColorFlares are able to communicate bilaterally as one ColorFlare can send its color wirelessly to another. The ColorFlares do not contain any predefined games or game rules.

Other examples of open-ended play are the Interactive Pathway [8], Flash Poles [2] and Morels [9]. The Interactive Pathway is an interactive playground installation, for young children. It consists of a pathway that can sense children's presence. When a child walks on the interactive pathway, objects that are placed alongside the pathway start spinning and in this way guide them on their walk. Flash Poles are interactive poles that are distributed on a field and can be used by children to play various physical games. Morels are mobile, cylindrical objects that can be carried around and thrown. The Morels can be 'loaded' by squeezing them and they can launch other Morels that are in the vicinity into the air. The Morels have no implemented games, only simple behavioral rules, with which players can create their own games.

Although the above-mentioned studies describe interesting concepts, these papers do not address the effect of multimodality on open-ended play. In this paper we explore the influence of multimodal feedback on open-ended play and evaluate the game experience and creativity of the children.

3   Prototype

To examine the influence of output modalities we designed the Multimodal Mixer: an open-ended play object for children in the age of 8-12. As described in [10], from eight years old onwards children start exploring the importance of rules and roles. Moreover, the children in this age group are able to create strategies and develop social skills [11]. Also, the children are independent and the group is easily within reach. These characteristics make this age group an interesting target group for open-ended play.

One of our first explorations of open-endedness for interactive play objects was done with the LEDball [1,3]. The LEDball is responsive to its environment and provides simple interactions like changing color when the object is shaken or rolled. A user study showed that children liked playing with the LEDballs and were able to create various games. It was also found that most of the games that were created were quite simple and did not explicitly use the feedback provided by the toys. As argued in the introduction, extending the interaction possibilities may lead to more diverse games and more fun. We therefore designed the Multimodal Mixer (see figure 1). The functionalities of the Multimodal Mixer are based on the LEDball (the Multimodal Mixer also requires shaking and rolling as input) and the ColorFlare (the Multimodal Mixers can also communicate wirelessly with each other) [6]. However, whereas the LEDball and the ColorFlare only provide visual feedback, the Multimodal Mixer triggers multiple senses having three different output modalities (visual, auditory and haptic feedback). We want to underline that in this paper we use the word *modality* to indicate a form of sensory output of the play object. We use the word *functionalities* to indicate the different options within a modality. For example: a unimodal play object has only one output modality (e.g. light), but may have different functionalities (e.g. rolling it changes color or shaking it causes it to start blinking).

The design of the Multimodal Mixer is simple, but it offers many play opportunities as a basis for game rules in open-ended play. No predefined game goals are linked to the design to allow children to create their own games (see figure 1).

Fig. 1. Children playing with the Multimodal Mixer during the play sessions

We deliberately used a fairly abstract shape for the Multimodal Mixer (see figure 2), because we wanted the children to make games inspired by the output modalities instead of the aesthetical features of the object. It was up to the children's imagination what could be the meaning of the object (and its output modalities) in the context of a game. Also, the interaction possibilities are uncomplicated. After all, the more specific the behavior of the objects would be to particular situations, the fewer games it can be used for.

The use of the Multimodal Mixer is independent on time and place: it is a flexible object that can be used anywhere. The Multimodal Mixer can be held in the hand (like a torch) or it can be put on the ground. In this way, the play object can be used both as a personal and as a shared play object depending on the game context, which improves the flexibility of the concept. The Multimodal Mixer responds to its environment: it

  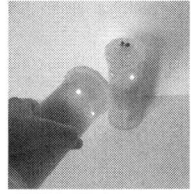 

Fig. 2. The Multimodal Mixers

reacts on physical input of the players, which triggers and encourages physical play. The objects are able to communicate through an infrared signal. One child can send a signal to another child through the play objects in order to stimulate social interaction.

In order to investigate the effect of multiple output modalities on creativity and user experience, two different versions of prototypes were created: one version of interactive play objects with one single output modality (light) and another version of objects (with the same aesthetical characteristics) with multiple output modalities. The functionalities of both versions are the same. We created one prototype with two modes: a slider for the unimodal and multimodal mode to be used by the test leader only. We made four of the same prototypes to be able to test in a group setting. The functionalities are visualized in the diagram below (figure 3).

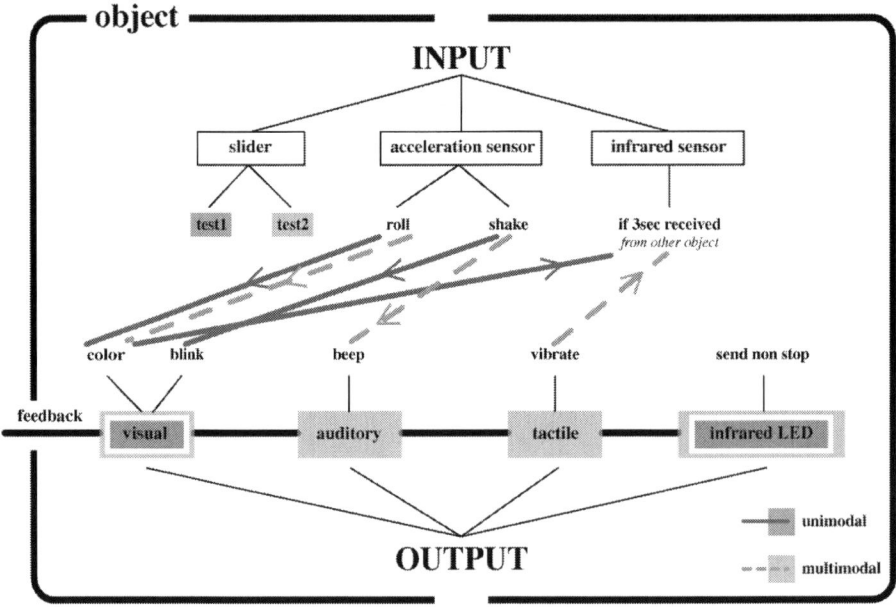

Fig. 3. Visualization of the functionalities of the Multimodal Mixer, where the straight lines indicate the interaction opportunities of the unimodal versus the multimodal version

The input side of the models contains a slider (for the mode of the object), an acceleration sensor (to detect the rolling or shaking of the object) and an infrared sensor (to detect infrared signals). The output features of the unimodal mode include full color RGB LEDs (visual) and an infrared LED (to send an infrared signal non stop). The output features of the multimodal mode include full color RGB LEDs (visual), a speaker (auditory), a vibration motor (haptic) and an infrared LED (to send an infrared signal non stop).

In the prototypes we used an Arduino Diecimilia microcontroller board for the software programming. Arduino is an open-source electronics prototyping platform based on flexible, easy-to-use hardware and software [12]. A general impression of the final prototypes is presented in figure 1.

4 Participants and Procedure

A study was carried out in which 10 groups of 3 or 4 participants (37 in total, 16 boys and 21 girls) played with the Multimodal Mixers in a free-play session. The participants of the study were children in the age of 8-12 years old.

We tested at a primary school and an after-school childcare in Eindhoven. The study was conducted with a between-subjects design. Five groups were assigned to the unimodal condition (in which they played with the unimodal play object); the other five groups were assigned to the multimodal condition (where they played with the multimodal play object).

All sessions were carried out according to the same protocol. A session started with a 5 minutes exploration phase in which the children would try and find out what they could do with the prototypes. After that, the test leader explained and demonstrated the interaction possibilities to ensure that all children started with the same understanding of the prototype. Subsequently, the children were asked to play with the prototypes for 30 minutes. The only instruction they got at this moment was to create a game. We wanted to keep the assignments in the experiment as open as possible, since we did not want to influence their play behavior. At the end of the test the children filled in a questionnaire. Every single test took approximately fifty minutes.

During the play sessions we made video recordings, which were the basis for our analysis. We counted the number of games played by each group, observed the type of games that the children created, and which functionalities they used as basis of the games they created. The categories that we used to analyze the children's play behavior were determined empirically on the basis of observations in other studies on open-ended play [7]. We defined the categories by analyzing the general descriptions of the games and the game rules: 1) *Assignment* – the children create small assignments that one person can win, e.g. roll the play object and if the object turns blue, the player wins the game; 2) *Tag* – a type of play where the children tag each other, for example by sending a signal to the other objects (inspired by games like *Catch Me If You Can*); 3) *Hide and Seek* – where either the children or the play objects are hidden in the environment and have to be found; 4) *Rolling* – in this type of play there is a central role for the interactive play objects that are rolled from one player to another; 5) *Role-playing* – the children pretend to be someone else in an act; 6) *Guessing* – a type of play where the players guess for example which object will turn yellow first; and 7) *Other* – those games that do not fit in the above-mentioned categories.

After the user experiment the participants filled in a questionnaire which was based on the Kids Game Experience Questionnaire (KGEQ) [13]. Our questionnaire addresses aspects of competence, flow and challenge, which were adopted from the KGEQ. In addition we created questions addressing creativity, social and physical aspects. Because this questionnaire has not been formally validated yet, we will not discuss the results of the questionnaire in detail in this paper. Instead, we will analyze the children's experience based on our own observations, supported by data from the questionnaire in terms of individual questions.

5   Results

First we portray how children used the objects in relation to some of our design decisions. Secondly, we describe the analysis of the data (the number and the type of games the children created and how the children used their creativity) – based on both our observations and the data derived from the questionnaire.

5.1   Design Considerations

The Multimodal Mixer has clear interaction possibilities: the children easily understood the working principles as they immediately start playing after the exploration of the play object. The aesthetics of the Multimodal Mixer triggered the children to shake or roll the object or to send a signal to another Multimodal Mixer. For instance: the shape of the head of the prototype triggered the children to send a signal and the circular form invited them to roll the prototype.

The size and shape of the object also allowed the Multimodal Mixer to be used both as a personal and as a shared play object during various games. For example: the objects were handheld and used as personal toys during *Tag* games, while in the *Assignment* category the prototypes were put upright. The flat bottom of the play object invited the object to be put on the floor – in contrast with the head of the Multimodal Mixer which is used for the sending of the signal: there is a clear difference between the upper and lower side of the object.

The children clearly made use of the flexibility of the object during the creation of new game elements. We conducted the test at two different locations and in both settings the players made full use of the entire space and its components – they even involved objects in the room as elements in the game. E.g. during a *Hide and Seek* game the players hide their Multimodal Mixer inside the furniture in the room. The flexibility of the prototype was not only reflected in the use of the environment, but also in the behavior of the children during the test. For some games the children ran around while for others they sat down at the floor, depending on the game goal. For example, during a *Tag* game where one player needed to catch the others, all players ran around, while the same children in another *Guessing* game sat down in a circle with one child in the middle who needed to guess whom of the players sent a signal to another player.

The Multimodal Mixer encourages the children to be physically active: the children used their motor skills in all of the games. Not only through the shaking and rolling of the play object, but also as a fundamental aspect of their games since most of the games that were created required physical activity. The children frequently were out of breath during and after the play session as indication that the level of physical activity was high throughout the test.

The Multimodal Mixer also stimulates social activity. Even though the test leader did not tell the participants to play *together*, all children played together in a group during the play sessions. There was not a single child that did not join a game, regardless of their age or personality. The fact that the different Multimodal Mixers were able to send and receive infrared signals contributed to this social interaction and stimulated the children to play together: the infrared communication played a crucial role in the encouragement of social play. By having an equal number of play objects and children in each group, all children were equally involved in the game. It was striking that when the objects were mixed during a previous game, the children wanted their *own* Multimodal Mixer back again during the next game – although all four Multimodal Mixers were exactly the same. Because of minor differences (like a small scratch on the casing) the children recognized their own object and claimed it as their personal one.

5.2 Creativity and Game Experience

The children in the multimodal setting created a few more games than the players who used the unimodal version of the interactive prototype (as visualized in table 1).

Table 1. Number of games per group for each test condition

	Unimodal	Multimodal
Average	6.5	7.1
Minimum	4	7
Maximum	13	11

In the unimodal condition the range of the number of games is quite broad. It is important to note that we did *not* stimulate the children to create as many games as possible. The group of children that created only 4 games had just as much fun as the group that created 13 games. More important was the fact that every group was able to come up with multiple games and that the children played nonstop for thirty minutes. The group that created 4 games simply played a game for a longer period. We observed that the number of games created also depends to a large extent on the character of the children, the composition of the group, the type and complexity of the games, etc.

In table 2 we describe which functionalities the children used as the basis of the games they created.

Table 2. Functionalities used per game for each test condition

Functionality	Number of games		
	Unimodal	Multimodal	Total
None	6	4	10
Rolling (Color)	18	15	33
Shaking (Flashing/Sound)	0	5	5
Sending (Color/Vibration)	13	14	27
Combi. of 2 functionalities	2[1]	2	4
Combi. of 3 functionalities	0	3	3
Total number of games	39	43	

---

[1] In this case both the sending and the color of the object play a distinctive role in the game goal. For example, in a game where a catcher needs to change the color of the objects of the other players by sending a signal. Once the object of another player changes to a specific color, that player needs to do an assignment depending on that color.

Table 3. Type of games per test condition

Type of game	Unimodal	%	Multimodal	%
Assignment	8	20.5	16	37.2
Tag	13	33.3	2	4.7
Hide and Seek	3	7.7	10	23.3
Rolling	4	10.3	5	11.6
Role-playing	4	10.3	4	9.3
Guessing	3	7.7	4	9.3
Other	4	10.3	2	4.7
Total	39	100	43	100

The use of color and infrared communication is used most frequent in both conditions. The flashing of the light (shaking) was never used in the unimodal setting, whereas sound (which requires the same input) was used in multiple game variations in the multimodal condition. Sometimes the children made combinations of two or three different functionalities. Occasionally the form of the interactive toy was more important than the functionality. In this case the players only used the tangible characteristics of the objects in their game, for example, they used the toy on the floor in the upright position.

An important finding is that the children in the multimodal condition used a wider range of functionalities in their games than the players in the unimodal condition (table 2). Apparently, offering various types of feedback made it easier to implement different functionalities in the game.

In the unimodal condition *Tagging* games are most popular, while in the multimodal condition games in the categories *Assignment* and *Hide and Seek* are played most often (table 3). The differences can be explained in terms of feedback modalities, for example, in the multimodal setting there are more diverse types of output modalities that can serve as inspiration for an *Assignment*. *Tagging* is much easier with a visible signal than an invisible one: it is clear for every single player who is tagged and who is not. Finally, it is more fun to play *Hide and Seek* with a sound or a vibration. For example: the vibration signal gives the *Hide and Seek* game a mysterious touch, because the children do not see the object, but indeed *feel* the presence of the object while they are searching. It is not exciting to look for the light of the object if an object or player is hidden in the environment (in the case of *Hide and Seek* the point is that players and objects are hidden).

We found that the children enjoyed playing with the Multimodal Mixer. The behavior of the players indicated that they liked creating their own games. The children showed that they had much inspiration for different games and indicated that they would create more games if they had the opportunity to play again. Our observations of the children's experience are supported by the results of the questionnaire. For example, children in both conditions were quite positive about whether they could use their fantasy while playing (Unimodal average: 4.05; sd.: 1.27, Multimodal average: 3.94; sd.: 1.21). The children also indicated that they had many ideas for new games (Unimodal average: 3.47; sd.: 1.35, Multimodal average: 3.29; sd.: 1.31) and that they would be able to create new games when they would have another opportunity to play with the Multimodal Mixer (Unimodal average: 3.89; sd.: 1.49, Multimodal average: 4.00; sd.: 0.97).

Although we observed that creating new games was not easy from the start (especially in the multimodal setting where the play object offered many different interaction possibilities), all children seemed to like the fact that they were left free: they found a challenge in creating their own games. The enthusiasm of the children was reflected in their behavior. Many of the players asked multiple times whether they could keep the play object or where they could buy it. These observations support the need for further development of interactive toys for open-ended play. However, only a longitudinal study can show whether open-ended play will remain to be so much fun on the long run and whether there are any differences between the different prototypes.

6 Conclusions and Discussion

Open-ended play is playing games without predefined game rules. The children create their own games inspired by the interaction with an (interactive) play object. Our aim was to explore the effect of multiple output modalities on the creativity and the game experience of the players during interactive open-ended play. We described a study in which we compared a unimodal and a multimodal interactive toy that is responsive to the behavior of the children and that provides feedback using different types of output. All children found open-ended play to be great fun.

6.1 Design Considerations for Multimodal Open-Ended Play

The qualitative results of our study provided valuable insights about the validity of our design decisions. We experienced that when designing interactive toys for open-ended play it is important to find a balance between offering an abstract shape and at the same time providing clear interaction possibilities. The more specific the aesthetics of the objects, the fewer games it can be used for. The abstract level of the aesthetical characteristics of the Multimodal Mixer (the shape, color and material) enabled the children to use their own imagination in determining what the function of the object was in a specific game context. The players assigned their own meaning to the design of the interactive toy. At the same time, it is important to note that the interaction possibilities should be clearly communicated through the shape of the object, for the children to know what they can do with the object. We recommend that an interactive play object should offer different interaction opportunities without being too complex.

The size and the shape allowed the Multimodal Mixer to be used both as personal and as shared play object: the design offered a flexible way of using the object in diverse types of play. We observed that the children find it important to have their own object in the game.

The Multimodal Mixer is not only responsive to physical input, but the physical activity is also essential in the games the children created. In this way open-ended play objects stimulate physical play. The Multimodal Mixer stimulated social play as well: all children who participated in the test spontaneously played together in a group setting. Supportive in this was the fact that the different Multimodal Mixers could communicate with each other.

6.2   The Influence of Output Modalities on Play Behavior

The quantitative results of our study research provide insights about how multiple modalities affect open-ended play behavior. Our study shows that multimodality in open-ended play is not too complex: children are able to assign meaning to the different types of feedback and translate the output to principles in different games they come up with. The children in the multimodal setting used all the different feedback modalities as inspiration in their games: they were able to assign meaning to all three types of output. They created different types of games by assigning meaning to the different types of output (where they occasionally even made combinations of the different functionalities).

The study shows that providing multiple output opportunities in open-ended play leads to richer games. That diversity has to do with the dispersal of the different functionalities used in the games and the type of games the children created depending on the modalities. However, this did not translate to a difference in experience between the multimodal and the unimodal condition; children were equally positive in both conditions.

It is important to mention that there is a limit to the number of interaction possibilities for interactive toys: the functionalities might get too overwhelming which may block the creativity of the children. Our study only shows that the step from traditional open-ended play to a richer type of open-ended play is understandable for children. Offering more interaction possibilities may make it easier for children to create games, but too many functionalities might be too complex and therefore daunting. It is important to find a balance in this by carefully choosing the functionalities of the object in such way it matches the intended function.

We expect that multimodal open-ended play will be more fun over a longer period of time, because it has more *diverse* interaction possibilities. For the further development of interactive toys for open-ended play future research needs to examine the effects of open-ended play on long-term use. Another interesting area of research is the development of intelligent interactive toys for open-ended play, that start with one output modality and gradually gains more interaction possibilities (for example in terms of output modalities): an intelligent object that increasingly grows along with the competence of its users.

Acknowledgments. We would like to thank Jos Verbeek for his help during the development of the prototypes, the people from the primary school and after-school childcare for their cooperation, and finally the children who enthusiastically participated in our study.

References

1. Sturm, J., Bekker, T., Groenendaal, B., Wesselink, R., Eggen, B.: Key Issues for the Successful Design of an Intelligent Interactive Playground. In: Proceedings of the 7th international conference on interaction design and children, Chicago, Illinois, pp. 258–265 (2008)

2. Bekker, T., Hoven, E., van den Peters, P., Klein Hemmink, B.: Stimulating Children's Physical Play through Interactive Games: Three Exploratory case studies. In: Proceedings of the 6th international conference on interaction design and children, Aalborg, Denmark, pp. 163–164 (2007)

3. Bekker, T., Sturm, J., Wesselink, R., Groenendaal, B., Eggen, B.: Interactive Play Objects and the Effects of Open-Ended Play on Social Interaction and Fun. In: Proceedings of the 2008 International Conference in Advances on Computer Entertainment Technology, Yokohama, Japan. ACM International Conference Proceeding Series, vol. 352, pp. 389–392 (2008)

4. Lin, T., Chang, K., Liu, H., Chu, H.: A Persuasive Game to Encourage Healthy Dietary Behaviors of Kindergarten Children. National Taiwan University (2004)

5. Bekker, T., Eggen, B.: Designing for Children's Physical Play. In: CHI 2008 extended abstracts on Human factors in computing systems, Florence, Italy, pp. 2871–2876 (2008)

6. Lemmelä, S.: Selecting Optimal Modalities for Multimodal Interaction in Mobile and Pervasive Environments. In: IMUx, Improved Mobile User Experience workshop of Pervasive 2008, the 6th international conference on Pervasive Computing, Sydney, Australia (2008)

7. Verbeek, J.: Graduation Project ColorFlare. University of Technology, Eindhoven (2009)

8. Seitinger, S., Sylva, E., Zuckerman, O., Popovic, M., Zuckerman, O.: A new playground experience: going digital? In: CHI 2006 extended abstracts on Human factors in computing systems, Montréal, Québec, Canada, pp. 303–308 (2006)

9. Iguchi, K., Inakage, M.: Morel: Remotely Launchable Outdoor Playthings. In: Proceedings of the 2006 ACM SIGCHI international conference on Advances in computer entertainment technology, Hollywood, California, vol. 266(35) (2006)

10. Acuff, D.S., Reiher, R.H.: What Kids Buy and why: The Psychology of Marketing to Kids. Simon & Schuster, Touchstone (1998)

11. Berk, L.E., Harris, S., Barnes-Young, L.: Development Through the Lifespan. Allyn & Bacon, Boston (2003)

12. Arduino, http://www.arduino.cc

13. Poels, K., IJsselsteijn, W.A., de Kort, Y.A.W.: Development of the Kids Game Experience Questionnaire: A Self Report Instrument to Assess Digital Game Experiences in Children. In: Extended abstract for Meaningful Play Conference, Michigan (2008)

Swinxsbee: A Shared Interactive Play Object to Stimulate Children's Social Play Behaviour and Physical Exercise

Martijn Jansen and Tilde Bekker

Department of Industrial Design, Eindhoven University of Technology
P.O. Box, 5600 MB Eindhoven, The Netherlands
m.e.p.jansen@student.tue.nl, m.m.bekker@tue.nl

Abstract. This paper describes a study on the influence of personal and shared play objects on the amount of social interaction. The study makes use of Swinxs, a commercially available game console that uses the strength of digital games to facilitate physically active games that can be played indoor or outdoor. A Frisbee-like object called Swinxsbee has been designed to support new game possibilities for Swinxs and stimulate social interaction. The results of a user evaluation show that children playing with shared objects engage in more social interaction than children playing with personal objects. Furthermore we observed that when games require much physical activity, this might have a negative influence on the level of social interaction, while games demanding creativity might have a positive influence.

Keywords: intelligent play objects, head-up play, social play behaviour.

1 Introduction

The popularity of digital games amongst children is huge. Digital games are engaging through their stimulating audiovisual effects and adaptability [1]. Despite the high score in engagement, most computer games do not stimulate social interaction and physical exercise. Nintendo Wii [2] and Sony Playstation's EyeToy [3] are recent attempts to make games more physical. Unfortunately these examples still keep the children in a setting that is not optimal for social interaction: play in front of a screen.

Traditional games like tag or soccer are both physical and social. The outdoor environment allows for freedom of movement and the children are playing with each other instead of with a computer. Pervasive gaming is a movement of digital gaming towards outdoor play. This genre blends real and virtual game elements to create new exciting game experiences [4]. Head-up play is a variation to pervasive gaming [5]. Where pervasive games still require children to pay attention to the technology, head-up play strives for games where children keep their 'head up' to stimulate social interaction. Swinxs [6] is a commercially available game console that supports a form of head-up play. It uses the strength of digital games to facilitate (physically) active games that can be played indoor or outdoor. This project has emerged from an interest in Swinxs as a platform for research on intelligent play and the request of the company

A. Nijholt, D. Reidsma, and H. Hondorp (Eds.): INTETAIN 2009, LNICST 9, pp. 90–101, 2009.

that has developed Swinxs to design a new play object for new game possibilities. In particular we are interested in the influence of the designed object in stimulating social interaction, because of the crucial role it plays in child development.

This paper describes the design of a new play object for Swinxs and the investigation of the influence of this design on social interaction. Our aim is to find specific game elements positively influencing social interaction as guidelines for game designers and researchers.

2 Background

Swinxs is a new game console for children aged 4 to 12. It facilitates physically active games that can be played indoor or outdoor. The most important technical features of Swinxs are the RFID-reader, speakers and USB-port. Swinxs comes with coloured armbands called XS-tags. Each XS-tag contains an RFID-tag for recognition of players. The range of the RFID-reader is approximately five centimeters above Swinxs, which requires the XS-tags to be really close to Swinxs for detection. The speakers are used for playing music and talking to the children by playing a set of professionally recorded sound samples. Swinxs explains the games, encourages the players and gives feedback on their achievement. This capability to talk enables Swinxs to communicate with the children without an attention-drawing screen. New games and supporting sound samples can be uploaded when connecting it to the computer via the USB-connection.

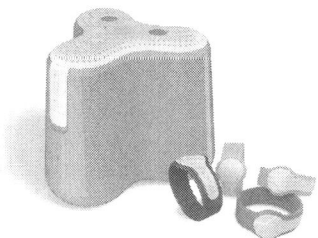

Fig. 1. The Swinxs game console and the XS-armbands

Swinxs games have a physical, creative or educational objective. Most Swinxs games are modern versions of traditional games like tag, hide and seek and musical chairs. The new version of musical chairs is called SwinxsCircle. The children are asked to run or dance in a circle on two meters distance of Swinxs while the music is playing. When the music stops, the children need to scan their XS at Swinxs. The player that first scans his XS wins the game.

One benefit of Swinxs over traditional games is that Swinxs acts as an objective referee. This can avoid arguments about the rules and about the score. Swinxs also encourages the children and gives positive feedback about each achievement. Swinxs can also play music during physical exercise, which leads to an increase positive affect and reduces perceived exertion [7].

2.1 Related Work

The interest in social gaming is quite recent. Researchers in interaction design have been creating several experimental social games for children. An example is aMAZEd, a tangible tabletop game [8]. The players have to go through a projected maze to rescue a princess. There are hurdles in the maze that force team members to meet somewhere in the maze and move together toward a certain location on the maze. The designers of the game have approached the stimulation of social interaction through cooperation. A quite similar approach has been applied in the development of Ely the Explorer [9], a game supporting a multi-user tangible interface. An Ely is a doll and an on-screen character. The children learn about different cultures through sending their Ely all over the world through a teleporter. The children are asked to help the Elys with documenting their travel. In the end the documentation of the children is combined as a common outcome. Another project is Camelot, a head-up game for outdoor play explores the potential of tangible interfaces [10]. In Camelot, two teams have to finish building a castle as fast as possible. Virtual resources need to be collected to earn parts of a physical castle.

All previously mentioned projects provide games to support social interaction, however they do not explicitly address the relationship between play objects and social interaction. This project hopes to find approaches how to positively influence social play behaviour through carefully designing game dynamics. This topic is also issued in current game design literature [11].

2.2 Theories

This subsection describes theories related to social interaction and player interaction patterns that inspired our work.

There are several theories that contribute to the field of social play behaviour. Parten defined the degree of participation in six sequential social participation categories: unoccupied behaviour, solitary play, onlooker behaviour, parallel play, associative play and cooperative play [12]. However this degree of participation does not describe in which way the children behave socially. Broadhead has created a methodology called the Social Play Continuum [13]. Here social play behaviour is measured by the level of reciprocity in language and action. The method describes four social domains: associative play, social play, highly social domain and cooperative play. The Social Play Continuum is a method to describe the level of social interaction.

Social interaction can be provoked by a game, but always requires other players. The type of relation between the players can influence the type of social interaction that will occur. The structure of interaction between a player, the game and other players is the so-called player interaction pattern [14]. Figure 2 shows the different player interaction patterns. A high level of social interaction can be provoked by the player interaction patterns cooperative play or team competition.

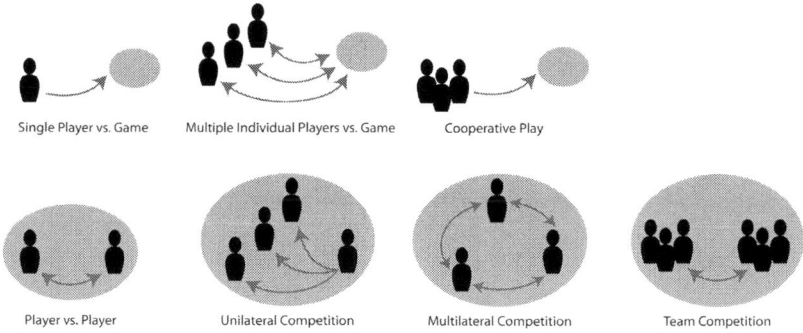

Single Player vs. Game   Multiple Individual Players vs. Game   Cooperative Play

Player vs. Player   Unilateral Competition   Multilateral Competition   Team Competition

Fig. 2. The different player interaction patterns (based on Fullerton et al., p.52 [14])

3 Design Case

The project has been approached through a design research process. In such a project, the design process and the research process run parallel to each other. We designed a play object for the purpose of addressing a research question about social play behaviour. The duration of the project was eight weeks.

3.1 Design of a New Swinxs Object

An analysis of Swinxs has shown that current Swinxs games do not include the player interaction patterns collaborative play or team play. Both patterns require collaboration, which can lead to a high degree of social interaction. To design a play object that requires collaboration is an opportunity for Swinxs to stimulate a high level of social play behaviour.

After several design iterations the concept Swinxsbee was created. Swinxsbee is a Frisbee that contains an RFID-tag (fig. 3). The fundamental difference between Swinxsbee and the existing armbands is that the armbands are *personal* objects and Swinxsbee is a *shared* object. Players are able to exchange Swinxsbee, because it is

Fig. 3. Swinxsbee, an interactive Frisbee for Swinxs

unattached, light in weight and floats on air. Handling a Frisbee is not easy; it requires skill of throwing and catching and a good sense of timing. Improving these skills is a very challenging activity and is a reason why it can remain fun on a long term.

Two Swinxsbee games have been developed for this study: Ultimate Swinxsbee and Multibee. For the design of the games the limited sensitivity of Swinxs' RFID-reader was kept in mind. It requires the players to hold the Swinxsbee close to Swinxs (approximately 5 cm) to scan Swinxsbee.

Ultimate Swinxsbee. This game is based on a Frisbee game called Ultimate Frisbee. It requires a Swinxs, a Swinxsbee and an even number of players (at least four players). Swinxs divides the group into two teams using the colors of the bracelets. The rules in this game are quite simple. The team that possesses the Frisbee can try to score a point by scanning the Frisbee at Swinxs. But the player holding Swinxsbee is not allowed to run or walk and has to throw Swinxsbee within ten seconds to his team member. The other team has to try to intercept the Swinxsbee by defending the free player. If they do so, they can try to score a point themselves. To recognize which team has scored, the XS-tags should be scanned after scanning Swinxsbee. After a point is scored, the scoring team throws the Frisbee away as far as possible to determine the location the other team can start from. The team with the most points after 3 minutes wins.

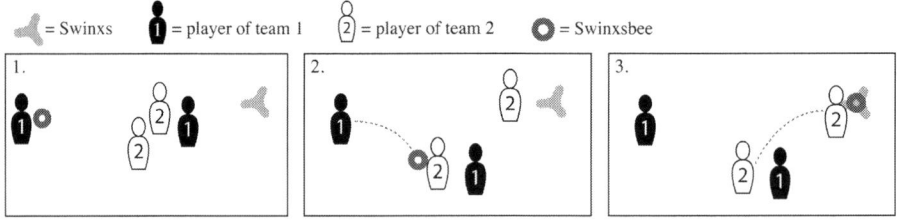

1 - The player holding Swinxsbee is not allowed to walk or run and has to throw Swinxsbee within 10 seconds. Team 2 defends the free player of team 1.
2 - Team 2 intercepts Swinxsbee and is able to attack.
3 - Swinxsbee is thrown to the free player of team 2, who scans Swinxsbee at Swinxs and scores a point.

Fig. 4. Scenario of Ultimate Swinxsbee

Multibee. The group is divided into teams of two players and each team has a Swinxsbee. The players have to draw a line of 10 meters long at about 15 meters from Swinxs. Each team has a thrower and a catcher. The thrower stands next to Swinxs and the catcher on the line. On Swinxs' signal the game starts and the player next to Swinxs throws Swinxsbee towards the catcher, but the Frisbee has to be thrown further than the line. The catcher should get Swinxsbee and run to Swinxs to scan Swinxsbee for scoring a point. On the same time the thrower runs to the line. The catcher becomes the thrower and the thrower becomes the catcher and this continues until the game ends after 3 minutes. The team with the highest score wins.

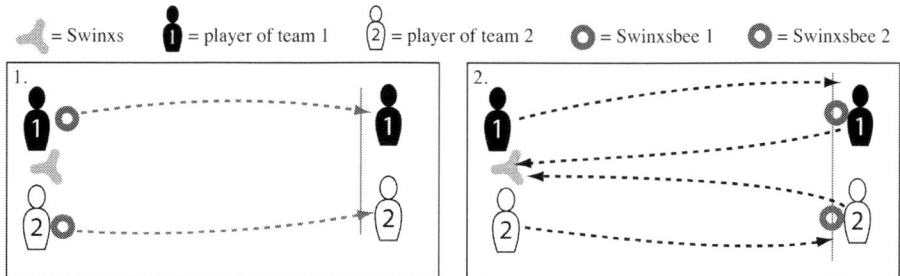

1. - Throw Swinxsbee to your team member
2. - The catcher runs with Swinxsbee to Swinxs and the thrower runs to the line

Fig. 5. Scenario of Multibee

4 Study

The study examines whether children playing with Swinxsbee engage in higher levels of social interaction than children playing with the bracelets. The game console Swinxs encourages physical play for children, but the current play objects especially stimulate play without collaboration. In contrast, the newly designed object Swinxsbee stimulates collaborative play. Using Swinxsbee we will examine our hypothesis: Playing with a shared object enhances social interaction as compared to playing with a personal object. Two conditions will be compared: play with a personal object versus play with a shared object.

4.1 Set-Up

The experiment is executed at a primary school in Eindhoven. In total 32 children between 8 and 12 years of age were asked to join the play sessions, of which 17 girls and 15 boys. In preparation for the experiment, the parents of the children have been informed and asked for permission to film and take pictures of the sessions.

The study exists of eight sessions with groups of four children. To decrease the influence of a specific game on social interaction, two games per condition will be played. All games should have a physical goal. The Swinxsbee games are Ultimate Swinxsbee and Multibee. The games for the XS-armbands are SwinxsCircle (explained in section 2) and Far and Away. In the game Far and Away Swinxs plays a music sample with a random length. The first time this sample is played, the children have to count and remember the duration of the sample. The second time the sample plays, the children have to run as far away as possible, but scan their XS-tag at Swinxs before the sample stops playing.

For this study we used a within subject design. Furthermore, both the order of playing with the shared and personal objects as the order of the games within both conditions was varied to reduce the chance of order effects.

4.2 Methodology and Analysis

This study approaches the analysis of social interaction in two ways: through video analysis and a questionnaire. The video is analysed using an observation scheme and the questionnaire provides data about the children's view on their social behaviour.

Video Analysis. Methodological research for evaluating children's interactive products is a relatively young field. Examples of observation methods for analyzing social behaviour are the earlier mentioned Social Play Continuum, the Play Observation Scale (POS) [15] and the Outdoor Play Observation Scale (OPOS) [16].

POS is not appropriate for this study, because it uses a too detailed scheme for our purposes. It also tries to examine the kind of play, which is not in the interest of this study as the kind of play is already given. OPOS aims at analyzing outdoor play. The social interaction module of OPOS codes the number of functional and non-functional interactions, but does not distinguish levels of social interaction. Therefore OPOS is not suitable for this study. The Social Play Continuum describes the level of social interaction through observing the reciprocity of actions and communication. However the Social Play Continuum is complex and not always clear about the boundaries between the domains. Therefore a new coding scheme is created for this study, which is intended for coding social interaction of players using intelligent play objects.

The coding scheme is based on the Social Play Continuum. The development of the observation scheme has gone through an iterative process of testing, evaluating and redefining the parameters. This process has eventually led to specific parameters (table 1) the observer should look at.

Table 1. Parameters of the observation scheme

Parameters	Values
Playing alone/together	Alone, parallel, teamwork
Communication	None, one-sided, reciprocal
Action	None, for own goal, for shared goal, constant reactive
Focus on game or other players	None, temporarily, constant

The values of the parameters form a basis for the interpretation of the children's play behavior. The coding scheme is shown in table 2.

Table 2. The observation scheme

Level of social interaction	Characteristics
Level 1 (low)	Alone, no focus on game or other children
Level 2 (mediocre)	Parallel/teamwork, one-sided communication/action
Level 3 (high)	Parallel/teamwork, reciprocal communication/action
Level 4 (rich)	Parallel/teamwork, cluster of reciprocal communication/action
Other	Children not in sight or intervention of the researcher

For the assessment of social play behaviour, the behaviour of each child needs to be coded separately. Providing an overall group score takes less time, but the observer's attention might be drawn to the active players. To give a realistic score of social interaction, the less active children have to be taken into account as well.

The procedure of coding is similar to the procedure of POS. Each child is observed while playing the four games. To get familiar with the behaviour of the target child and context, the observer watches the target child for 30 seconds before recording behaviours. Subsequently the target child is observed during intervals of 10 seconds. When the video is paused, the observer has to checkmark the appropriate level of social interaction within the next 5 to 10 seconds.

For each game the number of occurrences for each of the four social interaction levels is calculated. Because not all games have an equal duration, the numbers will be represented by percentages of the total play time of a game minus the play time coded as "other".

Because of time constraints only four play sessions with a total of 16 children have been analysed. The four groups have been chosen based on quality of the video. The first author has coded the play sessions.

Fig. 6. Ultimate Swinxsbee – the right girl tries to throw Swinxsbee to the left girl. The two middle girls try to defend the left girl.

Questionnaire. The questionnaire is used to find the children's perspective of their social play behaviour. It consists of 15 statements about social play behaviour during the play sessions. All 32 children have filled out the questionnaire twice, once after playing the bracelet games and once after playing the Swinxsbee games. The children were asked to give their opinion on how much they agree with the statements on a 5-point scale (not at all, slightly, moderately, fairly and extremely). The statements are derived from the social interaction module of the Kids Game Experience Questionnaire [17] extended by statements based on social interaction theories of Broadhead. The questionnaire has been written in a child friendly format and wording. Some examples of statements used are: "I was looking at others while playing", "We were mainly playing together" and "I was mimicking others while playing".

The mean differences between both conditions are calculated for all questions. To get an indication of how players perceive the social interaction, an average over all questions is calculated. A Wilcoxon signed rank test is used to test whether a significant difference between the two conditions exists.

5 Results

We will describe our findings on how the personal and the shared objects influenced the children's play behaviour. We will first present the social interaction scores from the video analysis, and then we will provide a more descriptive account of the children's behaviour. Secondly we will present the outcome of the questionnaire data.

A paired t-test was conducted on the average total social interaction scores for the two games with the bracelets versus the two games with the Swinxsbee. The total social interaction score was based on an average of the scores for social interaction levels 1 to 4. The paired t-test showed that children playing with the Swinxsbee had a significantly higher social interaction (average = 2.9, s.d. = 0.01) than children playing with the bracelets (average = 2.2, s.d. = 0.03) (n=16, p < 0.001). The average scores for social interaction for the two bracelet games are very similar, 2.4 (s.d. = 0.35) for SwinxsCircle and 2,1 (s.d. = 0.21) for Far and Away. The average scores for social interactions for the two Swinxsbee games were much more diverse: 3.4 (s.d. = 0.27) for Ultimate Swinxsbee and 2.5 for Multibee (s.d. = 0.21).

Figure 7 shows the average scores per social interaction level in percentages of all four games. The data of Ultimate Swinxsbee shows a peak for social interaction level 4. The videos of this game show that the children have a constant focus on each other and communicate both verbally and non-verbally. The ability to exchange the Swinxsbee leads to a high level of social behaviour. The players can actively ask for the Swinxsbee and carefully look at each other to defend the attackers or to make sure the defenders do not intercept the Swinxsbee. Remarkably, Multibee has scored on a similar level as a game played with personal objects, SwinxsCircle. The big difference between Multibee and the other games is the amount of physical exercise. Multibee demands all children to keep running for three minutes. The game clearly exhausted the children. This has had a big influence on the social interaction; in the end, the children were simply too exhausted to communicate and keep focus on each other and the game. The bracelet game SwinxsCircle has a higher percentage of social interaction level 3 than Multibee. The children are asked to run or dance in a circle around Swinxs. The silly tone of the music provoked funny dance moves. This creativity and humour in the game has regularly led to a high level of social interaction.

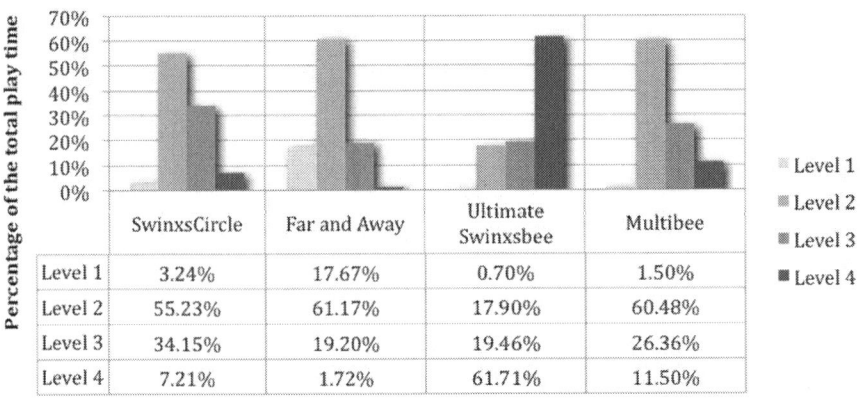

Level of social interaction

	SwinxsCircle	Far and Away	Ultimate Swinxsbee	Multibee
Level 1	3.24%	17.67%	0.70%	1.50%
Level 2	55.23%	61.17%	17.90%	60.48%
Level 3	34.15%	19.20%	19.46%	26.36%
Level 4	7.21%	1.72%	61.71%	11.50%

Level of social interaction per game

Fig. 7. Overview of the average scores for each level of social interaction of all four games

In total 32 children have filled out the questionnaire for both conditions. The mean differences show a few outliers. The statement "We helped each other while playing" scores much better for the Swinxsbee games (average c_1 = 2.4, average c_2 = 4.1). This is probably an effect of team play. The same reason counts the statement: "We played mainly together" (average c_1 = 3.0, average c_2 = 3.7). Another positive outlier is: "During the game we talked with each other about the game" (average c_1 = 2.1, average c_2 = 2.7). A negative outlier is: "We played mainly close to each other" (average c_1 = 3.4, average c_2 = 2.7). The negative result is likely an effect of one of the Swinxsbee games, Multibee. During this game children from the same team are separated and need to throw the Swinxsbee to each other.

The analysis of the questionnaire data has shown a higher total average score for the shared object games (average = 2.6, s.d. = 0.56) than the scores of personal objects for the shared (average = 2.1, s.d. = 0.49). The result of the Wilcoxon Signed Ranks Test shows a significant difference in social interaction of all groups (p = 0.039) where children felt they had more interaction during Swinxsbee games than during bracelet games.

6 Conclusions and Discussion

The current Swinxs games lack opportunities for cooperative play. A new play object called Swinxsbee, was created to support cooperative play and stimulate social interaction. Swinxsbee is a shared object and has the ability to be exchanged between players. This makes it likely that a higher level of social interaction occurs while playing with a shared play object than with a personal play object. The goal of this study was to examine the effect of shared and personal play objects on social interaction.

The data of both the video observation and questionnaire support the finding that playing with Swinxsbee leads to more social interaction than playing with the bracelet games. Even though the hypothesis was accepted; the differences in the video analysis data between the two Swinxsbee games have led us to a post-hoc examination of the other factors that influence social interaction. Our conclusion of this study is that collaboration is needed to achieve a high level of social interaction in a game. A shared object like Swinxsbee is able to evoke cooperation, but should be supported by the right game objectives and rules. Games for Swinxsbee are intended for physical play, but they can also be too focused on the physical objective. The amount of physical exercise in the game Multibee has led to a lower level of social interaction than the other Swinxsbee game. A balance between physical exercise and moments of rest might influence social interaction in a positive way. The game SwinxsCircle showed another game aspect that evoked social interaction. The children are asked to dance and the children use their creativity to dance in a funny way and leads to mimicking and laughing with other players. These game dynamics are aspects that influence social play behaviour and can be used as guidelines for the design of social games. Future research needs to examine the interaction between diverse design decisions such as game rules and other object properties and the amount of social interaction.

For the analysis of social interaction an observation scheme has been constructed. This scheme is based on social interaction theory and other observation methods. The next step is to determine the inter-coder reliability.

The newly designed object and the insights from the study were presented at the client company. They were surprised by the strength of such a simple concept like Swinxsbee. Looking at Swinxs from a player interaction pattern perspective has given them a different approach to design new games for Swinxs. Furthermore they were happy to see that in general Swinxs games scored well on social interaction.

Overall, the study has shown that using the theory of interaction patterns as an inspiration source for the design of play objects can lead to promising extensions to existing designs in terms of influencing levels of social interactions.

Acknowledgements

We would like to thank Govert de Vries and the employees of Swinxs for their input and help along the project. We also thank Janienke Sturm for her advice and expertise during the whole project. Many thanks go to the teachers of primary school 'De Driestam' that were willing to cooperate. Our greatest gratitude goes to the children that participated in the experiment. Without their help and enthusiasm, this project would not have been this successful.

References

1. Acuff, D.S., Reiher, R.H.: What kids buy and why: The psychology of marketing to kids. The Free Press, New York (1997)
2. Wii, N.: http://wii.com (date of last visit: 29-03-09)
3. EyeToy for Sony Playstation, http://www.eyetoy.com (date of last visit: 29-03-09)
4. Magerkurth, C., Cheok, A.D., Mandryk, R.L., Nilsen, T.: Pervasive games: bringing computer entertainment back to the real world. ACM Computers in Entertainment 3(3) (2005)
5. Soute, I.: HUGs: Head-Up Games. In: Proceedings of IDC 2007, pp. 205–208 (2007)
6. Swinxs, http://www.swinxs.com (date of last visit: 29-03-09)
7. Boutcher, S.H., Trenske, M.: The effects of sensory deprivation and music on perceived exertion and affect during exercise. J. Sport Exercise Psychology 12, 167–176 (1990)
8. Al Mahmud, A., Mubin, O., Octavia, J.R., Shahid, S., Yeo, L., Markopoulos, P., Martens, J.: aMAZEd: designing an affective social game for children. In: Proceedings of the 6th international Conference on interaction Design and Children (2007)
9. Africano, D., Eriksson, S., Lindbergh, K., Lundholm, P., Nilbrink, F.: Ely the explorer: A multi-user interactive play system to promote collaborative learning (2004)
10. Verhaegh, J., Soute, I., Kessels, A., Markopoulos, P.: On the design of Camelot, an outdoor game for children. In: Proceedings of the 2006 conference on Interaction design and children (2006)
11. Salen, K., Zimmerman, E.: Rules of Play: Game esign fundamentals. MIT Press, Cambridge (2004)
12. Parten, M.B.: Social participation among preschool children. Journal of Abnormal and Social Psychology (1932)

13. Broadhead, P.: Early years play and learning: developing social skills and cooperation. RoutledgeFalmer, London (2004)
14. Fullerton, T., Swain, C., Hoffman, S.: Game Design Workshop. CMP Books, San Francisco (2004)
15. Rubin, K.H.: The Play Observation Scale (POS). University of Waterloo, Waterloo (1989)
16. Bakker, S., Markopoulos, P., de Kort, Y.: OPOS: an Observation Scheme for Evaluating Head-Up Play. In: Proceedings of the 5th Nordic conference on Human-computer interaction: building bridges (2008)
17. Poels, K., IJsselsteijn, W.A., de Kort, Y.A.W.: Development of the Kids Game Experience Questionnaire: A self report instrument to assess digital game experiences in children. In: Poster Presentation at the Meaningful Play conference in Michigan (2008)

Affective Interface Adaptations in the Musickiosk Interactive Entertainment Application

L. Malatesta[1], A. Raouzaiou[1], L. Pearce[2], and K. Karpouzis[1]

[1] Image, Video and Multimedia Systems Lab., School of Electrical and Computer Engineering,
National Technical University of Athens
9, Heroon Politechniou str., 15780, Zografou, Athens, Greece
{lori,araouz}@image.ntua.gr, kkarpou@cs.ntua.gr
[2] XIM Ltd,
Fountain Court, 2 Victoria Square,
St.Albans, Herts, AL1 3TF, UK
laurence@xim.co.uk

Abstract. The current work presents the affective interface adaptations in the Musickiosk application. Adaptive interaction poses several open questions since there is no unique way of mapping affective factors of user behaviour to the output of the system. Musickiosk uses a non-contact interface and implicit interaction through emotional affect rather than explicit interaction where a gesture, sound or other input directly maps to an output behaviour - as in traditional entertainment applications. PAD model is used for characterizing the different affective states and emotions.

Keywords: affective interaction, adaptive interaction, interactive entertainment, PAD model.

1 Introduction

Nowadays the design of Perceptual User Interfaces (PUIs) constitutes a significant challenge for many researchers. These interfaces are characterized by interaction techniques that combine an understanding of natural human capabilities (particularly communication, motor, cognitive, and perceptual skills) with computer I/O devices and machine perception and reasoning. They seek to make the user interface more natural and compelling by taking advantage of the ways in which people naturally interact with each other and with the world, both verbal and nonverbal communications. The main directives of this research area are that devices and sensors should be transparent and passive if possible, and machines should both perceive relevant human communication channels and generate output that is naturally understood. These goals require integration of technologies such as speech and sound recognition and generation, computer vision, graphical animation and visualization, language understanding, touch-based sensing and feedback (haptics), learning, user modeling, and dialog management [9]. In the application presented in this paper, the interaction is focused on what is commonly referred to as affective interaction.

A. Nijholt, D. Reidsma, and H. Hondorp (Eds.): INTETAIN 2009, LNICST 9, pp. 102–109, 2009.

Berthouze et al. [3] identify three key points to be considered when developing systems that capture affective information: embodiment (experiencing physical reality), dynamics (mapping experience and emotional state with its label) and adaptive interaction (conveying emotive response, responding to a recognized emotional state).

Current work focuses on the third point of Berthouze, that of adaptive interaction. It is considered that embodiment and dynamics are sufficiently covered by the proposed architecture and the literature that supports each of the components used in the presented interface of entertainment. Adaptive interaction nevertheless poses several open questions since there is no unique way of mapping affective factors of user behaviour to the output of the system.

The proposed interactive application was chosen mainly for its requirement to entertain while using a non-contact interface and implicit interaction through emotional affect, rather than explicit interaction where a gesture, sound or other input directly maps to an output behaviour (as in traditional entertainment applications).

2 Affective Factors and Adaptive Interfaces

In a review on adapting interaction to affective factors [6], one of the key points is that personal goals are strongly linked to affective factors. Emotions control the process of goal achievement by informing the individual whether the monitored goals are compromised or have been achieved. So how are affective goals defined and which subset of these goals is relevant to entertainment interactions? According to Ford [7] there are three different kinds of within-person consequences that a person might desire: affective goals, cognitive goals and subjective organisation goals. Affective goals represent different kinds of feelings or emotions that a person might want to experience, or avoid. A well established psychological principle states that people are "intrinsically" motivated to seek and maintain an optimal level of arousal [8]. Ford classifies entertainment goals as a subgroup of affective goals. They represent a desire to increase one's level of arousal by doing something that is stimulating or exiting, dangerous or simply different from one's current activity. They are also defined as goals for avoiding boredom and stressful inactivity.

When talking of art and entertainment interfaces it is important to distinguish emotions represented in both of them from affective responses to them.

- Felt emotions / human affective responses to art/ entertainment. We refer to them as aesthetic emotions. By identifying and narrowing down this set of emotions in the case of interactive entertainment we can tackle the question how these emotions can be captured and interpreted so as to allow for affective interfaces to adapt accordingly.
- Perceived emotions in art/ entertainment/ interaction scenarios. How are affective changes/ adaptations of the environment perceived? For example, how is a change in music is perceived?

Having this distinction in mind we are trying to find the appropriate emotional model to be used in an affective interface.

A typical method of characterizing affective states and emotions is to focus on the underlying, often physiologically correlated factors and map these onto distinct dimensions. This approach leads to spatial/ dimensional models for emotions. Several such two or three dimensional sets have been proposed. Sets of emotion dimensions include "arousal, valence and dominance" (known in the literature by different names, including "evaluation, activation and power"; "pleasure, arousal, dominance"; etc.). Recent research provides additional evidence for the existence of three dimensions and suggests there should be a fourth one as well: [4] report consistent results from various cultures where a set of four dimensions is found in user studies: "valence, potency, arousal, and unpredictability". Unpredictability is the dimension that monitors reactions related with surprise and high novelty.

The Pleasure-Arousal-Dominance (P-A-D) model [1] is one of the most discussed models in the field. "Pleasure" stands for the degree of pleasantness of the emotional experience, which is typically characterized as a continuous range of affective responses extending from "unpleasant" to "pleasant". "Arousal" stands for the level of activation of the emotion, and it is characterized as a range of affective responses extending from "calm" to "excited". "Dominance" describes the level of attention or rejection of the emotion.

Within the PAD Model, there are eight basic and common varieties of emotion, as defined by all possible combinations of high versus low pleasure (+P and -P), high versus low arousal (+A and -A) and high versus low dominance (+D and -D). Thus, for instance, Anxious (-P+A-D) states include feeling aghast, bewildered, distressed, in pain, insecure, or upset; hostile (-P+A+D) states include feeling angry, catty, defiant, insolent, and nasty; and exuberant (+P+A+D) states include feeling admired, bold, carefree, excited, mighty, and triumphant.

In principle, if the P-A-D dimensions are continuous, this model is able to generate an infinite number of emotional states. In the case of adaptive interfaces and entertainment there is no need to account for this wide range of emotional states. It makes sense to limit the set of states to the ones related to the entertaining experience. One way of achieving that is by eliminating one of the dimensions. The literature supports such an action since the dominance dimension is useful mainly in distinguishing emotional states that have similar "pleasure" and "arousal" values. For example, the dominance dimension helps discriminate "violence" from "fear": "violence" has P-A-D values of (−0.50,+0.62,+0.38), and "fear" has P-A-D values of (−0.64,+0.60,−0.43) [1]. In our case in the monitoring of user experience dominance is of little importance since the affective states we aim to monitor are related with the aesthetic experience. A popular model that supports such a reduction is a simplified version of the P-A-D model that only uses the P-A dimensions which was introduced by Lang [2].

3   Description of Santa Cecilia

As interaction design continues to evolve for a plethora of interface types, a question that remains open is how affective factors can be accounted for in such design approaches. Current work focuses on a design of an interface built for entertainment purposes, called Musickiosk (Fig. 1).

Fig. 1. MusicKiosk: an interface built for entertainment purposes

Musickiosk is an exhibit in the National Academy of Santa Cecilia (*Accademia Nazionale di Santa Cecilia* [12], one of the world's oldest music institutes) in Rome. It uses multiple modalities as input and synthesizes a composite output comprised of music and visual animation. MusicKiosk is a walk-through installation of four consecutive rooms. Each room is equipped with cameras that monitor user behaviour. It takes inputs from "Shelf Components", accessed via the CALLAS Framework, and uses these to drive a cartoon-based story on the screen, and to generate music [14]. The design goal is to adapt the interface to the user's affective reactions and thus deliver a more engaging and customised entertaining experience. The audience is encouraged to interact with the showcase through words, emotional speech and facial expressions. The perceived emotion of these inputs is used to influence the mood of the main cartoon character, the animated musicians and of the music generated by the kiosk.

3.1 Scenario

The storyline was developed by Paola Pacetti, a children's author based at Santa Cecilia. It is inspired by a photograph in the museum of a 'Concerto Storico' which was held in honour of queen Margherita in the late 19th century. The historical photograph is used at the beginning and end of the animation.

The kiosk story centres on a boy in the Concerto Storico orchestra. He has arrived late for the special performance and needs the end user to help him find the concert. Without any physical contact with the computer the user can direct the boy to a series of rehearsal rooms – each featuring musicians playing a particular instrument group – and finally to the stage door itself, by speaking the numbers on the backstage doors. Within each rehearsal room, as the user expresses their mood, the music created changes accordingly. The stage door is only unlocked once the boy has entered all three rehearsal rooms, and in so doing the user will have created a unique piece of music.

XIM created a set of 2D animated characters and scenes in order to realise this story as a non-linear game-like kiosk application. Drawings were based on the characters and scenery in the historical photograph. A variety of instruments were drawn and animated, which are played in the rehearsal rooms according to the prevalent mood of the user [13].

As depicted in Figure 2 the user's behaviour is monitored by three components which in turn provide the input to the CALLAS Framework's blackboard. These components are a Multi-Keyword Spotting system detecting emotionally charged words and expressions, an affective speech detection system called EmoVoice ([10]) and a facial feature detection component ([11]) which monitors the movement of points in the face of the user and with the help of a neural network classifies the user's expressions in a two dimensional space of activation/ evaluation.

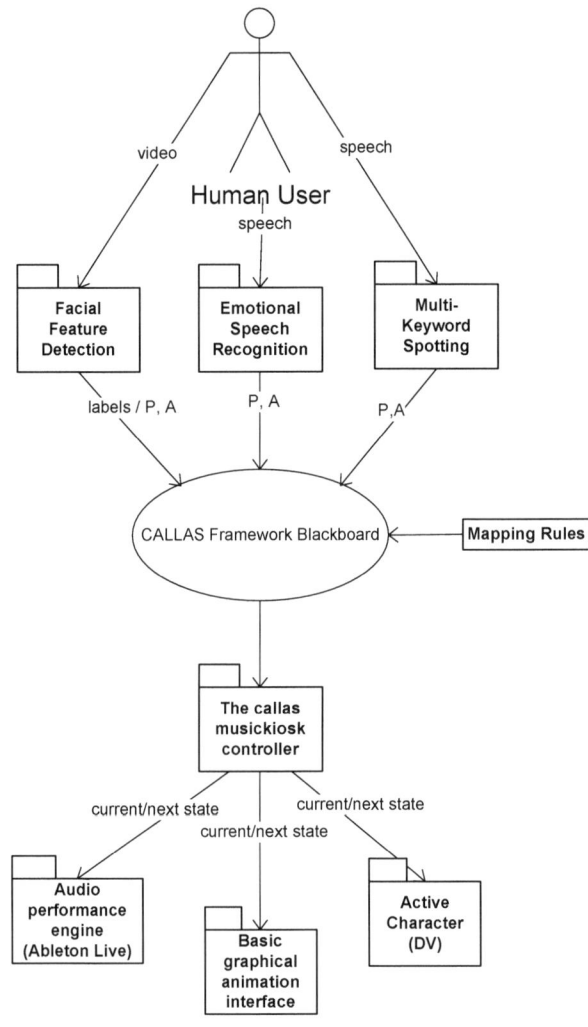

Fig. 2. MusicKiosk Architecture

Between blackboard and the system outputs resides the CALLAS Musickiosk controller. This is a controller application written in Java which manages all timing issues and is responsible for interpreting the blackboard events in the context of the application, mapping them to events in the audio and animation.

4   Adaptation of the Interface – State Transition Diagram

There is no unique way of mapping the overall pleasure, arousal values that the system calculates in each time cycle to a specific output. The idea is for the interface to adapt to the monitored dynamics of these dimensions. In order to achieve that in a systematic way we have put forward a set of rules. These rules are visualised in a state transition diagram (Fig. 3) and define the input conditions that fire specific changes in the environment. P and A stand for the two dimensions-pleasure and arousal- while the + and – are used when a predefined threshold is reached in the calculated values of these dimensions. Current design supports calibration of these thresholds such that their values are entered into a rule-mapping properties file that can be modified at run time. The rules are designed based on the fact that P-, A+ represents active disliking, P-, A- passive disliking, P+, A- serene liking and P+, A+ active liking. Interface adaptation is comprised of three actions:

- Change in the affective quality of music phrases played back
- Change in the facial expression of the virtual child
- Change in the number of instruments used to synthesise music playback.

These corresponding actions are triggered based the following rules:

- If arousal and/ or pleasure score less than the predefined threshold, neutral music phrases are played
- In the case of A+ the number of instruments is increased and A- leads to the decrease of the number of instruments used.
- In the case of significant changes in the pleasure variable the virtual child's facial expression mirrors this change (i.e. either negative, neutral or positive expressions are synthesised)
- In the case of active liking (A+, P+) joyful phrases are played
- Active disliking (A+, P-) triggers angry music phrases
- Serene/ passive liking (A-, P+) leads to sweet/ gentle music phrases being played back
- And finally if passive disliking (A-, P-) is recognised, melancholic music phrases are played.

These rules are applied in tandem meaning that the interface adapts in more ways than one depending on what changes are detected and in the current state of the system. For example if active liking is detected when neutral phrases are played and the virtual child has a neutral expression this will lead to a change in the child's facial animation to a happy one, an instrument will be added and music phrases will become joyful. In case no significant change is monitored in a cycle's duration the system remains in the same state. The overall interaction of the user with the system is bounded by a timeout limit. When the limit is reached the user is prompted to move to the next room.

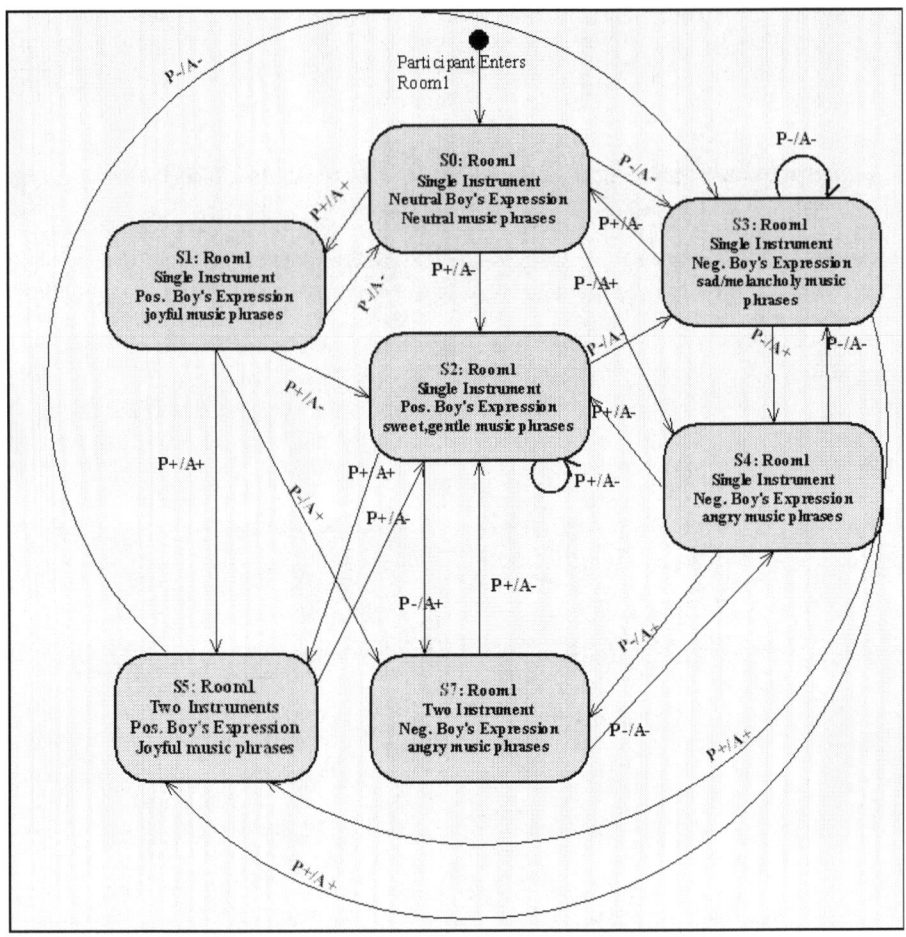

Fig. 3. State Transition diagram

5   Future Work – Adaptive Interface Evaluation

Choices in the mapping of affective factors and adaptations of the interface remain to be tested empirically with extended user studies. Our overall aim is to enhance the user experience and provide a more natural response to perceived emotional expressions. In order to achieve this goal we plan to adopt a two fold approach on interface evaluation, one taking place during the course of the interaction and the other taking place after its completion. In the first case the user interacting with the system will be given the opportunity to evaluate interface adaptations on the fly. In the second case, detailed, time-stamped data logs generated by the kiosk will be compared with collected user feedback on the perceived environment adaptations through self report questionnaires.

Acknowledgement

This work has been funded by the FP6 IP Callas (Conveying Affectiveness in Leading-edge Living Adaptive Systems), Contract Number IST-34800.

References

[1] Mehrabian, A.: Pleasure-arousal-dominance: A general framework for describing and measuring individual differences in temperament. Current Psycho. 14(4), 261–292 (1996)

[2] Lang, P.: Perspectives on Anger and Emotion, pp. 109–134. Lawrence Erlbaum Associates, Mahwah (1993)

[3] Bianchi-Berthouze, N., Lisetti, C.L.: Modelling multimodal expression of user's affective subjective experience. User Modelling and User-Adapted Interaction 12(1), 49–84 (2002)

[4] Fontaine, J., Scherer, K., Roesch, E., Ellsworth, P.: The world of emotions is not two-dimensional. Psychological Science 18(12), 1050–1057 (2007)

[5] Hudlicka, E., McNeese, M.: Assessment of User Affective and Belief States for Interface Adaptation: Application to an Air Force Pilot Task. User Modelling and User-Adapted Interaction 12, 1–47 (2002)

[6] De Rosis, F.: Towards Adaptation of Interaction to Affective Factors. User Modelling and User-Adapted Interaction (2001)

[7] Ford, M.E.: Motivating Humans. Sage Publishing, Newbury Park (1992)

[8] Berlyne, D.E.: Aesthetics and Psychobiology. Appleton-Century-Crofts, New York (1971)

[9] Turk, M., Robertson, G.: Perceptual user interfaces (introduction). Communications of the ACM 43, 32–34 (2000)

[10] Wagner, J., Vogt, T., André, E.: A Systematic Comparison of Different HMM Designs for Emotion Recognition from Acted and Spontaneous Speech. In: ACII 2007, pp. 114–125 (2007)

[11] Asteriadis, S., Tzouveli, P., Karpouzis, K., Kollias, S.: Estimation of behavioral user state based on eye gaze and head pose—application in an e-learning environment. Multimedia Tools and Applications 41(3), 469–493 (2009)

[12] http://www.santacecilia.it/

[13] FP6 IP Callas (Conveying Affectiveness in Leading-edge Living Adaptive Systems), Contract Number IST-34800 – Music Kiosk Installation Showcase Description

[14] FP6 IP Callas (Conveying Affectiveness in Leading-edge Living Adaptive Systems), Contract Number IST-34800 – Framework Description

iTheater Puppets
Tangible Interactions for Storytelling

Oscar Mayora, Cristina Costa, and Andrei Papliatseyeu

CREATE-NET, MISE
Via alla Cascata 56C - 38015, Trento, Italia
{oscar.mayora,cristina.costa,andrei.papliatseyeu}@create-net.org

Abstract. In this paper we present preliminary work on iTheater, an interactive integrated system for story-creation and storytelling, dedicated to young children. Based on the analogy with hand puppets' theatre, the system aims to create an interactive environment where children will be able to give life to their imaginary characters by creating, editing and recording computer animations in a simple and exciting way, through the movement and tactile manipulation of traditional hand puppets. The system merges the familiarity of use of physical objects with the engaging richness of expression of sounds, images and animations. The iTheater is conceived as a creative flexible toolkit to create and tell stories, taking advantage of the new opportunities based on the multimedia and interactive technologies.

Keywords: Tangible interfaces, children, puppetry, edutainment, new hardware technology for interaction and entertainment.

1 Introduction

Puppets are a powerful interface to fantasy and creativity. Its use provides a great potential to educators when working with children and their immediateness and simplicity makes them friendly and engaging. Besides, puppets provide children with a mean for expressing and experiencing emotions and interacting with other pairs.

All the physicality embedded in the use of puppets can be exploited as a tool for producing creative expressions. These expressions may vary from a projection of own thoughts and emotions through storytelling, to assimilation of the external stimuli through introspection. In this way, puppets could be used as a mean for reflecting and interpreting the perceived world and therefore as a way to bridge reality towards the internal cognitive processes of individuals. Based on the previous reflections, we can intuit the potential of puppets use in different cognitive experiences like education, cognitive therapy and artwork creation among others.

In this work, we propose iTheater as a way to expand the creative possibilities of puppets through the creation of puppet-like tangible interfaces augmented with embedded sensors (e.g. RFIDs and accelerometers) and multimedia capabilities integrating the different elements of a traditional puppets-theater (e.g. play setting, music, lighting, etc.) into a virtual representation. In this context the resulting tangibles

A. Nijholt, D. Reidsma, and H. Hondorp (Eds.): INTETAIN 2009, LNICST 9, pp. 110–118, 2009.
© ICST Institute for Computer Sciences, Social Informatics and Telecommunications Engineering 2009

would provide direct manipulation of physical objects enriched with more means of interaction and with persistence of actions in the digital world for further analysis.

In particular, the iTheatre takes advantage of the various aspects of puppetry for stimulating the user:

- *Puppet workshop*: the physical manipulation of the puppet, its creation, personalization and characterization, corresponds to the character creation in the multimedia piece of art.
- *Process drama*: the process of play creation by it self is full of opportunities for learning and creative work.
- *Make and believe*: tangible elements make it possible to the child to enter in the story and in the character
- *Storytelling*: the final result can be reviewed, manipulated, refined.

Besides the traditional advantages of using tangible interfaces with children, we should also add its versatility in catching all the expressiveness of gestures and richness of non verbal communication that otherwise would be lost. Indeed, when playing with a puppet, the borderline between the puppet and the kid's hand that is moving it is blurred: the puppeteer's hand is part of the puppet, but at the same time the puppet is an external entity. This that allows a great range of expression and non verbal communication, allowing to express feelings like aggressiveness as well as tenderness, stressing the make and believe effect, and giving to the child the sense of mastery.

2 Related Work

Based on the use of real puppets and other tangible representations of screenplay elements, iTheater allows children to have full control of the story. This is relevant according to the children needs pointed by Druin et al [4] regarding their interaction with technology - control, social experience and expressive tools - and in the fact that technology should support children's curiosities, love of repetition and need for control [5].

Traditional toys can be augmented in order to being used as tangible interfaces. Today children are used to interact with toys that are basically TUIs: indeed modern interactive toys have tactile interfaces, produce visual, audio and physical feedbacks, can be combined in various ways and sometimes 'programmed'. Objects such as soft and plush toys, puppets, etc., if used as TUIs allow children to interact complex systems in a very natural way. This is specially true for small children because we would use the objects that naturally attract their attention and curiosity. However, when a toy involves the child in a passive way, it is not able to support the child in their creativity. For example plush toys that tell stories do not support the child creating his or her own story. As Cassell and Ryokai point out in [8], these toys do not "empower them to express and create or co-create…and to use their imaginations."

An example of the use of child toys as TUI is the Rosebud [10] system, where toys based TUI is used in addition to the traditional graphical user interface (GUI). The child interacts with various toys and with a computer. The child tells his story his toys and the audio is recorded by the computer and associated to each toy. The software also generates the story-specific feedback and encouragement. The physical toy is enriched by the stories created the child, and the possibility to exchange it among children allows collaborative story creation.

In Storymat [8], toys based tangible interfaces were used for creating an familiar interactive environment where children could feel comfortable in telling stories making the storytelling very natural and easy. Children can play and tell stories on the Storymat using several toys and the mat itself (representing the world), "Storymat captures the stories, the motion of the toys, and the place they were told, for them or other children to see and hear later". In listening to the stories of others as well as their own, children react by telling more stories and telling stories collaboratively.

Another approach TUI based story telling can be found in Gorbet et al. [13] where the authors present *The Triangles* tool, that allow through the use physical building blocks (shaped as triangles) to create various applications based on object manipulations. One example of usage of *The Triangles*, is an application for interactive non-linear storytelling: depending on how the triangles are put together, different web pages or audio files are presented or played. Even if the results of the manipulation are shown in a traditional way (web pages and audio files), this early work already show how much physical building blocks can become "powerful tools for thought and play". The story telling example applications of *Triangles*, "provide a very simple means for interacting with a potentially very complicated set of character relationships and storytelling situations." These applications work with pre-configured story paths, but the use of physical building blocks allow users to use the application in a very straightforward way. This work shows how it is possible to exploit the physicity of the objects (in this case the triangle shaped blocks) and its affordances to give the user the actual feeling of holding and manipulating the content.

Other collaborative story making systems are the TellTale [14], and the DollTalk [15]. These story-making tools are based mostly on audio recording, without the use of computer graphics or animation that could enrich the final story. Kids Room [16], SAM [17], and ActiveCube [18] add the use of images and animation to record the story.

3   Envisioned Application Scenario and Education Goals

Besides of being entertaining and engaging for the children, iTheatre is designed for being an efficient and customizable tool for educational purposes. The system is conceived to provide a novel fertile tool both for educators and children to foster the crucial passage in learning from spoken language to written language, that, as E. Ackermann stresses in [3], can be a difficult one, "not just for children who grew up in dominantly oral traditions but, closer to home, for *digital* kids."

Storytelling and role playing encourages the child to develop his/her narrative skills, learning to contextualize a story, to organize ideas, keeping trace of a speech and elaborate the elements of a story [1]. Tangible interfaces have the role of facilitating this process, allowing children to naturally be engaged in playful interaction while creating the story.

The system will be evaluated in real scenarios such as schools and museums. To this aim, the iTheatre project involves teachers and educators with previous experiences on the use of new technologies in educational projects, with whom collaborate in the development of the interface and tool, working on usability/customizability/intuitiveness of the interface and on the design the interface best-suited for the specific activity of story creation. Besides, the ongoing collaboration with the local Natural Sciences museum (*Museo Tridentino delle Scienze Naturali*) will be important in the evaluation phase, for attracting users in a real context.

4   iTheater Description

The iTheater is an interactive integrated system for story-creation and storytelling based on tangible interfaces and animation editing, dedicated to young children of 4 to 8 years old.

iTheatre use a familiar context, the puppet theatre, for enabling storytelling as a game. Since the puppet theatre is also a social game that often involves more than one puppeteer and an audience, the collaborative involvement comes more spontaneous. The story created with the puppet do not have only an oral component but also a visual component given by the acting of the puppet that is translated into an animation on a video clip.

The iTheatre is characterized by two main complementary components:

(a) the core *Puppet Interface* for the control of one or more virtual characters;
(b) a set of physical objects constituting a *Tangible User Interface Toolkit* to perform the activity of animation-editing through physical intuitive objects.

The system is schematized in Figure 1, with a special highlight on the functional block tangible user interface.

The use of TUI allows to capture the expressiveness and creativity characteristic of the immediateness of the playing moment and use this material for creating content,

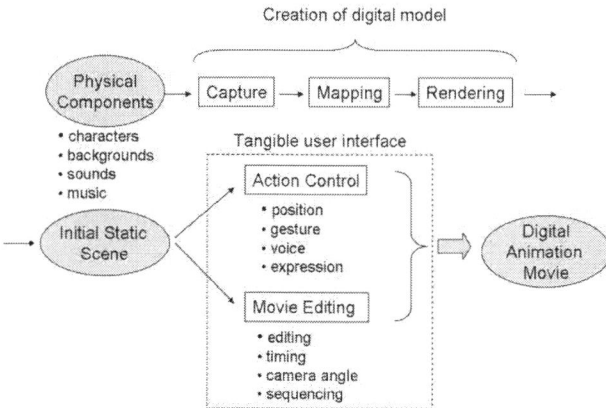

Fig. 1. Relationship between iTheatre components

based on animation techniques, that can be reviewed, modified and refined afterwards. The resulting system encourages creativity and expressiveness through the puppet interface and at the same time makes the complex task of animation editing easy and natural through the manipulation of physical objects though which create associations, control functionalities and manipulate multimedia material. Children can manipulate content in a very simple way, as if they were playing with toys in a playground, while the technology is completely hidden to them.

A particular emphasis is be given to simplicity, ergonomics and low-cost of the solution, based also on a deep analysis of user requirements. Participatory Design is used, taking into account both children and educators as final users.

4.1   Early Prototype

In order to have a quick first feedback from the teachers and educators that take care of the pedagogical design and assessment of the system, a basic prototype system has been developed (Fig.2).

The *Puppet Interface* was implemented using an IR vision system. Hand puppets were equipped with two infra-red (IR) leds placed on their arms. Puppet's movements were tracked by an IR camera able at the moment to recognize up to four IR lights, so that two it was possible to use two hand puppets at the same time (for this prototype we used the IR camera embedded into a Nintendo Wiimote Controller), allowing two users to play at the same time. The movement of the arms of the puppet are then tracked and interpreted. Movements that the user perform on the puppet are translated into various actions of the virtual character, including visual and audio effects, giving life to the virtual character. For this prototype, four pre-defined characters were created: *the princess, the bubble man, the pirate* and *the dragon*, with their own set of animations and audio effects. In addition to the movement of the virtual character in the screen, the player can induce his virtual character to perform pre-defined actions, depending on the profile of character chosen by the user. For example with a fast moving movement of the arms, the player can make *the dragon* to fly, or *the pirate* to fight, giving additional creative possibilities to the player.

Fig. 2. iTheater components

The *Animation-Making Toolkit* was implemented using as interface various objects with embedded RFID tags (in the example in fig.2 we used playing cards). Manipulating these objects, the user is able to set up the virtual puppet theatre and access to various functionalities. The player can use this interface for choosing his character and define the story context, for example adding/removing backgrounds (both audio and video), adding music effects to the narration, choosing style, etc… Selected objects (in this case playing cards) are collected on a bowl equipped with an antenna that reads the embedded RFID tag, allowing the system to recognize the user's choices and to set up the virtual puppet theatre.

Even being quite simple in its implementation, this first prototype met his objective of illustrating the concept behind the iTheatre system and received encouraging positive feedbacks.

5   Preliminary Users Feedback

Previous work on users requirements analysis has shown the difficulties of users for expressing requirements they are not aware of. This situation is typical in the development of emerging technologies [6]. One approach to mitigate this problem is the use of early prototypes that can give more concrete schemes and representations of these new technologies [7]. These assumptions motivated the development of the iTheater early prototype that is subject of this paper. In order to obtain preliminary users feedback for steering the future development of iTheater, we conducted the users study presented in this work.

The study was conducted with 10 users (5 Male and 5 Female) with different background (5 administrative workers, 4 researchers, 1 child;) and different age ranges (1 [< 10yy], 2 [20-25 yy], 4 [25-35 yy], 1 [35-45]yy, 2 [>45yy]) organized in three main stages: 1) demonstration of the main functionalities of the prototype, 2) direct usage of the iTheater prototype by users and 3) an interview based on a questionnaire regarding use and potentials of iTheater. Figure 3 shows two moments of the interaction of users with iTheater.

Fig. 3. Users interaction with iTheater system

The summary of the obtained results are shown in table 1.

Table 1. Users study summarized results

Familiarity with iTheater technology
From the analysis of interviews it was found that 7/10 users didn't found any similarities between iTheater technology with other systems they used in the past. However, the other three users recall their use of Nintendo-Wii as a similar technology stating as a main difference the fact that iTheater allows for more development of creativity while Nintendo-Wii was identified as a rather "close" system where interaction is more tight to predefined scripts (surprisingly the kid was one of this users that expressed iTheater can allow for more creativity "you can invent your own stories")..
General impression of iTheater prototype
All ten users expressed their likeness to iTheater prototype and six of them highlighted the potential of iTheater as a tool for developing creativity through richer storytelling means (involvement of audiovisual stimuli, physical interaction and eventually collaboration with other people). In general the system was perceived as "fun" and "entertaining".
Proffered/desired features:
During the interviews four features of the iTheater prototype were highlighted as the most interesting ones. The features are ordered according to the highest number of times that it was perceived as the most desirable one : 1) Virtual characters movements when moving physical puppet . Each character had three different states of movement when played (e.g. walk, sit, jump, etc.). 2) Manipulation of physical objects – effect in virtual world (e.g. physical drawings associated to virtual scene, physical objects associated to sound effects, etc.) 3) Interchangeable scenography and 4) Interchangeable audio effects and 5) multiple puppet interactions.
Difficulties of usage
All users recognized the system as an early prototype but highlighted the need to keep special attention when developing the final system on making the interaction easier. Indeed the current prototype require smooth movements of the puppets in order to be recognized and that was non immediate for users while interacting with the prototype. However after the first movements of the puppets users came naturally to move them slower to see better correspondence between physical movements and associated movement of virtual characters. Another relevant finding was the expression of users to use only one puppet in one hand while keeping the other hand free for manipulation of other objects such as the scenography, audio effects objects, etc. People wearing two puppets simultaneously show difficulties for doing such manipulations.
Potential applications for iTheater technology
Users manifested different potential applications of iTheater technology. The preferred potential application for iTheater was found to be for training and education. Other applications came out from the interviews such as the development of interactive toys, computer games and even as a tool for augment experience while shopping (e.g. supermarket) by manipulating products and obtaining more detailed descriptions in distributed displays.

The results show that iTheater users were able to express more concrete requirements after interacting with the prototype. In addition, the elicitation of the requirements was greatly simplified by the discussion with the experimenter mainly because they were grounded in practice and experiences. In any case, the requirements that came out from usage were still strongly related to the actual functionalities of the current low-fidelity prototype and only in few occasions were completely original. Thus, even if useful as a tool for early evaluations and identification of potential requirements, the use of low-fidelity prototypes may bias users' to focus more on current functionalities than in expressing new ones. Further work will consist in focusing on definition of new users studies motivating identification of new functionalities and requirements taking as starting point the findings of this study.

6 Concluding Remarks and Future Work

The preliminary work on iTheatre and the early involvement of users representatives allowed us to explore the many potentialities of our approach.

Furthermore, we believe that tangible interfaces are a powerful tool to fully exploit the physicality of the puppet theatre with all its creative richness, and the children confidence with puppets allows reduce the barrier to learn this new interface. Even if this specific research work is dedicated to a specific learning domain, findings from experimentation and system evaluation could open to many possibilities not just for edutainment projects but also for other application scenarios based on puppet theatre such as therapy and art creation. These include collaborative approaches to the iTheatre, such as remote multi user play creation and story-telling.

Future developments of the tangible interface will include the use of more sophisticated motion capture techniques, the possibility of customizing characters, the possibility of using user created content (e.g. background and sounds), recording the voices from users while playing their story, and the possibility of manipulating the story after creation.

After the preliminary positive results, we envision, for the next prototype version, to organize a more extensive user studies focused children, in order to obtain more targeted results and feedback.

References

1. Marshall, P., Rogers, Y., Scaife, M.: PUPPET: playing and learning in a virtual world. International Journal of Continuing Engineering Education and Life-long Learning 14(6), 519–531 (2004)
2. Popovici, D.M., Serbanati, L.D.: Using mixed VR/AR technologies in education. In: Proceedings of the International Multi-Conference on Computing in the Global Information Technology (ICCGI 2006) (2006)
3. Ackermann, E.: Bambini Digitali, Strumenti narrativi, scrittura dialogica. Tecnologie Didattiche 24(3), 24–48 (2001)
4. Druin, et al.: The Design of Children's Technology. Moran Kaufmann Publishers, Inc., San Francisco (1999)

5. Druin, A., Solomon, C.: Designing multimedia environments for children. John Wiley & Sons, Inc., Chichester (1996); Smith, T.F., Waterman, M.S.: Identification of Common Molecular Subsequences. J. Mol. Biol. 147, 195–197 (1981)
6. Anastassova, M., Mégard, C., Burkhardt, J.-M.: Prototype evaluation and user-needs analysis in the early design of emerging technologies. In: Proceedings of HCI International 2007, Beijing, China, July 22-27 (2007)
7. Anastassova, M., Ion, I., Mayora-Ibarra, O.: Elicitation of User Requirements for Mobile Interaction with Visual and RFID Tags: a Prototype-Based Exploratory Study. In: Proceedings of HCI International 2009, San Diego, USA (July 2009)
8. Cassell, J., Ryokai, K.: Making Space for Voice: Technologies to Support Children's Fantasy and Storytelling. Personal Technologies 5(3), 203–224 (2001)
9. Ullmer, B., Ishii, H.: Emerging frameworks for tangible user interfaces. IBM Syst. J. 39(3-4), 915–931 (2000)
10. Cassell, J.: Towards a Model of Technology and Literacy Development: Story Listening Systems. Journal of Applied Developmental Psychology 25, 75–105 (2004)
11. Glos, J., Cassell, J.: Rosebud: Technological Toys for Storytelling. In: Proceedings of the ACM Conference on Human Factors in Computing Systems (CHI 1997), pp. 359–360. ACM Press, New York (1997a)
12. Glos, J.W., Cassell, J.: Rosebud: A Place for Interaction Between Memory, Story, and Self. In: Proceedings of the 2nd International Conference on Cognitive Technology (CT 1997) (1997b)
13. Gorbet, M.G., Orth, M., Ishii, H.: Triangles: Tangible interface for manipulation and exploration of digital information topography. In: CHI 1998, pp. 49–56 (1998)
14. Ananny, M., Cassell, J.: Telling tales: A new toy for encouraging written literacy through oral storytelling. Presentation at Society for Research in Child Development (2001)
15. Vaucelle, C., Jehan, T.: Dolltalk: A computational toy to enhance childrens creativity (2002)
16. Bobick, A., Intille, S., Davis, J., Baird, F., Pinhanez, C., Campbell, L., Ivanov, Y., Schutte, A., Wilson, A.: The KidsRoom: A Perceptually-Based Interactive and Immersive Story Environment, E15, 20 Ames Street, Cambridge, MA 02139, Tech. Rep. 398 (December 1996)
17. Ryokai, K., Vaucelle, C., Cassell, J.: Literacy learning by storytelling with a virtual peer (2002)
18. Ichida, H., Itoh, Y., Kitamura, Y., Kishino, F.: Activecube and its 3d applications. In: IEEE VR 2004 Workshop Beyond Wand and Glove Based Interaction, Chicago, IL USA (2004)

Automatic and Interactive Key Posture Design by Combing the PIK with Parametric Posture Splicing

Shilei Li, Bing Wu, Jiahong Liang, and Jiongming Su

College of Mechatronic Engineering and Automation, National University of Defense
Technology, PhD candidate, Changsha, 410073, P.R. China
leeshileili@gmail.com

Abstract. Key posture design is commonly needed in computer animation. This paper presents an automatic and interactive whole body posture designing technique by combining the PIK (prioritized inverse kinematics) with the proposed parametric human posture splicing technique. The key feature of PIK is that the user can design a posture by adding high level constraints with different priorities. However, the PIK is essentially a numerical IK algorithm which relies on the iterative optimization starting from a good enough initial posture to get the final result. To speed up the running efficiency and ensure the lifelikeness of the final posture, the parametric posture splicing technique is proposed to generate the initial guess of the PIK. According to the set of the high level constraints, the whole body is divided into some partial parts, whose postures are then generated by the parametric posture synthesis from a single posture database. Then an initial posture guess with some main characteristics of the finally acceptable posture can be generated approximately by splicing these partial body postures together. Starting from this initial guess and with all constraints considered at different priority levels, the PIK can be initialized with a bias defined by this particularly initial guess and iterated step by step to get a final posture. The total process of the whole body posture generation is automatic and interactive. The experimental results show that this combination method can not only improve the computation efficiency of the PIK but also can simultaneously ensure the naturalness of the final posture.

Keywords: character animation, posture designing, prioritized inverse kinematics, parametric posture splicing.

1 Introduction

In the computer animation field, key posture design is a fundamental requirement of animators. Today, commercial animation software products, e.g. 3ds Max, Maya, all provide friendly interactive interface for character posture designing. However, key posture design is still a hand-driven technique which requires experience and long-timely humdrum labor.

When the animator designs a particular posture, she always has a rough outline of the desired posture in mind, which usually can be described by a set of high level

A. Nijholt, D. Reidsma, and H. Hondorp (Eds.): INTETAIN 2009, LNICST 9, pp. 119–130, 2009.
© ICST Institute for Computer Sciences, Social Informatics and Telecommunications Engineering 2009

constraints. The PIK [1,2] is an efficiently iterative algorithm which can enforce an arbitrary number of strict priorities to arbitrate the fulfillment of conflicting constraints and can run within an interactive environment. Given high level constraints, the whole body posture of complex characters can be generated automatically. However, the PIK is essentially a generalized Jacobian-pseudo-inverse based IK algorithm. The final posture is generated by iterative optimization starting from an initial guess of the posture configuration. Because of the redundancy of the human joints, different initial guesses can generate different final postures. The better the initial guess is, the less computation load and the more lifelikeness of the final result would be realized. Here, the goodness of the initial guess should be measured by the similarity between the initial guess and the final desired posture. In extreme cases, if we can give the final posture directly, there would be no need for the further PIK computation. Although we can never get the exactly final posture directly with only a set of high level constraints, we should set the initial guess close to the final result as much as possible. In this paper the motion capture database is used to generate the initial posture. Nevertheless, the diversity of the possible human postures makes it impossible to establish a posture database that includes all required postures in the future. To reduce the number of sample motions, the parametric splicing technique is purposed to synthesize the initial whole body posture by dividing the body into some partial parts. By combining the PIK with the parametric posture splicing technique, an automatic and interactive key posture designing framework is presented in this paper.

The remainder of this paper is organized as follows. Section *Related works and Contribution* reviews related literatures and outlines our contribution. Next, Section *Overview* gives an overview of our posture designing framework. In following two Sections, we detail our method for combing the parametric posture splicing with the PIK algorithm. Our results are shown and discussed in Section *Experimental Results and Discussion*. Finally, in Section *Conclusions and Future Work*, we conclude this paper and discuss some possible directions for the future work.

2 Related Works and Contribution

Key posture design is widely needed in computer animation. The motion quality of the traditionally hand-driven keyframing technique is basically determined by key postures. Nowadays, it is common to leverage on motion capture databases to generate virtual character animations as motion capture technique provides the most lifelike results by replaying the real human motions. However, motion capture data often need some adaptions to reuse in different environments. The adaption process often introduces artifacts and key posture design is still widely needed so as to correct and adjust any undesirable postures. Recently, to relieve the animator from the burden of enforcing physical plausibility, physical interpolation [3,4] is proposed to generate highly detailed and physically realistic motions. However, realistic key postures are still needed as the foundation of the final results.

While designing key postures can be done by directly given parameter values of different joints, it becomes rapidly tedious and time consuming as soon as the total number of animated object's DoFs (degrees of freedom) increases. For character animation, this is particularly noticeable as typical virtual characters may contain up to fifty DoFs even without considering the fingers. For this reason, specific algorithms have been developed to ease key posture design. IK (Inverse kinematics) is a process for determining the configuration of a character's parameters based on specifications of resulting features of the pose, such as end-effector positions. It can calculate the mid joints angles automatically, providing a goal-directed method in the human posture generation. The control of complex articulated figures using IK often requires that we can simultaneously apply multiple constraints, which may lead to conflicts between tasks because some are not achievable at the same time, whilst they can be separately. In references [1,2], a priority based numerical IK solver(PIK) is presented. The priority strategy ensures that the most important ones are satisfied first and the less import ones are satisfied as much as possible without disturbing the vital constraints. In references [5,6,7], the PIK is used for motion editing. In reference [7], to realize one particular key frame editing, the PIK is combined with the low dimension motion model constructed from a motion database using PCA. This approach provides faster and better quality results with less tuning from the user side compared with references [5,6], which use the PIK to realize motion editing based on the per-frame PIK paradigm. In this paper, the PIK algorithm is adopted to realize the process of conflicting constrains in key posture design. We also combine the PIK with a motion database but here the motion database are used to provide posture samples rather the motion model of one particular motion type like [7].

Our work belongs to the example-based IK methods. Style-based IK [8] is a robust and powerful technique for character posing using a statistical model learned from small datasets. However, it does not guarantee that poses still looks natural when desired poses are far away from the training data. Just like the parametric motion synthesis techniques [9,10,11] which generate new motions exactly corresponding to user-specified parameters, we propose the parametric posture splicing so that the combination of partial postures can be used as the initial guess of one particular set of high level constraints. To reduce the motion samples required for the parametric motion synthesis technique, Ha et al. [12] combined the upper and lower body splicing with the parametric motion synthesis. Here, we also use the splicing to reduce the required posture samples. But unlike these papers which generate motion sequences, we only generate a single posture without the need of the complex preprocess operation to determine the time, space and constraint correspondences between a set of motion primitives. Splicing is a technique to produce a new motion by cutting some part of one motion and attaching it to another. By combining different partial motions, the original motion database can be enriched without capturing new motions. Heck et al.[13] proposed a detailed method to splice the upper body of a motion with the lower body of another. Majkowska et al. [14] proposed a technique that splices hand gestures with body motions. Ikemoto et al. [15] introduced a way of enriching a motion database by changing the limb associated with a motion, and suggest rules for synthesizing motions that look natural. Recently Jang et al. [16] suggested an analogous combination technique which selects and combines coherent partial motions. In these papers, splicing is made just to ensure the naturalness of the final results without considering the exact feature of the finally combined results beforehand. In this paper, splicing is also used but we focus on the generation a posture entailing some main characteristics of user constraints so that it can be used as the initial guess of the PIK.

Compared with other example-based IK algorithm, the main contribution of our work is the high efficiency and quality of the final results by sequential apply the parametric splicing and PIK. Through the parametric splicing, a natural whole body posture can be generated without complex computation and used later as the initial starting point of the PIK algorithm. By combining the parametric splicing with the PIK, a more robust and efficient IK framework is presented.

3 Overview

The key feature of our posture designing framework is that the parametric posture splicing is combined with the PIK to realize automatic and interactive posture generation. Basically, our approach is divided into two main steps:

1. *Parametric posture splicing*: Posture databases are used to generate the initial guess of the PIK. To reduce the required posture samples, the splicing technique is used. Here, the main problem we need to solve is that how we can ensure the combined whole body posture can be used as an initial guess of the final desired posture. According to the certain set of high level constraints, we divide the whole body into some partial joint groups and generate these partial postures using the weighted interpolation of corresponding parts of different whole body postures. Then the posture of the whole body is spliced and used as the initial guess of the PIK.

2. *Further posture refining using PIK*: The feature of the PIK is its priority strategy. Using the PIK, the complex task with an arbitrary number of priority levels and parametric inputs can be processed. Using the parametric posture splicing results as the initial configuration, the PIK solves for the final results by considering all of user specified constraints with different priorities. As the initial guess generated through the partial interpolation of a posture database, the quality of the final results and the calculation efficiency can be improved compared to situations where only a random or a fixed initial posture configuration is used.

4 Parametric Posture Splicing

Our basic idea is to subdivide the body of a character into several parts, such as the lower and upper body. New postures can then by generated from the combination of partial postures. However, human is a complex life system which moves in a highly coordinated way and combining partial postures in an arbitrary way can not produce the harmony of real human posture. Furthermore, to synthesize a posture that can be used as an initial guess for a particular situation, we must ensure the combined posture have a certain similarity with the desired posture. In summary, we have two questions to solve. First, what division should we use to ensure the lifelikeness of the spliced posture? Second, how to use the same posture database to approximately generate different partial postures we want? In this section, we propose the parametric posture splicing to solve these two questions.

4.1 Posture Database Setup

To do the parametric posture splicing operation, first a posture database needs to be established as a preprocessing step. We use the motion capture data to setup the posture samples. A particular character posture is generally represented as a state vector P, described by the global position and orientation of the root node and a set of joint angles:

$$P = [p_0, q_0, q_1 \cdots q_n] \qquad (1)$$

Where p_0 and q_0 represent the 3D global position and orientation of the root joint and q_i is the local transformation of the ith joint expressed in its local coordinate system. It should be noted that a posture is unchanged if we translate it along the floor plane or rotate it about the vertical axis. Most papers adopt the similarity matrix proposed by Kovar et al.[17] to compare different postures. The optimized 2D transformation is used to get the optimal sum of squared distances between corresponding point clouds and the readers may refer to this paper for the details. However, when the posture database is used for the initial posture generation, the virtual character geometry may be different from the actual performer of the motion data. Consequently, when comparing the similarity between two postures, they are joint angles rather than some position values that determine the similarity level. For example, if an adult man and a child have the same joint angles of all of their joints, we think their postures are same in spite of their great differences in positional constraints. Although it is not always true that joint angles rather than position values determine the feature of a pose, for example, if we have a particular positional requirement of a posture (e.g. touch the nose, scratch the back of the head etc), it should be noted that here our purpose is to establish a posture database which can be used to generate the initial guess of the PIK algorithm to ensure the naturalness of the final posture result. The positional constraints of the particular posture will be further processed by the PIK component.

Before the similarity is computed, one of the two poses should be translated and rotated in the horizontal plane to remove differences in absolute position and facing direction. After removing differences in absolute positions and facing directions from the state of the pose, we calculate the similarity of the two postures simply using the following equation:

$$s = \sum_{i=0}^{n} [ws_i \times |q_i' - q_i|] \qquad (2)$$

Where s is the score for the posture similarity and the weighting vector ws_i is used because the angle variation of a joint located at the beginning of the human body kinematics chain has a greater influence on the generated posture than the same angle variation of a joint located at the end of the chain.

To generate the different posture samples, first different types of motion with a complete cycle, such as walking, running, kicking, reaching, sitting, etc. are collected. Then the posture database was established from these motions by adding a new pose only if the similarity score between that pose and all the poses currently in the database is greater than a threshold. Consequently, we finally get a database containing a set of unique postures, each stored as the joint angles.

4.2 Parametric Partial Posture Generation

Given a certain set of high level constraints, to reduce the number of required posture samples, we first need to divide the whole body into a certain number of partial parts and then generate these partial postures individually using the same posture database. Here unlike traditional methods [13,15,16] which simply divide the whole body into the same division, e.g. the upper and lower body parts, all the time, we divide the body part according to different situations. When a certain set of high level constraints is given, we first determine the underlying joint recruiting level of each constraint. For example, when a desired position of the hand is defined, we need to know if only the upper limb, the spine and the upper limb or even the lower body is needed to finish the task. This can be done automatically according to the relative positional constraints. For example, one constraint may require the character's hand in a certain position relative to its body. Then according to the particular geometrical length of its body model, we can approximately determine the joint recruiting level of this constraint. According to the character geometrical model and joint coupling relations, we establish a set of simple rulers of the recruiting level of different constraints. For example, for the reaching task, only the total stretching length is used to determine whether only the upper limb or the upper limb and other body parts is used for the posture generation. The users can also directly set the recruiting level of different constraints. For two different constraints, if they have common joints for the participation of their realization, they are put into the same partial body part. Here, by dividing the whole body into joint parts differently according to the exact set of constraints, we can ensure the coordination of the whole body posture as much as possible when splicing them together.

After the whole body is divided according to the constraints, we need to generate partial posture of these partial joint groups. For each sample in the database, we do the forward kinematics calculation to get the corresponding constraints value. Using these values, for each joint group JP_i ($1 \leq i \leq p$, p is the number of the partial body parts by dividing the whole body), we do the following calculation:

$$
\begin{pmatrix}
c_1^1 & c_1^2 & \cdots & c_1^{np_i} \\
c_2^1 & c_2^2 & & c_2^{np_i} \\
\vdots & \vdots & & \vdots \\
c_{nc_i}^1 & c_{nc_i}^2 & & c_{nc_i}^{np_i} \\
1 & 1 & \cdots & 1
\end{pmatrix}
w_i =
\begin{pmatrix}
c_1 \\
c_2 \\
\vdots \\
c_{nc_i} \\
1
\end{pmatrix}
\tag{3}
$$

Here, nc_i is the number of constraints which belong to the same joint group JP_i and np_i is the number of the used sample postures. The used partial posture samples are searched in the database through the k *nearest neighbors* according to the distance between the required constraints value and actually constraints value of each posture samples. The number of posture samples should satisfy $np_i \geq nc_i + 1$. c_{nc_i} is the representation of the value of required constraints and $c_{nc_i}^{np_i}$ is the representation of the actual constraints value of each sample postures. The equation is solved by using a singularity-robust inverse [18] to compute the weight for each sample postures. After the weight vector w_i is got, the joint angles in the partial joint group JP_i can be calculated as:

$$q_i(k) = \sum_{j=1}^{np_i} w_i(j)q_j \tag{4}$$

Where $w_i(j)$ is the jth element of w_i, k is the total number of the joints in the joint group JP_i and q_j denotes the angle of the corresponding joint k of the jth sample posture. In other words, the partial posture is generated by the weighted combined of similar postures in the joint space.

The calculation process above is repeated for each joint group JP_i ($1 \leq i \leq p$) so that the posture of every partial body parts is parametrically synthesized.

4.3 Whole Body Posture Splicing

After the joint angles of all body parts are calculated, we can combine them together directly to generate the whole body posture. Unlike the complex motion splicing operator [13,14], here we need no further processing of the temporal or spatial correlation between the postures of different body parts. Because we divide the whole body into partial body parts according to the exact constraints and the interpolation of joint angles rather than the joint positions are used for the partial posture generation, the whole body posture looks natural at most of the times. Nevertheless, combining partial postures together directly can never always ensure the lifelikeness of the whole body posture. However, through the parametric posture splicing technique proposed above, we realize the most important requirement that the initial guess should have a certain global similarity with the desired posture. It should be noted that here the spliced body posture is only used as an initial guess of the final posture and it will be refined by the PIK later. Furthermore, the animators can interactively change the whole body posture at this stage.

5 Automatic and Interactive Posture Generation

After the initial guess of the whole body posture is generated, we can refine the initial guess to get the desired whole body posture with the PIK. In this section, we first give an overview of the PIK algorithm and then we use the PIK to get the final posture with all constraints satisfied as much as possible.

5.1 Overview of the Prioritized Inverse Kinematics Algorithm

The PIK algorithm presented by Paolo Baerlocher et al.[1,2] is an extension to the Jacobian pseudo-inverse based numerical inverse kinematics method. The main originality is that they presented a recursive algorithm to speed up the traditional null space projectors computation and generalized the previous priority based approach to an arbitrary number of tasks with multiple levels of priority. Here, we give the final formulation directly. Considering t tasks T_p ordered from the highest priority ($p=1$) to the lowest ($p=t$), the algorithm can be summarized as follows:

$$\Delta q_p = \Delta q_{p-1} + (\tilde{J}_p)^{+\lambda_p}(\Delta x_p - J_p \Delta q_{p-1}) \tag{5}$$

$$\Delta q_1 = (\tilde{J}_1)^{+\lambda_1} \Delta x_1 \tag{6}$$

Where $\tilde{J}_p = J_p P_{N(J_{p-1}^A)}$, $P_{N(J_p^A)} = I - (J_p^A)^+ J_p^A = P_{N(J_{p-1}^A)} - (\tilde{J}_p)^+ \tilde{J}_p$ and

$P_{N(J_0^A)} = I$. $J_p^A = \begin{bmatrix} J_1 \\ J_2 \\ \vdots \\ J_p \end{bmatrix}$ is the so-called augmented Jacobian because obviously the

whole null space of these tasks (for tasks with the priority from 1 to p):

$$N(J_1, J_2 \cdots, J_p) = N(J_1) \cap N(J_2) \cap \cdots N(J_{p-1}) \cap N(J_p) = N(J_p^A) \tag{7}$$

In the formulation above, J^+ is the pseudo-inverse defined by $J^+ = J^T(JJ^T)^{-1}$ and $J_i^{+\lambda_i} = J_i^T(J_iJ_i^T + \lambda_i^2 I)^{-1}$ is the so-called damped least squares inverse using the damping factor λ_i to deal with singularities.

In addition, linear equality or inequality constraints, e.g. relative position constraints and joint limits, can also be processed in the framework of the PIK algorithm. Readers may refer to references [1,2] for further details.

5.2 Using the PIK Algorithm for Further Refining of the Spliced Posture

Using the PIK, we firstly need to prioritize all of the constraints. After the priority levels of different constraints are set, we can use the PIK algorithm directly. Here, besides using the spliced whole body as the initial guess, we further add an optimization item at the lowest priority level to make the final result resemble the initial guess as much as possible. We define a cost function as follows just like those used in motion editing [5,6]:

$$g(q) = \frac{1}{2}(p - p_s)^T K_w (p - p_s) \tag{8}$$

Where K_w is a weighting definite diagonal matrix setting relative importance of different joints and p_s is the initial posture. With this cost function, we can solve the finally desired joint increments by setting this optimization term as the lowest task using the same null space projection principle. At the PIK stage, the joints near the root node are often adjusted more than the joints at the end of the chain to exactly satisfy some positional constraints. Consequently, here we set very large values on the joints at the end of the chain and zero of the spine joints which near the root node. By setting the weighting matrix this way, we can ensure the final posture resemble the initially spliced posture as much as possible. During the priority loop, after the lowest priority constraint T_t ($p = t$) is processed, we can get the finally desired joints increments Δq by adding Δq_t with the following optimization term:

$$\Delta q = \Delta q_t - P_{N(J_t^A)} \alpha \nabla g \tag{9}$$

Where α is a positive constant and $\nabla g = \dfrac{\partial g}{\partial q}$. Here, we choose the negative gradient of the cost function $-\alpha \nabla g$ to ensure the final Δq ensemble the certain joint angles as close as possible. By adding this optimization item as the lowest task, we can ensure the lifelikeness of the final result by solving the redundancy with the certain joint angles of the initial guess.

6 Experimental Results and Discussion

This section presents some postures generated for a driving posture design task. The articulated character has 40 degrees of freedom (7 per upper limb, 7 per leg, 3 for back and waist respectively and 6 for the root joint). All postures are generated based on the same posture database. Tests were run on a single-core 3.5 GHz Intel Pentium 4 processor with 2GB memory under Windows XP operating system.

In this example, we use our framework to design a particular diving posture. We define five positional constraints: one for the hip, two for the hand and two for the foot. The hip constraint is given the highest priority level. The two hand constraints are given the second priority level and the two feet constraints are lastly considered. According to the recruiting level of each constraint, the whole body is divided into the upper and lower part. Two different geometrical character models are used. The initially spliced whole body posture of the character one is shown on the left of the figure 1 and the corresponding final whole body posture refined by the PIK is shown on the middle left. The initially spliced whole body posture of character two is shown on the middle right of the figure 1 and the corresponding final whole posture refined by the PIK is shown on the right. It can be seen that the initial guesses of the whole body posture for the two different characters are almost the same because the parametric posture splicing technique use the same posture database to generate them. These small differences come not only from the difference between geometrical models but also from the nonlinear relationship between the joint angles and the end-effectors' positions. The final whole body postures of the two characters have bigger differences because the PIK are used to generate the posture with positional constraints are satisfied as much as possible.

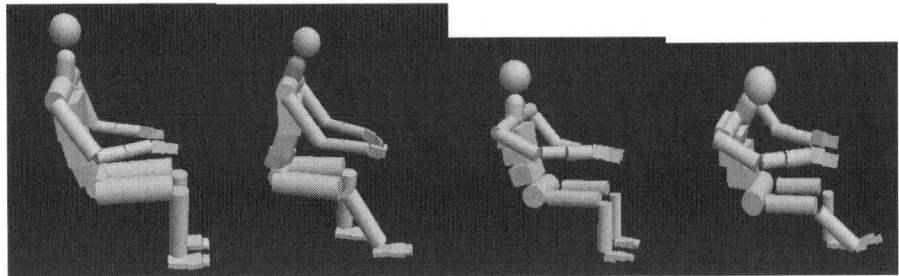

Fig. 1. The results of whole body posture: form left to right (a) initial guess of the character one (b) final result of the character one (c) initial guess of the character two (d) final result of the character two

From this experimental result, it can be seen that the final whole body postures are natural by using the initial guesses generated from the posture database. We also generate the whole body posture from the standing posture. For this experiment, the whole body posture generated by only using the PIK also looks natural. However, the computation time is approximately three times longer than our methods. For more complex tasks, we think the benefits of our method would be greater.

Currently, the main limitation of our method is that we search through all poses in the database according to the constraints and consequently the database needs to be small to use our technique in real-time situations. However, our method is more robust and intuitive than those using a statistical model learned for motion samples [8].

7 Conclusions and Future Work

In this paper, we have developed a whole body posture design framework that relies on the PIK, the parametric posture splicing technique and a library of example postures. At the preprocessing stage, we setup a posture library based on the motion capture data. To process the difference in the human's geometrical models, joint angles rather that joint positions are used. During the posture designing stage, after giving a set of high level constraints, we first divide the whole body into several body parts. Then a simple and efficient partial posture synthesis method is proposed to generate the partial body postures. The advantage of our method is that the posture samples need not be a perfect match for the constraints and the new whole body posture with the main characteristics of the constraints can be generated efficiently. Finally, the PIK is used to generate the final whole body posture. In essence, by combing the PIK with the parametric posture splicing, we divide the traditional PIK into two steps. The first step is to generate the initial guess using a posture database. The second step is to refine the initial guess using the PIK. Consequently, the whole body posture generation framework is automatic and interactive. Furthermore, the burden of the posture design is greatly reduced and simultaneously the quality of the final posture is improved.

In the future, firstly we want to integrate our framework into the commercial animation software products so as to provide a friendly interface to the users. Secondly we do not yet have a way of measuring how much the spliced posture is appropriate to the certain constraints or how many posture samples are sufficient to produce natural looking posture. We need do more research on how the whole body can be coordinately combined and search for more reliable methods for deriving good initial postures from observed motion samples.

Acknowledgments. The data used in this paper was obtained in part from mocap.cs.cmu.edu. This database was created with funding from NSF EIA-0196217.

References

1. Baerlocher, P., Boulic, R.: An inverse kinematics architecture enforcing an arbitrary number of strict priority levels. The Visual Computer 20(6), 402–417 (2004)
2. Baerlocher, P.: Inverse kinematics Techniques for the Interactive Posture Control of Articulated Figures. PhD thesis, Ecoles Polytechniques fédérale de Lausanne, Swiss Federal Institute of Technology (2001)
3. Fattal, R., Lischinski, D.: Pose controlled physically Based Motion. Computer Graphics Forum 25(4), 777–787 (2006)
4. Allen, B., Chu, D., Shapiro, A., Faloutsos, P.: On the Beat! Timing and Tension for Dynamic Characters. In: Proceeding of Eurographics/ ACM SIGGRAPH Symposium on Computer Animation, pp. 239–247 (2007)
5. Boulic, R., Le Callennec, B., Herren, M., Bay, H.: Motion Editing with Prioritized Constraints. In: Proceedings of 1st International Workshop on Interactive Rich Media Content Production - Architectures, Technologies, Applications, Tools (2003)
6. Le Callennec, B., Boulic, R.: Interactive motion deformation with prioritized constraints. Graphical Models 68(2), 175–193 (2006)
7. Carvalho, S.R., Boulic, R., Thalmann, D.: Interactive low-dimensional human motion synthesis by combining motion models and PIK. Computer Animation and Virtual World 18(4-5), 493–503 (2007)
8. Grochow, K., Martin, S.L., Hertzmann, A., Popovic, Z.: Style-based inverse kinematics. ACM Transactions on Graphics 23(3), 522–531 (2004)
9. Rose, C., Cohen, M.F., Bodenheimer, B.: Verbs and adverbs: multidimensional motion interpolation. IEEE Computer Graphics and Applications 18(5), 32–40 (1998)
10. Kovar, L., Gleicher, M.: Flexible automatic motion blending with registration curves. In: SCA 2003: Proceedings of the 2003 ACM SIGGRAPH/Eurographics Symposium on Computer Animation, pp. 214–224 (2003)
11. Kovar, L., Gleicher, M.: Automated Extraction and Parameterization of Motions in Large Data Sets. ACM Transactions on Graphics 23(3), 559–568 (2004)
12. Ha, D., Han, J.: Motion synthesis with decoupled parameterization. The Visual Computer 24(7), 587–594 (2008)

13. Heck, R., Kovar, L., Gleicher, M.: Splicing upper-body actions with locomotion. Comput. Graph. Forum. 25(3), 459–466 (2006)
14. Majkowska, A., Zordan, V.B., Faloutsos, P.: Automatic splicing for hand and body animations. In: SCA 2006: Proceedings of the 2006 ACM SIGGRAPH/Eurographics Symposium on Computer Animation, pp. 309–316 (2006)
15. Ikemoto, L., Forsyth, D.A.: Enriching a motion collection by transplanting limbs. In: SCA 2004: Proceedings of the 2004 ACM SIGGRAPH/Eurographics Symposium on Computer Animation, pp. 99–108 (2004)
16. Jang, W.S., Lee, W.K., Lee, I.K., Lee, J.: Enriching a motion database by analogous combination of partial human motions. The Visual Computer 24(4), 271–280 (2008)
17. Kovar, L., Gleicher, M., Pighin, F.: Motion graphs. ACM Transactions on Graphics 21(3), 473–482 (2002)
18. Nakamura, Y., Hanafusa, H.: Inverse Kinematics Solutions with Singularity Robustness for Robot Manipulator Control. J. Dynamic Sys., Meas., and Control, 108, 163–171 (1986)

Web-Enabled 3D Game Playing for Looped Knight's Tour

Gregory C.L. Lum and David Y.Y. Yun

Holmes 492, 2540 Dole St., Honolulu, Hawaii 96822 USA
{lumg,dyun}@hawaii.edu

Abstract. This paper elucidates the development of a 3D graphics display environment that facilitates the finding of a closed Loop Knight's Tour (LKT) that uniquely covers each grid in a 3D rectangular box. When LKT is played as a solitaire game in 3D space, it is not only mentally challenging but also difficult for the player to visualize the current or past (occupied) positions and to consider any follow-on possibilities (open grids). These graphic facilities simplify the visualization the global box as occupied and open grids and allow the convenient examination of the sequential chain of knight's moves. Relevant information and valuable relations are computed and displayed to assist the player in choosing the next grid to occupy and closing the ends to form a loop. This graphic game environment is Web enabled via Google's SketchUp. An online community may be developed as users challenge one another by increasingly difficult configurations.

Keywords: knight's tour, closed-loop, 3D grid box, solitaire game, community challenges, growing solved database, Web interaction, Google, SketchUp.

1 Introduction

Just as hard as imagining playing with the Rubik's Cube in an online virtual 3D display, visualizing all the pieces and (lines of) attacks for 3D chess is equally difficult. The fundamental difficulty lies in the visualization of 3D movements on a 2D screen. To achieve online display and enable Web-based playing of even solitaire games, therefore, must rely on motion support (turning, zooming, layering, etc.) in a 3D environment. Computed information such as available positions, attack points, blocking, etc. can be added advantages offered to players via the Web. More difficult aspects in 3D include look-ahead or even anticipating the ending can also be offered by an interactive display environment online. All these essential features (significantly different from those animations for arcade games) are considered and supported to enable an interactive game to be played over the Web. Online players can also post (mutual) challenges and help grow the common solution database for the collective Web community.

1.1 Background

The Knight's Tour (KT) problem originated in the 1700s by an English mathematician named Brook Taylor [8]. He wondered how to cover the 8x8 chess board uniquely by

A. Nijholt, D. Reidsma, and H. Hondorp (Eds.): INTETAIN 2009, LNICST 9, pp. 131–142, 2009.
© ICST Institute for Computer Sciences, Social Informatics and Telecommunications Engineering 2009

(exactly 64) knight movements. In 1991, Allen Schwenk, completely solved the KT problem for all 2D rectangular boards. His definition of Knight's Tour is one where the knight visits every square of the board and returns to the original position, hence forming a loop. In order to remove confusion, such closed-ended chain of knight moves will be considered as solving the Loop Knight Tour (LKT) problem. Schwenk [6] dealt with 2D problems only, an m x n chess board, where m is less than n, found that it has a solution unless: (a) m and n are both odd; (b) m = 1, 2, or 4; or (c) m = 3 and n = 4, 6 or 8. He also showed how to combine solutions from boards of smaller sizes. This LKT problem can certainly be extended to 3D and posed as a challenging and interesting solitaire game.

1.2 Motivation

LKT in 3D, unfortunately, cannot be physically realized. Hence, it is forced to use computer based visualization and support. A 2D display, or a sequence of 2D slices, will not be sufficient to clearly represent the LKT snapshots nor any knight's move possibilities among the open and occupied grids in 3D. An enhanced 3D environment is required. This paper demonstrates the design and implementation of a 3D game environment that assists a player with both local/global tracking tools and 3D visualization (with motion) for playing the LKT game. Presently, there is no visual system to make such 3D game playing (including true 3D chess) effective and enjoyable.

1.3 Loop Knight's Tour (LKT) in 3D

The LKT setting can be represented in 3D as a "Game Box" of dimensions l x m x n of $l*m*n$ grids for the knight to move to and from. Each grid is uniquely identified by the coordinate label of (x, y, z). A knight movement is ± 2 and ± 1 in any two directions and order along x, y or z axes. From any (x, y, z) grid in the Game Box there is a maximum of 24 grids that can be reached in one knight movement without getting out of the edges. As each knight movement occupies a grid, it gets a sequential move number, which also is a tally of the total number of grids "toured" so far. [10, 11].

The LKT solution is not completed until each grid of the Game Box has been occupied and the starting and ending positions are the same and a loop tour is accomplished. Before this happens the sequence of movements already completed is a chain of movements with two open ends. Each end can be extended in any order to complete the loop tour and cover every one of the lmn grids. Two chains can be linked together to form a longer chain so long as one end of one chain is a knight's move away from an end of another chain. In fact, since a loop can be "broken" at any link to form a chain, two (adjacent) loops can be broken at chosen links so that one end from each loop can be linked by a knight's move, then a longer joint chain is formed. If those two remaining ends of the joint chain happen also to be a knight's move apart, then a joint loop is found/constructed. Judiciously choosing the links to break from two loops so that two (opposite) pairs of ends are knight movements apart and form a joint loop is the method of "**stitching**" [6] for constructing larger 2D solutions from smaller ones. Such joining of loop solutions can be extended to 3D LKT problems (known as "**knight's crossing**") by stitching together two 2D layers or two 3D blocks in a similar manner. The simpler form is to stack two LKT loops (maybe the same) in 2D layers one on top of the other. In order to combine the solutions a knight's crossing needs to be found, the easiest of which is at one of the corners. When a knight's crossing is found, the corresponding links (in both loops) need to be broken and the opposite ends reconnected by night's moves to form a larger loop solution, now in 3D [10, 11]. In this way, LKT loops previously found in 2D or 3D can be combined to solve other larger Game Boxes. These loop checking and loop linking are necessary capabilities provided in the LKT game environment to assist the extension of solved boxes or layers into larger LKT solutions.

2 Game Features

Google's SketchUp program provides an online system for composite 3D objects to be accurately represented by 2D screen displays. SketchUp allows the user to control the environment by zooming, panning of an object, view angle or orientation control, and layer removal ("Section Plane") [7]. However, SketchUp needs additional features to properly support the LKT game environment. In order to determine what are required for an online LKT game player, a list of essential support features were developed, from which many 3D modeling tools were considered. SketchUp was selected as the implementation system by meeting most of the requirements of built-in features and its extension capabilities where essential game supports and displays can be created using a combination of Ruby, Java and HTML programming languages [2, 3, 4, 5, 9].

2.1 Two Move Directions

Before the loop solution for the LKT problem can be found, a chain of knight's moves always have two ends, both of which can be extended alternatingly, in a "forward" direction and a "backward" direction. These directions are, of course, arbitrarily labeled, where the ultimate goal is still to connect the ends together and form a loop. In fact, since a loop solution (if exists) can be broken anywhere, the ends of the chain or the starting position matters very little. Rather, they are merely convenient notions (or notations) for the game to continue.

2.2 Game Box

The 3D Game Box is a wire frame transparent grid system of size l x m x n, to allow maximum visibility through the entire game region. Other useful information can be placed within each grid. At the center of an occupied position is a knight piece, which is used to signify that the particular position has already been visited/toured. Next to the knight piece is its move number, which is both the sequence label and the present tally of the number of occupied grids. The move number is also mirrored in the move tables, and allows a quick scanning of the sequence to recognize the path the knight has taken to get to a particular position.

With all of the other features made to be invisible the Game Box would look just as if it was drawn on paper. The exception is that the Game Box will color the grids for both current positions of each direction. Figure 1 is an example of the Game Box. In

Fig. 1. Game Box View

this figure there is one grid colored red and another grid colored yellow. This is used to represent the two ends of the chain, corresponding to the two colored move tables (described below). By coloring the end points, it gives the user a clear indication of where the two ends need to meet in order to complete the game and which grids to avoid until every other position has been visited first.

2.3 The Window of 5x5x5

If the Game Box of l x m x n becomes very large, it poses difficulties for visualization and positioning in 3D, as the shading, coloring and grids can obscure and confuse the positions. A major feature that is designed to help the user to play the game is the 5^3 (or 5x5x5) window of the Game Box. This 5^3 window contains all the possible next moves for the knight's current (end) position. It is a tool for the user to make a more informed decision and can be made visible or invisible, i.e., turned on or off. Since its relation to the Game Box is always "rooted" at the knight's current position, it provides both a local view and a global perspective for the player.

There are two 5^3 windows, one for each end of the chain, distinguished by color. They can be displayed at the same time (possibly overlapping), or independently. At the center will be the current position, shown in Figure 2, which is marked by a red grid with a black knight piece and the number 16 next to it. Because of the unique movement of the knight piece there are only 24 possible legal positions that it can make from the center position. The positions that the knight is able to move to are shown in red. This is because the 5^3 window being shown is for the forward direction

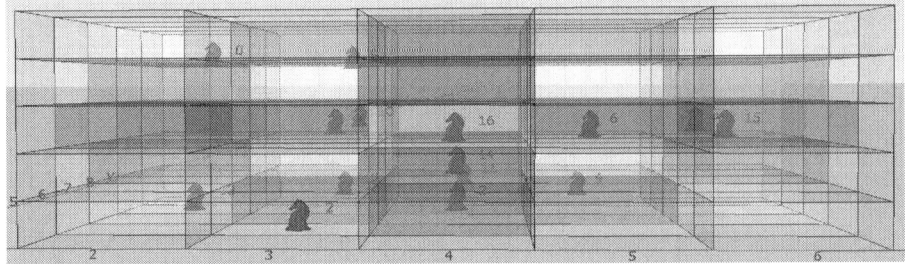

Fig. 2. 5^3 Window View

which is color coded as red. The backwards direction 5^3 window looks and functions in exactly same manner except that the current position is yellow and the grids that can be moved to in one knight move are also colored yellow. Positions that can be moved to but have already been occupied are colored gray and also contain a knight in the center.

The 5^3 windows will operate inside the Game Box as shown in Figure 7. As the next position is selected the current 5^3 window will center on the new position and all 125 grids of the 5^3 window will be updated with the new positions information. In Figure 7 there are different colored knight pieces, which indicate "move directions": a black knight is for the "forward" direction and a white knight is for the "backward" direction.

There are also special cases to the 5^3 window such was when the center grid is within two grids of the Game Box edge. This will result in some part of the 5^3 window being outside the actual game area. To resolve this, the illegal sections of the 5^3 window will not be visible outside of the game area and those outside points will not be selectable nor moved to. Another feature of the 5^3 window is that it displays those grids that can be moved to from either end of the move chain. Such grids are colored pink as seen in the Figure 3.

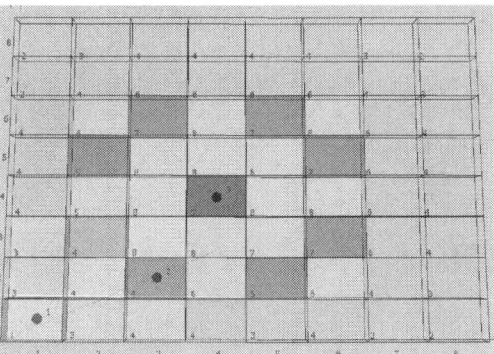

Fig. 3. Position Overlap

2.4   Selecting Next Legal Move

The LKT game environment allows the user multiple interactive options for selecting the next move. It also verifies that the next move selected is indeed legal, or else the user will be alerted and then given the opportunity to try another option.

With large Game Boxes the decision of picking the next move can be daunting and challenging with so many possibilities to track and visualize. The LKT game environment also keeps track of some useful counting heuristics (described below) to facilitate the decision (move) making process.

2.4.1   Text Input
Since the Game Box is a three dimensional grid system, each grid has an x, y, and z coordinate component. In order to select the next move the user has to input the x, y, and z value into the text boxes provided in the move tables. The use of the text input is more advantageous with larger 3D Game Boxes. This is due to the fact that the mouse's input, which will be discussed next, is only able to accurately select grids that are on the surface of the Game Box or relying on the user to zoom in to the critical 5^3 window. Therefore, if the user wishes to move to a grid that is not on the

outer surface, the user will have to "peel" away the grids that are in the way, obscuring a clear view. Not having to deal with this problem and just inputting the coordinates is a useful alternative.

2.4.2 Mouse Input

The mouse is used in the LKT environment for both overall controls and also for the selection of the next grid to move to. By clicking on the grid that the user wants to move to (when other grids are not in the way, or can be peeled away), the selected grid will be highlighted by a glowing blue outline. There is a confirmation button that must be pressed in order to actually move to that selected position. This insures that the user is confident with that move and that the mouse click was not a mistake.

A limitation of the mouse input is that it can only select grids that are on the surface of the Game Box or any 5^3 window. In order to select the inner grids, the view of just the 5^3 window can be used. Another method is to use the Section Plane tool [7] to peel away unwanted layers of grids until the desired grid is visible on the top viewing layer. With the unwanted grids removed for the time being, it is easy to select that particular grid by a mouse click.

2.4.3 Counting Heuristics

In order to successfully solve the LKT game, there needs to be some type of overall strategy that the user can heuristically rely on to make the next move and complete the loop solution. A few simple counting of open neighbors are provided in the visual display to track the current state and look ahead a step or two to help the user continue the play. It is still the user's decision to follow them or how to use them.

The Count of Open Successors (COS) is the number of open grids that the knight in the current position can move to. The grid with the lowest COS can be chosen as the next move. This criterion is derived from the most constrained (MC) strategy of [10, 11].

For such counting, it is inevitable and often for many grids to have the same integer COS. For grids tied with the same lowest COS, another counting estimate of Neighborhood Flexibility Count (NFC) is computed and displayed. The NFC value for each tied least-COS grid is the sum of all the COS values for each of its neighbors. Then the grid (among those tied) with the largest NFC value can be chosen as the next move. This criterion is derived from the least impact (LI) strategy of [10, 11].

Even after applying the tie-breaking NFC, it is still possible to have some grids tied with the same COS and NFC values. The tie breaking method is the Loop Targeting Measure (LTM). First, the current chain length is subtracted away from the ultimate loop length lmn to compute how far away from the current chain is to the final loop solution. The second estimate is the number of possible (open) grids that exist between the other end of the current chain and the tied grid. The LTM value is then computed as the difference between the first value and the second estimate. Such an LTM value is designed to provide an estimated measure to the goal of the final LKT solution loop, i.e., a heuristic estimate of the "distance to the goal state". To break the NFC tie, the smallest LTM value among the tied grids can be chosen.

If there is still a tie after applying these counting and tie-breaking values, then the final pick is a random grid among the remaining tied grids. These counting heuristic are merely computed for the convenience of the user and serves only as guidelines that can be deviated from at any step. They can and have helped to achieve some LKT solutions in one straight sequence of move selections without any backtracking. But they can, also, lead to dead ends that will require backtracking or look-ahead to complete the solution loop. But, it is clear that no heuristic can be infallible, so that these three values are computed and tabulated in the table of Neighbor Pool on the LKT game display, an example of which can be seen in Figure 5.

2.5 Move Tables

Solving the LKT problem is a process of extending a chain of moves (until the final closed loop). There are always two directions to extend the ends of the chain. Thus, there are two move tables, one for each of the directions. The starting position is move number 1 in both tables, from which the ends of the chain are extended as the tables grow. The Red move table is designated "forward" and the Yellow table is considered in the "backward" direction. The move tables contain the past movements sequentially in their respective directions, and can be scrolled down to check for any past positions. The more recent movements will put on the top of all previous moves. Figure 4 shows both move tables; however in the LKT game environment they are on opposite sides of the display. Blank boxes in each table allow the user to input the coordinates of the next move. There is also the "CheckLoop" button to test if the sequence of moves so far (in one of the two tables) is a loop or not. The "CheckLoop" button is not so useful until the two sequences are combined, since the move number 1 is the starting point for both sequences and only the last position in each table could possibly form a loop. Its value will be shown when the sequences in the two tables are combined by using the Control Panel (below) and the possibility of achieving a loop can be checked in one Move Table.

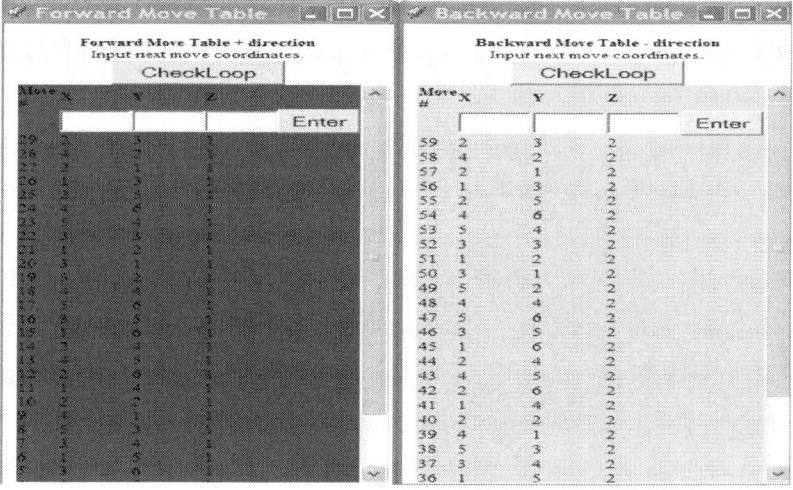

Fig. 4. Move Tables

2.6 Neighbor Pool

The neighbor pool contains a list of next move coordinates for each of the ends of the chain. It also contains the heuristic values of the COS, NFC and LTM for each grid with (x, y, z) coordinates. Figure 5 shows that the lines (coordinates) are colored according to which Move Table (or direction) they came from. The pink grids correspond to positions that can be reached by both ends of the chain. Each of the column labels of the Neighbor Pool can be clicked on, to sort the values in that column in increasing or decreasing order. For example, the user can sort all the next move positions by the COS value, to make it easier to select the move with the least COS. Then, sorting by the NFC and LTM columns simplifies the tie-breaking processes. One feature to easily improve the

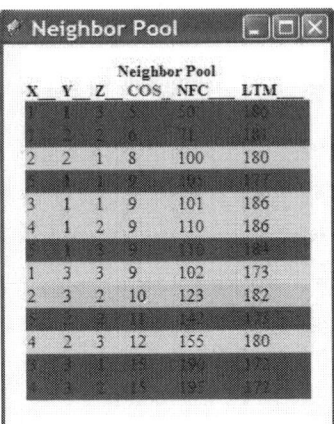

Fig. 5. Neighbor Pool

quality of game play is that of pointing and selecting a row, hence the coordinates as the next move.

2.7 Control Panel

The Control Panel (Figure 6) is where the user makes most of the interactions with the game. At the top of the control panel is the current direction information, shown either in red or yellow to keep track of which end of the chain is currently active.

The user is able to save the current game in progress to a file by pressing the "Save" button. The saved chain or loop can be loaded by the "Load" button. The user can also load another file to perhaps combine two solutions together in order to get

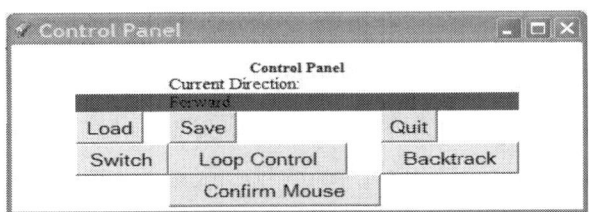

Fig. 6. Control Panel

a larger solution by pressing the "Load" button.

The "Backtrack" button allows the user to move back from the current position to the previous position, or to repeatedly backtrack several steps. Any backtracked move is forgotten, i.e., no history is kept so as to allow stepping forward again.

Another button in the control panel is the "Switch" button to change the direction (end) the moves are being made. Clicking the "Switch" button toggles between the forward (red) and backward (yellow) tables as the active direction. The current direction text and color will change accordingly to show the current direction or table.

By pressing the "Loop Control" button the user is then presented with the Loop Control window which has the ability to break a loop, reorder a loop, or combine two loops together to get a larger solution which is called stitching in 2D and knight's crossing in 3D. In the Loop Control window the user has five text boxes to fill in. The first and third text boxes are for the direction of loop that is being worked on. The second and fourth text boxes are the move numbers, and the last text box is to reverse the counting of the loop. The Loop Control breaks the loop at the designated point such that the first move and final move is where the break point occurs. This creates a chain of movements that can be combined with another chain of movements to create a larger chain of movements. After the two chains have been linked together into a larger chain, the "CheckLoop" button is then used to verify that the combination of the two chains does result in a new larger loop solution.

The "Confirm Mouse" button is used with Mouse Input (described above) to reaffirm that the mouse-selected grid is indeed the move that the user wants to make.

3   LKT Game Environment

Playing a 2D LKT game might be relatively simple (and theoretically solvable for any rectangular board [6]), since the entire board is viewable as seen in Figure 3. In a 3D Game Box, however, more viewing perspectives and manipulating tools are required and counting information (such as those provided in Sec. 2.4.3) to assist the user to monitor the current situation becomes more essential. The combination of the table displays with position information and the visual manipulation tools facilitates tracking during play. The ability to track and view positional relations, ranging from the local grid associations in the 5^3 windows, to the global perspectives offered by the entire Game Box, are what ultimately enables the user to understand the present situation and make decisions for the next move. Such capabilities, including the Neighbor Pool table that track the counting heuristics also facilitate user's understanding of the global relations (between the two ends of the chain in the "end game" and offer feasibility for completing a LKT loop.

In order to model, view and appreciate a 3D body with interior details through a 2D medium there needs to be a way to view the 3D object from all angles. Figure 7 is a sequence of snapshots taken as the Game Box is rotated in the counterclockwise direction. It illustrates a middle game stage where the user has made a multitude of moves in each of the forward and backward directions (tables). Both 5^3 windows are visible, and distinguished by the red and yellow colored grids. The difference between the sub-figures is a change of the orientation of the Game Box in the x-y plane, while the z plane remains constant. The axis labels also change as the view is changed to always be in the correct orientation to be read properly.

Being able to change the view of the Game Box is important in order to accurately assess the overall situation and make the best possible choice for the next move. It also allows the planning and strategizing of moves before committing to one. For example, in order to select a grid on the interior of the Game Box the user can to either input the coordinates into the appropriate "Move Table" or use SketchUp's built in "Section Plane" tool to peel away the grids that inhibit the mouse from

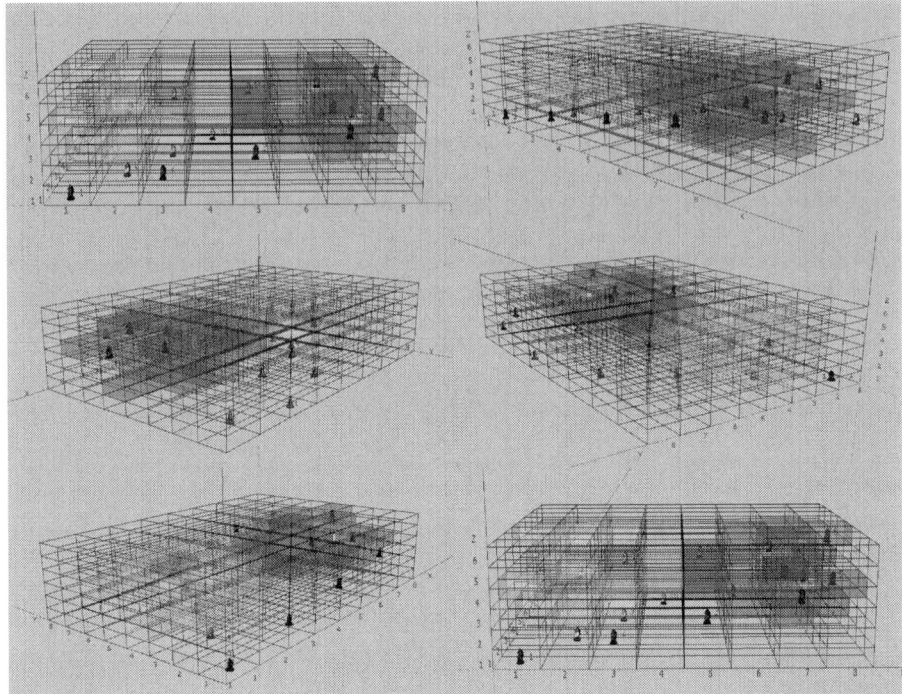

Fig. 7. Snapshot sequence showing the rotation of the Game Box in 3D (left to right, top down)

selecting the grid. Even by using the "Section Plane" or the 5^3 window, the viewing perspective may need to be changed in order to be able to see and select the appropriate grid.

4   Conclusion

Having a visual representation of problem states has demonstrated its power of a clarified view and understanding so as to enable the user to cut through the complexity of these problems and decide on the most logical steps to take. Furthermore, a visual system can stimulate different methods of thinking and attacking problems. This will, in turn, prompt new ways of approaching the same problem with more effectiveness or efficiency.

4.1   Solving the LKT Problems

The graphic environment for LKT game playing in 3D is supported and facilitated by the *LKT game environment* described above. The LKT game operates within Google's SketchUp 3D modeling software and utilizes Ruby, Java and HTML programming languages [7] for several features and extensions. Trying to play a LKT game mentally, without visual aid or computer assisted tracking, is extremely difficult, if not impossible, because the user must keep track of all position and move possibilities from both local and global perspectives in 3D. Using the LKT game environment, many variables (and open and occupied positions, and their relations) can be monitored and displayed for the user. The value of such a 3D graphic environment and computer assistance is, thus, demonstrated.

The overall solution approach towards a complete collection of solutions for all the 3D LKT problems will require a community of players challenging one another and cooperating to develop an increasing database of solutions. As smaller solutions are found and stored in a Web searchable database, larger sizes posed online can be solved by partitioning the size into smaller 2D layers or 3D blocks, some of which may have existing solutions, and composed together by 2D stitching or knight's crossing in 3D. Such a combination of top-down partitioning and bottom-up solution database yields a much more realistic, and interesting, solution method to solve all LKT problems in 3D, rectangular boxes or other shapes. Any time a larger size problem is solved; the database of solutions would not only index and store its loop solution, as a chain of knight's moves, but also its specific decomposition into smaller sizes. Such an indexed database developed by a community of players on the Web would grow with each new solution found and new game posed. The Web player community can blossom by using this LKT game environment via SketchUp and Google's world-wide distribution to achieve complete set of LKT solutions, while playing and enjoying the challenging game online.

4.2 Assessment of Potentials

3D games visually aided by motion, zooming and slicing and effectively assisted by computed tracking and counting information, facilitate the user decision making without diminishing the pleasure or challenge. The drawbacks of having to deal with 3D scenes and objects on 2D screens can largely be overcome. Computed assistance and visualizations can also help overcome certain physical difficulties to make the process of problem solving more interesting and enjoyable. The LKT game is such a demonstration of a computer enhanced environment to enable enjoyable playing of a 3D game.

The LKT environment can also be utilized to develop other types of games. There are games that claim to offer 3D chess, but in reality only the chess pieces are 3D while the game is still shown on a stack of 2D boards [1]. Due to the lack of computed tracking values and counting displays to facilitate decisions, playing such a 3D chess game is not much more than a stretch of the mental capacity beyond the 2D game. The LKT game environment described/offered here can be easily modified to support 3D chess and possibly trigger renewed interest worldwide via the Web.

Many games, including chess, are already played online. The 3D model system can offer a multitude of computed tracking to enhance the enjoyment, but maintain the usual challenges. The LKT game cannot be put into a physical realized model hence is only appropriate as a computerized game. As such, it has demonstrated the necessary 3D feasibility and added enjoyment and challenge through computer assistance and displays.

References

1. Bornet, R.E.: The Game of Three Dimensional Eight Level Chess (2004), http://www.hixoxih.com/games/chess/3D8L.htm#TRUE%203D%20CHESS
2. Duffy, S.: How to Do Everything with JavaScript. McGraw-Hill, Berkeley (2003)
3. Fitzgerald, M.: A Quick Guide to Ruby Pocket Reference. O'Reilly Media, Inc., Sebastopol (2007)
4. Flanagan, D., Matsumoto, Y.: The Ruby Programming Language. O'Reilly Media, Inc., Sebastopol (2008)
5. Koosis, D., Koosis, D.J.: Java Programming for Dummies, 2nd edn. IDG Books Worldwide, Inc., Foster City (1997)
6. Schwenk, A.J.: Which Rectangular Chessboards Have a Knight's Tour? Mathematics Magazine, pp. 325–332 (December 1991)
7. SketchUp. Ver. 6. Google (2008), http://sketchup.google.com/
8. Stewart, I.: Math Recreations Knight's Tours. Scientific American 4(97), 102–103
9. Thomas, D., Fowler, C., Hunt, A.: Programming Ruby The Pragmatic Programmers' Guide, 2nd edn. The Pragmatic Programmers, USA (2005)
10. Yun, D.Y.Y.: Achieving Computational Intelligence by Resource Optimization (Invited Paper). In: Proc. 2002 World Congress on Computational Intelligence. International Joint Conference on Neural Networks, Honolulu (May 2002)
11. Yun, D.Y.Y.: Intelligent Resource Management through the Constrained Resource Planning Engine. In: Kasabox, N. (ed.) Future Directions for Intelligent Systems and Information Sciences, ch. 18, pp. 373–386. Springer, Heidelberg (2000)

Robosonic: Randomness-Based Manipulation of Sounds Assisted by Robots

Filipe Costa Luz, Rui Pereira Jorge, and Vasco Bila

movlab – University Lusófona
Av. do Campo Grande, 376
1749-024 Lisbon
Tel.: +351 217 515 500; Ext.: 2389
{filipe.luz,ruip.jorge,vasco.bila}@ulusofona.pt

Abstract. In this text, we intend to explore the possibilities of sound manipulation in a context of augmented reality (AR) through the use of robots. We use the random behaviour of robots in a limited space for the real-time modulation of two sound characteristics: amplitude and frequency. We add the possibility of interaction with these robots, providing the user the opportunity to manipulate the physical interface by placing markers in the action space, which alter the behaviour of the robots and, consequently, the audible result produced.

We intend to demonstrate through the agents, programming of random processes and direct manipulation of this application, that it is possible to generate empathy in interaction and obtain specific audible results, which would be difficult to otherwise reproduce due to the infinite loops that the interaction promotes.

Keywords: Augmented Reality, Robots, Sound, Agents, Randomness, Communication, Collaborative Composing.

1 Introduction

Robosonic is an interactive application that seeks to manipulate sounds through interaction between people and robots. In the action space, a limited area of 80 x 60 cm, one or two Khepera robots move according to random programming. In the action space, there are one or two markers, objects with which the robot may collide and which may be moved from a given position by the user. Two axes (x and y) are considered in the robot's movement. The horizontal x-axis corresponds to frequency. If the robot is directed to the left (negative values on the x-axis), this value decreases; if the robot is directed to the right, the value increases. By prior determination, this increase and reduction does not exceed audible limits (20 to 20,000 Hz). Amplitude is considered on the vertical y-axis. Provided that the robot moves positively along the y-axis, the amplitude is increased; otherwise, it decreases. It was determined that if the robot approaches zero on the y-axis, sound will cease completely. The markers, which continue to be deployed by the user, fulfil two functions: they change the course of the robots provided that they detect the markers and change the tones that

A. Nijholt, D. Reidsma, and H. Hondorp (Eds.): INTETAIN 2009, LNICST 9, pp. 143–152, 2009.
© ICST Institute for Computer Sciences, Social Informatics and Telecommunications Engineering 2009

are to be reproduced. Every time that a tone is heard – provided that the robot finds a marker – this tone changes in a random fashion, based upon the library of effects previously loaded onto the application. Accordingly, we see the possibility of a simultaneous manipulation of three sound characteristics: the frequency and amplitude according to the robot's random behaviour in the action space and the tone according to the robot's collisions with the markers.

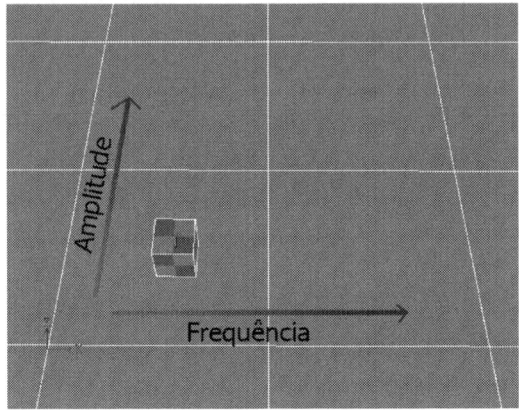

Fig. 1. Transformations in X and Y

The intended result is the modulation of sounds through the robot-designed course, which will depend upon human intervention (position of markers A and B). The user provides the markers with which the robots interact in the action space, thereby altering the existing sounds in a database loaded with passive sounds to be continually executed in audible loops. The objective is the creation of a space with multiple possible audible transformations that may generate unusual results.

This does not pertain to using the robot as a generator of sounds, or rather, as a synthesizer. The main aspect in this application's development is the use of robot behaviour as a form of sound manipulation. In this project, the sounds precede the application as they were synthesized on other platforms. What this application develops is the form of a robot, its random behaviour and the user's intervention in the possibilities of altering such random behaviour, producing manipulations of specific sound.

This application anticipates the possibility of an audio recording of the entire process. This means that the results obtained may be used subsequently in other contexts. In this document, we will refer to the possibility of using these modulations created during the process in later sampling processes, to then be included in other compositions.

Since 1863, when Henri Fourneaux invented a way to programme musical execution on a piano, which he called Pianista and that would later become Pianola, invented in 1876 by Edwin Votey, and which includes the possibility of a piano being able to execute sequences of previously determined notes on perforated tape, numerous robotic attempts at musical execution have been witnessed. An interesting development has recently been verified, which spans diverse areas such as academics, the arts, business and teaching. The level of complexity and development is great, allowing the robots to analyze, play and even compose music. However, we take the application presented in this document as a point of departure, especially the robot's role as interface and controller in which the user will elicit a specific type of behaviour in the robot with the deployment of markers. Since the control that the user exercises over the robot is far from complete – and even minimal – it is nonetheless an aspect that especially allows this application to explore the random possibilities of manipulation. We also discuss the controller so that we can compare the situation to that of a MIDI controller, such as a keyboard, for example, which serves to transmit information pertaining to frequency, amplitude, tone and duration. The robot will transmit information regarding frequency and amplitude through its course and tone through its collision with the markers. Accordingly, we underscore the idea that this phase does not pertain to generating sounds, but specifically to establishing a synthesis process. It is applied before manipulation, through the alteration of previously existing material, namely the looped tones previously loaded on a database.

An important aspect to consider is the fact that the results obtained with this application lead us back to hearing sound specificity, given that what is heard is always unexpected in the sense that the robot produces it. John Cage, a 20th century American composer and pioneer in the use of random processes in musical composition, paid particular attention to this possibility of us hearing basic sounds, avoiding any type of previous qualification. "The sounds enter the time-space centred within themselves, unimpeded by service to any abstraction, their 360 degrees of circumference free for an infinite play of interpretation." [1]

What is important to consider here, regarding the process of chance, is that it is more than simply randomness. It is also interesting to examine any type of imperfection, for example, that would otherwise not be obtained. "I myself use chance operations, some derived from the I-Ching, others from the observation of imperfections in the paper upon which I happen to be writing." [2]

2 Development of Application

The entire application was developed over a virtools platform based upon an augmented reality (AR) VirtoolKit library, VSL programming and webbots (robots) programming. A Mini DV video camera was used for video recognition (Tracking), in addition to two Khepera (K-team) robots and an interaction area. In support of the application, there is a sound library from which the robot will search for base loops.

The application is based on an AR mechanism, thereby catching a glimpse of a new visual dimension over the application to be subsequently developed. In this first stage, the AR allows us to detect the position of markers (interface manipulated by the user) and the robot's movements (artificial agent), thereby functioning as a tracking system for video processing. The marker's coordinates are then obtained in real time for use as frequency and volume variables for a specific sound.

Depending on the size of the interaction area, the factor that transforms the amplitude and the frequency will need to be adjusted. In the example presented, we multiplied the values of X and Y by 0.1, in order to better capture this application's dimensions (60 x 80 cm).

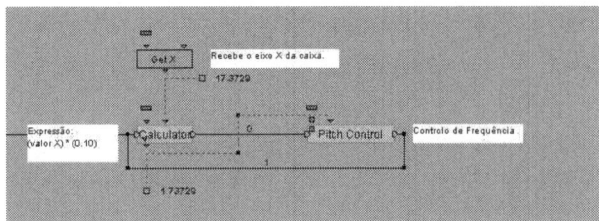

Fig. 2. Schematic view of X transformations

In figure 2, we can analyze the schematic programming view for the transformation of the x-axis (frequency) developed in Virtools.

According to the structure, this code is added to the Robot, while the remaining markers are placed to determine collisions with the robot and, consequently, require it to travel new paths within the interaction space. Provided that the robot detects a marker, the sequence of sounds associated with the database is reordered, replacing the tone that the robot is about to produce with another chosen randomly in the database, composed of a library of 12 sounds essentially with the character of texture. Meanwhile in the two-robot application version, it is associated with a second library with 12 sounds of a more rhythmic nature.

3   Robot Agency

During this interaction between the user and the robot, the intent is to blur the boundary between programming and the programmer given that in the space of this "musical game", the previous code in Virtools is merged with the robot's programming upon interaction with the user.

This does not apply specifically to studying the cyborg symbiosis between computers and humans, which occurs through the gaming experience [3], enhancing the human characteristic of attraction to the machine. At this moment, it is more important to emphasize that this type of application shows that humans "think" as agents, providing equalization between natural and artificial reasoning [4].

In the Robosonic application, we try to understand how the machine processes in order to seek control over its movements. It is through agency that the illusion of this human-computer communication process becomes stronger, given that the illusion that we are communicating with similar beings potentially increases the notion of "being present" in this interaction space [5].

According to Lahti, learning programming logic to construct computer games, where we may include other types of digital spaces such as software with a graphical interface, reveals a cyborg conscience that Ted Friedman indicates as a human extension of computational processes [6]. It pertains not only to understanding the machine, but also to working in unison with it in order to create. If, on one hand, the user tries to dominate the movements and sounds produced by the robot, then on the other hand the programming that the application's creator previously developed, trying to virtualize all possible operations in the "game" space, will be updated, or rather, the programmer creatively merges with the programming and hardware to produce this interactive space.

Fig. 3. User chaging fixed obstacle position to interact with two Khepera mobile robots

The programming ceases to be limited to the creation of a totally defined space, where the programmer, in a strategic and virtually ludic manner, projects a space for the user to experiment and subsequently create. It does not pertain solely to "thinking like a machine" but rather to thinking with the machine. "Are we using the computers, or are the computers using us?" [7]. Considering programming loops, John Maeda questions how far the computer will go without our direct interaction. Machines that function in constant cycles and that are provided with the ability to memorize may be considered autonomous and of an artificial nature, yet still the product of human technology.

Robosonic is therefore the materialization of an "inhabitable world" in the sense that it will be occupied by robots, bots, users and spectators. As a usual task, the intent to control this small world and, likewise, all of the restlessness that the lack of control may generate, is notable. Such a phenomenon occurs because the game space is inhabited by other agents who adapt to our form of interaction [8], trying to avoid control because of previous programming, or because they react in an apparently unpredictable manner due to "errors" in code.

The robot functions as an agent that seeks to move freely in the action space, interacting with the database that is reordered through a random programming factor and from the contact between the markers and the robot, or due to the detection of another robot. In this first phase, these agents present artificial intelligence at an elementary level, since they are limited to repositioning themselves in space (path finding) provided that their paths are marked by obstacles (markers). However, upon initial testing, it was immediately deduced that the agents completely revolutionized the application interface, creating a new paradigm for human-machine communications. A space inhabited by artificial beings that reacts with human interaction seems to provide personality to software [9] and generate special attention. When simulations of movement are shown to be synchronized with image and sound, they generate a type of "special attraction" over the audiences [10].

As an accepted definition, agents present their own properties [11] identified as: autonomy, by performing functions in a controlled manner without direct intervention by humans or other agents. They must respond to third-party elements whenever these contact them, while maintaining their individual objectives as a rule, conferring upon them autonomy, social aptitude and the ability to adapt to the surrounding environment, responding to transformations that may occur. Therefore, the agents must not be predictable in the performance of their tasks, demonstrating the sense of opportunity to surprise the user. To us, this concept seems to be an excellent reason to work towards the creation of a communications interface hypermediated by software, hardware and human agents, for the construction of sounds that cannot in any way be controlled exclusively by the user. Therefore, the agents have a fundamental role in the lack of control over manipulation, and, accordingly, in seeking unexpected paths that would carry us to unique musical results, abstracting the user through the transparency of connection that occurs in this interface of human-machine interaction.

4   Sound Manipulation

Above all, this application must be seen according to two different perspectives: sound manipulation and collaborative composing.

What should be observed in manipulation is the manner in which the course which the robot takes in a specific space provides modulation of the two sound characteristics, associated with the two axes of movement: on the horizontal x-axis, frequency, and on the vertical y-axis, amplitude. In the case of frequency, the application provides a central area in which the sound is reproduced with the base frequency and so forth. Whenever there is movement to the left, the sound becomes deeper, while in moving to the right, the sound becomes sharper. The programming initially defined that both the deep and sharp extremes will always be audible sounds, i.e., sounds that fall within the audible human range (between 20 and 20,000 Hz). In the case of the vertical axis, the possibility is assumed of sound going from zero – absence of sound – up to the application's maximum permitted volume. Given the application's functional type, fine tuning was intentionally set aside. What matters most is what is heard without concern for integration of that sound in the context of a scale according to musical notes.

The audible material is what matters.

"Ultimately, however, musical instruments, scales, and tuning systems are only the material and conceptual infrastructure onto which musical style is built. They may, in part, determine *what* sounds are played, but they have much less influence on *how* they are played." [12]

Another type of interface, such as MIDI controllers, allows for the manipulation of parameters along with frequency (notes). What emerges particularly and uniquely is that the robot's random movement in space suggests results in the context of unique amplitude / frequency combinations.

And, it is in this way that the issue of interface demonstrates interest in the context of this application.

"If a composer sets up a process which allows each player to move through the material at his own speed, for example, it is impossible for him to draw things together into some kind of calculated image, a particular effect or pattern of logical connections." [13]

Experimentation in the context of sound manipulation must be taken into account as the determining factor in this process. Beyond conducting the application as a tool, for the purpose of obtaining specific results – always conditioned given the fact that we are using this tool and that by nature it leaves its record of the result obtained – it is important to verify what such application has to offer us and that it has a unpredictable character: how can it surprise us?

By experimentation in this context, we mean this tool's attempt to take us to the limit in order to provide us with unexpected results.

"Experimental composers have evolved a vast number of processes to bring about 'acts the outcome of which are unknown' (Cage). The extent to which they are unknown (and to whom) is variable and depends on the specific process in question. Process may range from a minimum of organization to a minimum of arbitrariness, proposing different relationships between chance and choice, presenting different kinds of options and obligations". [14]

In this idea of experimentation, it is important to strengthen the concept of randomness and indetermination: these are critical to bringing about innovation. This statement of Qubais Gazala is characteristic of his practices of manipulation and alteration of musical instruments and other devices so as to infringe upon, as he says accordingly, the predictability of such instruments and devices as they are made available to the public: "We have now entered a world where music no longer adheres to human presumption in theory, circuit design and composition. Thus, great new sounds and musical realities can occur as one sits with one's out-of-theory instrument, a truly alien instrument, and listens to its metamorphosed output" [15].

At this level, we are particularly interested in raising the issue here of randomness in musical composition. The subject is not new, as it has been addressed many times in the history of music. Meanwhile, recent technological developments have permitted a broadening of this type of practice. Various hypotheses and methodologies may be considered here. In the particular case of the application, it would be interesting for us to call upon some of the assumptions considered by John Cage. Specifically, the issue is the presence of change in the compositional process. Perhaps what interests us most here is in the form of the unexpected. Unexpected because what the robot is going to produce with previously defined sounds on database translates into hearing unexpected effects. A certain type of x- and y-combinations could be attained in some other way with some degree of difficulty. If this adds up to the possibility that someone interacts with the robot by placing the markers in a specific position in the action space, within which the sounds will be altered, then variables increase and the possibility of unexpected results increases as well. "I was exploring chance electronics. While simple, the process is explosive in its startling audio output. Fantastic aleatoric music might result composed of either 'real' instruments (samples) or layers of evolving indefinable sounds" [15].

As a composer, John Cage occupied an illustrious position as regards the use of experimental musical composition processes throughout the 20th century. The concept of chance in musical composition is particularly important in this composer's work. He asserted that chance was completely legitimate as a compositional process. To him, in order for indetermination to be obtained, whether with traditional musical instruments, or through devices created for the purpose of proceeding with that type of manipulation, rules for indetermination in the context of contemporary composition

Fig. 4. Augmented Reality control PC providing randomess sound libraries for musician interact

need to be recognized. Cage clearly rejected a certain stubbornness on the part of many composers who did not consider that chance was part of the glossary and praxis of composition. To Cage, such rigidity of processes in seeking to group, include and catalogue everything is tragic and creatively inhibiting. This is especially the case because it rules out obtaining innovative results, which, *de rigeur*, should be part of any composer's guidelines.

The concept of collaborative composing plays an important role here. Above all, it pertains to verifying how the robot, as a technological device, facilitates this collaborative composing. At an elementary level, when two people interact with their instruments, they are already in a situation of collaborative composing. But the central point here is the collaboration between the behaviour of robots and whoever interacts with them. It pertains to collaborative composing to the extent that the robots offer a part of their material: their specific behaviour in the space that allows for a specific modulation of sounds. In turn, the users who interact with the robot, changing the position of the markers with which the robot collides, so prompting it to activate other sounds, represent the other part of material that is brought together in this collaboration. This allows the user to always have a margin for error – he knows, for example, that if he places the marker in front of the robot, the robot will run into it and change the sound. Likewise, he knows that if he moves the marker away from the robot, the robot will not collide with it and the same sound will persist. Nonetheless, the possibility of the user's control is limited by the unpredictability of the robot's random behaviour. The article of Kapur, A.; Eigenfeldt, A.; Bahn, C. and Schloss, A. should be consulted in this regard. Regarding collaborative musical composing using robots, it states: "The goal of many of the predecessors in the academic and artistic circles who build musical robotic systems has been to design new instruments to Express new musical ideas, not attainable by audio speakers, or human performers" [16].

With the first impulse in the sense of industrial production, the domain of robotics has expanded to other areas such as entertainment, for example. The use of robots in contexts of musical execution and creation are undergoing further development. We may even confirm that, within the arts world, music has exhibited the broadest use of robots. Certain characteristics contribute to this impact, namely the fact that the robot provides an interesting role as an interface for musical applications, as well as the fact that music is an art produced intrinsically by creation and manipulation – i.e. sounds – an activity in which robots, given their specific characteristics, may provide a valuable contribution.

5 Conclusion

The development of this application allows knowledge to be consolidated and information from different areas, such as robotics, augmented reality and musical composition, to be brought together.

Such development enables the establishment of a knowledge base that can be subsequently developed, namely through the integration of more robots, the integration of the video component related to sound manipulation developed by the application, and the interaction of other musicians and respective instruments with this application.

The possibility that the sounds manipulated by this application could be recorded for later use in other contexts should also be considered, strengthening the idea of using this application as a means rather than an end.

The performative aspect and the issue of interface are also clearly important in this study. The experience is performative, in the sense that the user, or users, are projected into a space for creation, simulation and visualization. They act at the moment of interaction and help to set into motion the action caused by the robots' movements.

Of future interest is the application's development in the context of its ability to integrate with other platforms in the creation and manipulation of sound and image.

Acknowledgments

We would like to thank Professor João MCS Abrantes and Professor Manuel Costa Leite for their support in terms of time, assistance and knowledge. We are also grateful to José Dinis and Fernando Marques for their unconditional help and to the *Fundação para a Ciência e Tecnologia* (Science and Technology Foundation) for supporting Project Evolutio: from Evolutionary Robotics to the Philosophy of Natural Cognition and Communication (PTDC/FIL/75060/2006).

References

1. Cage, J.: Silence: Lectures and Writings, p. 59. Wesleyan University Press (1973)
2. Cage, J.: Silence: Lectures and Writings, p. 17. Wesleyan University Press (1973)
3. Lahti, M.: As We Became Machines. In: The Video Game Theory Reader, pp. 157–170 (2003)
4. Friedman, T.: Civilization and Its Discontents: Simulation, Subjectivity, and Space. In: Smith, G. (ed.) Discovering Discs: Transforming Space and Genre. New York University Press (1999) CD-ROM, http://www.duke.edu/~tlove/civ.htm
5. Murray, J.: Hamlet on the Holodeck - The Future of narrative Cyberspace, pp. 154–182. The Free Press, New York (1997)
6. Lahti, M.: As We Became Machines. In: The Video Game Theory Reader, pp. 157–170 (2003)
7. Maeda, J.: The Infinite Loop. In: Code – The Language of Our Time, Ars Electrónica 2003, Germany, Hatje Cantz, pp. 168–171 (2003)
8. Tveit, A.: A survey of Agent-Oriented Software Engineering, Norwegian University of Science and Technology (2001), http://csgsc.idi.ntnu.no/2001/pages/papers/atveit.pdf
9. Johnson, S.: Interface Culture: How new technology transforms the way we create and communicate, 2nd edn. Basic Books, New York (1997)
10. Darley, A.: Visual Digital Culture, surface play and spectacle in new media games. Routledge, London (2000)
11. Jennings, J., Wooldbridge, M.: Software Agents. IEE Review, pp.17–20 (January 1996), http://www.ecs.soton.ac.uk/~nrj/pubs.html#1996
12. Théberge, P.: Music / Technology / Practice; Music Knowlwedge in Action. In: Bennett, A., ShanK, B., Toynbee, J. (eds.) The Popular Music studies reader, p. 285. Routledge, london (2006)
13. Nyman, M.: Experimental Music, Cage and Beyond, p. 29. Cambridge University Press, Cambridge (1999)
14. Nyman, M.: Experimental Music, Cage and Beyond, p. 4. Cambridge University Press, Cambridge (1999)
15. Ghazala, Q.: The Folk Music of Chance Electronics: Circuit-Bending the Modern Coconut. Leonardo Music Journal 14, 98 (2004)
16. Kapur, A., Eigenfeldt, A., Bahn, C., Schloss, A.: Collaborative Composition for Musical Robots in ARTECH, p. 67 (2008)

Turning Shortcomings into Challenges: Brain-Computer Interfaces for Games

Anton Nijholt, Boris Reuderink, and Danny Oude Bos

University of Twente, Faculty EEMCS,
P.O. Box 217, 7500 AE, Enschede
The Netherlands
anijholt@cs.utwente.nl

Abstract. In recent years we have seen a rising interest in brain-computer interfacing for human-computer interaction and potential game applications. Until now, however, we have almost only seen attempts where BCI is used to measure the affective state of the user or in neurofeedback games. There have hardly been any attempts to design BCI games where BCI is considered to be one of the possible input modalities that can be used to control the game. One reason may be that research still follows the paradigms of the traditional, medically oriented, BCI approaches. In this paper we discuss current BCI research from the viewpoint of games and game design. It is hoped that this survey will make clear that we need to design different games than we used to, but that such games can nevertheless be interesting and exciting.

Keywords: Brain-computer Interfacing, Multimodal Interaction, Game Design.

1 Introduction

Brain-Computer Interfacing (BCI) is finding its way in human-computer interaction [26,27]. In this paper we discuss the use of BCI in game and game-like applications. These applications are not that different from medical or military BCI applications. Medical applications, aiming at providing handicapped patients with communication and movement skills, have seen many research efforts. But we can also say that gamers, soldiers or, in fact, anybody is handicapped, in the sense that they will meet situations where it is desirable to have more skills and communication means than are available when using the usual verbal and nonverbal interaction modalities. The circumstances in which they have to perform challenge their abilities to control the environment and can demand control that cannot be delivered by conventional modalities (e.g. speech, gaze, keyboard, mouse). 'Induced disability' or 'situational disability' are words used to describe these circumstances. In fact, everybody, handicapped or not, will meet situations, in particular situations where they have to compete with others, where they would benefit from extra communication or movement modalities. This is particularly true in games, sports and entertainment.

There are other reasons that make games, gamers and the game industry interesting for BCI research and development. In particular, gamers are early adaptors. They are

A. Nijholt, D. Reidsma, and H. Hondorp (Eds.): INTETAIN 2009, LNICST 9, pp. 153–168, 2009.
© ICST Institute for Computer Sciences, Social Informatics and Telecommunications Engineering 2009

quite happy to play with technology, to accept that great efforts have to be made in order to gain a sometimes minimal advantage, and they are used to the fact that games have to be mastered by training, allowing them to go from one level to the next level and to get a higher ranking than their competitors. We may also expect interest from software companies for BCI games. There are enormous numbers of gamers. Being the first to introduce a new type of game, a new game element or a new interaction modality may bring them enormous profits. This is certainly an impetus for industry to invest in research and development into brain-computer interfacing.

We can use information made available to us from brain activity to adapt the interface to the user or to issue commands to the interface. Brain activity, whether it is consciously controlled and directed by the user or 'just' recorded in order to obtain information about the user's affective state, should be modeled and embedded in more general models of interaction in order to provide appropriate adaptation, feedback and a context where brain activity information is one of the many multi-modal interaction modalities that are provided to the gamer. From the traditional BCI point of view this is quite an unusual approach. Generally, BCI researchers prefer or assume that the only activity a subject performs is brain activity while any other activity (as extreme but nevertheless realistic examples, blinking of an eye or facial muscle movement) disrupts the activity in which the researcher is interested. We are not directly interested in designing games for ALS patients or designing games for gamers who have to behave like ALS patients and are punished for moving. Hence, measuring and interpreting brain signals and providing feedback in a particular game context is an aim that needs to be pursued. Employing measured brain activity to be used in everyday-life-like (domestic) applications is the next step.

BCI with the aim of obtaining knowledge about a user's experience of the game and maybe to adapt the game (interface) to the gamer is an important research issue. There are already several European research projects devoted to defining and measuring the game experience with the aim to use this knowledge for designing future games and to adapt games to their users [9]. One particular form of game experience is 'immersion' or 'flow' [5]. It can be considered as the ultimate goal of a game designer, being able to cause a flow experience where a gamer enters a situation where increasing challenges are to be met by increasing skills (see Figure 1). The gamer becomes immersed in the game, forgetting about time and other reality. Until now research aiming to understand this flow experience has concentrated on using more traditional physiological information, attempting to derive a user's affective state from, for example, heart rate, sweating, respiration, and blood pressure [10]. Recently, there have also been attempts to investigate how being in the flow can be read from body language [4]. It is certainly helpful if BCI

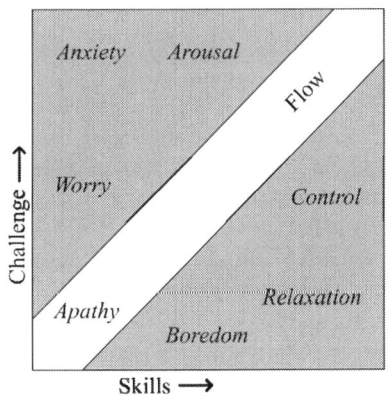

Fig. 1. Flow diagram, based on [5]

can tell us a gamer is bored, anxious, or frustrated. Then it is clear that a gamer is not in the flow envisaged by the game designer.

Hence, measuring experience and affect and adapting a game to the affective state of the gamer is an important issue. But probably even more interesting are games and game environments that have been designed to allow or require control from brain activity that is consciously produced by a gamer or that has been evoked from external stimuli that have been integrated into a game. There can be game situations where such control is an added modality to the other means a gamer has to play the game. It may help or it may be the only possibility to reach a next level in a game.

This paper provides a state-of-the-art survey of the field of brain-computer interfacing as far as it is of interest from the point of view of games. With this survey in mind we discuss possibilities for including BCI as an added modality in game design and we discuss developments and challenges.

2   BCI for Controlling and Adapting Games

When we look at possible BCI games we are asking for BCI theory that allows us to distinguish and employ activity in different regions of the brain (using machine learning algorithms) and that allows us to map each of these activities to commands to control or adapt a game. When we look at game applications we need to take into account that gamers will prefer not to game in a MRI scanner, that gamers will not want to wear heavy head sets that measure their brain waves, and that not all gamers are yet willing to undergo surgery to have implants that will improve measuring their brain waves or improve their brain functions. There are some exceptions, but in this paper we assume that brain activity is measured using an EEG cap. Such a cap has electrodes attached to it that measure activity in different regions of the brain. We can 'read' such information and make it available to a game engine that controls the environment, to use to adapt the game to a recognized mental state of the user or to translate consciously produced activity to commands that allow a gamer to change the environment, to navigate, and to make decisions that allow him or her to survive in the game. We can distinguish different kinds of brain activity:

- the gamer is experiencing the game, the task and the interface, and gets, among other things, frustrated, engaged, irritated, bored or stressed; in particular it would be useful to measure whether a gamer is 'in the zone' or 'in the flow'; currently, flow experience research is empirical, asking users about their experiences; however, there are already attempts to read the 'flow experience' from the nonverbally displayed expressions by gamers, and BCI can help to adapt the interface in order to get a better matching of skills and challenges in the game;
- there are external stimuli (visual, auditory, tactile, ...) designed and generated by the game environment to force the user to choose among certain possibilities (i.e., make decisions in the game) or that occur in a more natural way because BCI recognizes that a gamer is interested in a particular event that happens during a game; such externally evoked potentials can be generated by the game environment (an unexpected obstacle is introduced) or by a gamer's opponent (asking a gamer to react on a particular sword movement);

- the gamer consciously tries to evoke brain signals by performing a certain mental task; for instance, imagining a movement or doing a mental calculation, leading to brain signals that can be transformed in such a way that the application is controlled by this mental task, rather than by mouse, joystick or keyboard activity;
- the gamer consciously tries to control his or her global brain activity; that is, activity related to stress, attention, and relaxation, in order to control part of a game; this activity of the user or gamer is very much supported by performance feedback (visual or auditory) from the interface; this neurofeedback provides motivating rewards for the user and it stimulates the user to continue his or her efforts to control the game environment by thought.

2.1 Internally Evoked Potentials

We distinguish between internally and externally evoked brain signals. Motor imagery [20] is one of the possible ways in which we can have internally evoked potentials. In our motor cortex we can find a mapping from possible movements made by our body parts to brain regions in this cortex. That is, for example, imagining a movement of your left foot, imagining a movement of your index finger, or imagining a movement of the tip of your tongue, all these imaginary movements lead to distinguishable brain activity in the motor cortex of the brain. Moreover, imagining these movements leads to similar activity in similar or related regions of the motor cortex as executing or intending to execute such movements. By picking up these signals and translating them to commands, we can, for example, use brain activity to navigate in a virtual environment (see Figure 2), to guide our avatar, and also to add actions to our avatar or to the tools and weaponry used by our avatar in a game.

The mapping of 'thoughts' to actions in a virtual game environment does not necessarily have to be to 'natural'. A gamer can be asked to perform a difficult calculation (mental arithmetic) or to imagine a rotation of a geometric object. But preferably a required mental effort should be naturally embedded in a game because this helps a great deal to make the required game actions believable to the gamer and helps to keep the gamer immersed in the game. Mental efforts related to calculation or rotation, or other mental activities that have not yet been investigated, can become embedded in game environments. We can also look at more global levels of internally evoked brain activity. For example, changes in relaxation can be mapped on color changes in the environment and other changes in the landscape, or they influence the speed of changes in the environment, on the ability to move around, or on the fighting ability of game actors controlled by the gamer. Also, levels of relaxation can be mapped onto different game commands. However, generally we may expect that affect related brain signals are more useful to adapt the game to the particular gamer than to transform them to explicit commands that control game actions and events.

2.2 Externally Evoked Potentials

There are also many forms of externally evoked potentials that can be exploited by game designers. When looking at evoked potentials we should take into account what can be measured in a game situation. As an example, can we measure motor cortex brain activity that is evoked by looking at movements? On the other hand, it is well known that we can have externally evoked potentials in our brain. The stimuli that cause these potentials can be auditory (to be detected in the auditory cortex), visual (in the visual cortex), or somatosensory or tactile (in the somatosensory cortex), and combinations of these stimuli. Steady-state visually evoked potentials (SSVEPs), like flickering lights on a computer screen, have been used to allow a gamer to make binary decisions [16]. But there is no need to restrict ourselves to binary decisions since different frequencies cause different distinguishable brain activities. An example in with four SSVEP decision options are provided is shown in Figure 2.

Among the electrophysiological responses to external stimuli are also the event-related potentials (ERPs). While the evoked potentials reflect physical stimuli, the event-related potentials are more related to thoughts that are an automatic response to observed events. Hence, they are related to expectations and attention, and to changes in the mental state of the observer. A well-known example of these event-related potentials is the so-called P300 signal. Suppose you are playing a video game and you are anticipating certain events. Then, every time such an event takes place there is EEG measurable brain activity (a positive voltage deflection in the parietal cortex of the brain) about 300ms after the stimulus onset. See Figure 2 for an applied example.

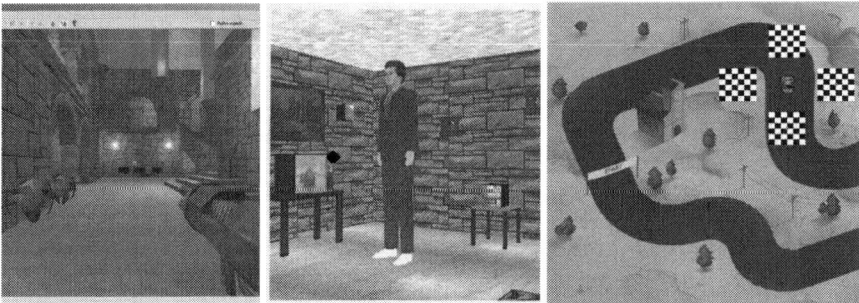

Fig. 2. Examples of games and virtual environments using imaginary movement [30], P300 [2], and SSVEP [21] paradigms respectively. To elicit the P300 potential, blinking spheres were connected with each controllable object in the room. For the SSVEP, each checkerboard was inverted at different frequencies. Imaginary movement is internally evoked, so no external stimuli are required for the interaction.

Less well-studied, but certainly interesting in the game context is the event-related N400 (a negative voltage deflection about 400ms after the stimulus onset) effect. It has been studied in the context of experiencing unexpected events, for example, when we recognize that a word we assume to have recognized does not have a semantic fit in the particular sentence context [8]. Detecting such semantic incongruity has also been studied in the context of humor studies [1] since incongruity and incongruity resolution are important concepts in humor theory [6]. Obviously, in game applications it is important to be able to measure brain signals, such as the EEG measurable N400-like signals, that are related to surprise.

3 Games That Employ BCI

In the previous section we mentioned various ways in which BCI can be employed in games. In research and demonstration contexts there are many attempts in which researchers 'play' with potential BCI game applications. Sometimes this is done for further developing ideas for research or medical applications. Game-like situations have also been designed to illustrate BCI research. Other reasons why researchers who aim at medical applications have looked at games are their potential for training environments for patients and to provide patients with entertainment facilities. Non-medical applications are also becoming important and we now see that game companies are starting to do their own research.

3.1 'Medical' Games

In neurofeedback applications, EEG data is made available to the user in a graphical or auditory way with the aim to train the user to perform in a desired way. Desirable behavior leads to immediate rewards, undesirable behavior is discouraged. Neurofeedback is usually based on asking the user to control slow (or ultra-slow) brainwave activity. Generally, slow brain activity is associated with relaxation, drowsiness, or sleep. Training brainwave activity may make it easier to enter a state of alertness, or, on the other hand, make it easier to enter a relaxed state. Treating mental disorders, for example, Attention-Deficit/Hyperactivity Disorder (ADHD) in children, has been a driving force for this kind of research. And, obviously, having an engaging training environment will help to keep children spending time on training.

In [31], neurofeedback experiments with Nintendo and PlayStation games are reported. In their 'neurofeedback-modulated' games the game pad or joy stick becomes easier to control when the children produce the right brainwaves. As another example, in [36] a training environment is introduced, again for ADHD treatment, where children have to steer a ball to a particular target using control of 'slow cortical potential' brain activity. BCI together with commercial video game software has also been used to allow epileptic teenagers to play games such as Space Invaders.

There are many small companies that now introduce neurofeedback games for non-medical applications on the market. We will return to these games in a later section.

3.2 'Research' Games

Simple and familiar video games have been given BCI control by researchers. The Berlin Brain-Computer Interface [14] has used motor imagery to play Pacman and Pong and similarly familiar games such as Tetris. Motor imagery applications exist for a First-Person Shooter game [30], navigating a ball in an environment where the ball has to jump over hills [24], navigating in Second Life [13] or other virtual environments, or controlling Google Earth [34]. Controlling the flippers of a virtual pinball machine by motor imagery also seems to be a promising application. A BCI game with brain activity related to real (finger) movements has been investigated in [18]. Externally evoked potentials have also been used in game-like implementations. Already in 1977 we saw the use of visually evoked potentials allowing the user to navigate in a maze [37]. Other examples are the control of a flight simulator [22] or the MindBalance game [16] where the user has to keep a tight-rope walker in balance. Some games that exploit more global brain activity have also been introduced. Well-known examples in this category are games where the gamer is asked to control the movements of a ball, either on a table or in a virtual environment. Brainball is one of them. In this game, gamers have to control a ball on the table through their state of relaxation [12]. A similar game [19] uses both relaxation and stress related activity. In the same category we find games where the gamer is asked to control a tight-rope walker, similar to the tight-rope walker of [16], but now by controlling left and right hemisphere brain activity [35]. More examples can be found in the literature.

A probably useful observation, and we will return to it in section 4, is that in many of these primitive games, we have visually rich 2D, 3D, or virtual reality environments, and moreover, there were experiments that included the use of head-mounted devices (HMDs). Rather than finding a decrease in performance of the gamer, it was found that such environments were stimulating and engaging, resulting in a better performance. This can be concluded from experiments that involved the use of ERPs, in particular the use of P300 (see [2] and [3]), the use of VEPs, and the use of motor imagery [17] Experiments in such visually rich environments also made clear that VEPs can be used for multiple directional controls [21].

3.3 Commercial Game Environments: Controlling the Game

All of the examples in the previous section concern game ideas that have, for various reasons, been found useful in a research context. As has become clear from the short descriptions, in all these examples we have one type of brain signals that are used for one type of control and mostly there is one object that has to be controlled. A similar observation can nowadays be made for the early companies that have attempted to introduce BCI in game products, either for entertainment or for medical and health purposes. For example, there is a commercial variant of the Brainball game, meant to be used in technology exhibitions and museums, and there are now 'commercial' games that aim at monitoring and influencing the brain state of ADHD children.

More recently, however, we see large software companies such as IBM and Microsoft, large console game companies such as Sony and Nintendo, and smaller specialized companies such as Emotiv, NeuroSky, and OCZ entering and defining a (future) market for commercial BCI games and other non-medical applications. In particular (still) small companies such as Emotiv and NeuroSky aim at developing games that are more interesting and therefore more engaging than the 'one-trick' games mentioned above. Apart from having to aim at commercial success, and apart from having to obey technological constraints, a BCI game designer does not have to take into consideration the limitations of an ALS patient, limitations of someone who has to control a prosthetic device, or limitations associated with military applications.

What kinds of game applications can be expected from commercial game companies? Obviously, there are the neurofeedback games that aim at training a patient or a healthy user to perform better on certain mental activities. We will return to them in the next section. Maybe more interesting are companies that aim at controlling a game by brainwaves. 'Passive' brain activity that is present because of the (multimodal) perception of events in the environment can be used to adapt the game to the mental state associated with this activity. 'Active' brain activity, for example motor imagery, allows the user to control a game: for example, making decisions about actions his or her avatar has to perform in the game environment.

A demonstration game developed by Emotiv [7] asks the gamer to rebuild Stonehenge. By motor imagery, using a wireless headset, the gamer can push, rotate and lift giant stones in a 3D environment until the desired stone structure has been obtained. A next version is under development by the well-known game company Demiurge. In this game, mood, facial expressions, mental tasks and head movements are input modalities. Fourteen electrodes are positioned on the head with a futuristic looking headset. Head movements are measured with a built-in dual-axis gyroscope. In the game the gamer is a student of mental martial arts that can walk around in a virtual world and who learns how to manipulate objects in the world with thought commands and facial expressions (scare away an evil spirit). According to the affective state of the gamer the environment can be adapted, for example, colors can be changed, or the difficulty of the game tasks can be tailored to this state. Mapping between mental tasks and the thought commands is done during a short training phase. One issue that may pop up with these kinds of games is how to remember the mental tasks and perform them in a consistent way. In the case of movements it may help to actually perform the corresponding movements.

Other companies that work on these next-generation video games are Hitachi, EmSense and NeuroSky. The latter company's headset has only one electrode. NeuroSky is also looking at BCI controlled games for mobile phones. NeuroSky partners with Sega Toys. Games that are developed use the mouse for directional movement and BCI (levels of focus and relaxation) to manipulate objects. In a multiplayer version, a player can throw objects to other players.

3.4 Commercial Game Environments: Neurofeedback Games

People may have fun playing simple games such as Pacman, Space Invaders, Tetris, a virtual pinball machine, or similar brain-controlled games. From a commercial point of view, there is a growing market for these so-called 'casual' games, where a user interacts with his or her PDA, mobile phone, notebook or PC to enter and get involved in games that employ neurofeedback. These games are meant to train healthy users to control their brainwaves in order to get better performance. For example, they can be used in attention management training, which can be useful for professionals such as pilots or crisis managers, for activities such as driving, and for sportsmen preparing for their performance. While for some situations it is useful to enter a state of so-called 'absorbed attention' (for example an athlete preparing for a high jump), in other situations too much focus or 'attentional tunneling' may lead to hazardous situations. Consider for example a pilot who, in a stress situation, loses awareness of the global situation. Especially when looking at sports where concentration and relaxation are extremely important, like darts, golf, and archery, we can expect attention from companies that are developing neurofeedback games. And indeed, for some of these sports such training games have already been developed.

There are many games that ask a gamer for qualities similar to those that are needed for real-life professions and activities. In particular this is true when such activities have been made part of virtual reality simulation environments. People find it fun to perform in a car or flight simulator, compete with others during a virtual golf game, and improve their performance by whatever the simulation environment offers them, including auditory or visual aids that aim at training the control of their attention and other aspects of the quality of their performance. But also in the more violent individual and multi-player video games these issues are important and there are many gamers willing to improve their performance by implicit and natural neurofeedback during their game playing. While playing they unconsciously train the desired brain activity that will allow them to perform better in real life in the future.

Looking at the future of neurofeedback-modulated games, Pope and Palsson [31] argue that "Entertaining games that incorporate biofeedback in the background may offer a palatable and effective way to systematically guide the cerebral rewiring occurring during prolonged video game playing towards fostering creativity, concentration skills, precision motor skills, and other valuable abilities."

4   Turn Shortcomings into Challenges

In medical BCI applications we are looking at improving imperfect communication and bodily skills of patients by using technological tools in which BCI knowledge is incorporated. Certainly, there is no need to change this viewpoint when we want to look at non-medical and, in particular, game applications for 'abled' users. As mentioned in the introduction, an abled person will also meet situations where only part of his or her available skills can be used and where an added communication, movement or control modality would be helpful. Moreover, having knowledge about the mental state of the user allows the application to adapt to it, leading to better performance. But, the applications can be designed in such a way that the user can always enter a built-in non-BCI mode where he or she uses the more traditional modalities for control and interaction.

Game designers have even more freedom. They can translate shortcomings in current BCI technology in challenges that need to be solved by a gamer and in decision moments that explicitly require a gamer to issue BCI commands, whether it is motor imagery, externally evoked potentials or by control of global brain activity. In game applications we can be satisfied with far from perfect 'solutions' since the game can be adapted to state-of-the-art theory and technology and nevertheless be interesting and challenging. Or maybe, because of such constraints, be even more challenging than when offering a gamer perfect BCI technology. We can have perfect game applications with imperfect technology.

Until now, in the academic BCI research community there are no or only modest research attempts to integrate BCI in multimodal interaction research and applications. Attempts to do so do not help ALS, Parkinson or epileptic patients. Now that BCI is becoming part of computer science and human-computer interaction research, multimodality is becoming an issue and there is both a 'technology push' to, and a 'technology pull' from potential application areas outside the medical domain. Nevertheless there is a controversy. Academics tell the industry that there are still lots of fundamental research issues that have to be investigated before a game with embedded intelligence and autonomous game agents can be developed and designed. Industry knows that imperfect interaction models and imperfect interaction technologies do not prevent the development of highly successful games.

As an example, consider the design of an air-traffic control system, the design of a remote surgery system, or the design of a crisis management system. Such systems aim at preventing, avoiding and managing surprise situations. The aim is to have a system that, as far as is possible, protects the user from making wrong decisions. In a game the situation is different. Games are meant to provide the gamer with challenges. A game designer should take care that gamers can match their skills with these challenges and they should take care that skills that are improved during game playing will meet new and higher challenges. Game design is challenging the gamer in such a way that the gamer remains convinced that his or her skills can match these challenges or can be sufficiently improved by spending more time on trying to meet these challenges. The game, the game environment, the game characters or other users in a multiplayer situation are opponents that try to force you to make wrong decisions rather than support you to make right decisions. A gamer is also allowed to lose.

Another view on the use of BCI in games is the following. Imagine a game situation where you have to fight an enemy. For example, you are engaged in a sword fight. You may try to kill your opponent. If you are not successful in your first attempt, try a second time. In a BCI game situation it is quite natural that BCI control is not immediately successful. You have to try a second time, for example by imaging a certain movement, making your opponent weaker by issuing a blow, or a third time, making your opponent even weaker, before, finally, in a fourth attempt, you are successful in eliminating your opponent. This is a rather acceptable and natural sequence of events in a game environment, but this is also a rather undesirable and unacceptable sequence of events in an air-traffic control or a crisis management situation. The example shows that in games a game designer can create situations where BCI signals can be used in a natural game-life-like way, and not necessarily a real-life-like way. In games there is no need to be realistic or supportive, as long as the events and their control are believable in the game context and environment.

As mentioned before, in game environments BCI can complement other modalities rather than replace other modalities. Usually, in BCI experiments the researchers try to prevent and get rid of EMG (ElectroMyoGraphy) activity. This is electrical activity caused by muscle movement and participants of these experiments are asked or forced not to move. This kind of research is necessary and useful from the point of view of BCI research and applications where a patient is not able to move. When, however, we look at applications for healthy users it is also useful to investigate how EMG activity and information from other modalities can help to get a more complete picture of the user, his or her intentions in controlling a game situation, and his or her affective state. Moreover, unlike an application for a patient such as to recover control of muscles, to control a prosthesis or to communicate by thoughts alone with the outside world, for games we have the freedom to combine approaches such as motor imagery with real movements, or to use brain activity that is associated with real movements to control an application. In our experiments [15] we found support for the hypothesis that actual movement as modality in BCI games is better recognizable than imagined movements. It does not necessarily mean that people prefer actual movements, but this is of course a matter of game design.

In game situations we can also expect and stimulate measurable brain activity at particular moments. The game designer can design situations that require interaction between gamer and artificially evoked and event-related potentials. These evoked potentials can give a gamer control of situations and events, which can be purposely introduced when designing the game. Evoked potentials can be used to let the gamer make a decision based on events explicitly asking for attention. To use event-related potentials the gamer does not have to be in control. Naturally occurring events in the game or the actions of the gamer's opponent evoke surprise, anticipation and response reactions of the gamer and they can be employed in the game design too.

The main message of this section is that game designers have the freedom to combine different BCI and other modalities and that they have the freedom to do, from a BCI point of view, very unusual things. Until now this freedom has not been explored. In addition, apart from the multimodal approach, embedding BCI in contexts where artificial intelligence (reasoning, common sense knowledge, knowledge of user goals and preferences) is another road to follow for designing BCI games. We are certainly aware of the problems that are associated with distinguishing and fusing the signals that come from different sources. But, this does not change our view that what are considered to be shortcomings of BCI in traditional BCI applications can be seen as game challenges from a game design point of view.

5 Developments and Challenges

In previous sections we have already mentioned many of the problems that prevent the design of full-fledged BCI games now and in the near future. In this section we mention further problems that need technical solutions or that need to be circumvented in one or other way by clever game design.

5.1 Multimodal Interaction and Artefacts

BCI game research requires the integration of theoretical research on multimodal interaction, intention detection, affective state and visual attention monitoring, and on-line motion control, but also the design of several prototypes. These may be games for amusement, but also (serious) games for education, training and simulation.

There are many challenges unique to BCI applications in Human Computer Interaction. One challenge is the inevitable presence of artifacts deemed to be "noise" in traditional BCI explorations. In our applications, we cannot typically control the environment as tightly as in many medical applications (e.g. we do not want to be gaming in a Faraday Cage) nor are we willing to restrict the actions of the user (e.g. tie them down so they do not move). Hence, we have to devise techniques that either sidestep these issues, or better yet, leverage the additional information available. A particular point of interest is how to fuse information coming from more traditional input modalities (e.g. touch, speech, gesture) with information obtained from the brain. Consciously produced brain signals need to be distinguished from other brain activity. This other brain activity is produced because the gamer is involved in other activities at the same time (responses to visual, auditory and tactile channels), because of physiological responses, because of movements needed to play the game because of natural movements beyond or almost beyond control of the gamer.

5.2 Measuring Brain Signals

In current BCI research EEG caps with 32 to 256 electrodes are used to measure brain activity. EEG is combined with EMG techniques as well, where the latter is about electrical activity that is obtained from face and body muscle movements. Rather than being happy with additional sources of information and including them in their research, BCI researchers often aim at pure mental BCI interfaces and consider the influence of muscle and eye movements as artifacts that have to be discounted.

We cannot expect that current EEG caps used in research (Figure 3a) will become part of a gamer's equipment. In addition to being expensive, for games we will not need up to 256 electrodes measuring activity from various parts of the brain. Moreover, setting up such a BCI session takes too much time, requiring the use of conductive gel, careful positioning of electrodes, and clean-up afterwards. But, both in research and commercial environments we see the development of 'dry-cap' technology. Experiments that investigate the consequences of using less electrodes and using a 'dry-cap' are reported in [27]. They report placing six electrodes at sites above the motor cortex and achieving 70 percent of full-gel-cap BCI performance.

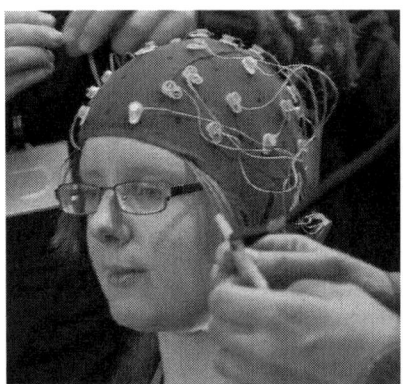 

Fig. 3. a) BioSemi EEG cap for research, and b) Emotiv EEG headset for gaming [7]

Clearly, game companies are interested in this technology. They are also aware of the effect of a beautifully designed cap on gamers and the game community. Hence, can a cap be designed to have similar effects as owning and using an iPod, an iPhone, or a Wii? Or, for more business-like applications, using a wearable microphone or teleconferencing equipment? The effect that design has on user acceptance should not be underestimated. The interest in the BCI company Emotiv is certainly due to the futuristic headset they offer (Figure 3b). It resembles a headset used in the cult movie Strange Days that is used to access earlier recorded memories and emotions. In such a headset other features that are interesting for gamers can be included. As mentioned earlier, the Emotiv headset also measures head movements that can provide input to the game. Adding a microphone to record speech commands is another possibility.

An alternative for EEG measuring is fNIR (functional Near-Infrared imaging). Changes in brain activity are accompanied with blood flow. By firing near-infrared rays into the brain and converting the reflected light to electrical signals changes in oxygen concentrations in the blood can be measured allowing one to draw conclusions about the brain activity in various regions of the brain. NIRS techniques have been used to power switches on and off by doing mental arithmetic. At this moment wearing the equipment required to do NIR measuring is certainly far away from applications outside the research laboratory. But also here, with an iPod and Wii user market in mind, unexpected things may happen.

Measuring brain signals from outside the scalp using EEG is far from ideal. Placing sensors directly on the brain would provide stronger and more accurate signals but this would require surgery. Nevertheless, we can expect that in the future this and more invasive surgery will be performed to extend human capabilities for non-medical applications, including games and entertainment.

5.3 Training and Illiteracy

Issues that should be mentioned when we look at measuring brain activity in order to use it to give commands to the game environment are training and BCI illiteracy. Looking at training, in research environments, during a training period, both the user and the system learns. The particular EEG patterns that are produced by one particular user are training material for the BCI system. Users, on the other hand, learn to modulate their brain patterns, by getting feedback about their performance, allowing the application to distinguish them and to map them on the commands that control the application. Users and BCI adapt to each other [11,27]. Users can be asked to perform different mental tasks in order to generate various brain commands. Although the BCI environment can help in strongly suggesting such mental tasks, it cannot fully control the way a user performs a task. In commercial games we sometimes see that up to thirteen game control commands have to be distinguished.

Rather than go through a training and calibration period that allows a BCI game application to get acquinted with a particular user, we foresee the development of game applications where training becomes part of the game, requiring the game designer to introduce game elements and game levels that require BCI activity to handle challenging game situations. Adding BCI to games fits in the current developments to exploit games that use all kinds of sensors and algorithms that know about speech characteristics, about facial expressions, gestures, location and identity of the gamer and physiological processes that can be used to adapt or control the game. Similar observations have been made for so-called exertion interfaces [23] where users are assumed to be engaged in physical activity and where it is suggested to include a 'warming-up' in the sports/fitness/exercise environment [32].

From research experiments we can learn that not all BCI users are able to perform at the same level. That is, not all users in these experiments are able to imagine movements or perform other mental tasks in such a way that a BCI system is able to detect them in a sufficiently reliable way, that is, allowing the system to interpret a particular and measurable brain activity and converting it into a particular command that affects the environment and its inhabitants. Performance is highly subject-specific. In [27] experiments are reported on motor imagery where 20 percent of the subjects show no effective motor imagery and where another 30 percent exhibit (too) slow (a) performance.

6   Conclusions

In this paper we surveyed the 'state of the art' of brain-computer interfacing in the context of games and entertainment. It should be clear from this survey that 'games and BCI' is an exciting topic. There are various possibilities in game design to provide a gamer with ways to control game situations using BCI and to add to other input modalities in order to modify them to control game situations. Games can be designed in such a way that game control by thought is possible and that game environments know how to adapt to cognitive and motoric skills of the gamer. Game companies involved in these activities (Microsoft, Emotiv, Hitachi, Sega Toys, IBM, etc.) are keen on filing patents and are very reluctant to share their ways of thinking about the BCI modality in games. From this survey it should be clear that at this moment there are many unexplored roads of research on the role of BCI in game research and game design.

Acknowledgments. This work has been supported by funding from the Dutch National SmartMix project BrainGain [28] on BCI (Ministry of Economic Affairs) and the GATE project, funded by the Netherlands Organization for Scientific Research (NWO) and the Netherlands ICT Research and Innovation Authority (ICT Regie). We made use of our earlier work [29,33] to compile the survey on BCI games that is part of this paper.

References

1. Bartolo, A., Benuzzi, F., Nocetti, L., Baraldi, P., Nichelli, P.: Humor Comprehension and Appreciation: An fMRI Study. Journal of Cognitive Neuroscience 18(11), 1789–1798 (2006)
2. Bayliss, J.D.: Use of the evoked potential p3 component for control in a virtual apartment. IEEE Transactions on Neural Systems and Rehabilitation Engineering 11(2), 113–116 (2003)
3. Bayliss, J.D., Inverso, S.A., Tentler, A.: Changing the P300 Brain Computer Interface. CyberPsychology & Behavior 7(6), 694–704 (2004)
4. Cairns, P., Cox, A., Berthouze, N., Dhoparee, S., Jennett, C.: Quantifying the experience of immersion in games. In: Cognitive Science of Games and Gameplay workshop at Cognitive Science (2006)
5. Csikszentmihalyi, M.: Flow: the psychology of optimal experience. Harper & Row, New York (1990)
6. De Mey, T.: Tales of the Unexpected: Incongruity-Resolution in Humor Comprehension, Scientific Discovery and Thought Experimentation. Logic and Logical Philosophy 14, 69–88 (2005)
7. Emotiv Systems, http://www.emotiv.com
8. FitzPatrick, I.: Effects of sentence context in L2 natural speech comprehension. Proc. of the Cognitive Neuroscience Master of the Radbout University 2(1), 43–56 (2007)
9. FUGA, Fun of Gaming: Measuring the Human Experience of Media Enjoyment. Project funded by the European Commission under the 6th Framework Programme: New and Emerging Science and Technology (NEST) (2006), http://project.hkkk.fi/fuga/

10. Gilleade, K., Dix, A., Allanson, J.: Affective Videogames and Modes of Affective Gaming: Assist Me, Challenge Me, Emote Me. In: Proc. DIGRA 2005 (2005)
11. Guger, C., Edlinger, G.: How many people can control a brain-computer interface (BCI)? In: Nijholt, A., Tan, D. (eds.) Proc. BrainPlay 2007: Playing with Your Brain. Workshop Intern. Conf. on Advances in Computer Entertainment Technology (ACE 2007), pp. 29–32 (2007)
12. Hjelm, S.I., Browall, C.: Brainball – Using brain activity for cool competition. In: Proceedings of NordiCHI (2000)
13. KEIO, http://www.bme.bio.keio.ac.jp/eng/01news/
14. Krepki, R., Blankertz, B., Curio, G., Müller, K.R.: The Berlin Brain-Computer Interface (BBCI)–towards a new communication channel for online control in gaming applications. Multimedia Tools and Applications 33(1), 73–90 (2007)
15. van de Laar, B., et al.: Actual and imagined movemnet in BCI gaming: Actually different? Manuscript, Human Media Interaction group, University of Twente, the Netherlands (December 2008)
16. Lalor, E., Kelly, S.P., Finucane, C., Burke, R., Reilly, R.B., McDarby, G.: Brain Computer Interface based on the Steady-State VEP for Immersive Gaming Control. In: Graz BCI Workshop (2004)
17. Leeb, R., Scherer, R., Lee, F., Bischof, H., Pfurtscheller, G.: Navigation in virtual environments through motor imagery. In: 9th Computer Vision Winter Workshop, CVWW, vol. 4, pp. 99–108 (2004)
18. Lehtonen, J., Jylanki, P., Kauhanen, L., Sams, M.: Online Classification of Single EEG Trials During Finger Movements. IEEE Trans. on Biomed. Eng. 55(2 Pt 1), 713–720 (2008)
19. Lin, T.A., John, L.R.: Quantifying Mental Relaxation with EEG for use in Computer Games. In: International Conference on Internet Computing, pp. 409–415 (2006)
20. Lotze, M., Halsband, U.: Motor imagery. Journal of Physiology 99(4-6), 386–395 (2006)
21. Martincz, P., Bakardjian, H., Cichocki, A.: Fully online multi-command brain-computer interface with visual neurofeedback using SSVEP paradigm. Computational Intelligence and Neuroscience 2007(1), 13 (2007)
22. Middendorf, M., McMillan, G., Calhoun, G., Jones, K.S.: Brain-computer interfaces based on the steady-state visual-evoked response. IEEE Transactions on Rehabilitation Engineering 8(2), 211–214 (2000)
23. Müller, F., Agamanolis, S., Picard, R.: Exertion Interfaces: Sports over a Distance for Social Bonding and Fun. In: ACM Conference on Human Factors in Computing Systems (CHI 2003), pp. 561–568 (2003)
24. Müller-Putz, G., Scherer, R., Pfurtschellcr, G.: Game-like Training to Learn Single Switch Operated Neuroprosthetic Control. In: BRAINPLAY 2007 Brain-Computer Interfaces and Games Workshop at ACE (Advances in Computer Entertainment) (2007)
25. Nijholt, A.: Playing and Cheating in Ambient Entertainment. In: Ma, L., Rauterberg, M., Nakatsu, R. (eds.) ICEC 2007. LNCS, vol. 4740, pp. 415–420. Springer, Heidelberg (2007)
26. Nijholt, A., Tan, D., Allison, B., del, J., Millán, R., Graimann, B., Jackson, M.M.: Brain-Computer Interfaces for HCI and Games. In: Proceedings ACM CHI 2008: Art. Science. Balance, Florence, Italy, pp. 3925–3928. ACM Publishing, NY (2008)
27. Nijholt, A., Tan, D., Pfurtscheller, G., Brunner, C., Del, J., Millan, R., Allison, B., Graimann, B., Popescu, F., Blankertz, B., Müller, K.-R.: Brain-Computer Interfacing for Intelligent Systems. IEEE Intelligent Systems, pp. 76-83 (May/June 2008)

28. Nijholt, A., van Erp, J., Heylen, D.K.J.: BrainGain: BCI for HCI and Games. In: Proceedings AISB Symposium Brain Computer Interfaces and Human Computer Interaction: A Convergence of Ideas, Aberdeen, UK, April 2, pp. 32–35 (2008)
29. Oude Bos, D.: BrainBasher: A multi-modal BCI game for research and demonstration. Masters Thesis, HMI, University of Twente, the Netherlands (September 2008)
30. Pineda, J.A., Silverman, D.S., Vankov, A., Hestenes, J.: Learning to control brain rhythms: making a brain-computer interface possible. IEEE Transactions on neural systems and rehabilitation engineering 11(2), 181–184 (2003)
31. Pope, A.T., Palsson, O.S.: Helping Video Games, Rewire our Minds (manuscript, 2004)
32. Powell, V.: CHI 2008 Exertion Interfaces: A Flexible approach. In: Exertion Workshop at CHI 2008, Florence (2008)
33. Reuderink, B.: Games and Brain-Computer Interfaces: The State of the Art. WP2 BrainGain Deliverable, HMI, University of Twente (September 2008)
34. Scherer, R., Schloegl, A., Lee, F., Bischof, H., Jan'sa, J., Pfurtscheller, G.: The Self-Paced Graz Brain-Computer Interface: Methods and Applications. Computational Intelligence and Neuroscience, Article ID 79826 (2007)
35. Shim, B.-S., Lee, S.-W., Shin, J.-H.: Implementation of a 3-Dimensional Game for developing balanced Brainwave. In: 5th ACIS International Conference on Software Engineering Research, Management & Applications (SERA 2007), pp. 751–758 (August 2007)
36. Strehl, U., Leins, U., Goth, G., Klinger, C., Hinterberger, T., Birbaumer, N.: Self-regulation of Slow Cortical Potentials: A New Treatment for Children With Attention-Deficit/Hyperactivity Disorder, Pediatrics (2006)
37. Vidal, J.J.: Real-time detection of brain events in EEG. Proceedings of the IEEE 65(5), 633–641 (1977)

Immersion in Movement-Based Interaction

Marco Pasch[1,3], Nadia Bianchi-Berthouze[2], Betsy van Dijk[3],
and Anton Nijholt[3]

[1] Faculty of Informatics, University of Lugano,
via Buffi 13, CH-6900 Lugano
marco.pasch@lu.unisi.ch
[2] UCL Interaction Centre, University College London,
Gower Street, London WC1E 6BT, UK
n.berthouze@ucl.ac.uk
[3] Human Media Interaction, University of Twente,
P.O. Box 217, NL-7500 AE Enschede
{bvdijk,anijholt}@ewi.utwente.nl

Abstract. The phenomenon of immersing oneself into virtual environments has been established widely. Yet to date (to our best knowledge) the physical dimension has been neglected in studies investigating immersion in Human-Computer Interaction (HCI). In movement-based interaction the user controls the interface via body movements, e.g. direct manipulation of screen objects via gestures or using a handheld controller as a virtual tennis racket. It has been shown that physical activity affects arousal and that movement-based controllers can facilitate engagement in the context of video games. This paper aims at identifying movement features that influence immersion. We first give a brief survey on immersion and movement-based interfaces. Then, we report results from an interview study that investigates how users experience their body movements when interacting with movement-based interfaces. Based on the interviews, we identify four movement-specific features. We recommend them as candidates for further investigation.

Keywords: Movement-based interaction, exertion, immersion, engagement, flow, games, entertainment.

1 Introduction

Moving our bodies for communication and interaction comes natural to us. We rely on our bodies to access our environment. In fact, it has been said, "all human actions (including cognition) are embodied actions" ([22], p. 692). Movement-based interfaces enable their users to employ active body movements as interaction modality. As such they can offer a more natural and richer interaction than traditional interaction techniques such as mouse and keyboard.

In particular in an entertainment context, exertion interfaces are becoming more and more popular. Wide-spread video game consoles such as Nintendo Wii, Sony Eye-Toy or Konami Dance Dance Revolution elicit exertion from

A. Nijholt, D. Reidsma, and H. Hondorp (Eds.): INTETAIN 2009, LNICST 9, pp. 169–180, 2009.
© ICST Institute for Computer Sciences, Social Informatics and Telecommunications Engineering 2009

their users. The Wii uses handheld controllers that the user has to wave and swing. The Eye-Toy captures the user's movements with a camera. To play Dance Dance Revolution the user has to jump and dance on a sensor mat. Apart from apparently being very entertaining, these games also offer a healthier interaction than traditional video games, by which we refer to video games that are steered via joystick, mouse and keyboard. These games promote sedentary behaviour and are seen as contributors to the growing obesity epidemic [10,17]. Initial studies [16,21] show that physical activity during gameplay increases energy expenditure significantly compared to sedentary games. They conclude that some exertion games exceed the cut-off for moderate intensity physical activity and are thus fit to contribute to recommended amounts of physical activity. But also ergonomic issues arise from this new type of interaction. Injuries and accidents related to exertion interfaces are described in [3,8]. Accidents are often attributed to the fact that users get too immersed and forget the real world around them. In exertion games, injuries like overstraining can be caused by the fact that players do not see their gaming as sport and omit stretching or by playing for too long.

In this paper we discuss movement-based interfaces in the context of immersion. Immersing oneself into a virtual environment has been described as a highly pleasurable experience. In HCI research, models of immersion have been put forward that describe different types [11] and levels [4] of immersion that users can experience during interaction. Yet, there is no account for body movements in these models. We speculate that physical activity has an influence on immersion, based on findings in [2]. Here, it has been shown that body movements as an input device do not only increase video gamers" levels of engagement, but also have an influence on the way a gamer gets engaged.

It is thus the aim of this paper to investigate if users immerse themselves differently in movement-based interaction and, if this is the case, which movement-specific features influence immersion. As there is only little existing knowledge on the relation between physical activity and immersion, our approach is an exploratory one: We interview users on their experiences with movement-based interfaces. Our aim is identifying features for further, quantitative investigation. A further goal is to point designers of movement-based interfaces to critical issues. For instance, how to make a movement-based game even more engaging for users and make them interact longer with the game and by that be physically active for longer periods of time.

The paper is structured as follows. We begin with a brief discussion of movement-based interfaces. This is followed by a description of the phenomenon of immersion and its modeling in HCI research. Our interview study and its outcomes are presented next. We then discuss the outcomes in the light of the existing immersion models. The paper concludes with an assessment of the current results and a call for further investigation.

2 Movement-Based Interaction

Movement-based interfaces enable the user to interact by means of movements of the body. Here, the user is freed from the need to relay commands via mouse and keyboard. Instead, active body movements are employed, e.g., playing tennis with a hand-held controller that the user has to swing like a real tennis racket. Since communicating and interacting via body movements (e.g., nonverbal communication) comes natural to us, we can speak of a more natural way of interaction (given that the movements required are resembling movements from real life).

A number of different types of movement-based interfaces have been proposed. Judging them by the intensity of movement they require, we can distinguish a wide range of approaches. Only minuscule movements are required by interfaces that use eye movements [20] as input modality. Other movement-based interfaces use moderate arm movements as input modality. Such approaches have been in particular employed in virtual environments. By using their hands, users can select objects by pointing at them and e.g. relocate them by moving their hand or rotate them by twisting their hand. This type of interaction is a very natural one, as it closely resembles the manipulation of objects in real life. The upper end of the intensity scale is represented by interfaces that require significant physical activity and that have been dubbed exertion interfaces [24]. Exertion interfaces can be found mainly in an entertainment and games context. The first examples of exertion interfaces were exercise devices like treadmills and exercise bikes that were connected to entertainment equipment in order to entertain and distract the user from strain.

In this paper we focus on exertion interfaces. They require high amounts of movements and we are specifically interested in the influence of body movements on immersion. Once we establish movement specific items we can check if they also apply to areas where only small amounts of movements are necessary.

Immense potential to increase the efficiency but also the user experience lies in making movement-based interfaces 'intelligent'. Intelligent movement-based interfaces are able to sense the movements and possible exertion of the user in order to adapt to it. In task-oriented environments they can help raise the efficiency of task fulfillment, by offering task-sensitive support. In entertainment, intelligent interfaces can monitor the user's affective state and adapt the gameplay accordingly. As pointed out in [26], intelligent exertion interfaces should be persuasive, motivating, and rewarding.

A number of approaches have been presented for detecting, sensing, and interpreting physical activity and affective state of a user: In the ball game presented in [24], there is no direct sensing of body movements. Solely the outcome of the exertion, i.e. force and trajectory, are measured and used for the gameplay. A boxing interface using gesture recognition is described in [18,27].

In [12], three types of adaptive responses of intelligent movement-based systems are envisioned: First, the system offers assistance if the user is frustrated. Secondly, the level of challenge can be adapted when the user is bored or demotivated. This applies in particular in a gaming context [6]. Finally, emotional displays can be inserted into the interface to minimize negative emotions and reinforce positive emotions.

3   Immersion in HCI

Immersion is a term used widely to describe the user experience, in particular in an entertainment context. The following definition is quoted widely and has been described as the most accepted one [23]:

> "The experience of being transported to an elaborately simulated place is pleasurable in itself, regardless of the fantasy content. We refer to this experience as immersion. Immersion is a metaphorical term derived from the physical experience of being submerged in water. We seek the same feeling from a psychologically immersive experience that we do from a plunge in the ocean or swimming pool: the sensation of being surrounded by a completely other reality, as different as water is from air, that takes over all of our attention, our whole perceptual apparatus..." ([25], p. 98).

Before further investigating the nature of immersion we delineate similar concepts that are all too often used synonymously with immersion. Several authors adapted Csikszentmihalyi's [9] theory of flow to an HCI context: The Game-Flow model [30] maps components of flow theory to elements from game design literature. The authors report that the model in its current state is useful for evaluation of games but needs further development to inform the design of games. An important item of flow theory is the flow zone: A person is in the flow zone when the person's abilities are matched by a challenge. Too much challenge leads to frustration, too little challenge to boredom. In [6], the author recommends games to adapt to the users' skills in order to keep them in the flow zone.

Presence is another term that appears in the literature to describe the gaming experience. The term originates from studies into virtual reality and is often defined as "the feeling of being there" [19]. In [5] it is argued that presence in a virtual reality context corresponds to immersion in a gaming context. Similarly, Ermi and Mäyrä prefer the term immersion as "it more clearly connotes the mental processes involved in gameplay" ([11], p. 19). We follow this line of argumentation and see immersion as the appropriate term when speaking of user experience in an entertainment context.

In the existing literature on immersion, two models have been proposed that focus on different aspects of immersion. The first model we discuss in the following focuses on the intensity of immersion into a virtual environment, while the second distinguishes different types of immersion.

3.1   Levels of Immersion

In the study presented in [4], Brown and Cairns investigate the intensity of immersion in video games. From interview data with gamers regarding their experiences during gameplay the authors identify three distinct levels of immersion, labeled engagement, engrossment, and total immersion. For each level barriers exist that have to be overcome to reach the level. Figure 1 shows the three levels and their respective barriers.

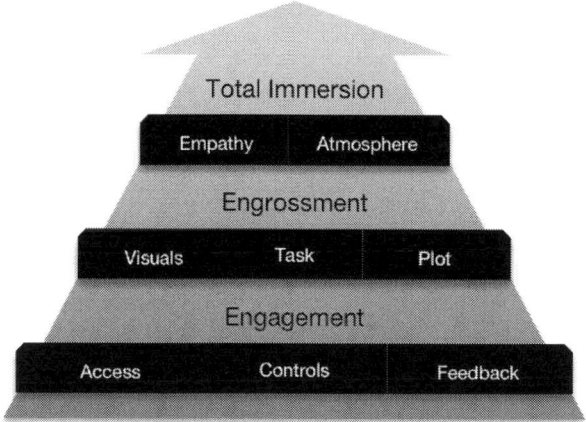

Fig. 1. Immersion Model of Brown and Cairns [4], own depiction. Barriers (shown in black) hinder the user from reaching (deeper) immersion.

Engagement is the first level of immersion. To reach it, gamers must first have access to a game. If gamers do not like a certain type or style of games, they will not even try to engage with it. So they must be willing to invest time, effort, and attention. In addition, controls and feedback must be provided: "Controls and feedback need to correspond in an appropriate manner so that the user can become an expert, at least at the main controls" ([4], p. 1298).

The barrier that has to be overcome to reach the second level, engrossment, is bad game construction, by which the authors refer to visuals, tasks, and plot. They point out that at this stage the gamers have already invested emotionally into the game and this makes them continue gaming.

Total immersion is the final level and it is described as being cut off from the world to an extent where the game is all that matters. Barriers to total immersion are a lack of empathy with game characters or a lack of feeling the atmosphere of the game. In a follow-up study [7], the stability of immersion is investigated. Here, the authors attempt to deliberately break the immersion of their test subjects and find that already low levels of immersion make subjects ignore drastic changes in the games behavior.

3.2   Types of Immersion

The second model is presented in [11] where the authors describe their investigation into different types of immersion, by interviewing gaming children and their parents. This way the authors identify three different types of immersion: sensory, challenge-based, and imaginative (SCI), from which they built the SCI-model of immersion, as shown in Figure 2. Sensory immersion refers to sensory information during gaming. Large screens and powerful sound are given as examples where sensory information of the real world is overpowered and the gamer entirely focuses on the game. Challenge-based immersion is described as most powerful when a balance between the abilities of the player and the challenge

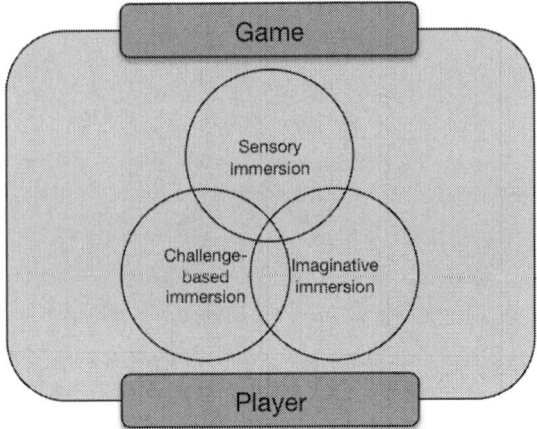

Fig. 2. Immersion Model of Ermi and Mäyrä [11], simplified. Three types of immersion are distinguished that can lead the user to immersive states: sensory, challenge-based, and imaginative immersion.

of the game is achieved and as such seems to correspond to the flow concept mentioned earlier. Finally, imaginative immersion happens when the player gets absorbed with the story line and identifies with the game characters.

Neither of the models contain movement-specific items. Yet we speculate that movement has an influence on immersion for several reasons: First, movement-based interfaces offer a more natural interaction as pointed out in the previous section. This should facilitate the experience of immersion, since users do not have to relay their commands via mouse or keyboard. In [2] it has been shown that body movements as an input device do not only increase video gamers" levels of engagement, but also have an influence on the way a gamer becomes engaged. Also, there is growing evidence that physical exercise increases mental well-being [13].

4   Movement-Based Interaction and Immersion

To investigate how users experience and interpret their interaction with movement-based systems we conduct an interview study. In the following we first present the setup of the study and then the movement-specific features that we can identify with the outcomes of the interviews.

4.1   Interview Study

To be able to compare the interview results we choose for one common interaction scenario as focus of our investigation. We choose the video game console Nintendo Wii as interaction platform, because it enjoys great commercial success and by this allows us to find interview subjects with sufficient familiarity to be able to reflect on their experiences. Four regular users of the Wii take part in this study.

A 20 minutes session of playing the Nintendo Wii Sports games primes the interviewees before the interview. The subjects are asked to play two different games on the Nintendo Wii, each for about 10 minutes. The particular games are changed for the different participants to avoid possible biases due to characteristics of a certain game. Still, in all sessions it is ensured that participants play one fast-paced game (boxing or tennis) and one slow-paced game (bowling, golf or baseball). We do this with the intention of asking about differences between the games later in the interview session, i.e., how the amount of physical activity and the type of movement may affect their gaming experience. The interview sessions take between 20 - 30 minutes and are held in a semi-structured style. Initial outcomes are used to update the interview guide for the following interviews.

The interviews are transcribed and analyzed using Grounded Theory [14,15] to identify relations between statements and establish concepts. In the following we present the outcomes of the interviews. To give the reader a better impression of general trends in the interview data, we show representative statements where they can help understanding.

4.2   Movement-Specific Features

Control appears to be a major factor in the gaming experience that includes body movements and is the first movement feature. How easy the game controls can be understood is an important point for the interviewees. The learning of the controls can be facilitated by appealing to the gamer's experience with similar activities in real life. It is seen as positive when gamers can transfer real world knowledge to learn the necessary movements for the game.

> "It is like tennis, I really like playing tennis in real life. And with the Wii I really like playing tennis, but you don't have as much as control, you can't move the players yourself. So I don't really see it as playing in real life. But then again bowling, it sort of involves the same movements [...] With the bowling you are doing the same as you would be doing in a bowling alley, except for the running. You know, the whole arm chucking movement. Whereas tennis, you're hitting a ball but you don't get that sort of feeling as you would have in real life." (i1)

> "The games I liked most so far are the sports games. I don't know why, but the principles are very simple, the controls are very easy and intuitive and its big fun to play with friends." (i2)

Interviewee 1 describes playing Wii tennis as an incomplete experience. It does not feel like playing real tennis, whereas she gets that feeling from Wii bowling. From the comments of interviewee 2 it seems that games that mimic real life activities should replicate the movements in those activities quite accurately. They should be "intuitive". For scenarios that mimic real life this is quite straight forward, but it also leads to the question of what determines the movements in a fantasy game with no reference to a real world scenario.

Another important concept can be described as *mapping of movements*. This refers to how well the gamers movements are replicated on screen and how the game reduces the high degrees of freedom of possible movements that a gamer can make.

> "... But I think with the technology that we have so far it might be limited how it can be really reflected. In boxing for example, what I said earlier, the type of punches that I can do are not really reflecting the diversity that I can have in real life." (i2)

The comment of interviewee 2 exemplifies this. He states that he is unsatisfied with the fact that the system does not replicate the movements exactly as he executes them. Still, he acknowledges that there are technical limitations involved. Interestingly, when it comes to the Wii Tennis game, interviewees are positive about the fact, that they cannot steer the movements of the avatar itself, but only execute the swings, stating that this is already difficult enough.

> "My movements were a bit larger and faster than the ones that the avatar was making. And sometimes the avatar was loosing its balance or something. It was leaning in one direction and I was in another and it was taking a while to catch up with me."(i4)

Feedback is another concept recurring in the data, though the term feedback itself is not mentioned explicitly by the interviewees. We interpret the statements in a way that the body itself is a source of feedback for the user. In the example above, interviewee 4 describes that he is physically leaning in one direction, whereas the avatar is still leaning in another direction. This discrepancy is of course also related to the feature "mapping of movements" that is described above. But it also shows that the positioning of the body is a source of feedback that at this moment is not in agreement with the visual feedback coming from the screen. Through the movements, the user receives additional feedback in form of proprioceptive feedback. In traditional video games sensory immersion is limited to sight, hearing and touch. These senses belong to the so-called exteroceptive senses (i.e. hearing, sight, smell, taste, and touch). The proprioceptive sense provides information about the relative position of neighboring parts of the body. It is for instance indispensable for moving without looking at where you go, e.g. walking in the dark (e.g., Sacks [29] reports of a patient that lost her proprioceptive sense and can only walk when she looks at her feet).

Challenge in movement-based interaction appears not only to have a mental, but also a physical component. The fourth feature that we can identify from the interview data is physical challenge. Frequently the interviewees state feeling physically challenged by the game and being exhausted afterwards.

5   Discussion

We discuss the results of our interview study by applying the four identified movement features to the two aforementioned models of immersion. The features

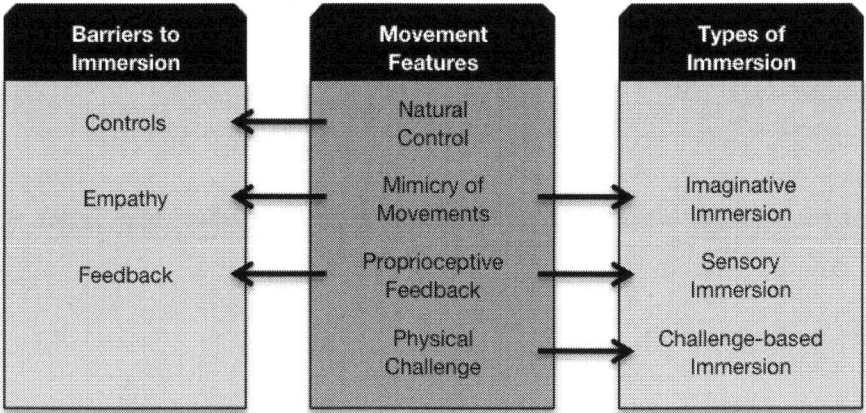

Fig. 3. Identified movement features and their potential influence on barriers to immersion [4] and types of immersion [11]

and the respective model constituents are shown in Figure 3 and we discuss each relation and how the respective feature can potentially influence immersion in the following.

Movement-based interfaces offer a more natural control than mouse, keyboard or joystick. Using body movements is often described as intuitive by the interviewees and also critized when it is not resembling movements in real life, as they expect. In Brown and Cairns' [4] model of immersion, control is a barrier to the first level of immersion. A more natural mode of control can lower this barrier and facilitate immersion, given that the interaction resembles movements in real life.

Mimicry of movements is the second movement feature identified from interview data. When the avatar copies the movements of the gamer, this appears to raise the level of empathy that is felt with an avatar. The following quotes exemplify this:

> "The boxing also felt more personal, because it feels like someone is hitting back at you, although that's not the case. So it's more emotionally engaging." (i3)

> "Keeping your arms up all the time and trying eagerly to punch and being in a situation where you can virtually be punched as well is maybe more stress than bowling." (i2)

Interviewee 3 reports about the Wii Boxing game that it "feels like someone is hitting back at you." Though he is immediately reflecting that this is not possible, there seems to be a strong emotional connection to the avatar. The same is true for interviewee 2 who finds a situation where he can be hit, though it is only virtual, as stressful. As shown in [1], mimicry can lead to increased empathy with a virtual character. In the case of movement-based video games like Wii Boxing, the avatar copies the movements of a gamer. It is conceivable that this mimicry of the gamer's movements leads to a stronger identification with the avatar, than in non movement-based games. Empathy is also a barrier to immersion and mimicry of movements appears to have the potential to lower this barrier. In terms of the different types of immersion it also seems to facilitate imaginative immersion.

Proprioceptive feedback is the third movement feature. With regards to the barriers to immersion this additional channel of immersion offers the potential of lowering the barrier feedback. When we look to the other model of immersion it appears to facilitate sensory immersion.

Physical challenge is our final movement feature. In sedentary games, challenge is usually put on mental capabilities of a gamer (Racing games and first-person shooter games form of course an exception here as they challenge the gamer's reflexes, but one might also categorize them as movement-based games). In movement-based interaction the physical challenge offers an additional channel of feeling challenged. Regarding the types of immersion model, it can open a new channel of challenge-based immersion.

6   Conclusions

We discussed the phenomenon of immersion in HCI and two models that focus on different types of immersion, respectively different levels of immersion and barriers to reach these. We also discussed movement-based interfaces, differentiated by the intensity of movement they require (or enable) and mentioned the potential of 'intelligent' movement-based interfaces that sense the movements of the user and adapt accordingly. With the results of an interview study on how users experience movements in their interaction with interactive systems we identified four features of movement-based interaction that potentially influence the constituents of the two immersion models: Natural control, mimicry of movements, proprioceptive feedback, and physical challenge.

For the moment, ensuring that the four mentioned movement features are considered, should help interaction designers to develop engaging movement-based user interfaces. Yet, still little is known on the relation between body movements as mode of interaction and immersion. The approach taken in this study is an exploratory one and the results are derived from a qualitative study. They represent trends that should be further investigated in quantitative studies. The current results hold a lot of potential for immersive, movement-based interfaces, but we need much more research on their validity and correct implementation. More knowledge on what makes an interface really engaging and fun to use, together with the potential of applications that can sense and interpret the state of the user (physical, affective, context, etc.) should result in a new generation of health promoting, challenging, supportive, and enjoyable interfaces.

Acknowledgments

The work described in this paper derives from the MSc thesis of Marco Pasch [28]. The thesis project was carried out at the UCL Interaction Centre in London, UK, with financial aid of the Twente Mobility Fund (TMF). Marco wishes to thank both institutions for making the project possible. The research of Nadia Berthouze has been supported by the Marie Curie International Re-Integration Grant "AffectME" (MIRG-CT-2006-046343). The research of Betsy van Dijk and Anton Nijholt has been supported by the GATE project, funded by the Netherlands Organization for Scientific Research and the Netherlands ICT Research and Innovation Authority (ICT Regie).

References

1. Bailenson, J.N., Yee, N.: Digital Chameleons. Automatic Assimilation of Nonverbal Gestures in Immersive Virtual Environments. Psychological Science 16(10), 814–819 (2005)
2. Bianchi-Berthouze, N., Kim, W.W., Darshak, P.: Does Body Movement Engage You More in Digital Game Play? and Why? In: Paiva, A.C.R., Prada, R., Picard, R.W. (eds.) ACII 2007. LNCS, vol. 4738, pp. 102–113. Springer, Heidelberg (2007)
3. Bonis, J.: Acute wiitis. New England Journal of Medicine 356(23), 2431–2432 (2007)
4. Brown, E., Cairns, P.: A grounded investigation of game immersion. In: Proceedings CHI 2004, pp. 1297–1300 (2004)
5. Cairns, P., Cox, A., Berthouze, N., Dhoparee, S., Jennett, C.: Quantifying the experience of immersion in games. Cognitive Science, Vancouver (2006)
6. Chen, J.: Flow in games (and everything else). Communications of the ACM 50(4), 31–34 (2007)
7. Cheng, K., Cairns, P.A.: Behaviour, realism and immersion in games. In: Proceedings CHI 2005, pp. 1272–1275 (2005)
8. Cowley, A.D., Minnaar, G.: Watch out for wii shoulder. British Medical Journal 336, 110 (2008)
9. Csikszentmihalyi, M.: Flow: the psychology of optimal experience. Harper and Row, New York (1990)
10. Epstein, L.H., Roemmich, J.N., Robinson, J.L., Paluch, R.A., Winiewicz, D.D., Fuerch, J.H., et al.: A Randomized Trial of the Effects of Reducing Television Viewing and Computer Use on Body Mass Index in Young Children. Archives of Pediatrics and Adolescent Medicine 162(3), 239–245 (2008)
11. Ermi, L., Mäyrä, F.: Fundamental components of the gameplay experience: analysing immersion. In: de Castell, S., Jenson, J. (eds.) Changing views: worlds in play, Selected Papers DiGRA conference, pp. 15–27 (2005)
12. Fairclough, S.H.: Fundamentals of physiological computing. Interacting with Computers (pre-print online version) (2008), doi:10.1016/j.intcom.2008.10.011
13. Fox, K.R.: The influence of physical activity on mental well-being. Public Health Nutrition 2(3a), 411–418 (1999)
14. Glaser, B., Strauss, A.: The discovery of grounded theory: Strategies for qualitative research. Aldine, New York (1967)
15. Goulding, C.: Grounded Theory: A Practical Guide for Management, Business and Market Researchers. SAGE, London (2002)
16. Graves, L.E., Ridgers, N.D., Stratton, G.: The contribution of upper limb and total body movement to adolescents' energy expenditure whilst playing Nintendo Wii. Eur. J. Appl. Physiol. (online version) (2008)
17. Hillier, A.: Childhood overweight and the built environment: making technology part of the solution rather than part of the problem. The ANNALS of the American Academy of Political and Social Science 615(1), 56–82 (2008)

18. Höysniemi, J., Aula, A., Auvinen, P., Hännikäinen, J., Hämäläinen, P.: Shadow boxer: a physically interactive fitness game. In: Third Nordic Conference on Human-Computer Interaction (NordiCHI 2004), vol. 82, pp. 389–392. ACM Press, New York (2004)
19. Ijsselsteijn, W., Riva, G.: Being there: the experience of presence in mediated environments. In: Riva, G., Davide, F., Ijsselsteijn, W. (eds.) Being There: Concepts, Effects and Measurements of User Presence in Synthetic Environments, pp. 3–16. IOS Press, Amsterdam (2003)
20. Jacob, R.K.J.: What you look at is what you get: Eye movement-based interaction techniques. In: Proceedings CHI 1990, pp. 11–18 (1990)
21. Lanningham-Foster, L., Jensen, T.B., Foster, R.C., Redmond, A.B., Walker, B.A., Heinz, D., et al.: Energy expenditure of sedentary screen time compared with active screen time for children. Pediatrics 118(6), 1831–1835 (2006)
22. Loke, L., Larssen, A.T., Robertson, T., Edwards, J.: Understanding movement for interaction design: frameworks and approaches. Personal and Ubiquitous Computing 11(8), 691–701 (2007)
23. McMahan, A.: Immersion, engagement and presence. The Video Game Theory Reader, pp. 67–86 (2003)
24. Mueller, F., Agamanolis, S., Picard, R.: Exertion Interfaces: Sports over a Distance for Social Bonding and Fun. In: Proceedings CHI 2003, pp. 561–568 (2003)
25. Murray, J.: Hamlet on the Holodeck: The Future of Narrative in Cyberspace. MIT Press, Cambridge (1997)
26. Nijholt, A., van Dijk, B., Reidsma, D.: Design of Experience and Flow in Movement-based Interaction. In: Proceedings Motion in Games. LNCS, vol. 5277, pp. 166–175. Springer, Berlin (2008)
27. Park, J.Y., Yi, J.H.: Gesture Recognition Based Interactive Boxing Game. International Journal of Information Technology 12(7), 36–44 (2006)
28. Pasch, M.: Bye-bye Couch Potato: Body Movement in the Gaming Experience. MSc Thesis, University of Twente, the Netherlands (2008)
29. Sacks, O.: The Man Who Mistook His Wife for a Hat, and Other Clinical Tales. Touchstone, New York (1998)
30. Sweetser, P., Wyeth, P.: Gameflow: a model for evaluating player enjoyment in games. Computers in Entertainment 3(3), 1–24 (2005)

Mood Swings: An Affective Interactive Art System

Leticia S.S. Bialoskorski[1,2], Joyce H.D.M. Westerink[1],
and Egon L. van den Broek[2]

[1] User Experience Group, Philips Research Europe
High Tech Campus 34, 5656 AE Eindhoven, The Netherlands
joyce.westerink@philips.com
[2] Center for Telematics and Information Technology (CTIT), University of Twente
P.O. Box 217, 7500 AE Enschede, The Netherlands
l.s.s.bialoskorski@alumnus.utwente.nl, vandenbroek@acm.org

Abstract. The progress in the field of affective computing enables the realization of affective consumer products, affective games, and affective art. This paper describes the affective interactive art system Mood Swings, which interprets and visualizes affect expressed by a person. Mood Swings is founded on the integration of a framework for affective movements and a color model. This enables Mood Swings to recognize affective movement characteristics as expressed by a person and display a color that matches the expressed emotion. With that, a unique interactive system is introduced, which can be considered as art, a game, or a combination of both.

Keywords: Mood Swings, affect, colors, movement, interaction.

1 Introduction

Emotions play a major role in judging (the use of) products [1]; for example we can feel great using a product that is not user friendly, but pleasing to the eye. Hence, next to usability other factors also play a role in user experience. In 2007 Sony introduced a photo camera with a "smile shutter" that recognizes whether or not the person in focus is smiling [2]. The camera can detect smiles, but is it possible to detect happiness? In the field of affective computing, systems are being designed that can recognize, interpret, and process emotions [3,4]. Picard states that computers need the ability to (at least) recognize and express affect to achieve natural and intelligent interaction with humans [4]. Interest shifts from intelligent to sensitive products.

In (interactive) art affective technologies can also be applied. An example is The Empathic Painting by Shugrina, Betke, and Collomosse [5]. The painting assesses the emotional state of a person through facial expression recognition, and uses this information to adjust the painting's color use and type of brushstroke. In this way the audience can experience digital art in a novel way.

Expanding research on this topic is interesting in order to acquire more insights in affective computing in different contexts. Therefore Mood Swings, an interactive light installation, was created. The installation consists of eight luminous orbs that

A. Nijholt, D. Reidsma, and H. Hondorp (Eds.): INTETAIN 2009, LNICST 9, pp. 181–186, 2009.
© ICST Institute for Computer Sciences, Social Informatics and Telecommunications Engineering 2009

Fig. 1. Mood Swings' luminous orbs in action

react on movement and take on certain colors with distinct movements, creating patterns of light. In this way users are challenged to express their emotion. Figure 1 depicts a person interacting with Mood Swings.

2 Related Work

Besides The Emphatic Painting, another example of affective interactive art is The Expressive Control. This system allows users to use their full-body for controlling the real-time generation of expressive visual and audio feedback. The system extracts expressive motion features from the user's full-body movements and gestures, and uses these parameters to project visuals on a screen and play audio [7].

The interactive art system Iamascope uses a video camera lens as the eye of a kaleidoscope and projects a kaleidoscopic image of the user onto a large screen. The image is also accompanied by musical notes, which are dependent on the speed and frequency of the participant's movements [8]. Special about this artwork is that it was used for a user experience evaluation. Costello, Muller, Amitani, and Edmonds aimed to find a methodology for recording and analyzing the experience of interactive art [8]. In examining the interaction with Iamascope, they discovered "The Trajectory of Interaction": common phases in interacting with interactive art. They labeled these phases: response, control, contemplation, belonging, and disengagement. In the response phase, the participants try to discover how the system works. In the control phase, the participants try to manipulate the device. In the contemplation phase, the participant reflects upon the meaning communicated by the artwork. The belonging phase is reached when a participant feels controlled by the installation itself. The disengagement phase is the final phase in the trajectory and encompasses the patterns of behavior that take place when the participant decides to stop interacting.

Evaluating this kind of interactive systems is common in Human Computer Interaction (HCI), but it is not common to test the interaction in art. This is because HCI evaluation strives to be objective, while in art it is all about the subjective opinion of a single observer [9]. Mood Swings was also evaluated to investigate whether the same phases as discovered by Costello et al. could be identified.

3   Mood Swings' Foundations

3.1   Emotions Expressed in Movement

The relationship between emotion and movement had been studied in many different ways, e.g. by looking at specific movements of certain body parts, or by studying qualities of body movement (e.g., speed and fluidity of movement). Laban, a famous dancer and choreographer, studied these qualities and developed a system to describe movement called: effort and shape. His description of movement features (weight, time, flow, space, and path) is used as a starting point in many researches [10, 11, 12].

In general, affect can be labeled in two manners; in discrete or dimensional emotions. Discrete emotions describe the affective state using basic emotions (e.g., fear, joy, sadness). A widely accepted approach of classifying emotions in a dimensional fashion is described by Russell [6]. He developed a circumplex model of affect that describes emotions in the two dimensions: valence (pleasure-displeasure) and arousal. In research by Lee, Park, and Nam [13] this model is transformed to be applicable to affective movements. They applied certain movement characteristics to the circumplex model by Russel, which led to the affective dimensions: velocity and smoothness (the regularity of a movement). These dimensions also appear to have a relationship to the features time and flow as described by Laban.

In the design of Mood Swings the model by Lee et al. [13] was incorporated. Arousal is related to the velocity of a movement, with slow movements linked to low arousal and fast movements linked to high arousal. Valence is related to the smoothness of a movement, with smooth movements being pleasant and jerky movements being unpleasant. Users interact with Mood Swings through moving the orbs. The orb's movement patterns are registered through an accelerometer placed inside the orb. Consequently, the orb is used to derive users' emotions.

3.2   Visualizing Emotion in Color

Mood Swings' feedback exists of colored light. Color is chosen because of the strong relation it can have with emotion. There is a reason why we can feel blue, become red with anger, or green with envy. Meaning is given to color due to evolution, personal experience, and cultural factors [14]. Artists use color to provoke emotions in people.

eMoto, a mobile messaging service developed by Ståhl, Sundström, and Höök, uses sub-symbolic expressions for expressing emotions [11]. A user can adjust the background (i.e., colors, shapes, and animations) of a text message to fit the emotional expression s/he wants to achieve. Emotion was linked to color according to Ryberg's color theory (as cited in [11]). In this theory, the most powerful and strong emotions are represented by red, and emotions with less energy are represented by blue, the color at the other end of the color scale. Ståhl et al. applied Ryberg's color theory to Itten's circular color model [11,15], which in turn can be adjusted to fit Russell's circumplex model of affect, as is shown in Figure 2. The colors fade to white towards the circle's center since in that point valence and arousal are neutral.

Itten's transformed color circle, as used in [11] is applied in Mood Swings, using six colors in combination with the emotion-movement relation framework of [13]. Six colors are used because results from a user test that investigated the functioning of

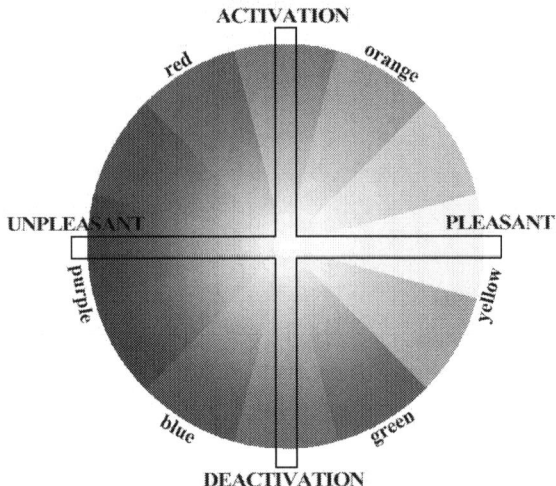

Fig. 2. Itten's color system [11,15] fitted to Russell's circumplex model of affect [6]

Mood Swings showed that using more colors made the installation's feedback harder to understand. The actual colors Mood Swings expresses are generated by six LEDs that are placed inside each orb. They react on the accelerometer inside the orb, hence displaying the color that reflects the emotional state of the user, based on the user's movements. The colors and their accompanying emotions are presented in Table 1. When Mood Swings is in rest, the orbs have a neutral/calm color, light mint green, to indicate to the audience the installation is on and the orbs have lights in them.

Table 1. Mood Swings interprets movements in terms of valence and arousal and subsequently provides feedback through colors. Mood Swings' translation of the dimensions of emotion to colors is denoted in this table.

Arousal	Valence	Color
High	Negative	Red
High	Positive	Orange
Neutral	Negative	Purple
Neutral	Positive	White
Low	Negative	Blue
Low	Positive	Green

3.3 User Test

Mood Swings was evaluated in a museum for contemporary art by 36 museum visitors. The preliminary results confirm The Trajectory of Interaction, although not all phases were reached. Few participants reached the contemplation phase, and none of the participants reached the belonging phase. A difference was found in the manner of interaction in the disengagement phase. This phase is characterized by the fact that the participants repeat a previous action sequence that they performed during their most intense control state. Unlike [8], the preliminary results show that trying to discover new things can also take place during the disengagement phase.

When asking the participants how they would define Mood Swings, most of the participants indicated they saw it as either art or a game. Other definitions were: living creature, computer application, living room lighting, and as a communication device for a public space or waiting rooms. Many participants saw Mood Swings as an application for children, in school, on a playground, or in a therapy room.

4 Discussion

In research by Pasch, Berthouze, Van Dijk, and Nijholt [16] on physical activity as interaction mode in video game consoles, they state there is a link between physical activity and engagement. If a game technology is able to interpret the affective state of the gamer and adapt the game to steer the gamer's movements, this will lead to a more enjoyable interaction.

In the current system, all the orbs work individually. This means that the emotion expressed by the user is visible in each orb individually. An example, if a user wants to express anger, s/he will move quick and random. In doing so, not all orbs will be touched equally. Maybe some orbs will barely move and light up in a color appropriate for relaxation. A nicer solution would be to let the orbs be aware of each other. In this way, the installation can let the orbs cooperate (e.g., through calculating a mean) and adjust the feedback more appropriately. The installation would be more cohesive, and including other feedback modalities like audio would be easier. Another advantage is that it would be possible to create more suitable games for Mood Swings, which will lead to a more natural and richer experience as discussed by [16].

Mood Swings is founded on a theoretical framework to facilitate the recognition of emotions as expressed in movements and reflecting them by displaying corresponding colors. Mood Swings was evaluated to identify The Trajectory of Interaction. All of the trajectory's phases, except one, were observed. Hence, Mood Swings' working was confirmed and the generic use of The Trajectory of Interaction was illustrated.

Mood Swings was originally designed as an affective interactive art installation, with no function and as its goal to be fun. While observing people interacting with the system, it became clear that Mood Swings indeed has the qualities of an interactive art installation, but furthermore was used as a game and a communication device. By adding cooperating orbs and/or other feedback modalities, Mood Swings could be more effective and even more suitable as a game or communication device.

Acknowledgments. The authors thank Jos Bax, Rene Verberne, Albert Geven, Frank Vossen, Tom Bergman, Albert Hoevenaars, Martin Ouwerkerk, and Paul-Christiaan Spruijtenburg for their contribution in the development of Mood Swings. Additionally, we thank Richard van de Sluis and the four anonymous reviewers, who provided valuable comments on the first version of this manuscript.

References

1. Norman, D.A.: Emotional Design: Why we Love (or Hate) Everyday Things. Basic Books, New York (2004)
2. Sony, `http://news.sel.sony.com/en/press_room/consumer/digital_imaging/digital_cameras/cyber-shot/release/31103.html`
3. Boehner, K., DePaula, R., Dourish, P., Sengers, P.: How Emotion is Made and Measured. International Journal of Human-Computer Studies 65(4), 275–291 (2007)
4. Picard, R.W.: Affective computing. MIT Press, Cambridge (1997)
5. Shugrina, M., Betke, M., Collomosse, J.P.: Empathic Painting: Interactive Stylization Using Observed Emotional State. In: 4th International Symposium on Non-Photorealistic Animation and Rendering, pp. 87–96. ACM Press, New York (2006)
6. Russell, J.A.: A Circumplex Model of Affect. Journal of Personality and Social Psychology 39(6), 1161–1178 (1980)
7. Castellano, G., Bresin, R., Camurri, A., Volpe, G.: Expressive Control of Music and Visual Media by Full-Body Movement. In: 7th International Conference on New interfaces For Musical Expression, pp. 390–391. ACM Press, New York (2007)
8. Costello, B., Muller, L., Amitani, S., Edmonds, E.: Understanding the Experience of Interactive Art: Iamascope in Beta_space. In: 2nd Australasian Conference on Interactive Entertainment, pp. 49–56. CCS Press, Sydney (2005)
9. Höök, K., Sengers, P., Andersson, G.: Sense and Sensibility: Evaluation and Interactive art. In: SIGCHI Conference on Human Factors in Computing Systems, pp. 241–248. ACM Press, New York (2003)
10. Camurri, A., Lagerlöf, I., Volpe, G.: Recognizing Emotion from Dance Movement: Comparison of Spectator Recognition and Automated Techniques. International Journal of Human-Computer Studies 59(1-2), 213–225 (2003)
11. Ståhl, A., Sundström, P., Höök, K.: A Foundation for Emotional Expressivity. In: 2005 Conference on Designing for User Experience. Designing For User Experiences, vol. 135. American Institute of Graphic Arts, New York (2005)
12. Zhao, L.: Synthesis and Acquisition of Laban Movement Analysis Qualitative Parameters for Communicative Gestures. Doctoral Thesis, University of Pennsylvania (2001)
13. Lee, J.-H., Park, J.-Y., Nam, T.-J.: Emotional Interaction through Physical Movement. In: Jacko, J.A. (ed.) HCI 2007. LNCS, vol. 4552, pp. 401–410. Springer, Heidelberg (2007)
14. Zammitto, V.L.: The Expressions of Colours. In: Digital Games Research Conference 2005, Changing Views: Worlds in Play, pp. 1–15. University of Vancouver, Vancouver (2005)
15. Itten, J.: Kunst der Farbe. Otto Maier Verlag, Ravensburg (1961)
16. Pasch, M., Berthouze, N., van Dijk, E.M.A.G., Nijholt, A.: Motivations, Strategies, and Movement Patterns of Video Gamers Playing Nintendo Wii Boxing. In: Facial and Bodily Expressions for Control and Adaptation of Games, pp. 27–33 (2008)

Navigating a Maze with Balance Board and Wiimote

Wim Fikkert, Niek Hoeijmakers, Paul van der Vet, and Anton Nijholt

Human Media Interaction, University of Twente
P.O. Box 217, 7500 AE, Enschede, The Netherlands
{f.w.fikkert,n.j.hoeijmakers,p.e.vandervet,a.nijholt}@utwente.nl

Abstract. Input from the lower body in human-computer interfaces can be beneficial, enjoyable and even entertaining when users are expected to perform tasks simultaneously. Users can navigate a virtual (game) world or even an (empirical) dataset while having their hands free to issue commands. We compared the Wii Balance Board to a hand-held Wiimote for navigating a maze and found that users completed this task slower with the Balance Board. However, the Balance Board was considered more intuitive, easy to learn and 'much fun'.

Keywords: H.5.2. User interfaces, Evaluation, Input devices and strategies.

1 Introduction

New forms of interaction keep flooding the market, introducing engaging and often unexpected new experiences to the public. Hand and other bodily movements now serve as input for game consoles. Similarly, input from the lower body in human-computer interfaces can benefit the interaction by enabling natural proprioception. In addition, users have their hands free to perform other, simultaneous tasks such as issuing commands to a virtual game world (World of Warcraft, Killzone) that they are navigating through with their lower body [1]. Such an interface has the potential to be more enjoyable because users can divide attention between tasks. In addition, lower body input can be highly entertaining, even enticing users to start interacting. This is, for example, illustrated by the Wii Fit game that is enthusiastically used in elderly homes for entertainment and in medical centers for rehabilitation[1].

Our contribution is an evaluation of the performance and, more importantly, enjoyability of users navigating a virtual maze world with their lower body while they are performing cognitive tasks with a hand-held device [2]. Section 2 describes related work on lower body HCI and ways to evaluate such interactions. In Sect. 3 we describe our evaluation of combining the Nintendo Wiimote and Balance Board for navigating through a simple maze. Sections 4 and 5 present the results and conclusions of this evaluation respectively.

2 Related Work

2.1 Lower Body Input

Navigating virtual worlds through virtual walking, where the user can physically walk freely through an entire world, has been addressed extensively in systems that fully

---

[1] In USA today, "Wii finds home in retirement communities, medical centers", on 2008-05-14.

A. Nijholt, D. Reidsma, and H. Hondorp (Eds.): INTETAIN 2009, LNICST 9, pp. 187–192, 2009.

immerse their users. The VirtuSphere[2] enables virtual walking by placing its users inside a large sphere in which they can walk, run, roll and even jump. See Kruijf's PhD thesis for a more extensive overview [3]. Interfaces that do not completely immerse their users typically require them to remain stationary for large displays or use users' mobility in portable interfaces. The JoyFoot uses accelerometers to detect ankle movements for controlling navigation in a virtual world [4]. The JoyFoot was evaluated with a large display in a game setting where users had to navigate an asteroid debris field game world in two dimensions by moving their feet on the floor. Reidsma et al. [5] presented their virtual dancer where users were enticed to engage in a dancing dialogue with a virtual dancer. A game dance mat[3] is used to detect the user's presence while a crude computer vision solution is used to detect dancing motions. Map manipulation has also been shown to benefit from combining a touch-sensitive wall-sized display for selection and activation with lower-body input from a Wii Balance Board for navigation [1]. It has also been suggested that the Balance Board can be a useful modality to perform 1 DOF control tasks by the feet [6].

2.2 Evaluating Input Devices

Input devices can be thoroughly evaluated on task completion times, error rates and user satisfaction on various tasks using the ISO 9241-9 standard [7] which is based on Fitts' Law on human motor control. The standard defines performance measures for evaluating input devices or techniques using basic interfaces tasks such as tap, drag and trace. Like [1], we are interested to explore the effect of tracing complex paths, for example, as found in map navigation. This goes beyond the underlying assumptions in Fitts' Law that eliminates the cognitive aspects of an interaction as much as possible in an effort to focus on the motor abilities of humans.

3   Methodology

Our large display interface, see Fig. 1, combines lower-body input (from a Wii Balance Board) with input from the hands (from a Wiimote). Users performed a time-crucial navigation task in a set of simple mazes during which they were required to input commands manually. These commands were issued at set locations in the maze, without which the user could not continue. The user controlled an avatar (green dot) in our maze task. Subjects in this study were selected based on sufficient computer experience. We hypothesize that the the Balance Board will be more intuitive for simultaneously navigating and issuing commands while not suffering loss in performance.

3.1 Devices for Navigating the Maze

The Nintendo Wiimote and Nintendo Balance Board were used in a within-subjects evaluation, see Fig. 1. The Wiimote has three perpendicular accelerometers and an IR

---

[2] Available online at http://www.virtusphere.com/, last checked feb. 2009.

[3] Dance Dance Revolution: http://www.konami.com/ddr/, last checked feb. 2009.

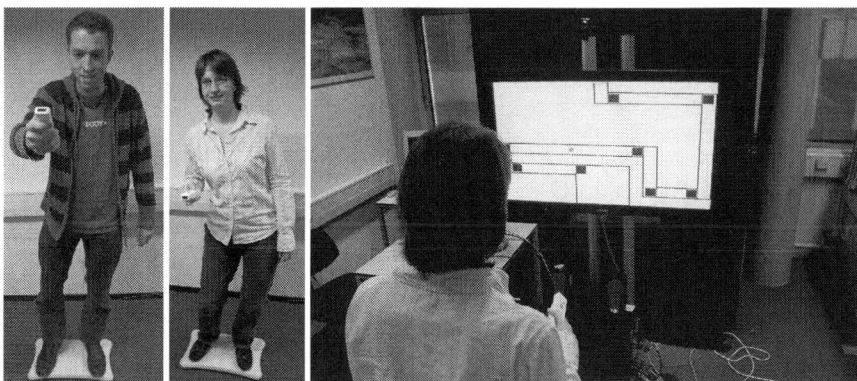

Fig. 1. The maze navigation task combines the input from a Balance Board and Wiimote alike. Subjects enjoyed both navigation approaches; using either the Wiimote or Balance Board. While navigating, users were required to press buttons on the Wiimote in order to complete the maze.

camera that detects fixed light sources for absolute pointing. The Balance Board (or board for short) has four pressure sensors at each of its corners.

Our test subjects completed two scenarios in counterbalanced order. The first scenario (BW) combined the board with a single Wiimote. In BW, the board was used for navigation; the subject stands on the board and shifts his center of gravity to move the avatar. Leaning forward moved the avatar up, left moved it left and so on. This is very similar to how a Segway works. The Wiimote could be held in the preferred hand (either left or right) and on set positions in the maze the subject was required to issue an command with it, see Sect. 3.2. In the second scenario (WM) our subjects only used one Wiimote to control both the avatar and issue the commands in the maze. A similar form of navigating the maze with the Wiimote was selected compared to BW; the accelerometers were used to detect roll (for moving left and right) and pitch (for moving up and down). We specifically chose not to use the embedded IR camera for detecting pointing (see [2]) because it could bias the avatar's movement speed. The avatar top movement speed was equal for BW and WM, matching the maximum pitch or lean.

3.2 The Maze Task

Subjects in our study navigated four mazes, seen from above, of varying difficulty, see Fig. 2. The four mazes were presented in the same order for both of the above scenarios. Before starting the first maze, our subjects were allowed a brief training session to get used to the device for navigation and to learn how to issue commands with the Wiimote. Each maze consisted out of a sequence of rooms that were connected by doors, ending with a maze exit. The subject had to navigate/walk to a each (closed) door and, while standing in front of the door on a doormat, press a button to open the door. The button to press was displayed on-screen only when a subject was standing on a doormat. After a correct button-press, the door would open so that the subject could proceed to the next room. Pressing an incorrect button would give a visual error signal.

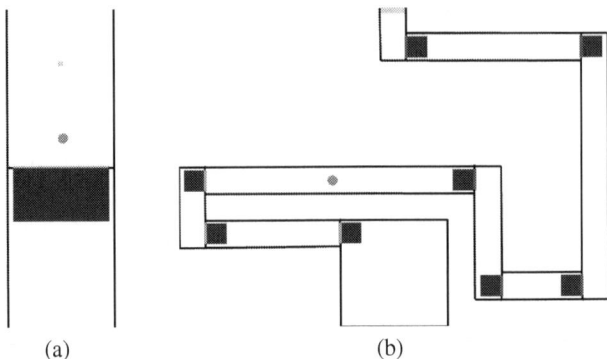

(a)   (b)

Fig. 2. The set of mazes consisted out of very simple (a) linear paths to (b) more complex paths. Maze components were identified by their color. In all cases, only one path existed.

3.3   User Evaluation

A paired t-test was used to compare our two scenarios (BW and WM) to each other. For each maze we measured the task completion time in addition to the time that a user stood still on a doormat as measure for performance. As a measure for error rate, we counted impacts with the walls of the maze and closed doors in addition to incorrectly entered commands. User personal data was gathered to assess their previous experience with the devices in this experiment or similar input devices. After completing each scenario, the user filled out a questionnaire in which they rated the interaction. Upon completing both scenarios the users rated which device they enjoyed the most for navigating.

4   Results

18 subjects participated in our evaluation, 4 female and 14 male ($\mu = 29$ years, $\sigma = 11$ years, ranging 18 to 56 years). 9 subjects held a Masters degree, 6 a Bachelors and 3 had no degree. On a 1-5 scale, our subjects were proficient with the Wiimote ($\mu = 3.4$, $\sigma = 1.2$) before taking part in the study but the Balance Board ($\mu = 2.3$, $\sigma = .9$) and other motion capture solutions ($\mu = 2.0$, $\sigma = .8$) were less familiar.

With respect to performance, we found that task completion time with WM was significantly faster (17 seconds faster, $p = 0.04$). After the test, most subjects (10 for WM, 4 for BW) also indicated that they experienced WM to be the faster solution for navigation. The number of wall and door hits did not differ significantly between BW and WM, nor did the number of incorrectly issued commands. However, 17 subjects indicated after the test that they experienced WM to be less prone to bumping into walls or doors (1 experienced no difference). We found that our subjects maintained their location on doormats more consistently for WM ($\mu = 4.3$ fewer drifts, $p < 0.01$). The total time spent on doormats did not differ significantly but on average each pass took significantly less time using BW ($\mu = 0.47$ seconds, $p = 0.04$).

We found no significant difference in ease of learning, the intuitiveness of the navigation and smoothness of the navigation between both techniques (BW and WM) for navigation in our user opinions after each scenario. However, in the evaluation after the test most subjects (10) indicated that BW was easiest to learn while 6 subjects found WM easier to learn. Likewise, BW was considered the most intuitive (13 subjects, 2 for WM). Our subjects rated the navigation accuracy significantly higher in favor of WM ($p < 0.01$) after each scenario and in the evaluation after the test (12 subjects, 2 for BW). Although we did not find a significant difference for opening the doors between BW and WM, five subjects indicated that they were not familiar enough with the Wiimote to find the required button right away. Although there was no significant difference in the extent that our subjects enjoyed using either WM or BW, they indicated after the test that BW was the most fun (12 while 2 had more fun with WM).

In observations during our trials we noticed that most subjects navigated in only one direction with WM at any one time. For example, a subject would move up first and then turn left rather than moving in both directions simultaneously. Similarly, we observed that our subjects would in most cases complete the navigation task first. Only after ensuring that they remained stationary on a doormat would they focus on opening the door. During the trials four subjects commented that they found our implementation for moving up and down with WM counter intuitive. They would rather invert it so that pitch down moves the avatar forward, arguing that that would be exactly the same as the BW implementation.

5   Conclusions and Future Work

By using the lower body to navigate a virtual world users keep their hands free to complete to perform other tasks simultaneously such as issuing commands. We have compared the Wii Balance Board to a hand-held Wiimote for navigating a series of simple mazes. While navigating the maze of consecutive rooms, our users had to open doors between these rooms on set locations directly in front of the doors. Users could navigate with the board by shifting their center of gravity through leaning or by changing the roll and pitch of the Wiimote in their preferred hand.

We hypothesized that the Balance Board would be more intuitive for the navigation task while not suffering a performance loss. Although we found that the board was easier to learn and use, the Wiimote was significantly faster in navigating the maze without resulting in an increase in navigation errors or errors in the issued commands. This suggests that using the same input modality (a hand-held device) performs better for navigating a virtual world while simultaneously issuing commands. However, we argue that the fun-factor of an interface is equally or even more important for many applications, especially games. Our subjects strongly indicated that they enjoyed using the combination of Wiimote and the Balance Board more, although it was not faster to complete the game. This raises a good point in that novelty is a very important factor for perceived the fun-factor. We expect that a comparison between Wiimote and joystick would provide similar differences. An unbiased assessment would require the users to become much more proficient with both devices.

Some subjects wanted to invert the pitch for navigating to match Balance Board navigation; leaning forward would move the avatar forward. We chose not to implement that approach in favor of mimicking ray-casting to the screen where pointing to the bottom of the screen would move the avatar down.

One aspect that we did not investigate was to what extent the lower body is suited to perform navigation as well as issuing the crude commands that we used in our evaluation. When compared with the current results we expect to find an increase in task completion time with a similar error rate. Trajectory analysis can be used to evaluate the distance to the ideal path through the maze. In addition, our observation that subjects moved the avatar along one axis at any one time could be grounded.

Acknowledgements. This work is part of the BioRange program carried out by the Netherlands Bioinformatics Centre, which is supported by a BSIK grant through the Netherlands Genomics Initiative, and the GATE project, funded by the Netherlands Organization for Scientific Research (NWO) and the Netherlands ICT Research and Innovation Authority (ICT Regie).

References

1. Schöning, J., Krüger, A.: Multi-modal navigation through spatial information. In: Cova, T.J., Miller, H.J., Beard, K., Frank, A.U., Goodchild, M.F. (eds.) GIScience 2008. LNCS, vol. 5266, pp. 151–154. Springer, Heidelberg (2008)
2. Fikkert, W., van der Vet, P., Nijholt, A.: Hand-held device evaluation in gesture interfaces. In: Gesture Workshop 2009 (February 2009)
3. Kruijff, E.: Unconventional 3D User Interfaces for Virtual Environments. PhD thesis, Institute for Computer Graphics and Vision, Graz University of Technology, Graz, Austria (October 2006)
4. Barrera, S., Takahashi, H., Nakajima, M.: Joyfoot's cyber system: a virtual landscape walking interface device for virtual reality applications. In: International Conference on Cyberworlds, pp. 286–292 (2004)
5. Reidsma, D., van Welbergen, H., Poppe, R., Bos, P., Nijholt, A.: Towards bi-directional dancing interaction. In: Harper, R., Rauterberg, M., Combetto, M. (eds.) ICEC 2006. LNCS, vol. 4161, pp. 1–12. Springer, Heidelberg (2006)
6. de Haan, G., Griffith, E., Post, F.: Using the Wii Balance Board^{TM}as a low-cost VR interaction device. In: VRST 2008: Proceedings of the 2008 ACM symposium on Virtual reality software and technology, pp. 289–290. ACM, New York (2008)
7. ISO: Ergonomic requirements for office work with visual display terminals (vdts) - part 9: Requirements for non-keyboard input devices. Technical Report ISO/DIS 9241-9:2000, International Organization for Standardization (2000)

Experiences with Interactive Multi-touch Tables

Wim Fikkert, Michiel Hakvoort, Paul van der Vet, and Anton Nijholt

Human Media Interaction, University of Twente
P.O. Box 217, 7500 AE, Enschede, The Netherlands
{f.w.fikkert,m.c.hakvoort,p.e.vandervet,a.nijholt}@utwente.nl

Abstract. Interactive multi-touch tables can be a powerful means of communication for collaborative work as well as an engaging environment for competition. Through enticing gameplay we have evaluated user experience on competitive gameplay, collaborative work and musical expression. In addition, we report on our extensive experiences with two types of interactive multi-touch tables and we introduce a software framework that abstracts from their technical differences.

Keywords: Interactive table display, User and developer experience.

1 Introduction

One of the promises of Ambient Intelligence (AmI) is to have intelligence embedded in our environments, whether it is the home environment, an office environment or public spaces. Intelligence is embedded in walls, floors, furniture, wearables, and other objects. The available intelligence is ubiquitous and pervasive. It can perceive activities and interactions. It can support, both in a reactive and pro-active way, the humans that inhabit or visit these environments. Natural implicit and explicit interaction with the environment requires an awareness of the activities and preferences the human inhabitant. Also, the environment and its interfaces should inform and communicate with their human partners using various modalities. Interactive surfaces where touch can be used to issue commands and to manipulate virtual objects are essential for natural interaction and for natural collaboration and entertainment activities. In this paper we report about our research on using interactive multi-touch displays for collaboration and entertainment applications. User experience is a main issue in our investigations.

The research reported here fits in our research on multimodal interaction in entertainment environments [1]. Touch is the main modality that we want to see explored in this work. Interactive surfaces that allow touch for multiple users and are connected with other touch-sensitive interaction surfaces can be expected to take flight in home, educational, professional and recreational environments. Multi-touch technology makes it possible for artists, designers, gamers and office workers to (jointly) interact with responsive surfaces, such as tables and walls. Interactive tables have already been introduced in restaurants, in museums, and at exhibitions to entertain visitors.

We are designing various applications for multi-touch tables with a particular interest in embedding such interactive surfaces in AmI and ambient entertainment environments. This requires research on how to embed such surfaces, how users want or are

A. Nijholt, D. Reidsma, and H. Hondorp (Eds.): INTETAIN 2009, LNICST 9, pp. 193–200, 2009.
© ICST Institute for Computer Sciences, Social Informatics and Telecommunications Engineering 2009

willing to interact with them and user experiences with diverse applications ranging from artistic and entertainment to decision making and crisis management.

The remainder of this paper is structured as follows. Section 2 provides an overview of multi-touch technology that possibly limits the interaction and defines research challenges for interactive tables. Section 3 introduces a software framework that abstracts from the interactive table hardware so that applications can run on any interactive table. Section 4 reports on our own experiences with two distinct multi-touch devices: a DI back projection table and the DiamondTouch [2]. With five distinct applications, we evaluated multi-touch interactions based on their fun factor, on performance and on the overall user experience in interacting with table displays. We conclude our paper in Sect. 5 with a discussion of our experiences and an outlook on open challenges for interactive surfaces in ambient intelligent environments.

2   Related Work

Previous multi-touch experiences. Interactions with interactive tables are influenced greatly by the application and its setting. Is the interaction time crucial [3]? Do users collaborate or do they compete with each other [4]? Do users casually interact with the table in passing [5] or do they perform complex and more time-consuming tasks [6]? How can hesitance to touch the table simultaneously be overcome [7]? Do we need to transfer the floor explicitly in collaborations [6] or can users operate cooperatively [8]?

Tse et al. [3] studied deictic input signals based on whole hand interaction with speech commands. Through collaborative time crucial tasks (Warcraft 3) and tasks where completion time was no issue (The Sims, Google Earth), Tse et al. showed that interactive table collaboration benefits from a shared view where users can communicate with each other directly through verbal utterances and manipulating the visualizations. Hardware and software limitations influenced the interaction greatly, resulting in coarse, counter-intuitive gestures. A later study found that users would actively engage in each other's tasks even insofar that tasks were jointly performed [8]. Also, deictic commands were observed to double as implicit communication between subjects.

A room furniture layout application (RoomPlanner) has been used for exploring interaction techniques that take advantage of multi-touch and hand shape input on table displays [9]. Two users on opposite sides of the table fitted furniture in a room. Private information could be projected on hands and objects by virtue of using a top-projection table. Three types of interactive table territories have been observed in both casual and formal interaction settings [5]. The personal territory allowed users to perform independent activities, the group territory served as a joint blackboard and the storage territory held unused icons in out-of-the-way spaces on the table.

Hardware. The most popular technique for optical recognition is Frustrated Total Internal Reflection (FTIR) is similar to fiber optics [4,10]. FTIR displays project IR light into an acrylic sheet. The internal reflection is frustrated by touching the surface, so that the refracted IR light can be detected with an IR-sensitive camera. FTIR scales up successfully but cannot support passive fiducials [4]. Active markers, however, might be used for FTIR displays [11]. Alternatively, Diffuse Illumination (DI) does support passive fiducials [12,13]. DI displays diffuse illuminate the surface so that a camera can detect all IR reflecting objects on and hovering over the surface: hands and fiducials alike. FTIR typically requires less computer vision (CV) filtering than DI.

The Apple iPhone is a well-known example of a capacitive coupling touch screen. This technology relies on the conductive properties of the human skin. A grid of electrically polarized transmitters and receivers can detect the small changes in capacitance triggered by a touch. Implementations vary: the iPhone is based on mutual capacitance, SmartSkin [14] has its receivers and transmitters under perpendicular angles and the DiamondTouch [2] touch panel contains two arrays of transmitters only with users standing on receiver mats. By design, the SmartSkin can detect conductive objects on its surface while The DiamondTouch can identify users through the receiver mats [6]. The signals received by the DiamondTouch are code division multiplexed which results in ambiguity of n^2 possibilities for n touches of the same user.

3   Abstract Software Layer - μ^3

Our multi-touch experiences are based on two distinctly different interactive tables, see Fig. 1, a DI back projection table and a DiamondTouch [2] top projection table. These two distinct platforms each have their pros and cons. The DI table can detect fiducials and hovering over the table while the DiamondTouch can identify users. Extracting touches is, due their distinct designs, quite different for each of our two interactive multi-touch tables. DI tables typically use the *tbeta*[1] framework which produces TUIO messages that hold information on location, orientation and recognized states [15]. TUIO cannot, however, handle multi-user information. The DiamondTouch can be accessed with the DiamondSpin toolkit [16]. DiamondSpin focuses on multi-user interaction and cannot handle multi-touch input adequately. Other similar frameworks such as TouchLib, reacTIVision [12] and LibTisch [17] have their own limitations so that there is no uniform framework that spans interactive multi-touch tables sufficiently.

The strengths of DI tables and capacitive coupling tables are combined in μ^3 which stands for *mu*lti-touch *mu*lti-tangible *mu*lti-user. With μ^3, we aim to overcome the shortcomings of existing multi-touch software. For multi-touch, we represent all possible touch points on a table in a 2D array (the table surface) as states. Each point is touched, untouched, a ghost touch[2] or an untouchable point (e.g. for non-rectangular tables). We generalize all touched points as tangible objects so that tangible object identification is made possible, also encompassing tracked fiducials [12]. Multiple users are also represented as the owners of tangible objects. Every 'tangible' can be assigned to at most one user for identification. The input arrays that represent touch point states and tangibles are combined into frames that, in turn, represent all touch activity on the table. To resolve overlapping touch points we use a collection of frames.

μ^3 can track, join and split touches. Developers need only to implement a preprocessing step to convert raw input to μ^3 frames, see Fig. 2. To illustrate, the DiamondTouch

---

[1] *tbeta* framework available: http://tbeta.nuigroup.com/, checked february 2009.
[2] Recall from Sect. 2 that the DiamondTouch suffers from touch ambiguity when 1 user touches the panel on 2 or more points.

Fig. 1. Two distinct interactive multi-touch tables with our AirHockey game on a diffuse illumination table (left) and on the MERL DiamondTouch table (right)

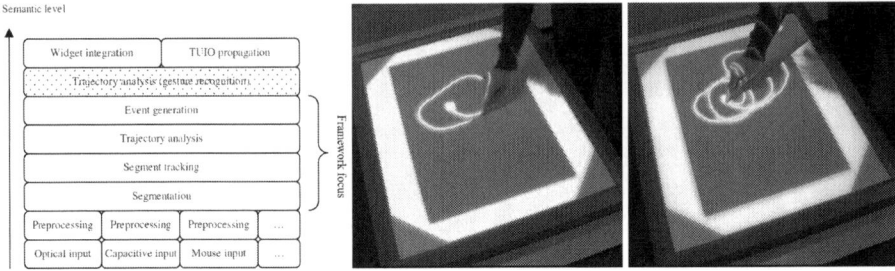

Fig. 2. The μ^3 framework architecture and our FeelSound musical application (see Sect. 4.4) build on top of μ^3 and composing on the DiamondTouch

is accessed in under 200 lines of code with μ^3. Adjacent points in the input are identified into a concave hull using marching squares and polygon simplification. Tracking searches for the best matching touch for each segment using a confidence measurement based on segment size and location. When exceeding a predefined threshold these segments are passed to the trajectory analysis where touches are possibly split or joined. Note that μ^3 is not capable of recognizing fiducials directly and expects this information from a preprocessing layer. μ^3 can also take TUIO messages as input.

4   Multi-touch Experiences

We present four applications for our interactive tables with which we explored the touch modality. First, turn taking is explored in manipulating a 3D molecule, based on [6]. Second, competitive and engaging behavior was explored with our AirHockey game. Third, MT-Pong crowds the table with competitive gamers. Fourth and final, we enticed creativity in passers-by to compose a musical performance in FeelSound.

4.1   Collaboration – 3D Molecule

Interactive tables are extremely suited for collaboration while users stand or sit around the table, sharing a common display [6]. We have evaluated collaborative behavior with

Fig. 3. One finger to rotate and two fingers or hands to zoom into and out of the 3D molecule

a biological visualization tool that fills the table with a 3D molecule. Bioinformaticians stand around the table to discover function from form. The interface is multi-user and multi-touch but only one task should be performed at any one time. Multi-touch and multi-hand gestures were implemented to control the molecule so that users can perform a task alone or together with a partner [8]. We were especially interested to find out how turn taking would take place: would users wait for their partners to finish?

Observations with two groups with no biological knowledge of the depicted molecules simply moved, rotated and resized the molecule. These users let a self-appointed chairman control the display. They argued that the simple goal did not require input from each of the participants. The chairman stood centralized, see Fig. 3. A group of three biologists jointly answered form-related questions; they located active sites on various simple and complex proteins. These biologists took turns to control the molecule by switching places and thinking out loud to solve the task.

4.2 Competition – AirHockey

What happens when the nature of the interaction shifts from collaborative to competitive? Our AirHockey game, based on the arcade version, is played by two gamers. The gameplay was tuned to this digital version, for example, touches in the goal area were discarded. In addition, we experimented with the number of balls, amount of friction and responsiveness to touches. Adding too many balls panicked gamers so that they tried to beat away as many balls coming towards them instead of applying some tactics. Players commented that they misjudged how fast the table would respond; the output initially lagged behind input, making real-time gameplay difficult. Players physically pushed the arms of their opponents out of the way to be able to score goals. This fast-paced game did entice gamers to great extent, making them very eager to win the game by any means possible.

4.3 Crowding – MT-Pong

Interactive tables are currently quite small. Multiple users easily crowd the display, inhibiting their own movements and those of others. We implemented a competitive game, MT-Pong which was similar to Gross' [4] Puh game. Up to four players would score points by playing balls in an opponent's goal. Players placed up to two paddles with two or more fingers; single touches were ignored, following [4]. Placing a third paddle would remove the first and paddles had a maximum length to prevent spanning the whole table. The game ended after a set time. An informal evaluation took place with passers-by gamers who played MT-Pong in our coffee room. These gamers initially started waving around their hands erratically at the balls, hoping to change their direction. They quickly caught on that two touches were needed to play. Most players noticed a minor delay in placing the paddles due to the update frequency of the DiamondTouch but found it of little influence to the gameplay as it was not as fast-paced as AirHockey. Like AirHockey, we observed that gamers physically pushed each other out of the way in order to win. MT-Pong was 'fun', 'engaging' and 'tiring' to play. Crowding the display is mostly fun for the gamers involved in competitive settings. Pushing opponents was not considered to be an issue, on the contrary, it added to the fun-factor.

4.4   Artistic Expression – FeelSound

Following reacTIVision [12] we explored how users would compose a musical performance on an interactive table using touches alone. FeelSound synthesizes real-time sounds based on touch trajectories, see Fig. 2. Composers draw shapes on the table to add samples to the performance. The horizontal and vertical axis represent the sample frequency and amplitude; complex shapes result in complex, long samples. Drawn shapes collapse into an icon on the table that can then be configured along the edge of the table to start replay. FeelSound can current only construct simple music samples for the performances. More complex samples such as singing and instruments is work-in-progress. During a public exhibition a large audience (50+ people) walked up to the table and started composing music with FeelSound; it was easy to entice passers-by to start composing. The interface proved to be not very intuitive; most users were unsure what to do without instruction. Often, composers would start out by tapping the table to see what would happen, cluttering the table with lots of brief sample icons. After receiving instructions, the composers found FeelSound very engaging for creating music.

5   Discussion and Future Work

Our experiences with interactive multi-touch tables are colored by the specifics of our two tables. Each table has its own, mutually exclusive strong points, see also Sect. 2. DI tables can detect hovering and fiducials while a capacitive coupling table can identify users and requires limited processing to access. Weak points were present in both tables. First, touch-calibration proved to be very fragile. The DiamondTouch is easily pushed aside, especially when leaning over the panel, because it simply lies on top of a table with minimal anti-slip precautions. In addition, when mounting the beamer on a tripod users tend to bump into it by accident as occurred often in our FeelSound exhibition. Similarly, the mirror set-up in the DI table is fragile and susceptible to users (unintentionally) banging against the table thus requiring recalibration. Second, the update frequency is rather limited. The DiamondTouch operates at 30 Hz while a DI table is limited by its camera. For both MT-Pong and AirHockey, players commented that the interface responded unexpectedly slow. Third, interactive tables are still rather small;

our tables are both roughly a meter across. However, our users typically did not experience lack in their freedom of movement due to this size.

We found that a DiamondTouch user not standing on a receiver mat can interact with the table by touching a user who is standing on a mat. This might offer some interesting forms of explicit collaboration on interactive tables taking into account that users can complement each other's commands as noted by [8].

A specific weak point of the DiamondTouch is its limitation to detect individual touch points by default. Touch ambiguity of n touches results in n^2 potential touches that the developer needs to handle. Tse et al. [3] worked around this by performing multiple selection with large bounding boxes and precise control with small ones. Our games required more precision that we were able to implement using μ^3. Our μ^3 framework abstracts from the table's underlying hardware so that developers can focus on applications rather than handling multi-touch hardware. μ^3 can track, join and split touches that originate from identifiable users or tangibles. μ^3 is under active development.

An extensive insight in developing for and using our DI table and DiamondTouch was given through informal evaluations of four very different applications. Through competitive gameplay (AirHockey) we found an eagerness to win that extended even beyond the interface by physically hampering opponents. This was intensified even more when the display was crowded (MT-Pong). Artistic expression was explored through composing music (FeelSound) and proved to be engaging in a public exhibition even though the interface was not very intuitive. In a collaborative setting (3D molecule) we observed that the display is controlled from a central spot from which the visualization can be observed upright. Turn-taking, in various forms, proved to be a very important aspect of the interaction with interactive tables. We showed the appreciation of physical interaction between users cooperating (jointly performing tasks) or frustrating other users in competitive gameplay (by pushing opponents away).

Acknowledgements. We sincerely thank our students Daan Scheerens, Jeroen Logtenberg and others for their collaboration on the works presented here. This work is part of the BioRange program carried out by the Netherlands Bioinformatics Centre, which is supported by a BSIK grant through the Netherlands Genomics Initiative, and the GATE project, funded by the Netherlands Organization for Scientific Research (NWO) and the Netherlands ICT Research and Innovation Authority (ICT Regie).

References

1. Reidsma, D., Poppe, R., Nijholt, A.: Games and entertainment in ambient intelligence environments. In: Aghajan, H., Delgado, R., Augusto, J.C. (eds.) Human-Centric Interfaces for Ambient Intelligence. Elsevier, Amsterdam (in press, 2009)
2. Dietz, P., Leigh, D.: Diamondtouch: a multi-user touch technology. In: UIST 2001: Proceedings of the 14th annual ACM symposium on User interface software and technology, pp. 219–226. ACM Press, New York (2001)
3. Tse, E., Shen, C., Greenberg, S., Forlines, C.: Enabling interaction with single user applications through speech and gestures on a multi-user tabletop. In: AVI 2006: Proceedings of the working conference on Advanced visual interfaces, pp. 336–343. ACM Press, New York (2006)

4. Gross, T., Fetter, M., Liebsch, S.: The cuetable: cooperative and competitive multi-touch interaction on a tabletop. In: CHI 2008: CHI 2008 extended abstracts on Human factors in computing systems, pp. 3465–3470. ACM, New York (2008)
5. Scott, S.D., Sheelagh, M., Carpendale, T., Inkpen, K.M.: Territoriality in collaborative table-top workspaces. In: CSCW 2004: Proceedings of the 2004 ACM conference on Computer supported cooperative work, pp. 294–303. ACM, New York (2004)
6. Forlines, C., Lilien, R.: Adapting a single-user, single-display molecular visualization application for use in a multi-user, multi-display environment. In: AVI 2008: Proceedings of the working conference on Advanced visual interfaces, pp. 367–371. ACM, New York (2008)
7. Ryall, K., Morris, M., Everitt, K., Forlines, C., Shen, C.: Experiences with and observations of direct-touch tabletops. In: TableTop 2006. First IEEE International Workshop on Horizontal Interactive Human-Computer Systems, pp. 89–96 (2006)
8. Tse, E., Shen, C., Greenberg, S., Forlines, C.: How pairs interact over a multimodal digital table. In: CHI 2007: Proceedings of the SIGCHI conference on Human factors in computing systems, pp. 215–218. ACM, New York (2007)
9. Wu, M., Balakrishnan, R.: Multi-finger and whole hand gestural interaction techniques for multi-user tabletop displays. In: UIST 2003: Proceedings of the 16th annual ACM symposium on User interface software and technology, pp. 193–202. ACM Press, New York (2003)
10. Han, J.: Low-cost multi-touch sensing through frustrated total internal reflection. In: UIST 2005: Proceedings of the 18th annual ACM symposium on User interface software and technology, pp. 115–118. ACM Press, New York (2005)
11. Malik, S., Laszlo, J.: Visual touchpad: a two-handed gestural input device. In: ICMI 2004: Proceedings of the 6th international conference on Multimodal interfaces, pp. 289–296. ACM Press, New York (2004)
12. Kaltenbrunner, M., Jorda, S., Geiger, G., Alonso, M.: The reactable*: A collaborative musical instrument. In: WETICE 2006: Proceedings of the 15th IEEE International Workshops on Enabling Technologies: Infrastructure for Collaborative Enterprises, pp. 406–411. IEEE Computer Society, Washington (2006)
13. Benko, H., Wilson, A., Baudisch, P.: Precise selection techniques for multi-touch screens. In: CHI 2006: Proceedings of the SIGCHI conference on Human Factors in computing systems, pp. 1263–1272. ACM Press, New York (2006)
14. Rekimoto, J.: Smartskin: an infrastructure for freehand manipulation on interactive surfaces. In: CHI 2002: Proceedings of the SIGCHI conference on Human factors in computing systems, pp. 113–120. ACM Press, New York (2002)
15. Kaltenbrunner, M., Bovermann, T., Bencina, R., Costanza, E.: Tuio: A protocol for tabletop tangible user interfaces. In: Gibet, S., Courty, N., Kamp, J.-F. (eds.) GW 2005. LNCS, vol. 3881. Springer, Heidelberg (2006)
16. Shen, C., Vernier, F., Forlines, C., Ringel, M.: Diamondspin: an extensible toolkit for around-the-table interaction. In: CHI 2004: Proceedings of the SIGCHI conference on Human factors in computing systems, pp. 167–174. ACM Press, New York (2004)
17. Echtler, F., Klinker, G.: A multitouch software architecture. In: Proceedings of the 5th Nordic conference on Human-computer interaction: building bridges. In: ACM International Conference Proceeding Series, vol. 358, pp. 463–466 (October 2008)

The Hyper-trapeze: A Physically Active Audio-Visual Interface for Performance and Play

Anne Hoekstra[1], Christoph Bartneck[1], and Michael J. Lyons[2]

[1] Eindhoven University of Technology, Department of Industrial Engineering
a.hoekstra@student.tue.nl, c.bartneck@tue.nl
[2] Ritsumeikan University, College of Image Arts and Sciences
lyons@im.ritsumei.ac.jp

Abstract. This paper reports the design, implementation, and application of a new interface for augmenting performance and play on the low flying trapeze. Sensors were used to gauge the motion of the trapeze and performer, mapping the data to control interactive sound and animation. The interface was tested in the context of a new multimedia composition entitled "Autumn".

Keywords: trapeze, performance interface, exertainment, exertion interface.

1 Introduction

Recently there is growing interest in the field of exertainment, which combines physical activity with interactive entertainment [1]. Interactive entertainment technology is being adopted in physical education settings to motivate exercise by offering players fun and novelty [2]. In this project we extend this concept to artistic and expressive play, using a performance medium, the low-flying trapeze, which is used by some modern dancers. We created a novel system that responds to the movements of the player to produce sound and animated graphics. Our intention is twofold: first to create a new performance interface, which we call the hyper-trapeze, which bridges the digital and physical world by augmenting an existing technology, the low-flying trapeze, with interactive multimedia. Second, to explore methods of interacting with the hyper-trapeze, both for purposes of artistic performance and for enjoyable physical activity.

2 Trapeze Background

The main inspiration for this project is the low flying trapeze, shown in figure 1, a performance technology used in some forms of contemporary dance. We were introduced to the low-flying trapeze by dancer/choreographer Peter GoLightly, of the Kyoto KyoRyuKan studio. In contrast to its circus cousin, the high-flying trapeze, it does not require a performer to risk life and limb: it hangs just high enough the ground to allow spinning, swinging, with legs airborne, and dance maneuvers with the feet on the ground. By allowing the dancer to leave the ground, and spin at high angular velocity, the trapeze expands the range of space and movement that may be

A. Nijholt, D. Reidsma, and H. Hondorp (Eds.): INTETAIN 2009, LNICST 9, pp. 201–206, 2009.
© ICST Institute for Computer Sciences, Social Informatics and Telecommunications Engineering 2009

Fig. 1. Overview of the hyper-trapeze system

used in a performance. This can greatly enhance the drama, variety, and excitement of a modern dance performance. At the same time, the novel appearance and perceived affordances of the trapeze invite play. With a soft studio floor, the trapeze is no more dangerous than a playground swing. These qualities of the trapeze suggest that, in addition to its role in performance, it may be suitable for use in exergaming.

The physical design of the low-flying trapeze is fairly straightforward. Unlike the circus trapeze, a wooden bar is suspended from a single point by a swivel attached to the ceiling with ropes, and a carabiner attached to the trapeze straps, allowing the user to use the same swivel with different trapezes. Soft grips are attached to the straps immediately adjacent to the wooden trapeze bar protecting the performer from rope burns.

The swivel allows the trapeze to spin without the support ropes twisting together; it must also safely support the performer's weight and spin freely. We used a Petzl P58 swivel [3]. This swivel is used by mountaineers when rappelling as well as in rescue work, and has been individually tested for a rated working load limit of 5 kN (kilonewtons), with a minimum breaking strength of 36 kN, more than sufficient to safely support an individual.

3 Hyper-trapeze Design Considerations

The trapeze acts passively to allow the performer a greater range of expressive movement. As a physical object responsive to the intentions of the dancer, the trapeze presents opportunities to interface with interactive digital media in a non-encumbering fashion. We asked whether augmenting the trapeze with sensors could allow it to become an audio-visual instrument, expanding the performers expressive scope.

This inspiration came from observing trapeze performances. To ground our design in expertise, we interviewed a trapeze performer (PG) about his approach to choreography and performance with the trapeze, and also carefully observed the trapeze while he demonstrated typical movements. To summarize, a lot of spinning movements are made, with the performer moving in a circular area centered below the swivel. The motion of the swivel itself is normally circular or linear depending on whether the trapeze is spinning or swinging. It can also be stationary when the performer climbs on the straps, or dances without the trapeze. PG also explained to us that he often moves his feet on the floor in painting movements in the circular area below the swivel and expressed a strong wish to have sensors responsive to these patterns. Our discussions produced a set of design requirements for the hyper-trapeze: the system should respond to the **performer's intentions**; the added technology must not interfere with the **safety**, or **comfort** of the trapeze; the system must be **robust** to vigorous movement; the design should be **trapeze specific**; and the **development time** required must be reasonable.

Based on these discussions we sketched several ideas for sensing movement of the trapeze and performer. Because the swivel is fairly isolated from the rest of the assembly and moves smoothly even for vigorous performances, we thought about various ways to sense its motion, including optical tracking of markers on the swivel, and magnetic tracking via a Hall effect sensor. Similarly, the ceiling support ropes are stationary during performance but experience variable load, leading us to consider force sensitive resistors (FSR) as a means to sense the shifting load and acceleration of the performer. We also considered directly sensing the dancer's body or the trapeze bar via optical tracking and reflective markers, finally, following the dancer's request, we considered adding sensors to the floor to allow the dancer to trigger effects with the feet. Here two alternatives were considered: tripping an optical switch with a laser beam and light sensor, or a similar arrangement but using the near infrared camera in

Table 1. Evaluation of design proposals for fulfillment of requirements (0 – low; 2 – high)

Sensed Variable	Sensor	Control	Safety	Robust-ness	Comfort	Trapeze Specific	Time	Total
Swivel Motion	Camera	1	2	1	2	2	1	9
	Hall Effect	1	2	1	2	2	1	9
Strap Pressure	Force Sensitive Resistors	1	2	2	2	2	2	11
Body Motion	Camera	1	2	1	1	0	0	5
Trapeze Motion	Camera	1	1	1	0	1	0	4
Foot Position	Laser Beam	2	2	0	2	2	2	10
	Wii Remote	2	2	2	2	2	2	12

the Wii remote with IR LEDs as light sources. Since this beam trigger resembles the famous Jean-Michel Jarre's famous "Laser Harp" musical interface, we call this a "Floor Harp". We evaluated the many ideas generated in terms of the design requirements listed above, with three score levels: **0** – the idea does not fit the requirement; **1**- the idea does fit the requirement; and **2** – the idea fits the requirement very well. Table 1 summarizes the idea evaluation process leading to the selection of the design elements to be implemented.

4   Hyper-trapeze Implementation

Based on an evaluation of the design concepts (Table 1), we implemented a prototype hyper-trapeze by eliminating low-scoring design ideas. The chosen design has: (a) a Hall effect sensor to gauge the motion of the trapeze swivel (b) two force sensors placed under the support straps and (c) a four "string" Floor harp with four Wii motes and four clusters of IR LEDs. Sensor data was acquired at approximately 200 Hz and sent wirelessly to a computer running Max/MSP [4] via a Bluetooth I-CubeX A/D convertor and microcontroller [5]. The Max/MSP patch also processed raw sensor data from the Wii motes and I-CubeX in real-time mapping the output to control sound synthesis. The Max/MSP patch sent data via a Flash server plug-in to a real-time Flash animation that was projected onto a wall adjacent to the trapeze. Small but

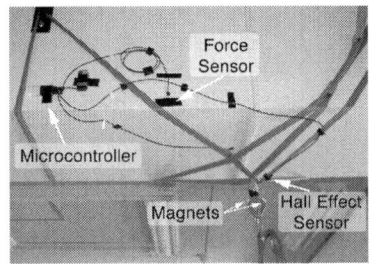

Fig. 2. Swivel motion and rope force sensors

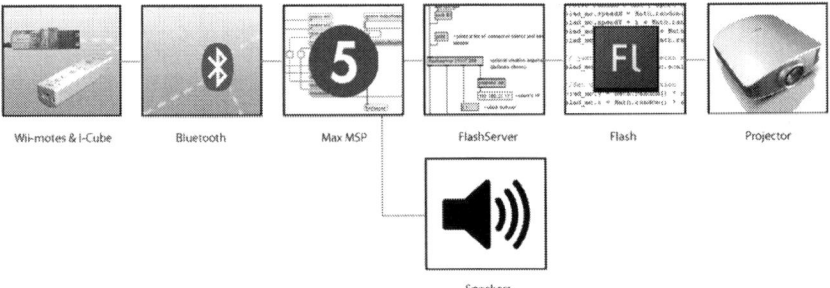

Fig. 3. System architecture of the hyper-trapeze

powerful neodymium magnets mounted on the swivel generate a signal in the Hall effect sensor which varies with the distance from the magnet; the maximum and minimum of the signal corresponding to the closest and furthest separations of the magnet and sensor. Analysis of this signal allows us to gauge the movement of the trapeze. The force sensors are calibrated to trigger events when a threshold is exceeded by pulling heavily on the straps.

5 Application of the Hyper-trapeze

Interactive audio-visual contents used with the hyper-trapeze interface were developed with a play/performance environment in mind: we chose the theme of "Autumn" inspired by the beautiful changing leaves of Kyoto's maple trees. The interactive animation shows falling coloured leaves blown here and there by the wind, while interactive Max/MSP patches play sounds of the blowing wind, raindrops and puddle splashes. The mapping from sensor signals to interactive effects was chosen to be simple, direct, and transparently understandable by novice players and spectators. The choice of mapping was informed both by discussion with a trapeze expert, and by many works presented at the NIME conferences [6] where the issue of performance interface sensor to output mapping has been studied. A review of musical interface design is beyond the scope of this paper, but we recommend two excellent foundational works [7, 8]. Briefly, the simple mapping we chose is oriented towards novices rather than virtuoso performers, as is appropriate for a completely new interface. The mapping is as follows: blocking a floor harp IR beam triggers playback of a water drop or splash and adds a leaf to the animation; rotation of the trapeze controls the cutoff frequency of resonant low-pass filtered noise, giving a remarkably convincing simulation of blowing wind. Spinning the swivel faster makes the wind blow harder both in the simulated sound and animation. Rotation direction is mapped to wind direction in the animation. Pulling a strap hard triggers bass notes or Japanese kana syllables, but is not currently mapped to visual output.

6 Related Work

Many prior works, too numerous to list here, have augmented dance performance with interactive audio and visual content. Two exemplary works are those by Winkler [7] and Camurri et al. [8]. In both, and most work in this area, cameras, or motion sensors capture movement of the dancers body. In contrast, in addition to having developed the world's first digitally augmented trapeze, we have taken a quite different approach in sensing the motion of a physical object other than the dancer's body. The hyper-trapeze is therefore akin to a musical instrument in that it is an object that responds to the conscious intentions and action of the player.

7 Conclusion

In collaboration with a dancer/choreographer we have designed and implemented a new interface for augmenting performance and play on the low-flying trapeze with interactive audio and animation. The first application of this system was a multimedia composition based on the theme "Autumn", but the system is flexible and can be adapted to offer new opportunities for creative expression by choreographers and dancers. We are also interested in the application of the hyper-trapeze to environments for fun, creative, and physically active play by both children and adults and we hope that this first study will facilitate future work in this direction.

Acknowledgement

This research was supported in part by a grant from the Japan Society for the Promotion of Science.

References

1. Brown, D.: Playing to Win: Video Games and the Fight against Obesity. Journal of the American Dietetic Association 106(2), 188–189 (2006)
2. Computer dance gets pupils active. BBC Online News, September 15 (2007)
3. Petzl Official website, http://www.petzl.com (accessed January 30, 2009)
4. Max/MSP, http://www.cycling74.com/ (accessed January 30, 2009)
5. I-CubeX Wireless microsystem, http://infusionsystems.com/ (accessed January 30, 2009)
6. Poupyrev, I., Lyons, M.J., Fels, S., Blaine, T.: New Interfaces for Musical Expression. Extended Abstracts. In: Conference on Human Factors in Computing Systems (CHI 2001), pp. 491–492 (2001)
7. Cook, P.R.: Principles for Designing Computer Music Controllers. In: Proceedings, New Interfaces for Musical Expression (NIME 2001) (2001)
8. Verplank, B.: A Course on Controllers. In: Proceedings New Interfaces for Musical Expression (NIME 2001) (2001)
9. Winkler, T.: Fusing Movement, Sound, and Video in Falling Up, an Interactive Dance/Theatre Production. In: Proceedings, International Conference on New Interfaces for Musical Expression (NIME 2002), pp. 188–189 (2002)
10. Camurri, A., Hashimoto, S., Ricchetti, M., Ricci, A., Suzuki, K., Trocca, R., Volpe, G.: EyesWeb: Toward Gesture and Affect Recognition in Interactive Dance and Music Systems. Computer Music Journal 24(1), 57–69 (2000)

Dead on Arrival: Adapting Games to Finish at a Given Time or Location

Arne von Öhsen[1] and Jörn Loviscach[2]

[1] Hochschule Bremen (University of Applied Sciences), 28199 Bremen, Germany
v.oehsen@googlemail.com
http://www.oehsen.com
[2] Fachhochschule Bielefeld (Univ. of Applied Sciences), 33602 Bielefeld, Germany
jl@j3L7h.de
http://j3L7h.de

Abstract. Casual and other games often serve as time-killing applications, be it on the commuter train or in the back seat of a shared car. When one arrives at the destination, the game has to be interrupted or aborted, which is annoying or even frustrating. Hence, we propose to continuously adapt the game's level of difficulty to the estimated remaining time to arrival. This can be preset as a number of minutes or can continuously be estimated from the player's position in relation to a predefined destination. Our dungeon-style prototype is based on an automated engine for content placement and can also make use of GPS data. We report on preliminary results from user tests.

Keywords: game difficulty adaptation, automated content creation, GPS, location-based service, casual games.

1 Introduction

Typically, the notion of location-based gaming [1] refers to using actual buildings etc. as part of a game, for instance as a playing-ground for a tag game or as a backdrop for a fictional story. This paper proposes a novel type of incorporating time and/or location into a game: The game—an otherwise standard video game—is finished in a satisfying way after a preset time has elapsed or when the player arrives at a predefined destination. This is achieved by a continuous adaptation of the game's difficulty.

The adaptation requires creating and placing game content appropriate to the strength the user has shown so far. For the prototype, we created a dungeon-style first-person shooter game in which both the number of rooms and their content (including monsters to be killed) are variable. The content is arranged in the rooms through a rule-based process. Depending on the player's progress, the system removes rooms or adds rooms that have yet to be visited and creates appropriate content for them, see Figure 1. The last room contains the master monster to be conquered so that the game possesses a satisfying end.

The software comprises four major components: A regular 3D game engine with standard game logic serves as the front end. The rules to create and populate

A. Nijholt, D. Reidsma, and H. Hondorp (Eds.): INTETAIN 2009, LNICST 9, pp. 207–212, 2009.
© ICST Institute for Computer Sciences, Social Informatics and Telecommunications Engineering 2009

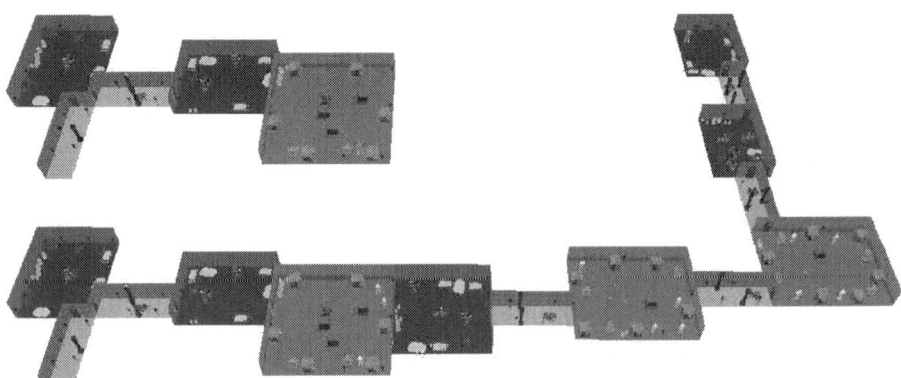

Fig. 1. To finish in the same time, a slower player will dynamically be presented with a simpler dungeon (top left) than will a quicker player (bottom and right)

rooms are stored in a database. A timing service provides an estimate on the remaining game time based on a direct setting by the user or on localization data obtained by a GPS device. These three components are tied together by the adaptation component that builds the gaming world and adapts it to the estimated remaining duration.

2   Related Work

Magerko [2] discusses domains in which game adaptation can be effective: storytelling (e. g., leading the player to decisions corresponding to the game author's intentions), player motivation (catering for different personalities and preferences), non-player character reasoning, and pedagogy. Most of these topics are connected to personalization [3], in contrast to the work presented here. For instance, Hunicke [4] describes a "dynamic difficulty adaptation" that intervenes to help the player's character stay at a given health level by placing helpful items or by manipulating the player's strength. This can already be perceived as a means to control the game's duration, namely to prevent from ending early.

Gustafsson et al. [5] describe another GPS-based adaptation of a game: Here, the game's story is adapted to the surrounding geographic items. Addressing a different type of entertainment by computers, Adcock et al. [6] introduce an audio player that tries to adapt the music selection to the available time.

3   Room Generation

The adaptation component employs an enhanced version of a system we introduced for automated placement of furniture [7]: A rule-based approach generates rooms, places immovable items in them and selects start positions and orientations for animated monsters. It operates on a collection of 3D content files such as models, textures, and animations that are described by a database. The entries of the database comprise low-level descriptions such as bounding boxes as

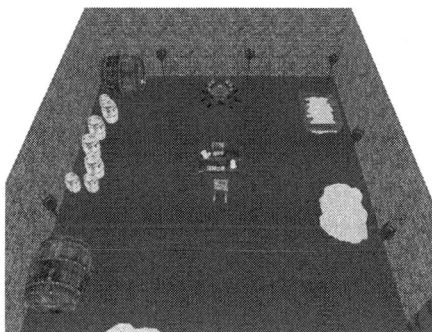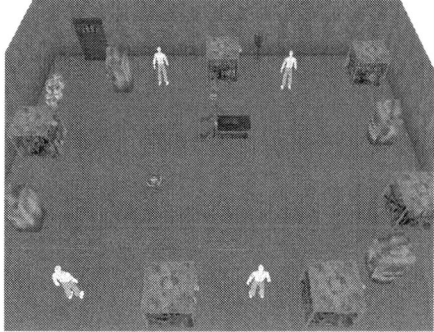

Fig. 2. Every room such as a lair (left) or a prison (right) is built and populated according to a set of rules associated with the room type and the items and monsters to be placed (bird's eye view, not available to the player)

well as high-level descriptions such as hierarchies and other relations between objects. The database entries for monsters are equipped with behavior scripts.

Rooms are not stored in the database in their finished form, but as collection of "room types," each of which comprises rules concerning the allowable size and frequency. Each room type possesses specific probabilities for the different kinds of items and monsters it may contain. To create a room, the system chooses among the room types obeying the given probabilities but not creating the same type in sequence. The room's size is determined at random. The room is attached to the rim of the existing dungeon with an appropriately placed door.

To populate a room, see Figure 2, a regular grid of about ten "room points" per square meter is created. These serve as hypothetical positions of items and initial positions of monsters. Items are picked according to their probability for the given room type. The placement process obeys the hierarchy prescribed in the database, which allows, for instance, to first place a table and then put the chairs around. Each item type is accompanied by rules in the database that specify how well such an item fits onto a given spare "room point." These rules can incorporate the vicinity of walls or other items of the same or other types. The optimum point is selected, proceeding from item to item in a greedy fashion.

The placement of the monsters proceeds in a similar fashion, with one difference: The ultimate room—i.e. the room entered when the time is about to expire—will always contain the master monster. Monsters in rooms that appear later in the game receive more life energy, meaning they are harder to kill. This increasing difficulty is intended to keep game more interesting. In a similar fashion, later rooms contain more loot, which can be picked up from the items and from dead monsters. It is distributed onto monsters and items alike.

4 Adaptation

On initialization, the system builds a dungeon of a size that would require a very good player to finish on time. If the player lags, the monsters in the ultimate room are made weaker. If they become weaker than those in the penultimate room, the latter room is removed—if the player is not already in it—and the strength of the monsters in the ultimate room is incremented again. This allows a more flexible control than only changing the number of rooms. If the player is ahead of schedule, additional rooms have to be appended. This can happen in particular with location-based control. For instance, the player may wait for a bus during the beginning of the game, so that the estimated required time skyrockets.

To determine if the player is ahead of or behind schedule, the system estimates the time required to finish the game. This includes the time for the movement from door to door (distance times a general estimate of the velocity) and the time to kill the monsters (damage to be made divided by the estimated power of the player), which depends on player's and the monsters' life energies.

Depending on the user's choice, the remaining target time is determined through a simple timer or from location data. In the latter case, the distance between the location at the game's start and the current location is used to determine the average traveling velocity of the player in the real world. The estimate for the remaining time is computed by assuming that the player continues traveling at this velocity to the destination defined upfront.

5 Prototype and User Test

Our prototype is based on Mogre 1.4.8—a .NET wrapper of the game engine Ogre 1.4.8—using standard commercial and freeware dungeon props. The user's input is handled through the Object-Oriented Input System (OIS), wrapped by Mogre MOIS. The adaption is run once per second and takes about 15 ms on a standard PC; building a new room takes about 200 ms. For easy setup and editing, the databases are created as a collection of XML files. The localization control runs in a separate thread that is periodically queried by the main game thread. The position data are collected from a standard BlueTooth GPS receiver; currently, the end position is specified as latitude/longitude, which can be determined with help of a Google Maps script, for instance.

To get initial feedback on how well the adaptation works and on how invasive it feels we conducted a preliminary user test with 14 participants (12 m, 2 f; age 18 to 30). All subjects but one had several years of computer gaming experience; half of the participants reported to play ten or more hours per week. In the test, each subject played one session of the game after initial familiarization; afterward, he or she completed a questionnaire. For simplicity and reproducibility we chose the timer-based version of the prototype instead of the location-based version. The intended playing time was preset to three minutes. The participants were not informed upfront about the adaptation mechanism.

Almost all subjects indicated that the placement of the monsters and the items and the sequence of the rooms were either good or inconspicuous (13 of 14 for three questions). The majority of the participants found the end to fit into the game (11 of 14), but half of them reported that the game felt too simple.

Table 1 and Figure 3 show excerpts of statistics we collected during the game sessions. Even if the player's strength varies drastically, as demonstrated by the

Table 1. The statistics (examples from the test, sorted by playing time) indicate that the duration can be kept relatively constant. See the text for a discussion of the outliers

Playing Time	Rooms Visited	Monsters Killed	Score (Loot and Monsters)
2:04	3	1	0
2:59	13	21	658
3:00	9	14	2911
3:00	12	20	74
3:06	14	23	1428
3:09	6	8	2061
3:10	5	4	2424
3:19	9	13	327
3:21	9	14	2712
4:20	6	3	3215

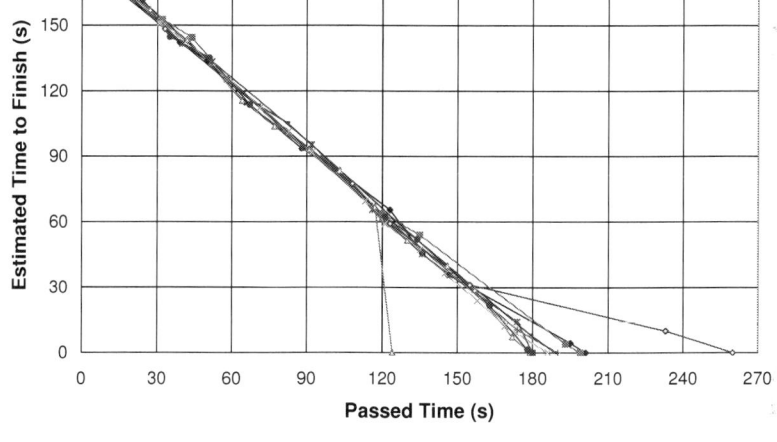

Fig. 3. Thanks to the repeated adaptation to the player's progress, the estimate on the remaining time remains closely tied to the eventual result (data of the same play sessions as given in Table 1)

scores, the game's duration only changes by some seconds. As the adaptation is not rigid, some fluctuation in the resulting duration cannot be avoided. We included the two most prominent outliers in the table: One user's character was killed early in the game; another user spent 77 seconds in the penultimate room, in which the game cannot be finished since this room was not scheduled to contain the master monster.

6   Conclusion and Outlook

We have demonstrated a method to let a video game finish at a certain time or when the player arrives at a given destination. The adaptation deals with a wide range of the users' abilities and remains mostly inconspicuous. We note, however, some uncommon situations in which the room-based adaptation fails. Handling these would require substantial ad-hoc changes to the game's rules.

The current prototype can be used on a notebook computer with the adaptation being controlled through a GPS receiver. This does not cover all mobile settings, however. For instance, GPS data are not available on a subway train. Thus, a next step will be a version for a mobile phone that employs cell IDs for localization. Other options would be in-flight and (car) rear seat entertainment systems, where localization data or even estimated arrival times are readily available. These applications would require scaling up the gaming times—and thus the game's content and story—to accommodate for hours of playing. The basic mechanisms, however, could still be in place.

To create a version of the game with open portals instead of doors, one could limit the adjustments to parts of the world that have so far been invisible to the player. Finally, one could overcome the simplifying limitations of the dungeon and procedurally build—and continuously rebuild—a virtual city [8].

References

1. Benford, S., Magerkurth, C., Ljungstrand, P.: Bridging the Physical and Digital in Pervasive Gaming. Communications of the ACM 48(3), 54–57 (2005)
2. Magerko, B.: Adaptation in Digital Games. IEEE Computer, 87–89 (June 2008)
3. Wong, K.K.W.: Player Adaptive Entertainment Computing. In: 2nd International Conference on Digital Interactive Media in Entertainment and Arts (DIMEA), p. 13. ACM Press, New York (2007)
4. Hunicke, R.: The Case for Dynamic Difficulty Adjustment in Games. In: 2005 ACM SIGCHI International Conference on Advances in Computer Entertainment Technology (ACE), pp. 429–433. ACM Press, New York (2005)
5. Gustafsson, A., Bichard, J., Brunnberg, L., Juhlin, O., Combetto, M.: Believable Environments: Generating Interactive Storytelling in Vast Location-based Pervasive Games. In: ACM SIGCHI International Conference on Advances in Computer Entertainment Technology (ACE), Article No. 24. ACM Press, New York (2006)
6. Adcock, M., Chung, J., Schmandt, C.: AreWeThereYet? – A Temporally Aware Media Player. In: 9th Australian User Interface Conference (AUIC), p. 29–32. Australian Computer Society, Darlinghurst (2008)
7. Brauer, R., Öhsen, A., Loviscach, J.: Automated Interior Design from A to Z. In: SIGGRAPH 2008 Poster (2008)
8. Wonka, P., Hanson, E., Müller, P., Watson, B.: Procedural Modeling of Urban Environments. In: SIGGRAPH 2006 Course (2006)

Design and Implementation of a Mobile Exergaming Platform

Laurent Prévost[1,2], Olivier Liechti[1], and Michael J. Lyons[2]

[1] HEIG-VD, Yverdon-les-Bains, Suisse
[2] Ritsumeikan University, Kyoto, Japan
{Laurent.Prevost,olivier.liechti}@heig-vd.ch,
lyons@im.ritsumei.ac.jp

Abstract. This paper describes the design, implementation, and initial testing of a reusable platform for the creation of pervasive games with geo-localization services. We concentrate on role-playing games built by combining several types of simpler mini-games having three major components: Quests; Collectables; and Non-player characters (NPC). Quests encourage players to be active in their physical environment and take part in collaborative play; Collectables provide motivation; and NPCs enable player-friendly interaction with the platform. Each of these elements poses different technical requirements, which were met by implementing the gaming platform using the inTrack pervasive middle-ware being developed by our group. Several sample games were implemented and tested within the urban environment of Kyoto, Japan, using gaming clients running on mobile phones from NTT DoCoMo, Japan's largest mobile provider.

Keywords: pervasive computing, exergaming, location-based service.

1   Introduction

Interactive entertainment systems traditionally offer a limited choice of user interface technologies and interaction styles that make little use of the human body and require low physical exertion. Video games, in particular, have been accused of contributing to sedentary habits and epidemic obesity amongst young people [1]. Recently, however, a new generation of video gaming devices is encouraging new styles of interactive recreation which are both more natural and involve greater physical exertion. A study at the Mayo Clinic in the USA found that children's energy expenditure increased greatly when playing a video game requiring physical activity, as compared to a traditional video game [2,3]. The spreading popularity of these new "exertion interface" games, or "exergames", is a social phenomenon of increasing benefit to the health and well being of millions of people worldwide.

In Japan, excessive interest in entertainment media, including video games, is a contributing factor to social phenomena such as the *otaku* [4] and *hikikomori* [5]. An *otaku*, (loosely "nerd" or "geek") is someone with obsessive level interest in a hobby, often involving fantasy media such as anime, manga, and games. Obsession with

A. Nijholt, D. Reidsma, and H. Hondorp (Eds.): INTETAIN 2009, LNICST 9, pp. 213–220, 2009.
© ICST Institute for Computer Sciences, Social Informatics and Telecommunications Engineering 2009

interactive entertainment media may complicate the socially pathological *hikikomori* ("severe social withdrawal") condition, which the Japanese Ministry of Health, Labour, and Welfare defines as individuals who isolate themselves in their homes for a period of more than six months [5].

In this work, we design and implement a platform for the development of interactive entertainment systems that encourages gaming outside the house, which is both physically and socially active. Mobile technology is reaching a stage of sophistication that can support collaborative location-aware interaction via media-rich contents. In the Japanese mobile phone market, for example, technologies such as GPS, internet connectivity, and touch sensitive high resolution colour displays have wide market penetration, offering opportunities for the development of mobile entertainment systems that area as engaging as home-based multimedia consoles. Mobile gaming platforms therefore has the potential to support a style of gaming conducive to the improvement of the physical and social health of game enthusiasts.

The development of mobile interactive entertainment systems is a relatively new area and expected to introduce new challenges for designers and engineers. For example, what genres of games will be most suitable to mobile platforms? How can game processes and data be managed in the context of mobile cooperative play? How can the (compared to home consoles) relatively limited resources of a mobile platform be most effectively used for a rich interactive entertainment experience? To explore these questions concretely we designed and implemented a geo-localized mobile gaming development platform. The work is motivated partly by the potential social benefits of mobile gaming, and partly by the interest in exploring novel forms of interaction offered by this nascent technology. The current paper is intended as a design report on lessons learned and new questions asked as a consequence of developing a working implementation of our mobile exergaming platform.

2   The Mobile Exergaming Platform (MEP): Game Play

For concreteness, we chose to focus this study on one style of interactive entertainment: the role-playing adventure game (RPG). This is usually a style of game requiring no physical activity, but the quests typical of RPGs should adapt well to movement in geographical space. Hence, one of the major technological objectives in the project was a generalized platform to provide the mechanisms for implementing mobile games adapted to specific locations and contexts. The platform should support tasks encouraging active exploration of the physical environment. Tasks should be general to support flexibility in site-specific implementation as well as the potential for extension and creative modification in the longer term. In this section we introduce the MEP conceptual architecture: introducing the primary components: players, non-player characters (NPC), quests, dialogs, an inventory of virtual objects, puzzles, and location data.

In keeping with the proposed mobile adventure RPG genre, tasks take the form of "quests" involving single players acting individually or multiple players in cooperative activity. Quests possess general features that were decided from the outset of the core MEP conceptual architecture design. For example, to obtain a new quest, a player uses a MEP dialog mechanism to communicate with non-player characters (NPC), a typical feature used by role-playing games to provide the narrative content of a game. Additionally, as is typical for role-playing games, MEP quests involve virtual items to be sought, collected, carried, dropped, given, traded and so on. Such items are essentially plot devices useful in motivating the player to engage in physically active, and sometimes socially cooperative play. Entertaining engagement with the physical, cultural, and social environment remains the primary goal of the mobile MEP, and the virtual objects serve to scaffold this engagement. Specific attributes of objects are undetermined in the core MEP architecture. It is intended that localized implementations of a MEP-based game will adapt objects to specific features of the geographical and cultural environs. For example, one quest might be to collect virtual flowers in the physical setting of a field or garden. To give another example, if the game is to be played in a market, a specified quest might require the player(s) to find, collect, and trade virtual foodstuffs or other goods.

Figure 1 shows the main mechanisms and entities of the game. Players, Items and Non-Player Characters are all derived from the generic entity at the basis of the MEP framework. This entity is normally associated with geographical localization data. For real players, the geo data corresponds to the player's location in physical space. For virtual entities such as items and NPCs, this is not constrained by physical reality.

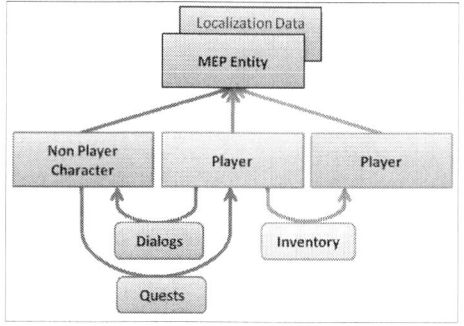

Fig. 1. MEP Game Conceptual Architecture

In keeping with our primary target of creatively augmenting the engagement of a player with their geographical surroundings, game play primarily consists of obtaining and completing tasks with a spatial aspect. The quest mechanism is also the primary means by which players interact with the game system as well as with other players. With the current implementation, for example, quests are obtained through interactive dialog with non-player characters. The quest mechanism is highly configurable, permitting the construction of a rich variety of tasks. For concreteness we have restricted the current implementation to three major types of quests:

- Reaching a target location
- Collecting an item (virtual object)
- Solving a rebus (picture puzzle).

The MEP mechanisms allow the association of virtual objects with real-world geography. This naturally suggests quests in which a player must move through a physical environment to search for, discover, and collect such items, encouraging the player to be physically active in the exploration of an environment. Items can be placed anywhere and arranged to form a path, or placed surrounding a building or geographical feature. The MEP architecture does not restrict the positioning of items, so that the quest designer may freely use their imagination.

The third type of quest we have studied is different from the others in that it explicitly requires interaction between players. One of the design questions we are interested in is how to provide a flexible way to scaffold interaction between players. We also asked whether such interaction could be verified without having to explicitly rely on geographical data, because, for various reasons, this data sometimes has variable accuracy or is not continuously available. We satisfied both of these design criteria with the quest described next. The key idea is to provide two users with a puzzle that can only be solved by comparing data they have each obtained from the game server. We implemented a solution using a popular children's puzzle where two different pictures are supplied to two players. The players obtain these pictures from non-player characters but then must locate another (real) player to complete the puzzle. When the two pictures are viewed together in the correct sequence, the solution may be found. This type of puzzle is known as a rebus, a class of puzzle that uses pictures to represent words or parts of words [6].

3 MEP Architecture

This section gives a technical description of the architecture of the system used to support the game design described in Chapter 2. The MEP Architecture is based on a multi-tier application (figure 2). The main application is composed of the two sub-systems: i) inTrack, which manages localization information and ii) the game engine, which manages game information.

The inTrack platform is being developed at the University of Engineering and Management of Western Switzerland. It integrates a middleware layer that offers mechanisms for the implementation of rich location-based applications. Two APIs are exposed by inTrack. The first one is used to send localization updates for various tracking technologies. The second one is used to retrieve the state of mobile entities via various types of queries. MEP uses both APIs, since the phone itself is used to track the players.

The game server manages the state of the game entities and implements the mechanisms to support quests, dialogs, and so on. It is important to bear in mind that the game server has to manage the data link between the inTrack platform and MEP. The inTrack platform provides an API needed for this linkage of the mobile entities (viewed from inTrack) and the game entities (viewed from MEP).

In the implementation studied here, the game server also provides the client user interface running via the player's web browser. This interface is specific to the iMode technology provided by NTT DoCoMo in Japan. iMode supports use of the Internet from a DoCoMo mobile phone [7].

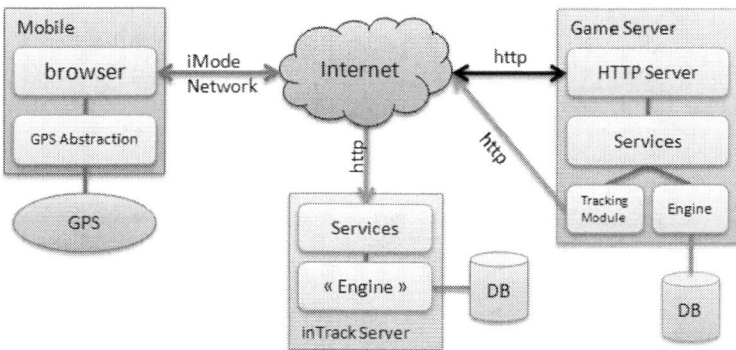

Fig. 2. MEP multi-tier application

Communications between the mobile client and the game server, or the game server and inTrack server take place via the HTTP protocol, integrating the diverse technologies involved in a specific MEP implementation. The game server embeds a configuration mechanism that allows building specific games based on the various mechanisms presented above. This is the main approach we have taken for adapting the platform for a specific gaming context. inTrack local mechanisms are directly integrated inside the game server application. This part of application ensures communication between the game server and inTrack server.

The mobile client in this project runs on a mobile phone from NTT DoCoMo, one of the major mobile service providers in Japan. NTT DoCoMo was selected not only for it's large share of the mobile market, but because the development environment provided by DoCoMo, a proprietary version of MIDP known as DoJa [8], seems to be more open for independent developers and better documented than those offered by the other major mobile providers.

Development of location aware applications under DoCoMo is possible by making use an attribute (known as "lcs") of the HTML tags A HREF and FORM that allows the developer to automatically add the local GPS data to the HTTP request. When this attribute is set, a dialog box appears with each HTTP request querying the user for agreement (or refusal) to send their location data. iMode-based interaction offers increased flexibility, compatibility and general ease of implementation of the game client.

4   User Experience with a Trial MEP Game

To evaluate MEP as a reusable platform, a concrete game was implemented in the context of the urban environment of Kyoto, Japan. This game is named the Kyoto Mobile Exergaming Project or KMEP. Figure 3 illustrates one of the KMEP game quests, "River of Flowers". This quest requires the player to collect some flowers while walking, running, or cycling along the Kamogawa (Kamo River), a popular location for leisure activities. The quest is received from an NPC, and then starting in the South, and walking northward, one searches for and collects virtual flowers.

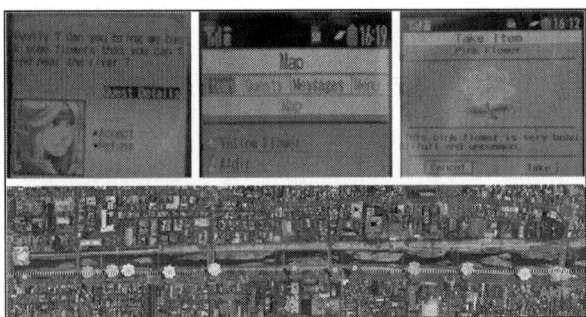

Fig. 3. The "River of Flowers" quest

The "River of Flowers" quest is of the second type described in section 2. After collecting a number of flowers, the player meets another NPC, who informs the player of the status of quest completion. "River of Flowers" is a single-player quest. It implicitly requires the player to walk or ride a bicycle, in order to collect virtual flowers. While this quest is primarily a demonstration of the MEP and inTrack platforms, it also illustrates the point that the gaming experience gains the richness of the physical environment that is not obtained with a desktop gaming platform. For example, during the first run of this game, our gamer was surprised by the unexpected sight of migrating birds – a memorable event he would never have experienced indoors at home with his computer.

In the Rebus category of quests, players compare pictures to solve a word puzzle. When the players obtain a solution they communicate with the MEP server for verification, which leads to the next stage of the game – for example they may then meet a new NPC and be given a quest. Rebus quests are not limited to two players. Indeed the complexity and challenge of finding the correct phrase for a rebus puzzle increases as the number of players increases.

5   Related Work

In this section we discuss the relationship of the current project to several prior works. The literature of ubiquitous and mobile computing is enormous, so we mention only key works that directly inspired KMEP.

City Explorer [9] is a game based on the board game Carcassonne. In City Explorer, players put some virtual tags in a real urban environment, with location categories such as bars, restaurants, and so on. Players must take a picture of the location where he has placed a virtual tag to prove he has actually visited that location. The others players can accept or refuse a player's virtual tag, based after examining the photo posted by the player. Hence localization is ensured both using GPS data and verification by the community of gamers, giving gamers an active role in validating localizations. This both authenticates physical movement in the urban environment (as opposed to purely virtual play) and introduces a social element to game play. In this project, the localization is ensured by the GPS and the acceptation of the players. The players have an active role to decide if the localizations are valid or not. In contrast to the quest-oriented RPG presented in the current paper (KMEP), the time frame of the City Explorer game is even more loosely specified and may last from one day to several weeks or longer. The game board is also not clearly defined before the game begins, but remains flexible and depends on the will of the players. By contrast, KMEP offers somewhat more structured game play, with quests being determined ahead of time by designers.

Another direct influence is the uBike project by one of the co-authors (OL) of the current paper. uBike also attempts to increase the motivation of people to do exercise [10]. In the uBike project it was found that supporting a social aspect of exercise by fostering encounters and interactions in the real world, was found to be a promising strategy for motivating exercise [11].

6 Conclusion

In this work we have provided a novel framework for the implementation of mobile role-playing games. We used the inTrack mobile middleware being developed at HEIG-VD to devise a new mobile exergaming platform (MEP). MEP is now fully operational and one of the positive outcomes of the work reported in this paper is the testing of this platform via its successful deployment in the local context of Kyoto, Japan.

Configuration of specific games was found to be a complex issue requiring the careful attention of the designer. To manage this complexity, game configuration was specified using a suite of XML files. This allowed a simple and flexible way to specialize the MEP for specific contexts. With its three major gaming components working solidly, the MEP allows designers to construct a variety of narrative quests, by mixing and matching quest types, collectables, and non-player characters, with no intrinsic limitations on how the types may be combined and configured.

Correctly designed, quests can offer a gaming experience conducive to physical exercise. This depends primarily on how the quest designer makes imaginative use of the geographical and cultural qualities of the context in which a game takes place. One of the quests implemented with in KMEP required a 4 km walk or bicycle ride, taking in several different terrains including shopping zones and riverside paths, leading to a fortuitous encounter with flocks of migrating birds. We believe that such games hold promise as a possible bridge for the otaku, stay-at-home technology addicts, to gently re-introduce them to the beauty and pleasure of the physical environment.

Early in this project, serious limitations of the Japanese mobile computing development environment were encountered: namely - that all Japanese providers restrict direct access to localization information of GPS enabled handsets, preventing implementation of games in which the MEP continually polled players location. This presented interesting challenges to our development process and led to some novel solutions. For example, we devised a novel method to authenticate player cooperation without building specific technical services. The Rebus puzzles, requiring real-world cooperation of multiple players, proved to be an effective way to extend existing MEP functionality and verify collaborative play.

Several aspects of MEP are points for our continuing efforts. First of all, a user-friendly authoring tool is needed to allow configuration and managing games by designers without having to edit XML files – an error-prone process which requires too much detailed knowledge of game data. Such a tool would also, ideally, provide checks for the integrity of game designs and other design support tools. We are plan to extend support for interactions between players to increase possibilities for social gaming. The current MEP architecture is sufficiently flexible to allow other types of interaction, so that research can proceed without a major revision of the platform described in the current paper. Lastly, we would like to port the user interface to other mobile providers.

Acknowledgement

This work was supported by research grants from the Japan Society for the Promotion of Science, HEIG-VD and the Hasler foundation.

References

1. Brown, D.: Playing to Win: Video Games and the Fight against Obesity. Journal of the American Dietetic Association 106(2), 188–189 (2006)
2. Lanningham-Foster, L., et al.: Expenditure of Sedentary Screen Time Compared With Active Screen Time. Pediatrics 118(6), E1831 (2006)
3. Let's Get Physical, The Economist, March 8 (2007)
4. McNicol, T.: Meet the Geek Elite. Wired Magazine (July 2006)
5. Itou, J.: Shakaiteki Hikikomori wo Meguru Tiiki Seisin Hoken Katudou No Guide-line (Guideline on Mental Health Activities in Communities for Social Withdrawal), Ministry of Health, Labor, and Welfare, Tokyo (2003)
6. Wikipedia, http://en.wikipedia.org/wiki/Rebus (accessed January 22, 2009)
7. NTT DoCoMo, http://www.nttdocomo.co.jp/english/service/imode/about/index.html (accessed January 27, 2009)
8. NTT DoCoMo, http://www.nttdocomo.co.jp/english/service/imode/make/content/iappli/architecture/index.html (accessed January 27, 2009)
9. Matyas, S.: Playful Geospatial Data Acquisition by Location-based Gaming Communities. The International Journal of Virtual Realities 6(3), 1–10 (2007)
10. Liechti, O.: Fun on the wheels: the ubike social application. In: International Workshop on Ubiquitous Computing and Wellness, UBICOMP 2007 (2007)
11. Liechti, O., Burnet, C.: Social data analysis and physical activity. In: Proceedings of the International Workshop on Social Data Analysis at ACM CHI 2008 (2008)

Affective Pacman: A Frustrating Game for Brain-Computer Interface Experiments

Boris Reuderink[1], Anton Nijholt[1], and Mannes Poel[1]

University of Twente, Faculty of EEMCS,
P.O. Box 217, 7500 AE Enschede, The Netherlands
{reuderin,a.nijholt,mpoel}@ewi.utwente.nl

Abstract. We present the design and development of Affective Pacman, a game that induces frustration to study the effect of user state changes on the EEG signal. Affective Pacman is designed to induce frustration for short periods, and allows the synchronous recording of a wide range of sensors, such as physiological sensors and EEG in addition to the game state. A self-assessment is integrated in the game to track changes in user state. Preliminary results indicate a significant effect of the frustration induction on the EEG.

Keywords: Brain-Computer Interfaces, EEG, physiological sensors, frustration, affective computing, Pacman.

1 Introduction

A brain-computer interface (BCI) provides a direct communication link between the brain of a subject and a computer. The brain signal can be used to control the computer, and indirectly other devices. BCI have mostly been applied in medical settings, for example to enable patients with Amyotropic Lateral Sclerosis (ALS) to communicate. In this paper however, we focus on the application of BCI in computer games.

The use of BCIs in computer games poses some additional challenges. We use electroencephalogram (EEG) sensors to record the electrical brain activity for the BCI. The EEG signal is known to be very sensitive to other sources of electrical activity, such as eye (electrooculogram, EOG) and muscle (electromyogram, EMG) movement. Besides these well-known influences, we expect that the user-state can be influenced by both the content of the game and the quality of BCI control, as current BCIs do not yet provide perfect recognition rates. Our goal is to make BCIs useful for gaming. Hence our BCIs should be robust against changes in the user state during game play, such as frustration caused by a malfunctioning BCI.

We will introduce the design of a Pacman game that we can use to investigate the influence of frustration on the EEG signal. We have chosen to focus on an actual movement paradigm, in contrast to the more common imaginary movement paradigm. This means that the user controls the game using real button presses, and we record the EEG only for off-line analysis. Because actual movement is

A. Nijholt, D. Reidsma, and H. Hondorp (Eds.): INTETAIN 2009, LNICST 9, pp. 221–227, 2009.
© ICST Institute for Computer Sciences, Social Informatics and Telecommunications Engineering 2009

very similar to imaginary movement [7], we expect our results to generalize to imaginary movement paradigms.

2   Previous Work

The induction of frustration has already been studied a few times in the context of interactive games. For example, Scheirer et al. [8] used a game in which the mouse failed to respond correctly at random intervals to induce a state of frustration in users, and collected physiological, behavioural and video data. A classifier based on Hidden Markov Models could correctly predict the user state based on the physiological signals of skin conductivity and blood volume pressure 67% of the time. Klein et al. [5] designed a human-computer interaction system that actively assists the user in recovering from negative emotional states using active listening. The experiment induced frustration by stalling the main character of an adventure game similar to the setup of Scheirer et al.. The system was evaluated by comparing with a condition in which the emotions are ignored and a condition in which the user could vent their emotions to the computer. Stalling the game did frustrate the user significantly more than the normal condition.

Diener and Oertel [4] performed a set of experiments using a modified Tetris game in which they identified, recognized and visualized affective states of the player. Affective states could be recognized from the physiological signals with accuracies of up to 70%. For evaluation of the affective states, the Self Assessment Manikin (SAM, [2]) was used. The four quadrants of of the valence-arousal dimensions were used as target affective states, as well as a "loss-of-control" condition in which 20% of the keyboard commands were ignored. These three studies seem to indicate that a malfunctioning control device can be used to frustrate the user on purpose.

A BCI controlled Pacman has already been created by Krepki et al. [6]. They implemented a BCI based on Lateralized Readiness Potential (LRP)[1] that was used to rotate Pacman. The BCI was trained using three to four sessions of seven minutes of training in which the user pressed keys at will (self paced), or performed imaginary movement in response to a cue. During the game, the user could make a decision every two seconds.

3   Design

In this section we describe the design of the Affective Pacman game. We will start with a short description of the requirements, describe the design of the game and finally the design of the experiment for frustration induction using Pacman.

3.1   Requirements

In our experiment we are comparing a condition with normal user interaction with a condition with frustration caused by malfunctioning controls and game

---

[1] The LRP is a slow negative EEG shift that develops over the activated motor cortex during a period of about 1 second before the actual movement onset.

response. As EEG is known to be a non-stationary signal, we need to spread our conditions evenly over the experimental session, and change conditions often. To verify that we are inducing frustration, we will use a self assessment after each condition. Because of our frequent changes of conditions, this self assessment has to be integrated in the game in order to minimize the strain on the user. And finally, the frustration manipulation needs to be hidden from the user to prevent the user from accepting it as a part of the experiment.

3.2 Game Design

The game is a Pacman clone close to the original: Four ghosts roam through a two dimensional maze, and for each level the goal is to eat all the pellets without dying. Points are scored for pellets eaten, and Pacman dies when touched by a ghost. When all the pellets are eaten, Pacman advances to the next level.

One major difference with other Pacman implementations is that our Pacman game implements **two button control**; the left shift-key of the keyboard turns Pacman 90° counter-clockwise, the right shift-key turns Pacman 90° clockwise. This allows us to let the user rest both hands on the keyboard, and play the game with index-finger movements. This configuration was chosen because the area on the motor cortex corresponding to left and right hand are far apart, and can therefore be used for BCI control. As in the original it is not possible to stop moving; only when Pacman hits a wall he stops. When Pacman turns in our game, he keeps moving in his last direction until he can move in the new direction. Corners can thus be taken far in advance, but reversing direction in a long corridor requires two turn commands to take effect. As this takes some time to get used to, the first level acts as a tutorial level in which the user can practise the two-button controls.

The game keeps track of the current high score, and displays this high score and the current score on the top-right screen corner to stimulate the user to set a new best.

3.3 Experiment Design

The experiment is built from 2 minute blocks in which frustration is, or is not induced. To keep the game enjoyable only one third of the blocks are of the frustration condition. The blocks are evenly distributed over the session by shuffling lists of 3 blocks (2 normal, 1 frustration) and adding these together. To frustrate the user we manipulate both the user input and the visual output. We randomly miss 15% of the key presses, resulting in a barely playable game. The screen freezes for two to five frames at 25 frames per second with a probability of 5%.

After each block, we assess the user state using the Self Assessment Manikin (SAM, [2]). The user can use the numeric keys on the keyboard to choose a point on the Likert-scale below the pictograms for respectively the valence, arousal and dominance axis (Figure 1). After pressing three digits, the experiment returns to the game that can then be resumed. We expect to measure a shift towards negative valence, higher arousal and lower dominance after each frustration block.

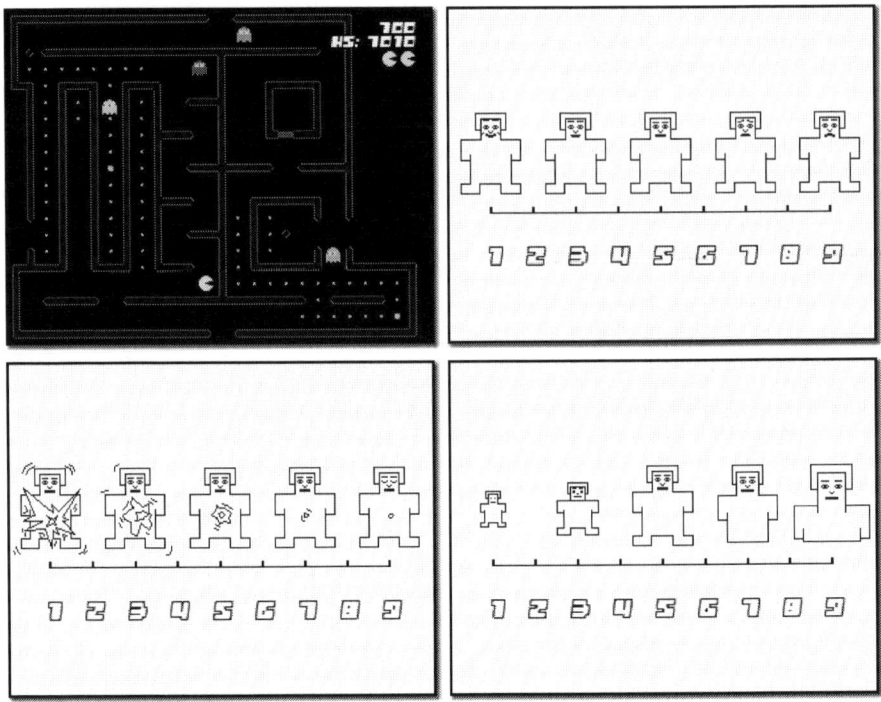

Fig. 1. From left to right, top to bottom: A screen shot of the third level, the SAM for valence, the SAM for arousal and the SAM for dominance

4   Sensors and Recording

We use our BioSemi ActiveTwo EEG system to record the EEG and physiological sensors. For EEG we use 32 Ag/AgCl electrodes at the positions of the Extended International 10-20 system. To measure and filter the influence of ocular and muscle artifacts we record the EOG (bipolar horizontal and vertical pairs) and EMG signals of the finger movement used to press the game controls.

In addition to these sensors, we measure the galvanic skin response (GSR), the heart rate, respiration, temperature, and the blood volume pressure (BVP). Both the EEG and physiological sensors are synchronized in hardware with event markers written from the game. The same physiological sensors were used by Chanel et al. [3] to detect boredom and anxiety in a Tetris game, resulting in significant differences for GSR, heart rate, respiration and temperature.

5   Preliminary Results

For our first subject we compared the Event Related Desynchronizatoin (ERD) related to the different key-presses in the game. The ERD is a decrease in band-power over the motor cortices related to motor activity. The EEG-data was

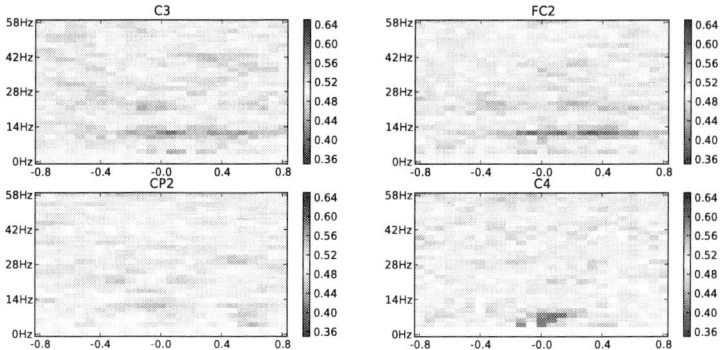

Fig. 2. Time-frequency plots for the EEG sensors C3 (left motorcortex), FC2, CP2, and C4 (right motorcortex). The colors indicate the AUC for left versus right, blue indicates more power in the left condition, red indicates more power in the right condition. Both C3 and FC2 show significant ERD-related differences around 12Hz. The key-presses are aligined at timepoint 0.

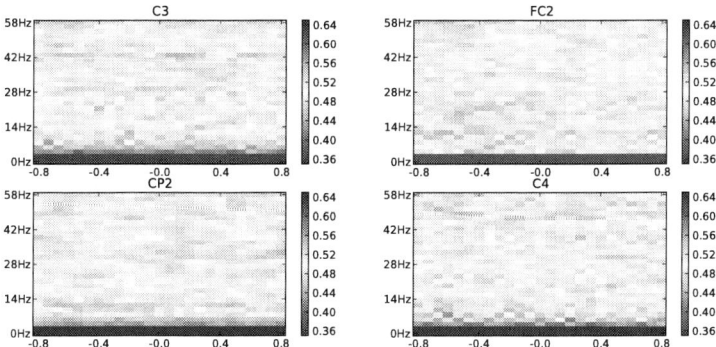

Fig. 3. Time-frequency plots for the EEG sensors C3 (left motorcortex), FC2, CP2, and C4 (right motorcortex). The colors indicate the AUC; blue indicates more power in the frustration condition, red indicates more power in the normal condition. The delta and theta-band are significantly different, but also around 12Hz differences can be observed (FC2, CP2).

re-referenced to the common average reference (CAR). After re-referencing, two seconds surrounding a key-press were extracted. These instances were transformed into a time-frequency representation using a Short-Term Fourier Transform (STFT). We used the area under curve (AUC)[2] of the Receiver Operating Characteristic (ROC) to compare left and right hand movements (Figure 2). Both motor cortices display significant differences ($p \leq 0.05$, Agarwal et al. [1]). This difference in bandpower indicates an ERD, that could be used for

---

[2] The AUC is a ranking statistic equivalent to the Wilcoxon-Mann-Whitney statistic.

classification. The right motor cortex (C4) displays an interleaving pattern around 8Hz that could be related to the LRP.

Now that we have verified the presence of ERD, we can compare the normal and frustration condition, hoping for a difference in the frequency ranges relevant for the detection of motor activity. Figure 3 show differences between the conditions. The differences in the delta-band (up to 3 Hz) and theta-band (4–7 Hz) are significant ($p \leq 0.05$), but also around 12Hz where the ERD for this subject manifests itself differences are visible. This is a observation that supports the hypothesis that the frustration could deteriorate BCI performance.

6   Conclusions and Future Work

We have presented the design of Affective Pacman, a game that allows us to research the effects of frustration on BCIs used in games. The game is designed to induce frustration for short periods, allows synchronous recording of a wide range of sensors.

The users report that the control of Pacman is challenging, and they assumed that the frustration induction was a bug in the game. This indicates that the method of induction is not too obvious, as is required for a successful experiment. Our preliminary analysis already revealed significant differences between the normal and the frustration condition, and indicates that features used for classification could be affected. A bigger test with ten to twenty users is planned in the near future. The real influence of frustration on BCI performance will be measured by training a BCI on data of the normal condition, and test on both unseen normal blocks and unseen blocks of the frustration condition.

A nice by-product of this experiment is that the SAM could indicate user changes over time, such as boredom, fatigue etc. If such a trend is found we could try to relate it to the BCI performance or even directly to the EEG. Future versions of the game could let the user play using the keyboard until the BCI has reached a acceptable performance level, and then transparently switch to brain-controlled game play.

Acknowledgements

The authors gratefully acknowledge the support of the BrainGain Smart Mix Programme of the Netherlands Ministry of Economic Affairs and the Netherlands Ministry of Education, Culture and Science.

References

[1] Agarwal, S., Graepel, T., Herbrich, R., Roth, D.: A large deviation bound for the area under the ROC curve. In: Advances in Neural Information Processing Systems, vol. 17, pp. 9–16 (2005)

[2] Bradley, M.M., Lang, P.J.: Measuring emotion: The self-assessment manikin and the semantic differential. Journal of Behavior Therapy and Experimental Psychiatry 25(1), 49–59 (1994)

[3] Chanel, G., Rebetez, C., Bétrancourt, M., Pun, T.: Boredom, engagement and anxiety as indicators for adaptation to difficulty in games. In: Proceedings of the 12th International Conference on Entertainment and Media in the Ubiquitous Era, pp. 13–17 (2008)

[4] Diener, H., Oertel, K.: Experimental approach to affective interaction in games. In: Edutainment, pp. 507–518 (2006)

[5] Klein, J., Moon, Y., Picard, R.W.: This computer responds to user frustration: Theory, design, and results. Interacting with Computers 14, 119–140 (2002)

[6] Krepki, R., Blankertz, B., Curio, G., Müller, K.-R.: The berlin brain-computer interface (BBCI) - towards a new communication channel for online control in gaming applications. Multimedia Tools and Applications 33(1), 73–90 (2007)

[7] McFarland, D.J., Miner, L.A., Vaughan, T.M., Wolpaw, J.R.: Mu and beta rhythm topographies during motor imagery and actual movements. Brain Topography 12(3), 117–186 (2000)

[8] Scheirer, J., Fernandez, R., Klein, J., Picard, R.W.: Frustrating the user on purpose: A step toward bulding an affective computer. Interacting with Computers 14, 93–118 (2002)

Stay Tuned!
An Automatic RSS Feeds Trans-coder

Patrick Salamin, Alexandre Wetzel, Daniel Thalmann, and Frédéric Vexo

VRLab - EPFL, Switzerland
patrick.salamin@epfl.ch
http://vrlab.epfl.ch

Abstract. News aggregators are widely used to read RSS feeds but they require the user to be in front of a screen. While moving, people usually do not have any display, or very small ones. Moreover, they need to perform actions to get access to the news: download a tool, choose to generate audio files from the news, and send them to e.g. an MP3 player. We propose in this paper a system that automatically detects when the user leaves the computer room and directly sends the trans-coded news onto the user Smartphone. All the aggregated news are then transmitted to the user who can listen to them without any action. We present in this paper such a system and the very promising results we obtained after testing it.

Keywords: User context awareness, RSS reader, Trans-coding, Geolocalization.

1 Introduction

Many people are using news aggregators but sometimes (e.g. while moving) they do not have at their disposal a screen, or a too small one to read the RSS feeds. A solution is to download one of the available-on-the-Internet tools. But in this case, the user must press a button to generate the audio files, connect his/her MP3 player to the computer, and accomplish the file transfer with a "drag and drop" operation onto the player.

We propose in this paper a solution executing an automatic transfer of the trans-coded RSS feeds onto the Smartphone that will directly continue to read the news.

We will first present an overview of the current technologies and researches on the fields of context awareness and trans-coding processes. After this, we will describe more in detail our concept and the needed system architecture. We will finally conclude with a discussion on the results of the previously described tests we made, but also on the further improvements of our application.

2 Related Works

As the user cannot read the news while walking, we need to trans-code the information. Some very promising researches were done within the trans-coding

A. Nijholt, D. Reidsma, and H. Hondorp (Eds.): INTETAIN 2009, LNICST 9, pp. 228–233, 2009.

domain, especially with the auditory and visual modalities. Jacquemin et al. e.g. developed a system involving audio- and visuo-rendering to mimic gusts of wind blowing a veil [1]. We also developed in 2007 an application allowing blind people to recognize 3D digital content with the help of a PDA [2]. By the way, there already exist several trans-coders to podcast; we could cite for instance Netvibes[1], Feedburner[2], Google reader[3], etc. But the main disadvantage of these tools resides in the manual operations needed to use them.

With the apparition of the "user context awareness" concept, the system must react according to the user context instead of requiring an interaction with the user like pushing a button. An invisible indoor geo-localization system could lead to a fully automated process and a real follow of the user [3]. The system, aware of the user context, must then be able to detect the user displacements, or at least the user location, in order to switch from the screen to another way to transmit the information. There exist several other technologies using specific hardware like infrared, magnetic, ultrasound, etc. But even if they are very precise, they are also very expensive and usually limited to one room. More recent systems tend to use cheaper and already deployed technologies like GSM, Wi-Fi, or Bluetooth. For example, RADAR [4][5] is a tracking system working with the signal strength of radio-based devices. This system inspired several researchers who tried to improve different aspects of the system: accuracy [6][7], localization in high signal fluctuation areas [8], and only using access points [9][10]. But in our experiment we only need to know if the user left his/her computer and the researches of Dhawan [11], [12], and [13] also inform us on range and possible co-existence of Bluetooth and Wi-Fi.

Based on the researches cited above, we decided to trans-code RSS feeds into audio files that will be read on a Smartphone. The user's proximity detection will be performed with the help of the Bluetooth and the data will be transmitted over IP with a previously installed Wi-Fi network. Our solution is described more in detail in the following sections.

3   Concept Description

Nowadays, most of people with a computer use news aggregators like Google News. But, when people are no more in front of their computer, they still should be able to get access to the news they have aggregated. They have then to find a way to trans-code the RSS feeds and to send them to a player they will wear while moving.

Our system performs all these actions automatically (Figure 1). It first stores the news aggregated by the user and automatically trans-codes them into audio files (with the help of the Free TTS[4] library) with a flag to indicate if the news

---

[1] http://www.netvibes.com/
[2] http://www.feedburner.com/
[3] http://www.google.com/reader/
[4] http://freetts.sourceforge.net/docs/index.php

is already read. Then, it detects when the user leaves the computer room and sends to the Smartphone all the unread aggregated news (already transcoded into audio files) to allow the user to listen to them. Finally, it updates the content depending on the possible newly added RSS feeds in the reader list.

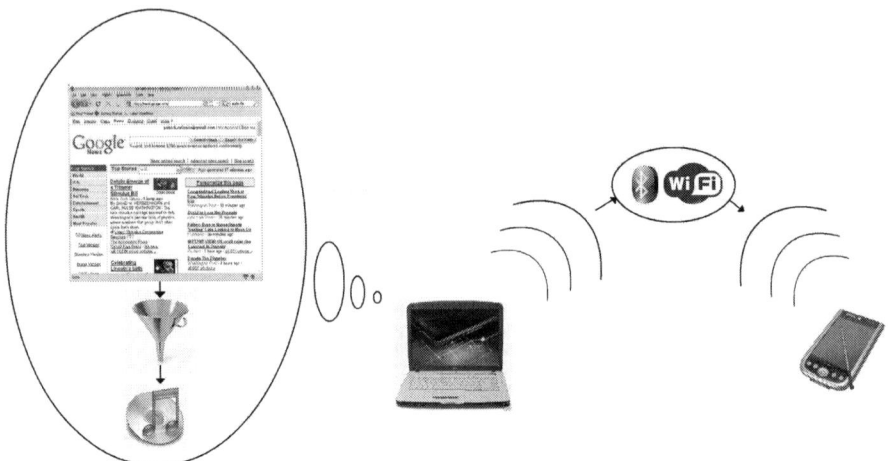

Fig. 1. Schema of our concept: from RSS feeds on the computer (from text into audio files) to an audio player on the smartphone

4   The Experiment

Twelve participants from 19 to 46 (mean: 26 years old) years old voluntarily took part to the experiment. Most of them (10) already read RSS feeds on the Internet and all of them had already used a Smartphone.

Before we start the experiment, we give to the users an overview (or reminder) of RSS feeds, the used material, and the purpose of the system. We then explain to them briefly the scenario of the experiment and which actions they will be asked to perform. Finally, we give them a Smartphone and show them the computer (server) on which they will start the experiment. At this moment, both applications (on the client and on the server) are already started.

Once the user is informed, we invite him/her to seat in front the computer screen (server) to aggregate some news and start to read them. As written above, each news is tagged as read or unread, depending on the user actions. After few minutes, we ask them to stand up and to leave the room with the Smartphone. At this step, our application detects the user is no more in front of the screen and sends the audio files to the smartphone After this, the user can listen the sent news and then to come back to the computer, which lead our system to make an update concerning the status of the pieces of news (to consider them as read or not).

4.1 Questionnaire

Once the experiment performed, we proposed a SUMI-like (Software Usability Measurement Inventory) questionnaire[5] [14] to the users in order to validate the efficiency and intuitiveness of our application. Indeed, several types of validity studies [15][16][17] have already been conducted with SUMI, whose one of them concerns laboratory-based studies (carried out in the Human Factors Research Group). This questionnaire is composed of two parts that we describe here.

The first part is composed of questions about the user profile like the age, gender, but also if the user is used to work with a computer and a Smartphone. This part concludes with questions about the training for using the system (availability and length) and if the time to use the system was also adequate.

The second part of the questionnaire is composed of fifty statements. The user must answer to all of them by marking one of the three proposed boxes labeled: "Disagree", "Undecided", and "Agree". It is also firstly noticed that marking the "Undecided" boxes means that the user cannot make up his/her mind, or that the statement has no relevance to the software or the situation. Secondly, it is added that marking the "Disagree" or "agree" boxes does not necessarily indicate a strong disagreement (respectively agreement) but only a general feeling most of the time.

The questions of this second part concern various topics: responsiveness of the software, quality of proposed instructions, global satisfaction about the software, possible improvements, intuitiveness, and attractiveness of the software. In the next section, we will analyze the users' answers and their behavior during the experiment.

5 Results

Globally, most of the users enjoyed the system. Every step was performed by every user, even if some of them needed more time to adapt to the system. We will now first present the users' behavior during the experimentation and then the answers they give to our questionnaire.

5.1 Questionnaire Trends

Our adapted SUMI questionnaire was filled by every participant. Its first part, concerning the users' profile, reveals us that one experiment loop for training was widely enough for all the participants.

The questions of the second part reveal us that our software is very accurate and fast enough for everyone but two. Indeed, the Bluetooth detection seems not to be fast enough for people rushing out of the room because they are very late. Notice also that the update action (to add new RSS feeds and delete already read ones) was considered as "a bit too long" by eight people. Finally, they seem to be a bit surprised at the beginning with the Smartphone that automatically starts to read news but after the first loop, they really enjoyed our application.

---

[5] http://sumi.ucc.ie/

Our system was then considered as very attractive, easy to use, and intuitive enough, even if improvements can be done in the future.

6   Conclusion and Further Works

The obtained results confirm our hypotheses. Being able to have access to one's aggregate news all the time (and not only in front of a computer screen) is a very attractive concept.

It seems also that our application reached the planned objectives: attractiveness, intuitiveness, and efficiency. Because of the users' enthusiasm, we may deduce that our application is attractive. As mentioned above, some users even asked us if there already exist a similar version of our application to read emails. In addition, most of the users did neither need any help nor too much time to feel comfortable with our application. Finally, the users really appreciate the concept of the "following trans-coded news".

Nevertheless, some users deplored the "update" and "sending information" steps speed. In order to solve this problem, a first solution would be to send the RSS feeds as text files to the Smartphone and trans-code them after. Another solution would be to send data via 3G [6] instead of Wi-Fi.

Acknowledgments

This research has been partially supported by the European Coordination Action: FOCUS K3D (http://www.focusk3d.eu).

References

1. Jacquemin, C., de Laubier, S.: Transmodal feedback as a new perspective for audiovisual effects. In: NIME 2006: Proceedings of the 2006 conference on New interfaces for musical expression, Paris, France, pp. 156–161. IRCAM — Centre Pompidou (2006)
2. Salamin, P., Thalmann, D., Vexo, F.: Visualization Learning for Visually Impaired People. In: The 2nd International Conference of E-Learning and Games: Edutaiment 2007, pp. 171–181 (2007)
3. Abowd, G.D., Dey, A.K., Brown, P.J., Davies, N., Smith, M., Steggles, P.: Towards a better understanding of context and context-awareness. In: Gellersen, H.-W. (ed.) HUC 1999. LNCS, vol. 1707, pp. 304–307. Springer, Heidelberg (1999)
4. Bahl, P., Padmanabhan, V.N.: Radar: an in-building rf-based user location and tracking system. In: INFOCOM 2000. Nineteenth Annual Joint Conference of the IEEE Computer and Communications Societies. Proceedings, vol. 2, pp. 775–784. IEEE, Los Alamitos (2000)
5. Bahl, P., Balachandran, A., Padmanabhan, V.: Enhancements to the radar user location and tracking system. Technical report, Microsoft Research Technical Report (February 2000)

---

[6] http://en.wikipedia.org/wiki/3G

6. Astrain, J.J., Villadangos, J., Garitagoitia, J.R., González de Mendívil, J.R., Cholvi, V.: Fuzzy location and tracking on wireless networks. In: MobiWac 2006: Proceedings of the 4th ACM international workshop on Mobility management and wireless access, pp. 84–91. ACM, New York (2006)
7. Kumar, R., Apte, K.V., Power, Y.A.: Improving the accuracy of wireless lan based location determination systems using kalman filter and multiple observers. In: Wireless Communications and Networking Conference (WCNC), Las Vegas (April 2006)
8. Ho, W., Smailagic, A., Siewiorek, D.P., Faloutsos, C.: An adaptive two-phase approach to wifi location sensing. In: PERCOMW 2006: Proceedings of the 4th annual IEEE international conference on Pervasive Computing and Communications Workshops, p. 452. IEEE Computer Society, Washington (2006)
9. Zàruba, G.V., Huber, M., Kamangar, F.A., Chlamtac, I.: Indoor location tracking using rssi readings from a single wi-fi access point. Wirel. Netw. 13(2), 221–235 (2007)
10. Hopmann, M., Thalmann, D., Vexo, F.: Thanks to geolocalized remote control: The sound will follow. In: CW 2008: Proceedings of the 2008 International Conference on Cyberworlds, pp. 371–376. IEEE Computer Society, Washington (2008)
11. Dhawan, S.: Analogy of promising wireless technologies on different frequencies: Bluetooth, wifi, and wimax. In: AUSWIRELESS 2007: Proceedings of the The 2nd International Conference on Wireless Broadband and Ultra Wideband Communications, p. 14. IEEE Computer Society, Washington (2007)
12. Patrick, D., Morrow, R.: WiFi and Bluetooth Coexistence. McGraw-Hill Professional, New York (2004)
13. Member-Corvaja, R.: Qos analysis in overlay bluetooth-wifi networks with profile-based vertical handover. IEEE Transactions on Mobile Computing 5(12), 1679–1690 (2006)
14. McSweeney, R.: Sumi – a psychometric approach to software evaluation. Unpublished MA (Qual) thesis in Applied Psychology, University College Cork, Ireland (1992)
15. Ravden, S., Johnson, G.: Evaluating usability of human-computer interfaces: a practical method. Halsted Press, New York (1989)
16. Saunders, C.S., Jones, J.W.: Measuring performance of the information systems function. J. Manage. Inf. Syst. 8(4), 63–82 (1992)
17. Wong, G., Rengger, R.: The validity of questionnaires designed to measure user-satisfaction of computer systems. Technical report, National Physical Laboratory report DITC 169/90, Teddington, Middx, UK (1990)

An Experiment in Improvised Interactive Drama

Ivo Swartjes and Mariët Theune

Human Media Interaction group, University of Twente, P.O. Box 217, 7500 AE
Enschede, The Netherlands
{swartjes,theune}@ewi.utwente.nl

Abstract. To inform the design of interactive drama systems, we investigate the experience of an interactor being part of a story that they can have a fundamental influence on. Improvisational theatre might serve as a model for this experience, where there is no pre-scripted plot; each of its actors shares responsibility for the collaborative emergence of a story. This requires a performer attitude from the interactor. We describe an experiment in which improv actors create a story together with subjects who have no improv experience, to find out how we can characterize this experience, and how it might be achieved. Our results support a recent hypothesis that an interactor in interactive drama might be treated as a collaborative performer rather than an (antagonistic) player.

Keywords: Interactive Storytelling, Dramatic Presence, Interactive Drama, Improvisational Theatre.

1 Introduction

Recent advances in computer game development and virtual reality have opened up the potential for creating *interactive drama* systems, a particular form of interactive entertainment where a user interacts with a story world by assuming the first-person role of one of its characters. A number of interactive drama systems have been developed within the interactive storytelling community (perhaps the most famous being Façade, [1]). One major difficulty that the community still faces, is that the high level of interaction freedom that virtual reality and computer games as media provide, may clash with the long-term dramatic structure or closure that would give the interactor a story experience. A common assumption underlying this 'narrative paradox' is that interactors are willing to sacrifice dramatic development to exert their interaction freedom to do 'whatever they want', and should therefore be restricted or corrected in their choices. Recently it was hypothesized that interactors might be acting as collaborative *performers* rather than antagonistic *players*, if they are expecting to be rewarded by meaningful dramatic interaction rather than ludic incentives common in contemporary computer games [2]. This view implies that interactors will be carrying part of the authorial responsibility for the drama, not dissimilar to actors in improvisational theatre. Here, improvisational actors co-create scenes without any explicit guidance or centralized direction as to what the story should be, and none of its participants can control its outcome.

A. Nijholt, D. Reidsma, and H. Hondorp (Eds.): INTETAIN 2009, LNICST 9, pp. 234–239, 2009.

We conducted an experiment to investigate whether improvisational theatre could serve as a model for interactive drama. If we give improv actors the task not to entertain an audience, but to engage a participant who has no improv experience, and as such might *not* be employing the same techniques that improv actors have acquired in their training, will they succeed in delivering a story-like experience to the interactor? What would the actors have to do to compensate for the user's lack of experience in improvised story making? Does the interactor indeed take on the role of a performer rather than a player?

This experiment is related to the live interactive drama experiment within the OZ project [3]. In this experiment, actors played out a performance on a theatre stage in order to engage an interactor participating in the drama. A director used a predetermined graph of desired scene sequences to give private directives to the actors, in order to ensure a certain dramatic development. The experiment was designed to investigate how it feels for an interactor to be immersed in a dramatic virtual world. The lesson learned from this experiment is that the experience of dramatic presence, as they call it, can be engrossing and powerful and that interactors experience a story very different from spectators. Interactors found interactive drama to easily cause immediate and personal emotions. The main difference is that in our experiment, there is no premeditated plot, giving the interactor a fundamental influence on the story.

2   Setup of the Experiment

In the experiment we conducted, we tried to achieve meaningful improvised interaction between two improv actors and a participant with no particular improv experience. Two improv actors (5+ years of experience) from the local Theatresports[1] group Pro Deo were found willing to participate.

The experiment was performed using a chat client to avoid potential issues of stage fright and performance anxiety. Pilot experiments were conducted to investigate potential problems of using text-based chat as a medium for improvised interaction, but none of relevance to the experiment were found. The client was extended with a `narrate` command, allowing the participants to state information which appears without their chat name (e.g., "It was a stormy night."").

The setup of the experiment can be seen in Fig. 1. The actors were placed in the same room and were instructed to use out-of-character communication whenever they felt like it. We hypothesized that out-of-character communication between the improv actors would improve their ability to collaborate in engaging the interactor. There is evidence from studies of adult improvisation theatre that professional acting ensembles create more complex plot structures if they are allowed to use out-of-character techniques [5]. The communication of the improv actors was recorded using a webcam.

---

[1] Theatresports is a form of improvisational theatre in which two teams challenge each other to play short improvised scenes in order to earn points issued by a team of impartial judges [4].

Room 1   Video   Room 2
                                  recording

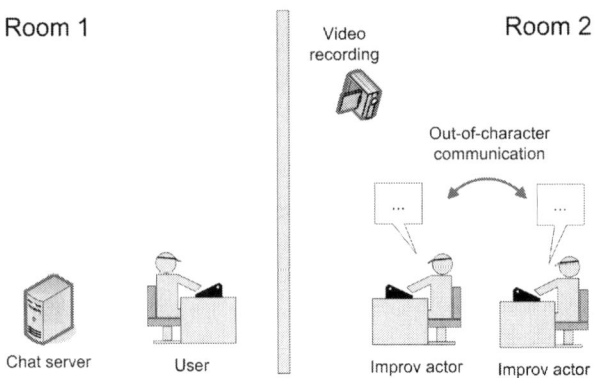

Fig. 1. Experimental setup

We had three subjects, one male and two female, aged 21, 20 and 35 respectively, and asked them in advance whether they had experience with any kind of RPG, with chatting, with virtual communities such as Second Life, with improv theatre (either as spectator or as participant) and whether they liked role playing. Experience with chatting was required for participation.

Each subject played the role of a character in one improvised story. Each story lasted between 30 and 45 minutes. We kept the pre-briefing as minimal as possible; we made it clear that the subjects would be interacting with two other participants (rather than with a computer program), and told them that they would be entering a story world, without giving them any task to achieve. We told them to relax and "see what happens". The only information given in advance was the location of the starting scene of the story, the rest of the story world was completely filled in by the three participants.

After the experiment, we held semi-structured interviews with the subjects after their individual story experience, using questions about narrative presence factors [6] (e.g., identification with their role, control over the experience and affect) to guide the interview. We included the improv actors in these interviews, expecting that the interview would also function as a discussion between the participants, and might reveal important information about their experiences. We held a separate interview with the improv actors after the whole experiment. We also analyzed the chat transcripts and the video material, annotating any out-of-character communication between the actors.

3 Results

This section describes the results of the experiment, discussing our observations and the interview results. Quotes have been translated from Dutch into English, taking care to stay close to the original meaning.

3.1   Participants and Stories

The first subject was a 21 year old male computer science student. He indicated that he had ample experience with RPG, online chatting, multiplayer online computer games and that he really liked role playing. He had some experience with virtual communities and with improvisational theatre, both as participant and as spectator. The initial location for the story was given as a forest, which resulted in a medieval tale about revenge for damaged pride. During the experience, the subject seemed a bit rebellious, making out-of-character remarks about inconsistencies ("Weren't you already standing still?"), joking and testing the characters' reactions.

The second subject was a 20 year old female law student. She indicated that she had ample experience with online chatting, some experience with multiplayer online computer games and some affinity with role play. She had little experience with role playing, virtual communities and improv theatre as a spectator, and never participated in improv theatre. The starting location was a bar, which resulted in a thriller about coke smuggling. The subject did not seem short of inspiration and was really dominating the input.

The third subject was a 35 year old female high school teacher. She indicated that she had ample experience with online chatting, some experience with role playing and improv theatre as a participant, and some affinity with role play. She had no experience with virtual communities, multiplayer online games, or with improv theatre as a spectator. The starting location was a beach, which led to a horror story in which a shark attacked a happy family. The subject seemed really immersed, expressing in-character panic and staying in character during the whole experiment.

3.2   Interview Results

The first subject's main point was that he found his role in the story and the open-ended starting conditions confusing. He felt that he could resolve any problem by further filling in the situation (the subject gave the example that if he were to encounter a locked door, he could blow on a whistle to have a battering-ram appear). He characterized his experience as a game rather than a story, and clearly indicated a need for rules that constrained what he could do. He described his own role to be that of a 'dungeon master within his own dungeon'. As a result, he did not feel very much immersed in the story. He did however enjoy the creative side of the experience, wondering what he could create and how the other characters would react to his actions.

Unlike the first subject, the second subject felt that she played out the story as if she was really there. She found it an enjoyable story and could visualize it. She felt that she had a fundamental influence on the story, and felt satisfied with this amount of influence. She didn't feel there was anything she was supposed to do. The actors commented that they felt that the subject was making the story, and they were going along with it, rather than the other way around. This had the effect that at times they were struggling to ensure story development. At times, the subject provided massive amounts of backstory without any development forward in time.

The third subject felt like she was both playing a role, and immersed in the story. She observed that the actors kept changing roles and considered doing the same, but felt it was not necessary. She really felt as if she was there in the water and had vivid images of the story world. She also felt that she had an influence on the story (e.g., she 'planted' a red flag on the beach, from which the whole shark-attack horror theme had sprung). She had the feeling that things were happening continuously and that she had to keep on providing input. Just like the second subject, she did not feel like she needed any more or less guidance; the location was enough for the feeling that "something would happen." She said the story could have easily lasted ten times longer, which contrasted with the remark of the actors, who found the story becoming a bit boring because they were in the water all the time and nothing really happened. The subject did not know how they would be saved, but considered the solution to be the actors' responsibility. The subject mentioned she was not sure whether the characters were allowed to die, which indicated a certain expectation of constraints. She said she had much fun playing the story, and would also have enjoyed it had the story been different.

3.3 The Actors: Observations and Interview Results

During the three stories, the improv actors conferred with each other by (1) discussing story control issues (e.g., "There is still no relationship [defined] between you and Annie"), (2) discussing possible story direction (e.g., "Shall we see if we can make her transport our drugs?"), (3) establishing common ground in the interpretation of the participants' intent (e.g., "She doesn't dare to go into the water.") and (4) expressing out-of-character experience (e.g., "Haha, she's gonna play her own extra character, great!"). After the experiment, there was a discussion with the actors about their experiences with the three stories.

Although the first subject had indicated a need for more constraints, the actors had reacted in the second and third story by providing *less* initial constraints, leaving more initiative to the subjects. This seemed to have the effect that participants felt that it was *their* story they were acting out, and that the actors went along in the story world of the subject, rather than the other way around. They mentioned this as a possible explanation for the fact that the second and third subjects had no feeling of needing more guidance and reported that it was 'just right'. The actors were very aware of their task as managers of the story, and of the input they were providing to the story. They described this task to be fairly similar to improv acting; they were looking for ways to introduce and resolve conflict. There were times during the experiment where this happened effortlessly, whereas at other times they were heavily deliberating and discussing their options, which they mentioned to be different from normal improv acting. Their greatest fun was in seeing how the subjects responded to their offers, especially when it went as predicted, to see that 'it worked'. They had much more difficulty 'predicting' the first subject than the second and third.

4 Discussion

The described experiment explored the application of an improvisational theatre model to interactive storytelling, and in particular the hypothesis that interactors in such a setup can be viewed and treated as performers, collaborating with the story construction, rather than as players, acting against it. Although the number of subjects was small, the results mainly support this view in that the subjects enjoyed the aspect of being present in the story as well as the aspect of actively seeking to achieve dramatic development, being collaborative, creative and explorative, co-creating stories by providing input to the fictive reality of the story and finding out its consequences. The second and third subjects demonstrated highly collaborative behaviour, rarely blocking input and actively participating in the story development, not only by reacting to the story world events, but also by proactively providing input to the fictive reality. The first subject seemed more antagonistic. He was clearly looking for constraints, indicating he expected to play a game offered to him, rather than perform and create a story in collaboration. It is likely that he had strong expectations based on his RPG experience. His remark that he was the 'dungeon master of his own dungeon' was indicative of these expectations. This might explain his limited sense of dramatic presence compared to the second and third subject.

Acknowledgements. This research has been supported by the GATE project, funded by the Netherlands Organization for Scientific Research (NWO) and the Netherlands ICT Research and Innovation Authority (ICT Regie). Thanks to Marijn van Vliet and Joost Kroes of the Theatresports club Pro Deo for helping as improv actors in the experiment.

References

1. Mateas, M., Stern, A.: Façade: An experiment in building a fully-realized interactive drama. In: Game Developers Conference: Game Design Track (2003)
2. Tanenbaum, J., Tanenbaum, K.: Improvisation and performance as models for interacting with stories. In: Proceedings of the First Joint International Conference on Interactive Digital Storytelling (ICIDS 2008) (2008)
3. Kelso, M.T., Weyhrauch, P., Bates, J.: Dramatic presence. PRESENCE: The Journal of Teleoperators and Virtual Environments 2(1), 1–15 (1993)
4. Johnstone, K.: Impro for Storytellers. Faber and Faber (1999)
5. Sawyer, R.K.: Improvisation and narrative. Narrative Inquiry 12(2), 319–349 (2002)
6. Rowe, J.P., McQuiggan, S.W., Lester, J.C.: Narrative presence in intelligent learning environments. In: Working Notes of the 2007 AAAI Fall Symposium on Intelligent Narrative Technologies (2007)

Big Fat Wand: A Pointing Device for Open Space Edutainment

Toru Takahashi[1], Miki Namatame[2], Fusako Kusunoki[3], and Takao Terano[1]

[1] Tokyo Institute of Technology, Nagatuda, Midori-ku, Yokohama, Japan
{toru,terano}@trn.dis.titech.ac.jp
[2] Tsukuba Institute of Technology, Tsukuba, Ibaragi, Japan
miki@a.tsukuba-tech.ac.jp
[3] Tama Art Univeristy, Hachioji, Tokyo, Japan
kusunoki@tamabi.ac.jp

Abstract. This paper presents principles, functions, and experiments of a new edutainment tool: Big Fat Wand (BFW). BFW is developed from a conventional laser show device, however, it is modified to a small enough one to be used at an open apace. BFW is connected to a laptop PC, which provides character, symbol images, and/or animations. From experimental results, we conclude that BFW is a good gear for a facilitator to educate and educate hearing-impaired students.

Keywords: Laser Show Device, Edutainment in an Open Space, Education for Hearing-Impaired Students, Interactive Sessions.

1 Introduction

Although there are various methodologies for education of hearing-impaired or deaf people, it is still difficult to give lectures to them at out-of-classroom environments, for example, the explanations of artistic materials at a museum. Because the students cannot focus on both of the materials or hand languages at a same time, a teacher meet the troubles to manage students' interests about the objects and their explanation.

To cope with the issues, we are developing a new intelligent pointing device: Big Fat Wand (BFW). BFW is a handy smaller version of a conventional laser show device. A programmable laser-light show device will allow the user to specify the pattern displayed via any charactcrs and/or symbolic patters on the targeted object [10], [11]. BFW stands for the very big magic wand. The device aims at presenting the learners both the focus points and the contents information about the target object (Figure 1). This paper describes basic principles, functions of the device, and experimental results of BFW.

The rest of the paper is organized as follows: in the next section, we discuss the motivation of the research. Then, we explain the basic principles and the architecture of BFW. Next, we describe the preliminary experiments on a lecture with and without BFW at a large room for sketch exercises of traditional plaster figures of Tsukuba University. Finally some concluding remarks will follow.

A. Nijholt, D. Reidsma, and H. Hondorp (Eds.): INTETAIN 2009, LNICST 9, pp. 240–245, 2009.
© ICST Institute for Computer Sciences, Social Informatics and Telecommunications Engineering 2009

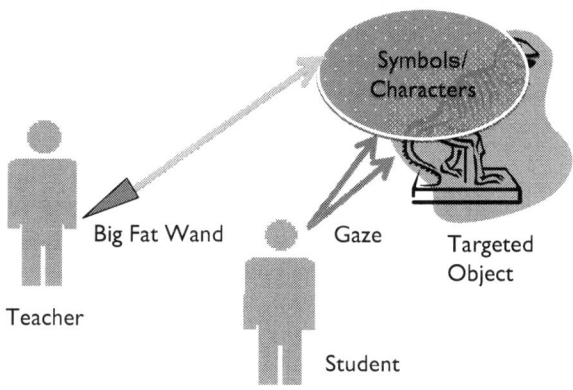

Fig. 1. BFW Directly Presents the Focus Points and Explanation

2 Background and Motivation

In the literature of the study of hearing-impaired peoples, there are several researches on their understandings on the explanations of a targeted object.

Gentry, M. M., et al. [5] present that additions of image information to language or character information remarkably help their understandings of the explanations of the targeted object. Jensema, C.J., et al and Jelinek Lewis, M.S., et al. [2], [3], [4] have reported that when native hearing-impaired people enjoy a TV drama with captions, they are divided to the two groups: the ones tend to focus on the mouth moves and the others tend to focus on the characters and that too many characters are hard to be recognized. Wilson, M., et al., [6] have discussed the roles of the working memories to the processes of encoding and decoding of hand language and character information. Also, we have analyzed that hearing-impaired people have the wider focus areas about their environments [8].

There are other various studies on the development of support systems for hand language educations and communication skills [7], [8], [9]. However, they do not cope with the out-of-classroom lectures.

These researches suggest that the following design guidelines of a new pointing device: i) It is desirable to dynamically show the explanation among the targeted object, but it is not so severe to show the information at the same place; ii) The smaller numbers of simpler information, the better; and iii) Both character and symbol information are necessary for good explanation.

To follow the guideline, we have not found good devices for the lectures. A conventional laser pointer has too poor information. Conventional PC projectors are too dark and too heavy at out-of-classroom environments. Because of financial and technical reasons, we have no chance to develop the pointing devices from scratch. Therefore, we have decided to develop a new one from conventional laser show devices.

3   Big Fat Wand: Handy Laser Show Device

Big Fat Wand system has the following components: i) A laptop PC with line drawing image generation, image display and editing software, ii) A one-board micro-computer to convert the digital information of the drawings to the analog ones to control the device, and iii) Laser show device with laser light generator, small dynamic mirror devices to control displays of the drawings, and power supplies. Very unique points of BFW are summarized as follows: i) A one-board 16 bit micro computer manages DA conversion of explanation and controlling the images, ii) The cylinder part is carefully designed to avoid heat damages of the laser devices, iii) the components of the devices are packaged in separated two parts to easily use the system, and iv) special purpose authoring tools are developed for naïve users to prepare the lectures.

Figure 2 shows each component and Figure 3 depicts the photos of an integrated BFW. A user or teacher uses the cylinder like device to show the desired information. The box behind the cylinder contains devices such as one-board micro-computer, power supply,

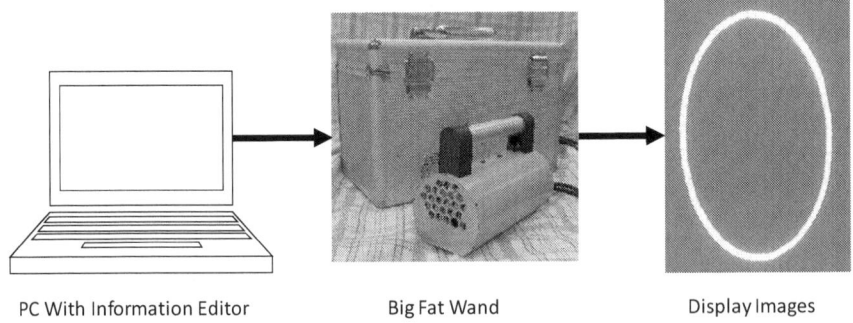

PC With Information Editor   Big Fat Wand   Display Images

Fig. 2. Architecture of BFW

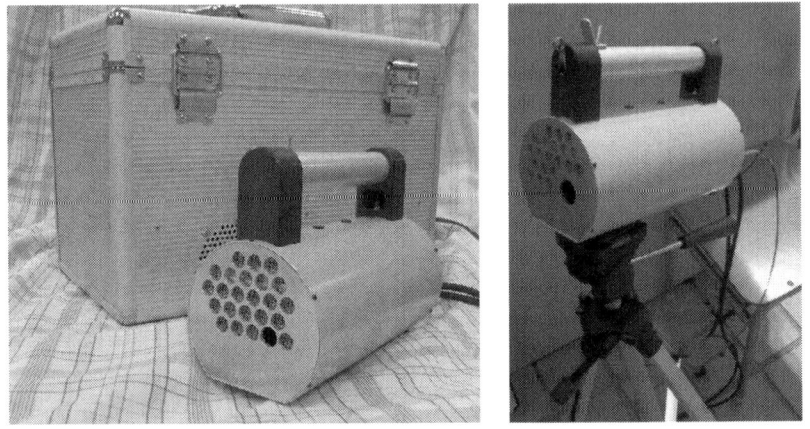

Fig. 3. Outlook of the Integrated Device

laser light generator, and so on. The information is prepared beforehand and/or at the learning site using special purpose authoring tools equipped on a laptop PC.

The current version of the tools are able i) to process static bitmap images (both characters and symbols), which are converted to line drawings, ii) to generate simple animations combined with the bitmap images, and also processes line drawings written with the postscript language. This means that the user is able to both design and generate the necessary information with bitmaps beforehand and draw pictures and character in a real time environment.

Fig. 4. Making Drawings from Bit-map Images

Figure 4 shows the processes to generate laser animations from bit-map images. Users of BFW are easy to make such drawing images and moving animations.

4 Experiments

Following preliminary experiments reported in [12], we have carried out intensive experiments of BFW for out-of-classroom lectures to evaluate the basic functionality of BFW on November 4, 2008 at Tsukuba University Art Department.

We have had two instructors: the one is a professor of Art Department, Tsukuba University and the other is the second author of this paper, who is a specialist to teach hearing-impaired students. They gave a 30 minute lecture to twelve subjects, who are the third grade under-graduate hearing-impaired students of Tsukuba Institute of Technology. Their specialty is art and design. The objective of the lecture is to explain the characteristics of big traditional plaster figures, which ware made from original ones in real size scales, in the room for drawing exercise (Figure 5). The subjects were the first time to visit the room. We have made two explanation materials of the Figure 5, beforehand. They are developed under the advices of the professor on the art domain. The explanation materials consist of both traditional paper forms and laser drawing forms. Figure 5 also shows a sample of the laser display information.

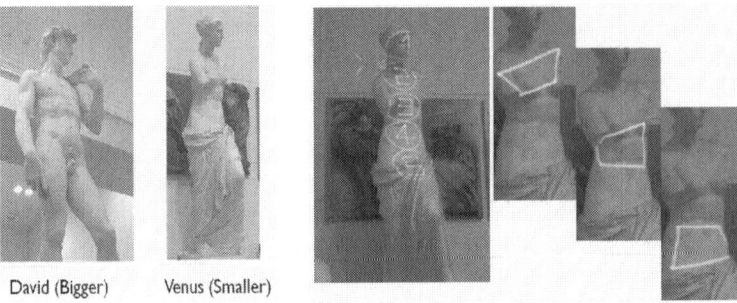

David (Bigger)   Venus (Smaller)

Fig. 5. Targeted Sculptures and Sample Laser Explanations

Fig. 6. Photos of Learners at the Sketch Room

Subjects are divided into sub-groups based on the experimental design methodology [1]. We have designed all the subjects have both paper and laser explanation twice for the different plaster figures. After each lecture, subjects are required to answer simple questionnaire. Also, they were required to describe free answers. After the al the explanations, they were required to make rough sketches, which aim at to evaluate their understandings on the target sculptures (Figure 6).

From the experimental results, the observations of experiments, and free descriptions of the questionnaire, we have drawn the following statements:

- BFW device is usable for instructors, who are not familiar with any other interaction devices.
- Operations of BFW are sometimes disturbed by the lecture environments, for example, obstacles of the room prevent smooth displays and movements of information.
- Although the number of the subjects is very small, there are comparative evaluation with BFW and traditional explanation.
- The figures are the bigger, the effects of the laser explanation will become the superior.
- We expect that the number of students becomes larger, the effectiveness of BFW will increase.

5   Concluding Remarks

This paper has proposed a new laser pointing device Big Fat Wand for education aid to hearing-impaired students. The objective of the device is to effectively give lectures at the out-of-classroom environment. The paper has also reported some experimental results to evaluate the effectiveness of BFW.

Our conclusion is simple: although BFW is at beginning stage of the development, the idea is effective to develop a new methodology for education of hearing-impaired students. The usage is not limited to the current purpose. Future work is to improve BFW to Small Smart Wand.

References

1. Jacko, J.A., Sears, A. (eds.): The Human-Computer Interaction Handbook: Fundamentals, Evolving Technologies and Emerging Applications. Lawrence Erlbaum Assoc Inc., Mahwah (2002)
2. Jensema, C.J., Danturthi, S., Burch, R.: Time Spent Viewing Captions on Television Programs. American Annals of the Deaf 145(5), 464–468 (2000)
3. Jensema, C.J., Sharkawy, S.E., Danturthi, R.W., Burch, R., Hsu, D.: Eye Movement Patterns of Captioned Television Viewers. American Annals of the Deaf. 145, 275–285 (2000)
4. Jelinek Lewis, M.S., Jackson, D.W.: Television Literacy: Comprehension of Program Content Using Closed Captions for the Deaf. Journal of Deaf Studies and Deaf Education 6(1), 42–53 (2001)
5. Gentry, M.M., Chinn, K.M., Moulton, R.D.: Effectiveness of Multimedia Reading Materials When Used with Children Who are Deaf. American Annals of the Deaf 149, 394–402 (2004)
6. Wilson, M., Emmorey, K.: Working Memory of Sign Language: A Window into the Architecture of the Working Memory System. Journal of Deaf Studies and Deaf Education 2, 121–130 (1997)
7. Michaud, L.N., McCoy, K.F., Christopher, A.: An Intelligent Tutoring System for Deaf Learners of Written English. In: Fourth Annual ACM Conference on Assistive Technologies, pp. 92–100 (2000)
8. Namatame, M., Harada, Y., Kusunoki, F., Inagaki, S., Terano, T.: To Use PYA Tool or Not for Learning Japanese. In: Proceedings of the ACM SIGCHI International Conference on Advances in Computer Entertainment Technology (ACE 2006), pp. S17–a79 (2006)
9. Su, S.A., Furuta, R.K.: VRML-Based Representations of ASL Fingerspelling on the World-Wide Web. In: Third Annual ACM Conference on Assistive Technologies, pp. 43–45 (1998)
10. http://www.laserfx.com/
11. Qijie, G., Yanyan, L.: Development of an Intelligent Laser Show System - A Novel Application of Mixed Reality Technology. In: 2005 ASEAN Virtual Instrumentation Applications Contest (2005)
12. Takahashi, T., Namatame, M., Kusunoki, F., Ono, I., Terano, T.: A Laser Show Device Works in An Open Space for Hearing-Impaired Students. In: Proc. Asia Modeling Symposium (AMS 2008), vol. F-12, pp. 385–389 (2008)

Enhancing Mediated Interpersonal Communication through Affective Haptics

Dzmitry Tsetserukou[1], Alena Neviarouskaya[2], Helmut Prendinger[3],
Naoki Kawakami[1], Mitsuru Ishizuka[2], and Susumu Tachi[1]

[1] Department of Information Physics and Computing, University of Tokyo, Japan
dima_teterukov@ipc.i.u-tokyo.ac.jp,
{kawakami,tachi}@star.t.u-tokyo.ac.jp
[2] Department of Information and Communication Engineering, University of Tokyo, Japan
lena@mi.ci.i.u-tokyo.ac.jp, ishizuka@i.u-tokyo.ac.jp
[3] National Institute of Informatics, Japan
helmut@nii.ac.jp

Abstract. Driven by the motivation to enhance emotionally immersive experience of real-time messaging in 3D virtual world Second Life, we are proposing a conceptually novel approach to reinforcing (intensifying) own feelings and reproducing (simulating) the emotions felt by the partner through specially designed system, iFeel_IM!. In the paper we are describing the development of novel haptic devices (HaptiHeart, HaptiHug, HaptiTickler, HaptiCooler, and HaptiWarmer) integrated into iFeel_IM! system, which architecture is presented in detail.

Keywords: Affective haptics, affective user interface, wearable devices.

1 Introduction

In a real world, whenever one person interacts with another, both observe, perceive and interpret each other's emotional expressions communicated through a variety of signals. Valuable information is also transferred by non-verbal communication (e.g. social touch). Nowadays, communication in 3D virtual world through instant messenger and chat is very popular. However, during on-line communication people are concentrating on textual information and are only slightly affected emotionally. Conventional mediated systems usually (1) support only simple textual cues like emoticons; (2) lack visual emotional signals such as facial expressions and gestures; (3) support only manual control of expressiveness of graphical representations of users (avatars); and (4) completely ignore such important channel of social communication as sense of touch.

To deliver emotions through instant messenger, Shin et al. [1] developed a tactile interface. However, in the proposed methods users have to memorize the vibration or pin matrix patterns and cognitively interpret the communicated emotional state. Moreover, such device cannot evoke user's emotion in a direct way. To our knowledge,

A. Nijholt, D. Reidsma, and H. Hondorp (Eds.): INTETAIN 2009, LNICST 9, pp. 246–251, 2009.

the only work concentrated on the physical emotion elicitation through physical means is described in [2].

Driven by the motivation to enhance social interactivity and emotionally immersive experience of real-time messaging, we are proposing a conceptually novel approach to reinforcing (intensifying) own feelings and reproducing (simulating) the emotions felt by the partner through specially designed system, iFeel_IM!. The philosophy behind the iFeel_IM! (intelligent system for **Feel**ing enhancement powered by affect sensitive **I**nstant **M**essenger) is "*I feel* [therefore] *I am!*". The emotion evoked by physical stimulation might imbue our communication with passion and increase the emotional intimacy, ability to be close, loving, and vulnerable. We argue that interpersonal relationship and the ability to express empathy grow strongly when people become emotionally closer through disclosing thoughts, feelings, and emotions for the sake of understanding.

In this work, we focus on implementation of novel devices for generation of physical stimulation aimed to convey (and influence on) the emotion experienced during online conversations.

2   iFeel_IM! Architecture

In the iFeel_IM! system, great importance is placed on the automatic sensing of emotions conveyed through textual messages in 3D virtual world Second Life, the visualization of the detected emotions by avatars in virtual environment, and enhancement of user's affective state and reproduction of feeling of social touch (e.g., hug) by means of haptic stimulation in a real world. The architecture of the iFeel_IM! system is presented in Fig. 1.

In order to communicate through iFeel_IM! system, users have to wear innovative haptic devices (HaptiHeart, HaptiHug, HaptiTickler, HaptiCooler, and HaptiWarmer) developed by us. As a media for communication, we employ Second Life allowing users to flexibly create their online identities (avatars) and to play various animations (e.g., facial expressions and gestures) of avatars by typing special abbreviations (e.g., '/laugh' for laughing) in a chat window.

To automate emotional behaviour of avatar and to avoid thus manual control by user, we developed EmoHeart object [3] (invisible in case of 'neutral' state) that listens to each message of avatar, sends it to the Affect Analysis Model [3] located on the server, gets the result (dominant emotion and intensity for each sentence), and visually reflects the sensed affective state through avatar facial expression and EmoHeart texture and size. The motivation behind using the heart-shaped object as an additional channel for visualization was to represent the communicated emotions in a vivid and intense way.

In addition to communication with Affect Analysis Model, EmoHeart is responsible for sensing symbolic cues or keywords of 'hug' communicative function conveyed by text, and for visualization (triggering related animation) of 'hugging' in Second Life. The results from the Affect Analysis Model and EmoHeart are stored along with chat messages in a file on local computer of each user. Haptic Devices Controller analyses these data in a real time and generates control signals for Digital/Analog converter (D/A), which then feeds Driver Box for haptic devices with control cues. Based on the transmitted signal, the corresponding haptic device (HaptiHeart, HaptiHug, HaptiTickler, HaptiCooler, or HaptiWarmer) worn by user is activated.

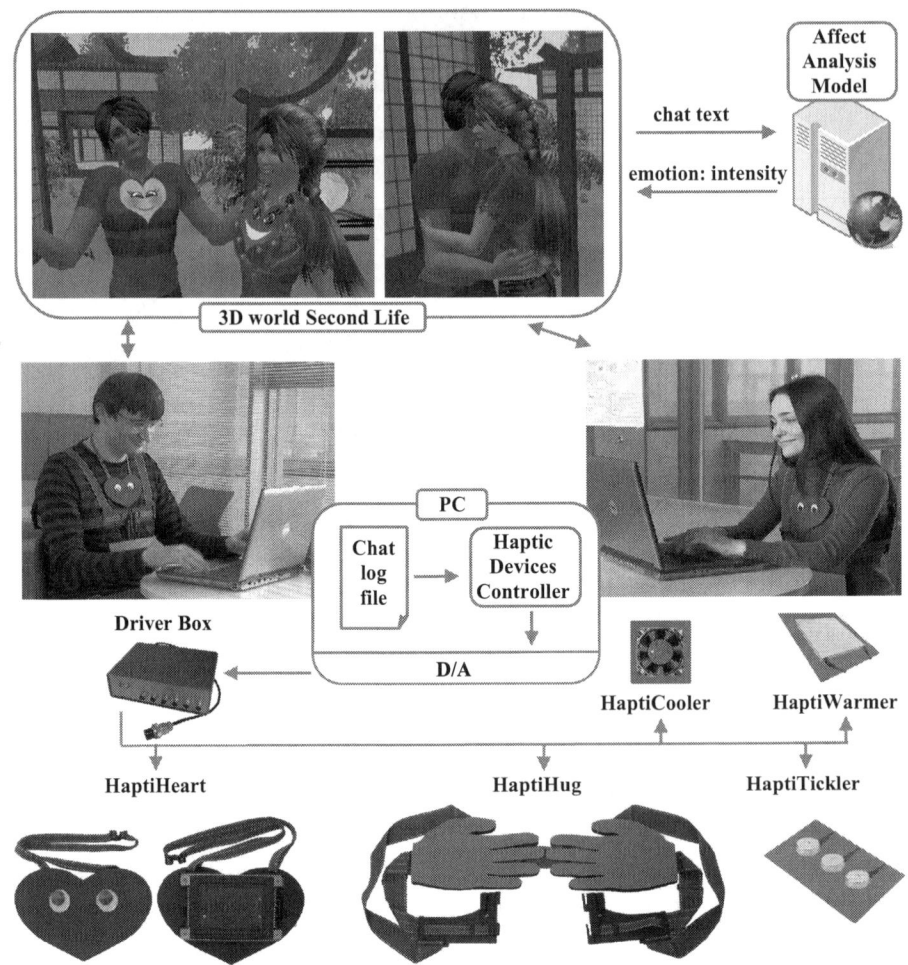

Fig. 1. Architecture of iFeel_IM! system

3   Affective Haptic Devices

In order to support the affective communication, we implemented several novel haptic gadgets embedded in iFeel_IM!. They make up three groups. First one is intended for emotion elicitation implicitly (HaptiHeart, HaptiCooler, HaptiWarmer), second type evokes affect in a direct way (HaptiTickler), and third one uses sense of social touch (HaptiHug) for mood influence. All these devices produce a sense of touch including kinesthetic and coetaneous channels. Kinesthetic stimulations, produced by forces exerted on body, are sensed by mechanoreceptors in the tendons and muscles. This channel is highly involved in sensing stimulus produced by HaptiHug device. On the other hand, mechanoreceptors in the skin layers are responsible for cutaneous stimulation perception. Different types of tactile corpuscles allow us sensing thermal property of the object (HaptiCooler, HaptiWarmer), pressure (HaptiHeart, HaptiTickler), vibration frequency (HaptiTickler), and stimuli location (localization of stimulating device position enables association with particular physical contact).

3.1 HaptiHug: The Way of Realistic Hugging over Distance

When people are hugging, they generate pressure on the back of each other by the hands, and on the chest area simultaneously. The key feature of the developed HaptiHug is that it physically reproduces the hug pattern similar to that of human-human interaction. The hands for a HaptiHug are sketched from a real human and made from soft material. The important point is that the hands were designed in such a way that the user feels as if the friend's hands actually contact him. Couple of oppositely rotating motors are incorporated into the holder placed on the user chest area. Soft Hands, aligned horizontally, contact back of the user. Shoulder strips, supporting the motor holder and Soft Hands, allow aligning the vertical position of device. Once 'hug' command is received, couple of motors tense the belt, pressing thus Soft Hands and chest part of HaptiHug in the direction of human body (Fig. 2).

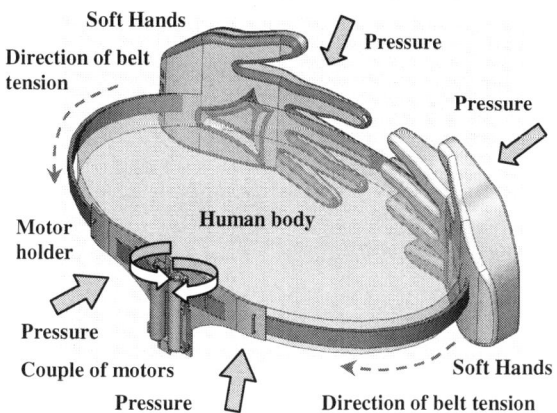

Fig. 2. Structure of wearable HaptiHug device

The duration and intensity of the hug is controlled by the software according to the detected emoticon or keyword. The Driver Box regulates the current magnitude in DC motor from 0 mA to 500 mA. For presentation of plain hug level (e.g., '(>^_^)>', '{}', '<h>'), big hug level (e.g., '>:D<', '{{{}}}'), and great big hug level (e.g., 'gbh', '{{{{}}}}'), the pressure of 200 N/m^2 with duration of 2 sec, the pressure of 300 N/m^2 with duration of 3 sec, and the

pressure of 450 N/m^2 with duration of 4 sec, was applied on the user's back and chest, respectively.

The technical specification of the device is as follows. DC motors RE 10 1.5 W in combination with planetary gearhead GP 10 A (gear ratio of 64:1) generate stall torque of 192.6 mNm. The pressure produced on the human chest by tensed belt equals 450 N/m^2 at the most. Motor holder was manufactured on 3D printer Dimension DS 768 from ABS plastic material. Special slots were provided to make the pass for pressing belt.

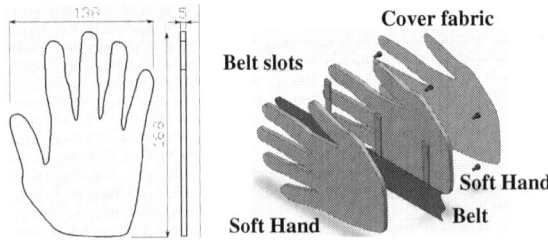

Fig. 3. Left: Soft Hand dimensions. Right: sandwiched structure of Soft Hands.

Preliminary, Soft Hands were produced on 3D printer from ABS plastic material with thickness of 1 mm. However, plate flexibility was not enough to achieve touch sensation similar to human hand. Therefore, we decided to make hands from compliant rubber-sponge material. The contour profile of Soft Hand is sketched from the male human and has front-face area of 155.6 cm^2. Two identical pieces of Soft Hand of 5 mm thickness were sandwiched by narrow belt slots and connected by plastic screws. Such structure provides enough flexibility to tightly fit to the human back surface while being pressed by belt. Moreover, belt can loosely move inside the Soft Hands during tension. The dimensions and structure of Soft Hands are presented in Fig. 3.

HaptiHug device has lightweight tri-glide bucklers and side release fastener integrated into the motor holder to facilitate easy adjustment of the belt size to her/his body sizes and detaching it in a natural and rapid manner.

3.2 HaptiHeart, HaptiCooler, HaptiWarmer, HaptiTickler. Or How We Can Enhance and Influence on Our Emotions by Haptics

We selected four distinct emotions with strong and unique physiological patterns: 'anger', 'fear', 'sadness', and 'joy' [4].

There is no doubt that feelings are intuitively connected with the heart, and our lexicon confirms this. The research on interplay between heart rate and emotions revealed that different emotions are associated with distinctive patterns of heart rate variations. We developed heart imitator HaptiHeart to produce special heartbeat patterns according to emotion to be conveyed or elicited (sad is associated with slightly intense heartbeat, anger with quick and violent heartbeat, fear with intense heart rate).

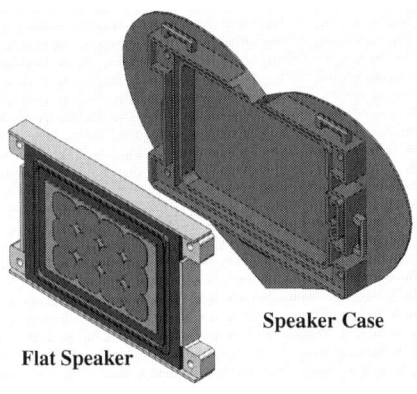

Fig. 4. HaptiHeart layout

We take advantage of the fact that our heart naturally synchronizes with the heart of a person we hold or hug. Thus, the heart rate of a user is influenced by haptic perception of the beat rate of the HaptiHeart.

The HaptiHeart consists of two modules: flat speaker FPS 0304 and speaker holder. The flat speaker sizes (66.5 x 107 x 8 mm) and rated input power of 10 W allowed us to design powerful and relatively compact HaptiHeart device producing realistic heartbeating sensation with high fidelity. The 3D model is presented in Fig. 4.

We recorded the heartbeat patterns for the cases of experiencing fear, anger, and sadness. The pre-recorded sound signal with low frequency generates the pressure on the human chest through vibration of the speaker surface.

HaptiTickler is responsible for joy emotion evocation. The idea behind this device is to reproduce effect of "*Butterflies in the stomach*" (fluttery or tickling feeling in the stomach felt by people experiencing love) by means of circular arrays of vibration motors attached to user abdomen area. HaptiWarmer is intended for the rise of skin temperature to evoke either aggression or pleasant feeling (hot or warm, respectively). In order to boost fear emotion physically, we designed HaptiCooler interface that sends "*Shivers down/up human body's spine*" by means of a row of vibration motors, and "*Chills down/up human body's spine*" through both cold airflow from DC fan and cold side of Peltier element.

4   Conclusion

In a nutshell, while developing the iFeel_IM! system, we attempted to bridge the gap between mediated and face-to-face communications by enabling and enriching the spectrum of senses such as vision and touch along with cognition and inner personal state.

In the paper we described the architecture of iFeel_IM and development of novel haptic devices, such as HaptiHeart, HaptiHug, HaptiTickler, HaptiCooler, and HaptiWarmer. All devices were designed with particular emphasis on ergonomic design. The user can comfortably wear them and easily detach from torso. We believe that iFeel_IM! will encourage users to get in "touch" with their emotions and to make social contact with other people in on-line communication.

Acknowledgments. The research is supported in part by a Japan Society for the Promotion of Science (JSPS) Postdoctoral Fellowship for Foreign Scholars.

References

1. Shin, H., Lee, J., Park, J., Kim, Y., Oh, H., Lee, T.: A Tactile Emotional Interface for Instant Messenger Chart. In: Proceedings of Symposium on Human Interface (HCI International 2007), pp. 166–175 (2007)
2. Kok, R., Broekens, J.: Physical Emotion Induction and Its Use in Entertainment: Lessons Learned. In: Proceedings of First IFIP Entertainment Computing Symposium, pp. 33–48 (2008)
3. Neviarouskaya, A., Prendinger, H., Ishizuka, M.: EmoHeart: Automation of Expressive Communication of Emotions in Second Life. In: Proceedings of International Conference on Human-Computer Interaction (2009)
4. Wallbott, H.G., Scherer, K.R.: How Universal and Specific is Emotional Experience? In: Scherer, K.R. (ed.) Evidence from 27 Countries on Five Continents. Facets of Emotion: Recent Research, pp. 31–56. Lawrence Erlbaum Inc., Hillsdale (1988)

Opinion Elicitation in Second Life

Marijn van Vliet[1,2], Alena Neviarouskaya[3], and Helmut Prendinger[1]

[1] National Institute of Informatics, Japan
helmut@nii.ac.jp
[2] University of Twente, Department of Human Machine Interaction, The Netherlands
w.m.vanvliet@student.utwente.nl
[3] University of Tokyo, Department of Information and Communication Engineering, Japan
lena@mi.ci.i.u-tokyo.ac.jp

Abstract. The paper describes a novel method for opinion elicitation, which is based on the popular 3D online world of "Second Life". Here people, as avatars, are put into a somewhat realistic context related to the topic for which opinions are sought. We hypothesize that this kind of concrete, interactive context supports the evocation of opinions better than non-context methods, e.g. only showing related images. To confirm our hypothesis, we conducted a small pilot study, which compares the influence of static and interactive context methods on the opinions expressed by subjects. The opinion elicitation scenario in Second Life is supported by the automatic retrieval of opinions from the web. The results of a study indicate that subjects show more reasoned opinions in the interactive condition. A demo illustrating the content of this paper is available.

Keywords: Opinion elicitation, virtual worlds, avatars, subjectivity analysis.

1 Introduction

Testing new laws or policies in the real world is costly and risky. Usually, new laws are first investigated in laboratory settings, where their effects on people are observed, and assessed by questionnaires. However, there is often a gap between laboratory conditions and the experience in a real-world setting. Therefore, two lawyers [1] suggested to first test new regulations in a virtual world, before commencing real-world implementation.

We adopted a variant of this approach in order to investigate opinions about genetically modified tomatoes. Specifically, the virtual world setting is employed to assess people's attitude towards a somewhat controversial topic, like genetically modified food. As the virtual world, we chose Second Life, a three-dimensional (3D) networked environment (www.secondlife.com), which is based on user-generated content rather than a pre-defined game plot. Here, we created small (virtual) fields with natural and genetically modified tomatoes. In order to evoke the opinions of users, who are represented as avatars (graphical self-representations) in Second Life,

A. Nijholt, D. Reidsma, and H. Hondorp (Eds.): INTETAIN 2009, LNICST 9, pp. 252–257, 2009.

computer-controlled agents (bots) were designed and 'fed' with opinions derived from web sources using the developed (simple) opinion mining system.

2   Opinion Extraction from the Web

The document collector is a program that automatically crawls for information from the web. It takes as input a set of keywords from the user, queries several search engines with the keywords and parses the results to a data structure.

Unlike other crawlers, it tries to extract metadata from the retrieved documents, like the publication date, the name of the author and an article–comment hierarchy. This is accomplished by parsing the HTML with manually created XSL templates, which results in a list of articles, associated comments and possibly new URLs that will be crawled next. The XSL templates will remove all HTML markups, leaving the data in a polished format ready to be processed by natural language systems.

The result of the document collector is a database with articles and comments. The next step in the process is to extract single sentences from this data, which are expected to be useful for provoking the users' to express their opinion. In this research, we concentrate on extracting subjective sentences that directly relate to the topic. To accomplish this, the OpinionFinder system [4] has been used in combination with a method described in [2].

Each article and each comment is parsed with OpinionFinder. The output of the system is an annotated version of the text. For each sentence, a subjectivity score is given. The subjectivity score consists of a flag indicating the sentence as objective or subjective and a number indicating the confidence of the classifier. The higher the subjectivity score, the more confident the OpinionFinder result.

Any sentences classified as being subjective are extracted and passed to the next step, where the query originally entered by the user is used. For each subjective sentence provided by the previous step, any words which correspond to a word in the query are marked as keywords. For example, for the query "genetically modified tomatoes" we obtained (among others) the sentence: "I *dislike unnatural* food, genetically modified food is *rubbish* and *unnatural*, do you know genetically modified tomatoes can cause genetic *disorder?*" It was given a subjectivity score of 32.0. The subjectivity hints are set *in italics* and the keywords are underlined.

For each word that was marked as a subjectivity hint in the sentence by the OpinionFinder system, the distance to the nearest keyword is calculated, resulting in a set of distances. The distance to a keyword is a measure for the probability of a semantic relation between the two. The exact probabilities for adjectives are calculated in [2]. In our work, subjectivity hints are restricted to adjectives (as marked by the POS tagger of the OpinionFinder system).

For the previous example sentence, the following {subjectivity hint, keyword} pairs would be identified: *{unnatural, genetically}, {rubbish, modified}, {unnatural, genetically}.* The corresponding distances are {2,-3,4} and the associated probabilities are {0.1504, 0.0585, 0.0141}.

The sum of the calculated probabilities is stored as the 'filter score'. The higher the filter score, the more likely it is that the opinion is about the topic the user was searching for. If the subjectivity score of a sentence is over a certain threshold and the filter score is more than zero, the sentence is classified as containing a relevant opinion. Such sentences, sorted by their filter score and additionally annotated by polarity (positive or negative), are included in the final relevant data set.

3 Pilot Study

The goal of the pilot study was to investigate the impact of the virtual environment on the way users formulate their opinion. Two types of virtual environments were created. One environment is 'static', showing pictures of genetically modified and natural tomatoes. The other one is 'interactive' (or immersive), allowing participants to visit a virtual field, and perform some (limited) interaction with the environment. The interview was conducted by computer-controlled agents, which stimulated the expression of subjects' opinions by first telling their 'quasi-own' opinion (extracted from web sources) regarding genetically modified food.

The main hypothesis is: *When placed in a virtual environment, which exemplifies the given topic of the opinion target, a user will express more reasoned opinions when the environment is interactive, as opposed to a static environment with only images.*

The hypothesis states that when a person is asked about his or her opinion by an automated system, the context, i.e. local environment in which the person is situated in, has an impact on the resulting opinion. In our case, the opinion target is genetic modification and in particular the genetic modification of tomatoes.

An environment consisting of just text and pictures describing genetically modified food is considered as 'static' (non-context control condition). On the other hand, a rich 3D environment with a tomato field where tomatoes can be picked and examined more closely is considered 'interactive' (the context experimental condition). The hypothesis states that in the latter environment, the opinions of the users will be more elaborate, because they are 'grounded' in a realistic (albeit virtual) experience.

3.1 Experimental Design

The verbal and non-verbal behavior of the computer-controlled agents (telling and asking for opinions) was driven by MPML3D, which is an authoring language for virtual agents. The agents use a text-to-speech system (Loquendo), whereby the utterances are also written into the standard chat channel of Second Life, effectively providing subtitles. Subjects respond to the agents by using the same chat functionality. We used a between-subjects design and created two scenarios.

- *Static (non-context) condition*: Two computer-controlled agents (bots) tell preselected opinions about genetically modified (GM) tomatoes to subjects, and poll them for their opinion. There are pictures of both GM and natural tomatoes.
- *Interactive (context) condition*: The same computer controlled agents do the same as in the static condition. Instead of pictures, there are virtual fields with both GM and natural tomatoes, which the users can pick and examine.

Figure 1 shows screenshots of both environments.

Fig. 1. Top: static environment. Bottom: interactive environment.

3.2 Subjects and Procedure

In total 10 subjects (7 male, 3 female), with an average age of 24 (std-dev 2) participated in the study. They were randomly split into two groups of 5. The subjects were all students from the Netherlands (while the conductor was in Japan). Subjects were paid 500 Linden Dollars, the official currency of Second Life, for their efforts.

Subjects' avatars visited the specified location in our Second Life environment individually. The experimental conductor asks if the subject has any questions. Then the conductor informs that the experiment will start, and his avatar (i.e. the avatar of the first author of this paper) will disappear from sight.

In the static condition, the subject will look at three pictures (about the tomatoes) and approach the two bots when finished. In the interactive condition, the subject is instructed to select five natural and five GM tomatoes from the virtual field by clicking on them. The selected tomatoes will appear in the basket.

Subsequently, in both conditions, the subject will *first* hear an opinion promoting genetic modification, presented by a male bot. Having said its opinion, the bot will use a trigger sentence like "What do you think?" to enquire about the opinion of the subject. The subject will give his or her opinion using the local chat functionality. *Next*, the subject hears an opinion contra genetic modification, spoken by a female bot. Likewise, the bot will try to trigger a response from the subject. This process was repeated five times. Finally, the bots will thank the subject for his or her cooperation and direct the user to a website with a questionnaire.

Examples of pro/contra opinions presented to the subjects include:

- "Genetically modified food may increase the world's crop by having stronger genes and a longer preservative time." (Pro)
- "I dislike unnatural food. Genetically modified food is rubbish and unnatural. Did you know genetically modified tomatoes could cause genetic disorder?" (Contra)

The presented utterances were manually selected from a list of automatically collected opinions in order to increase the controllability of the experiment. Each subject was presented with the same opinions as the others.

3.3 Results

The responses made by the subjects were analyzed using our new SVM-based discourse parser (http://nlp.prendingerlab.net/hilda/). The parser identifies 19 distinctive rhetorical relations between units of sentences. Relations were divided into two classes: 'specific' relations (often) indicate some underlying argumentation within responses whereas 'generic' relations (often) relate two or more sentences. The results presented in Table 1 seem to support our hypothesis, that the interactive environment triggers more reasoned opinions in people.

Table 1. Rhetoric relations in the responses by eight subjects (one excessively verbose subject in the static version was omitted, and one subject in the interactive version, because of a system error towards the end of the session)

Type of relation		Interactive env.		Static env.	
		Number	Percentage	Number	Percentage
Specific	Contrast	14	13.86	6	6.06
	Condition	5	4.95	3	3.03
	Comparison	3	2.97	1	1.01
	Explanation	2	1.98	1	1.01
	Manner-Means	1	1.01	0	0.00
	Enablement	0	0.00	1	1.01
	Total	14	13.86	7	7.07
Generic	Elaboration	38	37.62	46	46.46
	Attribution	29	28.71	23	23.23
	same-unit	5	4.95	3	3.03
	Joint	3	2.97	9	9.09
	Temporal	1	0.99	1	1.01
	Background	1	0.99	4	4.04
	Total	39	38.61	50	50.51

After the experiment, the subjects answered a short questionnaire, with four questions regarding *fun*, *impact of the environment*, *impact of the bots* and *task difficulty*. A 7-point Likert scale was used: 1 for "completely disagree" and 7 for "completely agree". The collected data shows mostly consensus between both conditions. However, the difficulty dimension ("It was difficult to give my opinion") indicates that users might feel more comfortable in the interactive environment (an average score of 2.6 for the interactive vs. 4.2 for the static). We can only speculate that the easiness of opinion expression can be attributed to the interactive, immersive nature of the environment.

4 Conclusions

In this paper, we show how virtual worlds like Second Life can serve as a platform for contextualized opinion elicitation, and in a further step, support e-rulemaking. We describe our first study, which involves the evocation of opinions in the field of genetically modified food. Opinions were automatically retrieved from the web through a simple, but effective process, and fed into Second Life bots, who presented the opinions to visitors. Keeping in mind that we conducted a pilot study, the main result is that in the condition which exploits the power of a virtual environment (e.g. interaction with virtual tomatoes), subjects showed more argumentation patterns in their responses. We take this as a non-trivial promising outcome, which will still have to be confirmed by a larger-scale study.

Acknowledgements

The first author was supported by an NII Grand Challenge project grant. We would like to thank Hugo Hernault for helping with the discourse parser.

References

1. Bradley, C., Froomkin, M.: Virtual Worlds, Real Rules. In: Law Review, pp. 103–146. New York Law School, New York (2004)
2. Skomorowski, J., Vechtomova, O.: Ad Hoc Retrieval of Documents with Topical Opinion. In: Amati, G., Carpineto, C., Romano, G. (eds.) ECIR 2007. LNCS, vol. 4425, pp. 405–417. Springer, Heidelberg (2007)
3. Ullrich, S., Prendinger, H., Ishizuka, M.: MPML3D: Agent Authoring Language for Virtual Worlds. In: Proceedings International Conference on Advances in Computer Entertainment, pp. 134–137. ACM Press, Yokohama (2008)
4. Wilson, T., Hoffmann, P., Somasundaran, S., Kessler, J., Wiebe, J., Choi, Y., Cardie, C., Riloff, E., Patwardhan, S.: OpinionFinder: A System for Subjectivity Analysis. In: Proceedings of HLT/EMNLP 2005 Interactive Demonstrations, Vancouver, British Columbia, Canada, October, ACL, pp. 34–35 (2005)

Hidden Markov Models Implementation for Tangible Interfaces

Piero Zappi[1], Elisabetta Farella[1], and Luca Benini[1]

DEIS University of Bologna, Bologna, Italy
{piero.zappi,elisabetta.farella,luca.benini}@unibo.it

Abstract. Smart objects equipped with inertial sensors can recognize gestures and act as tangible interfaces to interact with smart environments. Hidden Markov Models (HMM) are a powerful tool for gesture recognition. Gesture recognition with HMM is performed using the forward algorithm. In this paper we evaluate the fixed point implementation of the forward algorithm for HMM to assess if this implementation can be effective on resource constraint devices such as the Smart Micrel Cube (SMCube). The SMCube is a tangible interfacet that embeds an 8-bit microcontroller running at 7.372 MHz. The complexity-performance trade off has been explored, and a discussion on the critical steps of the algorithm implementation is presented.

Keywords: Smart Object, Hidden Markov Models, Tangible interfaces, Fixed point.

1 Introduction

The development of smart objects is an active field of research. With the objective of enhancing the interaction with smart environments, smart objects can be used as tangible interfaces and play a fundamental role in improving human experience within interactive spaces for entertainment and education [1]. The SMCube is a tangible interface developed for the *TANGerINE* framework, a tangible tabletop environment where users manipulate smart objects in order to perform actions on the contents of a *digital media table* [2]. Previous work showed how a simple ad-hoc technique and a standard tree classification algorithm can be implemented on the SMCube to include basic gesture recognition and improve interaction modalities [3].

Hidden Markov Models (HMMs) allow to handle temporal dynamics and classify more complex gestures than the ones already recognized. Typically, classification with HMMs is performed using a recursive algorithm called *forward* algorithm. Although this process is a lightweight task, several issues must be considered in order to implement it on a low-power, low-cost microcontroller such as the one embedded on the SMCube.

In this paper we evaluate the fixed point implementation of the forward algorithm. Discussion of ad-hoc solution to solve numerical problems while keeping low overall computational complexity is presented. Considerations about the

A. Nijholt, D. Reidsma, and H. Hondorp (Eds.): INTETAIN 2009, LNICST 9, pp. 258–263, 2009.

complexity of the algorithm, both in terms of computational and memory cost, and its performance are discussed through the paper.

2   Hardware Overview

The SMCube is a smart object equipped with sensors (a digital tri-axes accelerometer from STM, LIS3LV02DQ, and 6 photo transistors) and actuators (infrared LEDs) (see figure 1). It embeds an ATMega 168 low-power, low-cost microcontroller to sample and process data from its sensors, and a Bluetooth 2.0 transceiver from BlueGiga (WT12) to wirelessly communicate with a PC. The ATMega 168 features a RISC architecture that can operate up to 24MHz and offers 16 KB of Flash memory, 1 KB of RAM and 512 Bytes of EEPROM. The microcontroller includes a multiplier and several peripherals (ADC, timers, SPI and UART serial interfaces etc.). The firmware has been implemented in C using the Atmel AVR Studio 4 IDE that provides all the APIs necessary to exploit the peripherals and perform operations with 8, 16, and 32 bit variables.

Fig. 1. The Tangerine SMCube. The cube edge is 6.5 *cm* long.

3   Hidden Markov Models

A HMM is a probabilistic model used to describe sequences of observations $O = \{o_1, o_2, ..., o_T\}$ and their corresponding hidden state $Q = \{q_1, q_2, ..., q_T\}$.

A discrete HMM is characterized by a set of N states (s_i), M possible observable (measurable) values (v_k), a $N \times N$ matrix state transition $A = \{a_{ij}\} = P(q_{t+1} = s_j|q_t = s_i)$, a $N \times M$ observation matrix $B = \{b_i(k)\} = P(o_t = v_k|q_t = s_i)$, and a $N \times 1$ starting probability vector $\Pi = \{\pi_i\} = P(q_1 = s_i)$. The compact notation for an HMM is $\lambda = (A, B, \Pi)$.

Two hypotheses are given: (1) the state at time t depends only on the state a $t - 1$, $P(q_t|q_{t-1})$; (2) each observation is independent given its state, $P(o_t|q_t)$.

There are three problems associated with HMM: (1) the classification problem, (2) the decoding problem, (3) the training problem [4].

Given a model λ and a sequence of observations O, the classification problem consists in finding the probability that λ generated O and is solved using the *forward* algorithm. When we use HMMs for gesture classification, we train one model, λ_i for each class of gestures, then we apply the forward algorithm with all the models and find the most probable one, $G_{out} = argmax_i[P(O|\lambda_i)]$.

3.1 The Forward Algorithm

The forward algorithm is a recursive algorithm that relies on a set of support variables $\alpha_t(i) = P(o_1, o_2, ..., o_t, q_t = i|\lambda)$ and is made up of three steps.

1. Initialization: $\alpha_1(i) = \pi_i(O_1)b_i(O_1)$, $1 \le i \le N$
2. Induction: $\alpha_{t+1}(j) = [\sum_{i=1}^{N} \alpha_t(i)a_{ij}]b_j(O_{t+1})$, $1 \le j \le N$ and $1 \le t \le T-1$
3. Termination: $P(O|\lambda) = \sum_{i=1}^{N} \alpha_T(i)$

3.2 Normalization

According to the definitions in the previous section we can see that the $\alpha_t(j)$ are sum of a large number of terms in the form ($\prod_{s=1}^{t-1} a_{q_s,q_{s+1}} \prod_{s=1}^{t} b_{q_s}(O_s)$). Since both the a_{ij} and the $b_i(k)$ are smaller than 1 as t become large $\alpha_t(j)$ tends to zero exponentially and soon it exceeds the precision of any machine.

In order to avoid underflow, the $\alpha_t(j)$ are normalized at every step using the scaling factor $c_t = \dfrac{1}{\sum_{i=1}^{N} \alpha_t(i)}$. The scaled $\hat{\alpha}_t(j)$ are used in place of the $\alpha_t(j)$.

This normalization procedure is not suitable for low-power microcontrollers since it requires to perform N divisions each time a new sample is processed.

Thus we propose an alternative approach:

1. check if all $\alpha_t(j)$ are smaller than $\frac{1}{2}$, otherwise scaling is not needed;
2. calculate the number of shift to the left (l) needed to render the highest $\alpha_t(j)$ greater than $\frac{1}{2}$;
3. shift all $\alpha_t(j)$ to the left of l bits.

This procedure requires only shifts and can be efficiently implemented on a microcontroller.

3.3 Likelihood

To compute the final sequence probability we can not use the scaled $\hat{\alpha}_t(j)$. However we can notice that:

$$\sum_{i=1}^{N} \hat{\alpha}_T(i) = \prod_{t=1}^{T} 2^{l_t} \cdot \sum_{i=1}^{N} \alpha_T(i) = \prod_{t=1}^{T} 2^{l_t} \cdot P(O|\lambda) = r \longrightarrow P(O|\lambda) = \frac{r}{\prod_{t=1}^{T} 2^{l_t}} \quad (1)$$

Since $P(O|\lambda)$ can be very small, we compute $\log P(O|\lambda) = \log(r) - \sum_{t=1}^{T} \log 2^{l_t}$.

If we decide to use $\log_2$ we already have the value of $\sum_{t=1}^{T} \log 2^{l_t}$ by keeping track of how many shifts we performed for scaling. Furthermore, we do not need to compute $\log(r)$ since logarithm is a monotonically increasing function. Thus, to compare 2 models, we simply check for the one that required less shifts for scaling, in case of tie the one with higher r is the most probable model.

4   Evaluation

To evaluate this implementation we used a dataset made up of 10 complex gestures collected on the car assembly scenario [6]. These gestures can be compared to the ones that may be used within role-playing games. The dataset has been extended since its first use and now it includes 70 repetition for each gesture. We used 4 fold cross validation technique to extend the validation set up to all 70 samples.

To recognize these gestures we used a set of discrete HMMs with 4 states ($N = 4$). Accelerometer' streams have been quantized to 3 symbols ($M = 3$).

To assess the complexity of the forward algorithm we assumed the values presented in tables 1a and 1b, where N is the number of HMM states and C is the number of gestures we want to recognize (here $C = 10$). The memory cost is given by $\frac{\text{data size}}{8} \cdot C \cdot (N^2 + N \cdot M + 2 \cdot N)$. Where M is the number of symbols in the accelerometer stream.

4.1   Classification Accuracy

To evaluate the performance loss due to the use of fixed point data representation, we classified the dataset using a floating point representation of the data and the traditional normalization algorithm (optimal performance), and using a fixed point representation and the shift scaling algorithm.

Table 1. Computational complexity

(a) Computational complexity

Operation	Cost
Shift	1
Variables comparison	1
Sum 8 bits	1
Sum 16 bits	2
Sum 32 bits	4
Multiplication 8 bits	2
Multiplication 16 bits	4
Multiplication 32 bits	6

(b) Algorithm complexity

Algorithm	Cost
$\alpha_{t+1}(i)$ Calculation	$(N+1)$ mul. $+ N$ sum.
Normalization	$2 \cdot N + 1 + 2 \cdot$ data size
Single step (8-bit)	$C \cdot [N \cdot (3 \cdot N + 2) + 2 \cdot N + 17]$
Single step (16-bit)	$C \cdot [N \cdot (6 \cdot N + 4) + 2 \cdot N + 33]$
Single step (32-bit)	$C \cdot [N \cdot (10 \cdot N + 6) + 2 \cdot N + 65]$

Performances are evaluated using the following indexes (see table 2):

- *Correct Classification Ratio*: $CCR = \dfrac{\text{number of correctly classified instances}}{\text{total number of instances}}$;
  is a global indication of the performance of the classifier.
- *Precision*: $PR_i = \dfrac{\text{number of instances correctly classified for class i}}{\text{number of instances classified as class i}}$;
  is an indication of the exactness of the classifier.
- *Recall*: $RC_i = \dfrac{\text{number of instances correctly classified for class i}}{\text{total number of instances from class i}}$;
  is an indication of the performances of the classifier over a specific class

5 Discussion

Table 2 and 3 present PR, RC, CCR, computational and memory cost for our implementations when using the given dataset. The implementations that use 16 and 32 bits fixed point data representation achieve similar or even equal CCR than the floating point solution. On the other hand the 8 bits fixed point implementation worsen the CCR by 14.15 %. However, the 32 bit solution can not be implemented on the ATmega168 since it requires more RAM than available, therefore the 16 bits solution is the optimal choice for the SMCube.

Table 2. Classification performances

Class	PR 8b	PR 16b	PR 32b	PR fl	RC 8b	RC 16b	RC 32b	RC fl
Gesture 1	1.00	1.00	1.00	1.00	0.99	0.99	0.99	0.99
Gesture 2	0.50	0.66	0.66	0.66	0.01	0.64	0.64	0.64
Gesture 3	0.38	0.54	0.54	0.54	0.41	0.56	0.56	0.56
Gesture 4	0.54	0.60	0.61	0.61	0.64	0.67	0.69	0.69
Gesture 5	0.29	0.67	0.69	0.69	0.36	0.50	0.50	0.50
Gesture 6	0.36	0.53	0.53	0.53	0.43	0.36	0.36	0.36
Gesture 7	0.53	0.65	0.65	0.65	0.59	0.86	0.86	0.86
Gesture 8	0.47	0.56	0.56	0.56	0.52	0.63	0.63	0.63
Gesture 9	0.77	0.87	0.87	0.87	0.81	0.89	0.89	0.89
Gesture 10	0.93	0.96	0.96	0.96	0.90	0.99	0.99	0.99
CCR					56.71%	70.71%	70.86%	70.86%

Table 3. Performance and cost comparison

Variables Size (bits)	CCR (%)	Memory cost (bytes)	Computational cost
8	56.71	360	810
16	70.71	720	1370
32	70.86	1440	2090
Floating point	70.86		

6 Conclusion and Future Works

In this paper we presented our evaluation of a fixed point implementation of the forward algorithm for HMM. Furthermore, we presented our solutions to the peculiar numerical problems of this classification algorithm. The 16-bit implementation is the best solution that can be implemented on our target microcontroller (ATMega168). This solution shows performance only slightly worse than the optimal ones of the floating point implementation (70.71% CCR, 16 bit fixed point; 70.68% floating point) and makes this implementation suitable for smart objects equipped with low-power, low-cost microcontrollers such as the SMCube.

HMM is a common approach in gesture recognition, thus the possibility to implement this algorithm on a smart object greatly enhances potential for using it as an effective HCI device. In future works we plan to augment human computer interaction within a tabletop environment allowing the interaction through a set of complex natural gestures.

References

1. Ishii, H.: The tangible user interface and its evolution. J. Comm. ACM 51(6), 32–36 (2008)
2. Baraldi, S., Del Bimbo, A., Landucci, L., Torpei, N., Cafini, O., Farella, E., Pieracci, A., Benini, L.: Introducing tangerine: a tangible interactive natural environment. In: Proc. of ACM International Conference on Multimedia (MM), pp. 831–834. ACM Press, Augsburg (2007)
3. Cafini, O., Farella, E., Benini, L., Baraldi, S., Torpei, N., Landucci, L., Del Bimbo, A.: Tangerine SMCube: a smart device for human computer interaction. In: Proc. of IEEE European Conference on Smart Sensing and Context (2008)
4. Rabiner, L.R.: A tutorial on hidden Markov models and selected applications in speech recognition. Proceedings of the IEEE 77(2), 257–286 (1989)
5. Mitra, S., Acharya, T.: Gesture Recognition: A Survey. IEEE Transactions on Systems, Man and Cybernetics - Part C 37(3), 311–324 (2007)
6. Zappi, P., Stiefmeier, T., Farella, E., Roggen, D., Benini, L., Tröster, G.: Activity Recognition From On-Body Sensors by Classifier Fusion: Sensor Scalability and Robustness. In: Proc. 3rd Int. Conf. on Intelligent Sensors, Sensor Networks, and Information Processing (2007)

Author Index